A CENTURY OF GRACE

A HISTORY OF THE MISSOURI SYNOD

1847—1947

by

Walter A. Baepler

CONCORDIA PUBLISHING HOUSE

Saint Louis, Missouri

1947

Copyright by
Concordia Publishing House
Saint Louis, Missouri
1947
Slightly revised 1963

Printed in U. S. A.

ISBN: 978-0-7586-1843-6

FOREWORD

*T*HIS centennial history of the Missouri Synod is published under the auspices of the Centennial Committee appointed by the venerable President of Synod, Dr. J. W. Behnken, pursuant to the resolution of the General Convention of 1941: Dr. Theo. Hoyer, Chairman; Rev. H. W. Romoser, Secretary; Dr. L. Fuerbringer; Dr. H. B. Hemmeter; Dr. E. T. Lams; Teacher A. H. Kramer; Mr. G. A. Fleischer.

As the century ends, we pause, and our eyes naturally turn to the past; we see abounding evidences in this history that God has been with us; and as a memorial of our gratitude to Him we inscribe it: "A Century of Grace." And as we turn again and look toward the future, we are encouraged by the history of the past to take up the work anew, and with confidence we pray with Solomon: "The Lord our God be with us, as He was with our fathers" (1 Kings 8:57).

PREFACE

THE preparation of this brief history of the Evangelical Lutheran Synod of Missouri, Ohio, and Other States has been undertaken at the request of the Centennial Committee of the Missouri Synod. It forms a volume in the series of Centennial publications now being issued to commemorate the one-hundredth anniversary of this Lutheran church body.

This book makes no claim to be an exhaustive study or a documentary history of the Missouri Synod. Its purpose is to acquaint the reader with the antecedents, organization, growth, and doctrine of this important part of the Lutheran Church in America. Nevertheless, all historical data are taken from primary or secondary sources. In complete understanding with the Centennial Committee, the author, owing to the abnormal pressure of routine work, used the labors of those who worked before him in this particular field of church history — Fischer, Vehse, Hochstetter, Koestering, Schieferdecker, Loehe, Fritschel, Polack, and others. The periodicals of the Missouri Synod, *Der Lutheraner*, *Lehre und Wehre*, *The Lutheran Witness*, and especially the *Proceedings* of the regular conventions of the Synod, were carefully scanned. Owing to the limitations of space and the mass of available material, some sections of this history have become more statistical than was originally planned.

The author desires to thank Dr. Theo. Hoyer, Dr. H. B. Hemmeter, and Prof. L. Blankenbuehler for helpful suggestions, and his former student Pastor Geo. C. Derwig of Kampsville, Illinois, for clerical assistance. He is indebted especially to the venerable Dr. L. Fuerbringer, who read the manuscript critically and whose intimate knowledge of the subject matter was of inestimable value to the writer.

May Jesus Christ, the Head of the Church, who abundantly blessed the Missouri Synod during the first century of its existence, grant that in the new century to come the pastors and people of our congregations may serve Him with true faith, pure zeal, and consecrated life.   WALTER A. BAEPLER

CONTENTS

CHAPTER	PAGE
1. Lutheranism in America and in Germany in 1846	1
2. The Saxon Emigration	15
3. Carl Ferdinand Wilhelm Walther	41
4. Friedrich Conrad Dietrich Wyneken	53
5. Johann Konrad Wilhelm Loehe and His Efforts on Behalf of the Lutheran Church in America	65
6. Wilhelm Sihler	75
7. Preliminary Meetings Leading to tne Organization of the Missouri Synod	83
8. The Organization of the German Evangelical Lutheran Synod of Missouri, Ohio, and Other States	97
9. Lengthening the Cords (1847—1872)	107
10. The Evangelical Lutheran Synodical Conference of North America	155
11. Strengthening the Stakes (1872—1897)	167
12. Steadily Forward (1897—1922)	217
13. Abounding More and More (1922—1947)	275
14. The Centennial of 1947	355
Notes	359
Officers, Boards, and Committees of the Missouri Synod	362
Synodical Officers, Districts, and District Presidents, 1847—1947	364
Brief Statement of Doctrinal Position of the Missouri Synod	371
Topical Index	385

1

LUTHERANISM IN AMERICA AND IN GERMANY IN 1846

*T*HE nineteenth century is a glorious chapter in the history of our country. It is the story of the conquest of the vast territory lying between the Atlantic and the Pacific. It sets forth the transformation of this area from a sparsely settled wilderness to one filled with growing cities and improved farms; it tells of the discovery and development of the natural resources, the growth of commerce, and the development of great transportation and communication systems. In brief, the nineteenth century is the history of the maturing of our country as a nation.

Of particular interest for our purpose is the account of the spread and growth of population during these hundred years. The frontier line in 1800, broadly speaking, paralleled the Appalachians, with occasional bulges penetrating Ohio and extending into Kentucky and Tennessee. By 1820 it touched the Mississippi in Louisiana and in the southern parts of Illinois and Missouri. Decade after decade it moved slowly towards the West, crossing the 95th meridian in 1850 and the 100th in 1880. In the meantime, settlements on the Pacific Coast and in the Rocky Mountain area preceded the advancing tide of population from the East, but by 1900, and even prior to this, East and West had met, and the frontier line disappeared from the map of the United States. During the century the population of our country rose from 5,308,483 to 75,994,575.

Midway in this epic century — on April 26, 1847 — the German Evangelical Lutheran Synod of Missouri, Ohio, and Other States was organized in Chicago. Coming into being when the tide of Lutheran immigration was beginning to surge, cradled near the frontier of a rapidly growing country (Fort Wayne, Chicago, St. Louis), and establishing strategic outposts in Milwaukee, Detroit, Buffalo, New York, Baltimore, and Cleveland, the young synod, favored by time and geography, enjoyed a remarkable growth, and after a century of existence has developed into a body of more than 1,500,000 baptized members.

The territory in which the Missouri Synod established itself and which for decades was its stronghold in membership comprised Missouri, Illinois, Indiana, Ohio, Michigan, and Wisconsin. The first settlements in these States followed the chief rivers and their tributaries. Traveling was made easier through the development of the rivers and the building of canals. The Erie Canal from Buffalo to Albany, completed in 1825, connected the Eastern seaboard with the Middle West. The Illinois-Michigan Canal from Chicago to La Salle, Ill., opened in 1848, linked the Eastern route with the Mississippi Valley, and the Miami Canal (running from Cincinnati north to "The Junction") and the Wabash Canal (leading from Toledo, Ohio, through Fort Wayne to Evansville, Ind.), begun in 1832 and finished in 1845, offered means of transportation north and south. Leading to the canals and rivers were plank roads, corduroy roads, and government pikes. Between 1827 and 1850 the Cumberland, or National, Road was the principal route overland between the East and the West.

The first steamboat went up the Mississippi from New Orleans in 1812, and soon St. Louis became the center of industrial life in the West. This city was the terminus of steamboat lines from New Orleans and the starting point for navigation for the upper Mississippi, the Illinois, the Missouri, and the Ohio. Before the days of the railroad, Chicago could not compete with St. Louis.

There were no railroads in this territory to speak of at the time under consideration. From 1830 to 1848 only 149 miles of track were laid in the Western States. The first railroad in Illinois was the Northern Cross, from Springfield to Meredosia, begun in 1837 and completed in 1842.

Using the available transportation facilities, settlers began to filter into the Middle West in the early twenties of the nineteenth century. Many of them were discontented or ambitious elements from the East, many were immigrants from the Old World. Among the newcomers were Lutherans in large numbers. The physical hardships and especially the spiritual plight of these pioneers are described by Pastor F. C. D. Wyneken, who traveled among them from 1838 to 1841. He writes:

"Either singly or in small groups our brethren go into the forest with their wives and children. In many cases they have no neighbors for miles around, and even if they have such near by, the dense forest so separates them that they live in ignorance of one another. . . . Husband and wife and children must work hard to fell the giant trees, to clear the virgin forest, to plow, sow, and plant. Bread must be procured; but this can be gotten only from the ground which they till. . . . Small wonder, then, that everybody works in order to support this body and life. No difference is made between Sunday and weekdays, especially since no church bell calls them to the house of God and no neighbor in his Sunday outfit arrives to call for his friend.

"It is not to be wondered at that the pioneers' tired limbs seek their couch without prayer and that dire need drives them to leave it and return to work without prayer; even the prayer at mealtime has long since been banished by inveterate infidelity or recent trouble. Alas, Bible and hymnal also in many cases have been left in the Old Country, as the people, owing to rationalism, had lost taste for them. No preacher arrives to rouse them from their carnal thoughts and pursuits, and the sweet voice of the Gospel has not been heard for a long time.

"Picture to yourself thousands of families scattered over these extended tracts of land. The parents die without hearing the Word of God, no one arouses and admonishes, no one comforts them. Now behold, young and old are lying on their deathbed; their soul perhaps has not as much as given a thought of preparation for the solemn judgment. But a servant of the Lord would be able to direct the lost one to the holy God, who outside of Christ is a consuming fire, but in Christ a reconciled father; he might, by the grace of God and the power of the Word, lead the heart to repentance and faith, and the dying souls would be saved. How many thousands go forth unprepared and uncomforted into eternity!" [1]

Was there no Lutheran Church in America to minister to these members of the household of faith? Indeed, there was. The Lutheran Church had come to America more than 200 years before this time and was now organized into twenty corporate bodies. But evil days had fallen upon the Church of the Reformation. In many instances the name Lutheran stood merely for a historical fact but gave no sure index to the doctrines and practices of those who bore it.

In the territory in which the Missouri Synod later found its constituents a number of Lutheran synods were represented at the time of the organization of the new body. Pastor Wilhelm Loehe of Neuendettelsau, Bavaria, becoming acquainted with the Ohio Synod (organized 1818) in 1842 through his missioners Ernst and Burger, advised his emissaries to join this group. But these and other Loehe men, charter members of Missouri Synod, did not find a confessionally true Lutheranism in the Ohio Synod. It was at that time, as Dr. Loy states in his *Story of My Life,* a "unionistic corporation" ministering to Lutheran and Reformed elements in the same congregation, and the Loehe men left this body because they realized that the majority of its members had no sincere willingness to fight against the religious unionism of those days.

Another group of the Loehe men joined the Michigan Synod, which had been established in 1840. But one year later — in one instance two years — they, too, were compelled to leave this synod for conscience' sake. Not only did this body minister to "union" congregations, that is, to congregations composed of Lutherans and Reformed, it received into its membership a minister who had refused to subscribe without reservations to the Confessions of the Lutheran Church.

The Buffalo Synod, founded 1845 by Prussian immigrants who had come to America in 1839, desired to be a confessional Lutheran body. The hierarchical doctrines, however, which this group propagated were abhorrent to the Saxon Lutherans in St. Louis and in Perry County, Mo., likewise charter members of the Missouri Synod, because they were in direct opposition to the principles of the Reformation.

There was the Synod of the West, organized in 1835 and claiming for itself the territory of Illinois, Indiana, Kentucky, and Missouri. Wyneken, a strong proponent of confessional Lutheranism, had been a member of this group. The Synod of the West went from bad to worse, as far as confessional Lutheranism was concerned, when it joined the General Synod in 1841.

The General Synod, existing since 1820, was at this time a federation of fifteen Lutheran synods, comprising more than half of the Lutherans in America. Its leaders were avowed enemies of the Lutheran Confessions. They denounced the Lutheran doctrines of Baptism, the Lord's Supper, absolution, and the personal union of the two natures of Christ. They loved the doctrines of the Reformed Church, championed the revival, and advocated a union with the sects. Wyneken severed his connection with this organization in 1845 when he failed in his attempt to win it back to Lutheranism.

The Ministerium of Pennsylvania, organized in 1748, also had its representatives in the West. Pastors Chr. Fr. Heyer and Ezra Keller journeyed through Indiana, Illinois, and Missouri in 1836 and reported the sad plight of the German Lutherans in these States. But this body was fraternizing with the General Synod in 1846, shared its non-confessional position, and affiliated with it in 1853.

The Tennessee Synod had several clergymen in the territory occupied later by the Missouri Synod. This small group, in existence since 1820, had made valiant efforts to promote confessional Lutheranism in America. However, it lacked the resources in manpower required for the work in the Middle West and, besides, at this time was rapidly changing from a German to an English synod.

The Lutheran Church as it was organized in America in 1846 was unable to meet the challenge of the Lutheran immigration. It was not merely the geographical remoteness which prevented the Eastern Lutherans from making an impact upon the West, nor was it only the dearth of ministers that handicapped the Western Lutherans in their efforts to provide for the newcomers in their territory. The trouble lay deeper. It was the lack of confessional Lutheranism within these bodies that unfitted them for the task of giving spiritual care to the thousands of fellow Lutherans arriving in America. And, on the other hand, it was the desire to promote confessional Lutheranism in America that brought the Loehe men and the Saxons together in the Missouri Synod and which stimulated the new body to gather the Lutheran immigrants into congregations which were truly Lutheran.

The situation in the Lutheran Church in America and the striving for confessional Lutheranism reflected the state and tendencies within the Lutheran Church of Germany at that time.

Germany in 1846 was not the Empire of 1871. After the Congress of Vienna (1815) there were in Germany 39 states, of which four were free cities—Hamburg, Bremen, Luebeck, and Frankfurt on the Main — the others had monarchical constitutions. They formed a union whose common organ was the Diet at Frankfurt. The chief aim of this confederation was the common defense of federal territory against foreign attacks, but the individual states retained full sovereignty of their internal affairs. In 1834 the greater part of Germany formed an economic entity through the customs union which simplified internal communication, established uniform systems of weights, measures, and currency, but for the time being exercised no important influence on political life. It was not until 1871 that the German Empire was created.

The Napoleonic Wars caused much devastation in Germany. There followed economic insecurity, political persecution, and religious oppression, all of which combined to stimulate a huge emigration to America, the land of economic stability, political freedom, and religious liberty. While 6,761 Germans arrived in America during the second decade of the nineteenth century and 152,454 in the third, the high tide of German immigration set in after 1840. In that decade the new arrivals numbered 434,626; in the next, 951,667. Immigration from Germany reached its apex between 1881 and 1890, when it numbered 1,452,970. During the nineteenth century a total of 5,009,280 Germans arrived at American ports.

The Church in Germany was controlled by the State. In

fact, it was a department of the State. The administration of the Church was in the hands of the consistory, composed of clerical and non-clerical members, which not only regulated the external affairs of the parishes but also prescribed what liturgies, hymnbooks, and doctrinal standards were to be used. The future pastors had to pass an examination before the consistory and, if successful, were placed into their parishes by this governmental agency. A candidate of theology who did not share the doctrinal views of the consistory had little chance of obtaining an appointment. In some parts of Germany the so-called "Patronatssystem" prevailed, which gave certain men who belonged to the nobility the power of appointing ministers to the congregations on their estates. Such a "Patron" was Count Detlev von Einsiedel, who appointed Pastor E. G. W. Keyl to the congregation at Niederfrohna and Pastor C. F. W. Walther to Braeunsdorf. Another "Patron" was Gottwerth Friedemann Loeber, through whom his brother, G. H. Loeber, became pastor at Eichenberg. Likewise Pastor E. M. Buerger obtained his charge through his "Patron," Count von Schoenburg.

The congregations and their pastors were supported by taxes levied by the State. Everyone born in a parish was a member of the church and could demand the services of the pastor regardless of his personal conduct or religious convictions. Under such order of things church discipline could not function properly and, in fact, did not function at all in most parishes. The result was spiritual deterioration. Spiritual deterioration within the Lutheran Church in Germany appeared already at the end of the 17th century, which is known in church history as the age of dead orthodoxy. Dead orthodoxy had a high regard for doctrine but little concern for Christian life. Generally speaking, religion was reduced to mere formalism and externalism. Dead orthodoxy was followed by the age of pietism, which was fully developed in the first part of the 18th century. Pietism emphasized Christian life but had an utter disregard for purity of doctrine. A third and fourth resultant evil of the State-controlled Church was rationalism and unionism.

Rationalism, today called modernism, made reason the arbiter of religious truth. Claiming that the Bible was a book of myths and legends, rationalism proclaimed the doctrine of God, virtue, and immortality: It changed the appearance and life of the Church. Churches were made lecture rooms, the pulpits became desks above the altars and dwindled into insignificance. All distinctively Christian thought was removed from the hymns and replaced by rhymes of the shallowest thought, praising the joy of nature, the exercise of virtue, and the care of the body. Sermons were long-winded discourses on the utility of things. The old church orders were mutilated. Baptism was robbed of its meaning, the Lord's Supper emptied of its significance, private confession totally abolished, and confirmation degraded into a promise of civic righteous conduct. The catechism contained nothing but natural religion and an inane moralizing on the happiness of man.

Rationalism was rampant especially in Saxony. In the biography of his brother-in-law, Pastor J. F. Buenger, Prof. C. F. W. Walther presents a detailed account of rationalism as he himself experienced it while serving the congregation at Braeunsdorf. He writes:

"Just as in that time the binding oath upon the Book of Concord was only an empty comedy, so the most important regulations of the established Church were merely so many denials of the Confessions of the Church. Only by applying Jesuitical moral principles could one maintain that the Church of Saxony was Lutheran, because the Confessions of this Church still prevailed in it. Already in 1812 a Book of Forms, or *Agende,* had been introduced which a true Lutheran pastor could use only with a bad conscience, since it contained forms which, on the one hand, openly denied divine truth and, on the other hand, watered Christian doctrine. While nobody questioned or cared when the rationalistic, unbelieving clergyman, to whom it still sounded too Christian, merely guided himself by the Book of Forms, the confessional Lutheran pastor did not dare to deviate in the least from the prescribed forms. If he did and it came to the attention of his superiors, he was most severely called to account. . . . The confessional Lutheran pastor was more distressed in his conscience when he was expected to read from his pulpit the miserable prayers especially prepared by the consistory for special occasions. Furthermore, a hymnal beyond all measure rationalistic had been introduced. The schoolbooks were almost without exception completely leavened with modernism, so that the Lutheran clergyman, as the spiritual supervisor of the school, was constantly in dire distress of conscience.

"Furthermore, it was in the highest degree offensive to the conscience of a confessional Lutheran pastor that by reason of his office he was compelled not only to maintain ecclesiastical, sacramental, and fraternal relations with errorists, yea with most notorious heretics, but to recognize them as his spiritual superiors, suffer himself to be examined, ordained, and installed into office by them, and to permit them to blaspheme divine truth before his own congregation. . . . Finally, it also caused the confessional Lutheran pastor no little trouble that the practice of announcement before Communion, the suspension of impenitent persons from the Lord's Supper, in short, every exercise of church discipline was denied him.

"Confessional Lutheran laymen in Saxony at that time likewise were in much spiritual distress. They were required to recognize notorious false prophets as their shepherds and pastors, permit their children to be baptized and confirmed by them, suffer themselves to be absolved by them at confession and to receive Holy Communion from them. They were required to place their children into the charge of godless schoolmasters for their instruction in religion and Christian training, and for this purpose to purchase and themselves place into their hands schoolbooks containing false and blasphemous doctrine.

"Hard as it was for many poor pious laymen to walk for miles if they desired to hear a Lutheran sermon, this was the least they had to bear. Many of them, after having labored the whole week from early dawn until late at night to earn their meager daily bread, set out at the approach of Sunday, soon after midnight, in order to refresh their famishing souls with the preaching of the pure Word of God in some distant church. When this was done, on Sunday evening they began the journey homeward with rejoicing and on Monday, refreshed spiritually, again took up the weekly task which barely supported them and their own." [2]

The spiritual deterioration of the German State-controlled Lutheran Church manifested itself also in religious unionism. The Congress of Vienna had decreed religious toleration for all Christian denominations in the German states. This caused considerable confusion, especially in those states in which the Lutheran and the Reformed Churches were represented. Some State governments endeavored to end the religious confusion by uniting the two Churches. Prussia proposed such a union when on September 27, 1817, King Frederick William III issued a proclamation announcing that on October 31 both the Reformed and the Lutheran Court and Garrison Churches at Potsdam would be united in an Evangelical-Christian Church to observe the tricentenary of the Reformation in a joint Communion service. The King was a member of the Reformed Church; his wife, who died in 1810, had been a Lutheran.

The Union met with the approval of the rationalists and the pietists, the former having no doctrine to defend, the latter being indifferent to Scriptural truths. It provoked opposition, however, in some sections of the Lutheran Church. These opponents were called Confessional Lutherans, sometimes also Old Lutherans. One of the leaders of the Confessional Lutheran School was Claus Harms of Kiel, who on October 31, 1817, published not only Luther's Ninety-Five Theses, but also ninety-five theses of his own, in which he attacked rationalism and the Union and pleaded for a return to the fundamentals of the Reformation. Other prominent men of the conservative school were E. W. Hengstenberg, H. E. F. Guericke, A. G. Rudelbach, and G. C. A. Harless.

After 1830 the Prussian government took stern measures against those who resisted the Union. Lutherans not conforming to the decree of 1817 were removed from civil service, pastors were imprisoned, congregations disbanded. Dr. Johann Gottfried Scheibel, the leader of the Confessional Lutherans in Breslau, was exiled. In order to escape further persecution, 700 Lutherans with their pastor, A. L. C. Kavel, left Prussia in 1838 for Australia. The following year Pastor J. A. A. Grabau for the same reason emigrated with 1,000 Lutherans to America. The fear of this Union, which, however, never became effective in Saxony, was by no means an insignificant factor in the decision of the 700 Saxons to leave for America in 1838 under the leadership of Pastor Martin Stephan.

Thus many Lutherans left Germany because of their religious convictions and came to America. Their contending for the faith of their fathers had a wholesome effect on many who remained in Germany. A reawakening of true Lutheranism took place in Saxony, Bavaria, Hannover, and in other German states. The State governments had to modify their policies with reference to the churches. Prussia granted Lutherans the privilege of establishing free congregations, that is, congregations independent of the State, in 1841. The Lutheran Church in Saxony obtained the same privilege in 1848.

Confessional Lutheranism originating in Germany found its fullest development in America in the Missouri Synod and in its associate synods of the Synodical Conference. The secret of the growth and achievements of the Missouri Synod, accordingly, must be sought not in the time in which it was organized nor in the territory in which it established itself, but in its adherence to confessional Lutheranism. Wrote Dr. R. C. H. Lenski of the Ohio Synod in the *Kirchenzeitung* of May 20, 1922: "If there ever was a strictly conservative Lutheran body, it surely is the Missouri Synod. Nevertheless, this growth! Here is a historical fact that refutes all talk trying to persuade us that we must be liberal, accommodate ourselves to the spirit of the time, etc., in order to win men and grow externally. The very opposite is seen in the Missouri Synod. Missouri has at all times been unyielding; it is so still. In this body the Scriptures and the Confessions have been, and still are, valued to their full import. There was no disposition to surrender any part of them. With this asset Missouri has been working in free America, which abounds in sects and religious confusion, and now exhibits its enormous achievements. What so many regard as Missouri's weakness has in reality been its strength. This fact we might write down for our own remembrance. It is a mark of the pastors and leaders of the Missouri Synod that they never, ay never, tire of discussing doctrine on the basis of the Confessions and of Scriptures. That is one trait that may be called 'the spirit of Missouri.'"

2

THE SAXON EMIGRATION

THE charter members of the Missouri Synod came from two groups: the Saxons and the Loehe men. While the latter were the prime movers in the endeavor to establish a confessional Lutheran Synod in America and gave the stimulus for the organizing of the Missouri Synod, the Saxons quickly assumed the theological leadership in the new organization. Moreover, to the Saxons, the first of the two groups to arrive in America, credit is due for the Scriptural principles embodied in Synod's constitution.

The leader of the Saxon emigration was Martin Stephan. Born in Stramberg, Moravia, August 13, 1777, he came to Breslau at the age of 22, a journeyman linen weaver. Here he was introduced to a group of confessional but pietistic Lutherans who had gathered about Dr. John Ephraim Scheibel, principal of the Elizabeth *Gymnasium*.

Persuaded by Scheibel and assured of financial support, Stephan, in 1802, enrolled in the *Gymnasium*, although his schoolmates were from 12 to 15 years his juniors. He continued his studies at the universities of Halle and Leipzig, graduating in 1809.

After serving a small congregation at Haber, Bohemia, for one year, Stephan came to Dresden, Saxony, in 1810, as pastor of the Bohemian congregation in that city. This congregation had been established by exiles driven from Bohemia during the Thirty Years' War. Settling at Pirna, a suburb of Dresden, they worshiped in the Nikolai Church. In 1639 they sought the shelter of the fortified city of Dresden and for ten years met for worship in their pastor's home. After the Peace of Westphalia (1648), when it became apparent that these Bohemians could not return to their native country, they petitioned Elector John George III on March 29, 1650, "to be received as his faithful subjects and brethren in the faith and to be given a church building for their evangelical services." By a rescript of May 15, 1650, St. John's Church at Dresden was turned over to them for their sole use. From Bohemia they had carried with them a considerable amount of money which they invested and whose proceeds they used for the support of their pastor and the poor in the congregation. In 1837 the amount invested amounted to 50,000 German Thaler (about $32,000).[1]

Martin Stephan

By the time Stephan became pastor of this congregation, it had lost its original complexion. The Bohemians had been assimilated by intermarriage, and, more as a matter of form than of necessity, Stephan conducted a service in the Bohemian language at 10 A. M. in addition to the main German service at 7 A. M. Later, in 1837, German services were held in the morning and Bohemian services in the afternoon. A school was maintained for teaching the Bohemian language.

In Dresden, Stephan soon drew the attention of many people. Walther writes in his biography of Buenger: "The less God's Word resounded at that time in the other churches of Dresden, the more Stephan's church was filled with souls of that locality who were eager for salvation, for Stephan really preached the Gospel, and that on the basis of his own personal experience. Like a house of bread, in which every

St. John's Church, Dresden

beggar during a period of most bitter famine might come and take fresh, nourishing bread, stood Stephan's church, in that day the smallest and plainest in that splendid city. Stephan possessed none of the arts of worldly oratory; at least the richly endowed man did not employ them. Hardly moving a hand, seldom modulating his voice, without any force of expression, he plainly and simply declared the counsel of God for man's salvation, showing in the same manner the spirituality and strictness of the Law and the condition of every man by nature, as well as the riches of the Gospel's grace and the sure help which every sinner may find in Christ. Whoever heard him once, if he was not filled with the spirit of scoffing, felt himself moved to the inmost depths of his being, without really knowing how this had come to pass. Although his sermons were not what is usually called attractive, they, nevertheless, had such power that many people, determined never again to enter his church lest they become more disquieted, after a short time were drawn back again with irresistible force. In his sermon Stephan aimed to influence not so much the emotions as the conscience. His wonderful knowledge of men and of the human heart was of great service to him in his ministry. It could never be said of Stephan that he ever designed merely to arouse the emotions. Whoever persuaded himself to go to him for advice and comfort found the most cordial reception and, as a rule, most reliable counsel and true comfort actually drawn from the Word of God and a rich Christian experience."

Although the Bohemian congregation was under the supervision of the consistory of Dresden, its peculiar church organization was permitted to function unmolested. Like his predecessors, Petermann and Czapowitz, Stephan conducted private religious meetings in his parsonage and later in the schoolhouse. Opening and closing these assemblies with hymns and prayers, he reviewed in a catechetical manner the sermon of the previous Sunday.

These meetings, to which more and more souls came seeking salvation, provoked public opposition to Stephan. On August 21, 1821, he was attacked in the public press and branded as the founder of a new fanatical sect. Stephan promptly replied in the *Nationalzeitung der Deutschen*, stating among other things: "I am neither the founder of a sect nor the leader of a sect. I belong neither to an old nor to a new sect. I hate all sectarianism and fanaticism. I am an Evangelical Lutheran minister and preach the Word of God as it is written in the Bible. I build my congregation on the foundation of the Apostles and the Prophets, Jesus Christ being the chief Cornerstone. I have and preach the apostolic religion, preached so purely and courageously by Luther. I preach the Law and the Gospel, the knowledge of sin and the knowledge of grace in Christ, the God-man. I preach faith in Christ, who by His death on the Cross atoned for the sins of the whole world. I preach this plainly, not in any strange, mystic sense, but in the same sense in which our pious forefathers honestly and plainly expressed it in the symbolical writings. I have no peculiar religious opinions; my religion stands neither above nor below the Bible, but it is in the Bible; it leads to Christ and keeps men with Christ."

In 1823 Stephan published two sermons. In the preface he insisted that he taught no other doctrine in his private meetings than that which he proclaimed from his pulpit. The members who came to his private meetings, he said, came and went as they pleased, without placing themselves under any obligation to him. Since his meetings were open to the public, they could not be classified as conventicles.

In 1825 he published a volume of sermons. The advance list of subscribers numbers more than 500, who lived in more than 107 cities, towns, and villages. Stephan says in the introduction: "What I have preached I myself believe with my whole heart. I am firmly convinced that only the Bible can be the fountain of pure doctrine. Out of this our pious forefathers have drawn and preserved for us the pure doctrine in the Confessional Writings of our Evangelical Lutheran Church. The spreading of this doctrine is my sincere *effort* in this book."

From this time on Stephan's prestige and influence began

to grow. Into the orbit of his influence were drawn not only prominent laymen, such as Count Detlev von Einsiedel, Dr. Adolph Marbach, Dr. C. E. Vehse, and others, but also a number of outstanding clergymen. Among these were E. G. W. Keyl of Niederfrohna; G. H. Loeber of Eichenberg, C. F. Gruber of Reust, both in the duchy of Altenburg; E. M. Buerger of Lunzenau and, later, O. H. Walther of Langenchursdorf and C. F. W. Walther of Braeunsdorf. Likewise a number of candidates of theology had become followers of Stephan. While not all these men followed Stephan blindly, they did consider his doctrinal position sound and his judgment of the times and of the state of the Church in Saxony true.

The Lutheranism which some of these clergymen and candidates of theology professed was very much colored by pietism. Moreover, some of the pastors used methods in their parish work which were anything but evangelical. A system of espionage was developed, particularly in Dresden, causing husband to spy on wife, children on parents, and then reporting anything derogatory to Stephan and his followers unto designated authorities. The result was domestic disturbances in the homes of many parishioners. The missionary activities of zealous "Stephanites" produced a state of religious excitement in the Mulde Valley and in Dresden, and members of parishes turned from their duly appointed pastors and teachers to seek out Stephan for spiritual advice. All this served to increase the opposition to Stephan.

The political upheavals of 1830 affected also Stephan and his adherents. Count Detlev von Einsiedel, a Royal Councilor and Minister of the Interior in the Saxon cabinet, was looked upon by the revolutionaries as a reactionary and had to resign his governmental offices and retire to his estate. Thus Stephan lost the immediate protection of an influential man. The same year gave the press more liberty of expression, so that the public assaults upon Stephan multiplied. His personal life, in particular his excursions at night in mixed groups, was attacked. When Stephan did not answer the charges, his congregation, in 1833, through Candidate Poeschel, refuted the accusations brought against its pastor in a pamphlet of 74 pages, entitled *Confession of the Congregation of St. John at Dresden*. Although Stephan's opponents persisted in maligning and persecuting him, even haling him before court on charges of holding conventicles and of unseemly conduct, he was completely exonerated through the efforts of Dr. Marbach, an adroit lawyer and a city official of Dresden.

It was about this time that Stephan began seriously to consider leaving Germany with his flock. Dr. Benjamin Kurtz of Baltimore, who had visited Stephan in Dresden in 1827, wrote in the *Observer* of November 16, 1839: "A few years after our return [1830] to the United States, we received a letter from Mr. Stephan, stating that he and his people still cherished the pleasing prospect, painful as in many respects it might be, of bidding adieu unto the place of their nativity and childhood, their homes, their relations, their favorite old house of worship, etc., and of locating in the land of the free. At the same time Mr. Stephan made many inquiries as to the best mode of arranging the great work of emigration, the relative price of land, the climate, healthfulness, etc., of several states. We consulted a few of our friends in this city [Baltimore], especially Mr. C. W. Karthaus and Mr. F. L. Brauns, intelligent and highly respectable merchants. We then advised Mr. Stephan to send a delegation of two or three intelligent members of his church to this country to spy out the land, select a location, etc., or, if this should not be approved of, to embark at Bremen or Amsterdam in the autumn, sail for New Orleans, then up the Mississippi, and settle in the State of Missouri, etc., but if they should set sail in the spring, then their better plan would be to direct their course to Baltimore, thence to Wheeling, down the Ohio, etc." [2]

Christopher Friedrich von Ammon, chief court preacher at Dresden and vice-president of the Superior Consistory, a decided rationalist, published in 1833 *The Development of Christianity as a Universal Religion,* in which he endeavored to square the Bible religion with the results of science. He advocated Christianity as a universal religion, which would appeal to both religionists and scientists. This book, written by an official of such high rank, was considered by many of Stephan's followers as the death knell of confessional Lutheranism. When, in 1835, Ammon, Roehr, and Bretschneider — all Lutheran church dignitaries — attended the jubilee of the Reformed Church at Geneva; when in the same year a Lutheran candidate of theology was appointed preacher of the Reformed church in Dresden, the Old Lutherans in Dresden no longer doubted that a church union was inevitable.

Accordingly, a number of Stephan's friends, pastors, theological candidates, and laymen, met in his home during the latter part of May, 1836. The religious situation in Saxony was canvassed and this resolution adopted: "Emigration to a country where the Church may enjoy perfect religious liberty has become an urgent necessity." A general committee was appointed to draw up regulations governing the emigration, to select applicants, collect necessary funds, to charter ships, and to purchase essential equipment for a colony to be established in America.

To finance the undertaking, a common treasury was arranged, into which $80,900.74 were paid. With this the Dresden committee bought a theological library, a pipe organ, band instruments, church music, Communion vessels, four church bells, materials for clergy vestments, and many other items to be used in church and school.

Missouri was chosen for the site of the new colony. Reports of Dr. Gottfried Duden had directed attention to this State. In 1834, in company of an agriculturist, Louis Eversmann, Duden had bought 270 acres of Government land near Dutzow, on Lake Creek, Warren County, Missouri. In 36 letters he issued an *Account of a Journey to the Western States of North America and of a Several Years' Sojourn on the Missouri in the Years 1824—1827*. His book, circulating in numerous editions during the social, religious, and political upheavals of the thirties, led many thousands of Germans to Missouri.

In 1835 the Council of Dresden forbade Stephan to extend his evening religious meetings beyond 10 P. M., under the pretext that they were becoming subversive of the welfare of the city. In reality, however, the City Council was moved to issue this order by the Chief Consistorial Councilor Ammon, who thought thereby to counteract the influence of the pastor of St. John's. On November 8, 1837, Stephan was caught transgressing the edict of the city authorities. His suspension from office followed immediately. Candidate G. Kluegel preached in St. John's Church the following Sunday on Matt. 24:15, emphasizing the abomination of desolation as manifested in the procedure of the Dresden city officials against Pastor Stephan. Three charges were placed against him: immoral conduct, misappropriation of congregational funds, and neglect of pastoral duties. Although Stephan was able to clear himself in court, he was no longer permitted to preach in St. John's Church.

In the following year, 1838, meetings of Stephan's followers were held in Dresden, Leipzig, and Niederfrohna under the leadership of Dr. Marbach, and it was resolved to leave Germany even if Stephan were detained by the Saxon authorities and should not be able to accompany the emigrants. On May 17, 1838, the committee of the emigrants prepared and adopted a set of regulations for emigrants, of which Paragraph Two reads:

"Emigration: its cause, end, and aim. After the calmest and purest reflection they [the emigrants] see the human impossibility before them to retain, confess, and transmit to their descendants this faith in their present homeland. They are, therefore, constrained by their conscience to emigrate and search for a land where the Lutheran faith is not endangered and where they can serve God unhindered according to the Word of Grace and where they can enjoy the use of the Means of Grace, ordained by God for the salvation of all men, in their completeness and purity and preserve them for themselves and their descendants." [3]

It was at this time that Stephan sent word to his followers that "the hour to depart has struck; the time to flee from Babel has come; whoever desires to save his soul should get ready to leave." Keyl announced to his people: "Whoever does not emigrate is no Christian." These words of the Savior were thrown at the people: "And a man's foes shall be they of his own household. He that loveth father or mother more than Me is not worthy of Me." Likewise Matt. 19:29, "And everyone that hath forsaken houses, or brethren, or sisters, or father, or mother, or wife, or children, or lands for My name's sake shall receive an hundredfold and shall inherit everlasting life," was often quoted. The time had come when God was calling to the faithful in the manner He had called to Abraham: "Get thee out of thy [idolatrous] country and from thy kindred and from thy father's house unto a land that I will show thee."

Excitement ran high among the followers of Stephan. Dr. Walther writes that by September 4, 1838, the following numbers presented themselves: from Dresden and vicinity (Pastor Stephan): 240 souls; Eichenberg (Pastor G. H. Loeber): 108, among whom were Teacher J. F. F. Winter's group from Planena, near Halle, whose pastor, Dr. H. E. F.

Guericke, refused to join the movement; Frohna (Pastor E. G. W. Keyl): 109; Lunzenau (Pastor E. M. Buerger): 84; Paitzdorf (Pastor C. F. Gruber): 48; Braeunsdorf (Pastor C. F. W. Walther): 19; Langenchursdorf (Pastor O. H. Walther): 16; Leipzig: 31; and 20 individuals. Total: 707 souls. Very few of the emigrants realized that Stephan and not God was calling them. Preachers, schoolteachers, State officials, resigned their positions; farmers sold their lands, lawyers and physicians gave up their practice, artisans and craftsmen laid down their tools. It even happened that married people left their spouses, parents their children, children their parents, all under the delusion that thereby they were saving the true Church. A number of country girls whose parents had refused permission for them to leave, so that they could not obtain passports, left their homes disguised as students or as ladies of fashion and made the journey to Bremen on foot in order to join the emigrants.

Besides the seven pastors the group numbered the following candidates of theology: Theo. J. Brohm, J. F. Buenger, E. F. A. Froehlich, O. Fuerbringer, C. L. Geyer, J. Goenner, G. Kluegel, G. A. Schieferdecker, E. J. M. Wege, and K. W. Welzel; schoolteachers: F. Winter, F. Koch, J. Hellwig, J. G. A. K. Zoege, C. A. Schuetzler, and C. J. O. Nitschke; two doctors of medicine: Schnabel and Schroeder; two renowned lawyers: Dr. Franz Adolph Marbach and Dr. Carl Eduard Vehse, several civil service employees and merchants. The largest number, however, were tradesmen and craftsmen. There were 160 children, 110 of school age.

On September 30, 1838, the *Leipziger Allgemeine Zeitung* published a declaration of nine pastors with reference to the disturbances within the Saxon State Church caused by Stephan and his adherents. The statement, signed also by Dr. A. G. Rudelbach, condemned the emigration as premature, sinful, and unnecessary. (Rudelbach himself resigned his ecclesiastical offices in 1845 and returned to his native

Denmark in protest against the abuses tolerated in the Saxon Church.)

A more favorable opinion appeared in the *Bremer Zeitung* of November 7, 1838. "Pastor Martin Stephan of Dresden has arrived in our city and with him two hundred of his fellow Lutherans to embark for New Orleans. More than four hundred persons, who arrived from Saxony via Hamburg, have already set sail. . . . The more we learn to know these well-mannered, law-abiding, and, in fact, highly educated people, the more we are strengthened in the conviction that the various newspaper reports about Pastor Stephan and his congregation may have originated from very sordid and malicious sources and that they are greatly distorted, if not entirely false. It is to be deplored that Germany, and especially Saxony, is losing in them a part of its peaceable, industrious, and well-to-do inhabitants, against whom no other charge can be adduced than that they strictly adhere to the teachings of Luther. It gives us some satisfaction, however, to visualize a colony growing up along the Missouri River which will be a credit to the German name, and we wish our departing countrymen the best of success for their undertaking." [4]

Ludwig Fischer in his "False Martyrdom of the Stephanites," quoting the *Leipziger Allgemeine Zeitung*, states that the emigrants left Dresden in three groups on October 4, 18, and 28, respectively, traveling on barges down the Elbe to Hamburg, thence overland to Bremen.

Pastor Stephan was the last to arrive. He had once more run afoul of the law and was detained in his home by the authorities from October 15 to 24. The charges against him were suppressed by royal abolition, and after posting a bond of 500 thaler (about $325.00), he left Dresden at midnight. October 27, leaving behind his wife and seven children. One son, Martin, was among the emigrants. Stephan arrived at Bremen November 4.

Before sailing from Bremerhaven, the emigrants published their *Exulantenlieder* (Hymns of the Exiles), composed by Pastor O. H. Walther. Stephan published the following "Farewell" in the Bremen papers.

"FAREWELL OF THE OLD LUTHERAN CONGREGATION,
TRAVELING FROM SAXONY TO NORTH AMERICA

"Before we leave Germany and Europe, we desire to transmit friendly greetings and farewells to our friends who are remaining behind. After many years of defamation we are at long last delivered from the hands of our enemies and are traveling in peace to that part of the world where they who are slandered have the privilege of defending themselves publicly. Though we are parting with painful memories of many bitter experiences, we are not unmindful of the manifold favors bestowed upon us by people of high and low estate. Our hearts are filled with sincere thanks to all who showed solicitude for us. We ask God to compensate them richly for this in their hour of need. With reference to our many enemies, we wish to heed the words of our Lord Jesus Christ: 'Love your enemies,' etc., Matt. 5:44. If you, dear friends, desire to travel with us in spirit to America, you will find an Old-Lutheran congregation, sailing on five ships under the protection of God. Six clergymen with about 700 souls, among them 10 candidates of theology and four schoolteachers, are joyfully traveling to a land where, unpersecuted and according to their best knowledge and conscience, they can preserve the faith of their fathers, serve God therein, and in this faith travel the way through time to eternity in peace.   STEPHAN"[5]

The uncompromising attitude of the emigrants had an effect upon the consistory of Sachsen-Altenburg, Pastor Loeber's home, for on November 13, 1838, it ordered all its pastors and teachers henceforth to preach the Gospel in its purity and all the fundamental doctrines of the Christian Church.

The first ship to set sail from Bremerhaven was the *Copernicus*, weighing anchor on November 3 and reaching New Orleans December 31, 1838. Pastor Buerger was the officiating clergyman of this ship. On the same day the *Johann Georg*, in charge of Pastor Keyl, assisted by Pastor C. F. W. Walther, sailed, arriving in port on January 5, 1839. On November 12, the *Republik* left, its passengers being ministered to by Pastor Loeber. It arrived at New Orleans on January 12, 1839. The fourth vessel, the *Olbers*, set out to sea on November 18, making port on January 20, 1839. Pastors Stephan and O. H. Walther were on this ship. The *Amalia* likewise left on November 18, but was lost at sea. Pastor C. F. W. Walther had been designated chaplain of this boat, but in order to avoid useless detention on a charge of having abducted some children, sailed on the *Johann Georg*, using the reservation for Candidate Goenner, who transferred to the *Olbers*. Walther later was exonerated from the charge in the public press of Germany.

After a stay of several days in New Orleans, the passengers reshipped to the river steamers *Rienzi, Clyde, Knickerbocker,* and *Selma*, arriving in St. Louis on January 18, 24, 30, and February 19, respectively. When the *Rienzi* arrived in St. Louis, it was met by Pastor Maximilian Oertel. Oertel, who had been in touch with the Stephan movement in Germany, had been sent to America by the Barmen Mission Society, arriving in New York with Pastors John Muehlhaeuser and L. Nollau, October 3, 1837. Here he ministered to a group of Lutherans from Berlin, who, on Stephan's advice, had left for New York. Arriving in St. Louis on January 3, 1839, Oertel immediately identified himself with the Stephanites.

During the sea voyage Stephan persuaded his fellow passengers to elect him bishop. He urged the necessity of

THE SAXON EMIGRATION

central authority and stated that while he wished to be only the bishop's adviser, it would be best, since there was no one else for the position, to give it to him. While traveling up the Mississippi, he had a "Declaration of Submission to the Bishop" drawn up by virtue of which all signatories were to submit to his authority in temporal as well as in spiritual matters. His election as bishop as well as the Declaration was ratified by the immigrants from the other ships in St. Louis.

When the different groups arrived in St. Louis, they moved into rented quarters, which eventually cost them $500 to $600 a month. A committee was entrusted with the selection of a suitable tract of land upon which the colony might establish itself. On April 8 the committee purchased 4,472.66 acres of land in Perry County, Missouri, for $9,234.25 and paid an additional $1,000 for the landing place at Wittenberg.

Where the group met for divine services from January 18 until March 3 while in St. Louis is not known, but it may be inferred from some statements of Schieferdecker that they used the public school buildings for this purpose. After March 3 they were given the use of Christ Church Cathedral basement, in which they worshiped until December 4, 1842, when they dedicated their own church. Bishop Jackson Kemper, missionary bishop of the Northwest (Missouri and Indiana), read the following notice to his congregation:

"A body of Lutherans, having been persecuted by the Saxon government because they believed it their duty to adhere to the doctrines inculcated by their great leader and contained in the Augsburg Confession of Faith, have arrived here with the intention of settling in this or one of the neighboring States, and having been deprived of the privilege of worship for three months, they have earnestly and most respectfully requested the use of our church that they may again unite in all the ordinances of our holy religion. I have, therefore, with the entire approbation of the vestry, granted the use of our church from this day, from 2 P. M. until sunset, to a denomination whose early members were highly esteemed by the English Reformers and with whom our glorious martyrs Cranmer, Ridley, and others had much early intercourse."

For these services Stephan appointed Pastor Keyl as the official salaried preacher until April 26, when Pastor Loeber

St. Louis in 1839

was made Stephan's vicar. Schools were established immediately for the children. On April 26 Stephan, accompanied by Keyl, O. H. Walther, Brohm, Dr. Marbach, and a second group of workmen — the first having preceded them on April 10 — left for Perry County. The larger part of the immigrants, including Pastors Loeber, Buerger, C. F. Walther, and all candidates except Brohm, remained in St. Louis.

The American population of St. Louis was friendly towards the Saxons. Not so, however, the *Anzeiger des Westens,* founded in 1835 by Herr von Festen and Christian Bimpage. This paper was the mouthpiece of political and religious liberalism and the leading representative of "en-

St. Louis Levee Scene, 1839

lightened German thought" in the Middle West. Obsessed by memories of the priest-ridden Church in Germany, it loudly objected to all forms of organized religion and designated all preachers as despicable "Pfaffen," whose one aim was to fleece their victims and to hold them in ecclesiastical bondage. Stephan and his groups did not escape the ire of this publication, which for many years applied opprobrious terms to the Stephanites.[6] On April 27 a public defense signed by the Saxon clergy was published in the *Anzeiger des Westens* against its attacks. A similar defense was inserted by the twelve lay deputies of the Saxons on May 4.

The colony in Perry County was strengthened on May 18 by the arrival of Candidate J. F. Buenger with 95 "Berliner" at Wittenberg. They had come from New York by way of the Ohio and the Mississippi Rivers. This group, mostly Prussian and Hessian peasants, was part of the flock served by the aforementioned Pastor Oertel. Buenger joined the "Berliner" because he was unable to leave Germany with his fellow Saxons. When he arrived at Bremen on November 7, 1838, he learned to his dismay that his mother had been arrested because "she had abducted two orphans without their guardian's consent." In spite of every effort he could not effect her release. He therefore remained with her and his two sisters until she was acquitted on December 11, 1838. Then Buenger, together with his mother and sister Clementine (his sister Emma remained in Germany), sailed for New York on December 21 via the *Constitution,* arriving in port on February 18, 1839. At Stephan's suggestion he accompanied the "Berliner" to Perry County.

The immigrants' cause received a severe blow when it was discovered that their leader had become unworthy of the trust reposed in him. Pastor C. F. W. Walther was dispatched by the St. Louis clergy and candidates to Perry County to confront Stephan with the evidence and secure for the immigrants the support of the colony trustees. The immigrants who had remained in St. Louis went down to Perry County, May 23, on two steamboats, the *Toledo* and the *Prairie*. On the following day the Council, which consisted of the pastors and five laymen, deposed Stephan from office. On May 31 he was taken by boat across the Mississippi to the Devil's Bakeoven on the Illinois side, where he found temporary refuge in a farmhouse. Later Stephan became pastor of the congregation at Horse Prairie, near Red Bud, Ill., where he died on February 26, 1846. An Evangelical pastor, A. Baltzer, preached the funeral sermon.

On June 1, 1839, through the medium of the *Anzeiger des Westens*, the Saxons formally renounced all association with Stephan. The statement bears the date May 27, 1839.

With the unfrocking and removal of Stephan, bewilderment, confusion, and consternation seized the immigrants. The Committee on Administration was reorganized, and every attempt was made to continue the communal way of living. However, the cost of the voyage, the purchase of land, the extravagant living of Bishop Stephan, and other unwise expenditures had so depleted the treasury that on June 22, 1839, it was reported that only $2,000 of the original $80,000 remained. Dissatisfied with the way affairs were being managed, the vice-president, secretary, and treasurer of the Administration Committee, Dr. C. E. Vehse, Henry Fischer, and Gustav Jaeckel, resigned their positions, after having shown the futility of continuing a communal form of living and having urged private enterprise.

The process of decentralization soon followed. The land was divided among the immigrants, and colonies were established. Under date of September 30, 1839, Loeber wrote his brother: "We are now divided into five congregations, whose five clergymen form a joint ministry. The older Walther serves the congregation which remained in St. Louis and is permitted to worship in the Episcopal Church. To this congregation belong chiefly craftsmen, who find abundant work in the city and who intend to accumulate some funds before coming to settle with us in the country. Many inhabitants of St. Louis attend our services, so that the Sunday collections suffice to maintain the pastor and the teacher (Candidate Geyer) and to support the sick and the poor. ... The younger Walther serves the congregation at Dresden and the Berliner' group. At Dresden are a number of houses, built of boards, erected when the colony was established, in one of which the three married pastors (Keyl, Loeber, Buerger) live, somewhat crowded, but without being in each other's way. Walther, together with Candidate Fuerbringer, lives with the 'Berliner.' Opposite our home many families live together in a much larger shack of flimsy build. In this house we have our common services and give the most necessary instruction to the children until our college and the church and school of each congregation are completed. Next to the Dresden congregation are the Altenburgers with their families from Planena and Halle, several from Saxony, Dresden, Hannover, and New York, who have called me as pastor. Two farmhouses are available, which will serve after some time as parsonage and schoolhouse. Bordering on my congregation is the group of Pastor Keyl, which numbers least in membership but which should be strengthened yet this year by the arrival of Pastor Gruber. Towards the Mississippi is the congregation of Seelitz, served by Pastor Buerger. And finally there is a group at the landing place (Wittenberg), served by one of us pastors or by Candidate Schieferdecker." [7]

Pastor Oertel, dissatisfied with existing conditions, left Perry County and returned to New York, where he joined the Roman Catholic Church. Of his former members, some went to St. Louis, others joined the congregations in Perry County. Sixteen of the "Berliner," Catholics and Reformed, were received, after due instruction, into the Lutheran

Altenburg's First Parsonage

Church by the rite of confirmation by Pastor Loeber, the senior of the clergy, in the presence of his colleagues.

Distressing times now came for the settlers. Reduced to stark poverty and unaccustomed to the tasks before them, they had a difficult time becoming acclimatized. Writes Schieferdecker: "Not only the poorer, but also the wealthier ones faced need in view of the coming winter. The fevers peculiar to the climate soon made their appearance and caused terrible ravages, a fact which was intensified by the lack of sufficient shelter, conveniences, and other necessities of human life as well as by the hardships and labors under a burning sun, the danger of which was not yet appreciated. The new population was soon decimated, death claiming the strongest people. Others lay sick with the fever for weeks and months, lacking the most necessary care, because those who would gladly have done the nursing were themselves ill. The present writer remembers that in a rude frame house on the bank of the Mississippi not only the lower story, but the upper story as well was filled with sick people, who, in addition to the heat of the fever, languished with the oppressively hot atmosphere; he remembers that in the following autumn, in one part of the colony, called Seelitz, there was not one of the buildings which had been erected in haste out of logs and in part had to house several families that was not filled with several sick persons suffering severe cases of fever. The buildings were literally hospitals, and often there was hardly anyone in a position to dispense the necessary care to the sick one." [8] "All this," remarks Koestering, "had to come, that they might be weaned away from putting their trust in man, and cast themselves into the arms of God's gracious protection." [9]

While the colonists were laboring under these physical tribulations and were suffering bitter, biting poverty, there appeared in the *Anzeiger des Westens* an item dated August 13, 1839:

"An Institution of Instruction and Education

"We, the undersigned, intend to establish an institution of instruction and education which distinguishes itself from ordinary elementary schools, especially by this, that it comprises, besides the ordinary branches, all college sciences (*Gymnasialwissenschaften*) necessary to a true Christian and scientific education, as religion, the Latin, Greek and Hebrew, German, French and English languages, history, geography, mathematics, physics, natural history, elementary philosophy, music, drawing. The pupils of our institution are to be so far advanced in the above-named studies that, after absolving a complete course of study, they will be qualified for university studies. The esteemed parents who may desire to place their children into our institution are requested to make inquiries regarding its plan and arrangements of Pastor O. H. Walther in St. Louis, 14 Poplar Street, between First and Second Streets. Instructions are to begin, God willing, on the 1st of October of this year.

"The settlement of the German Lutherans in Perry County, near the Obrazo, August 13, 1839.

"C. Ferd. W. Walther
"Ottomar Fuerbringer
"Th. Jul. Brohm
"Joh. Fr. Buenger"

The log-cabin college was erected by Pastor C. F. W. Walther and Candidates Buenger, Brohm, and Fuerbringer. It was opened for classes on December 9, 1839. The first enrollment consisted of F. J. Biltz, J. A. F. W. Mueller, C. H. Loeber, H. Buenger, Theo. Schubert, Columbus Price, Theobald von Wurmb, Lydia Buenger, Martha Loeber, Marie and Sarah von Wurmb. The girls were instructed by Candidate Buenger.

Pastor C. F. Gruber arrived from Paitzdorf, Saxony, on December 13, 1839, with a good part of his own congregation as well as stragglers from Frohna and Dresden, 141 souls in all, to found the settlement of Paitzdorf in Perry County.

Great as were the physical hardships which the immigrants in Perry County had to endure, the spiritual tribulations which engulfed them were even more severe and dangerous. They were the results of Stephan's false teaching regarding the doctrine of the Church and the office of the ministry. He had taught that the visible Lutheran Church was the only Church in which salvation was possible. Accordingly, they who wished to be saved must join him in his emigration. Concerning the office of the ministry he had maintained that this office, instituted immediately by God, had been given by Christ to His Apostles and by these transmitted to others. Only through the ministry could the grace of God be offered,

Log Cabin in Altenburg

O. Fuerbringer

J. F. Buenger

through the means of grace indeed, but they had to be dispensed by ordained ministers. The office of the ministry continued even if the minister had no congregation and no hearers. They who accepted the preaching formed the flock of Christ and together with the ministry constituted the Church.

When Stephan had been deposed, a natural reaction followed. Men like Vehse, Fischer, and Jaeckel repudiated the false teaching of Stephan regarding the office of the ministry and the Church and insisted — in an extreme manner — upon the prerogatives of their spiritual priesthood and upon the rights and privileges of a congregation. Men like Marbach, Barthel, Sproede, Candidate Kluegel, and others, on the other hand, maintained that the immigrants by leaving their congregations in Germany had severed themselves from the Church and that they could not establish the office of the ministry in their midst. In the resulting confusion Pastor Buerger resigned his office as pastor of the congregation at Seelitz, convinced that he was not and could not be lawfully called by this congregation. Pastor Loeber, who had left his congregation in Germany, was inclined to resign and then either to return home or to remain in America as a layman.

Dr. Vehse addressed a memorandum to Pastor O. H. Walther on August 5, 1839, in which he endeavored to set forth the Scriptural and confessional doctrine of the ministry. On September 19, 1839, a "Public Protest against the False Medieval Papistic and Sectarian Stephanite System of Ecclesiastical Government," signed by Vehse, Jaeckel, and Fischer, with a supplement as of November 20, was addressed to the clergy members of the group.

The result was that "the discussions and debates were unending. It was impossible to escape them. In the homes, in the gatherings of the neighbors, in the meetings of the clergy, the same questions were raised again and again.

Their solution seemed impossible. A splitting up of the colony into a pitiable number of little separatistic groups seemed inevitable. The pendulum, which under 'Bishop' Stephan had swung so far toward Rome, now swung back just as far toward the Donatistic error, which denies the character of the Church to any but a perfectly pure and sinless church body. These people, who had held themselves to be the only true visible Church on earth, now doubted or denied that they were Christians or a Church at all. They who had been inclined to make the validity of the holy Sacraments dependent upon ordination at the hands of Stephan now questioned the validity of any and every official ministerial act. They who formerly had been tempted to limit salvation to a use of the means of grace dispensed by Stephan and his adherents now questioned the possibility of their being saved under any condition or circumstance whatsoever. In short, their whole emigration, which they once had looked upon as a great work of God, now seemed to be only the work of the devil." [10]

For two years these questions agitated the minds of the people. The man who was to be the instrument in God's hand to dispel the doubts and misgivings of the immigrants by setting forth the Scriptural truth concerning the doctrine of the Church and the ministry was Carl Ferdinand Wilhelm Walther.

3

CARL FERDINAND WILHELM WALTHER

WALTHER came from a family of Lutheran clergymen. His father and grandfather were pastors of the Lutheran congregation at Langenchursdorf, Saxony. There Carl Ferdinand Wilhelm was born, October 23, 1811, the eighth child and the fourth son.

After having been taught the elementary subjects by his father and the village schoolmaster, he attended the school at Hohenstein, near Chemnitz (1819—1821). He then entered the *Gymnasium* at Schneeberg. Magister H. F. W. Schubert, who had married Walther's older sister, was co-principal at this school. Here Walther remained for eight years, until 1829.

During these years, the age of rationalism, Walther heard but little of the Bible. He writes: "I was eighteen years old when I left the *Gymnasium,* and I never heard a sentence of the Word of God coming from a believing heart. I had never had a Bible, neither a Catechism, but only a miserable *Leitfaden* (guide), which contained heathen morality. My dear God-fearing father taught me from childhood that the Bible is the Word of God. But I soon left my parental home — in my eighth year — to live in unbelieving circles. I did not lose this historic faith. It accompanied me through my life like an angel of God. But I spent my more than eight years of college life unconverted." [1]

Walther desired to study music, but the reading of a biography of the famous J. F. Oberlin by G. H. Schubert determined him to devote his life to the study of theology. He entered the University of Leipzig in 1829. Only two of the members of the faculty taught the doctrine of faith, namely Profs. August Hahn and F. W. Lindner, Sr. But they did this somewhat indifferently.

Not long before Walther entered the university, a small group of students had established a so-called "pious fraternity." The small circle of friends met regularly for mutual edification through prayer, reading of Scripture, religious books, and the discussion of things pertaining to their salvation. Among other members of this group were Theodore Brohm, who later became secretary to Stephan at Dresden; Joh. Fr. Buenger, a descendant of a family of Lutheran clergymen reaching back to the Reformation, and Ottomar Fuerbringer.

The leader of this group was Candidate Kuehn. He had come to a joyful, full assurance of faith only after a long period of spiritual conflict under the most agonizing conviction of sin and unspeakable terror of God's holy Law. Therefore he attempted to lead the young men who sought his guidance into the same path he himself had gone, testing every man's religious experience by his own. He insisted that a person's Christianity did not rest upon a firm foundation unless, like himself, one had experienced the keenest sorrow for sin and had known the very terrors of hell in agonizing struggles of repentance. Consequently, a joyful, evangelical Christianity developed into one of gloom and legalism in these young hearts.

The books chiefly read by this circle were of the pietistic school, whose weakness consisted in disregarding pure doctrine and espousing a religion of emotion and practical benevolence. "The less a book invited to faith," says Walther, "and the more legalistically it insisted upon contrite brokenness of heart and upon a complete mortification of the old man, the better we held it to be. Even such writings we read only so far as they described the griefs and exercises of remorse; when a description of faith and comfort followed, we usually closed the book, for, so we thought, this is as yet nothing for us." [2]

Occasionally the young men would walk out to Frohna to hear Pastor Keyl preach. Walther was deeply impressed by his sermons. While at Leipzig the group attended the services of Pastor F. A. Wolf of St. Peter's Church and later worshiped at St. George's Church, F. M. Haensel, pastor.

Soon most of the men who had formed this circle completed their studies and departed from the university, leaving only Brohm, Buenger, and Walther, who united in lifelong friendship. When Brohm, who lived with Buenger, left, the latter and Walther became inseparable companions.

The only family which understood the spiritual condition of these men and whose home was at all times open to them was that of Friederich Wilhelm Barthel, who later joined the Stephanist movement and was Treasurer of the Missouri Synod from 1847 to 1859.

The blessings of his association with this family are related by Walther in the funeral sermon which he preached for Mrs. Barthel in 1881. "Fifty years have just passed," said Walther, "since I had the good fortune to be introduced by a pious friend to the family of the deceased. A youth without God lay behind me, and having come to the knowledge of Jesus Christ only a short time before, a new outlook on life was opened to me. I saw a truly Christian household, a family in which Jesus was all in all, in which the Word of God was daily food for souls. Thus I found my spiritual parents here, a father and mother in Christ, who now cared for me, spiritually and bodily, as for a son.

"At that time I was in deep spiritual affliction, famished in body and soul, doubting my salvation, wrestling with despair. No praying, weeping, fasting, or struggling seemed able to help. The peace of God had departed from my soul. It was then that the dear departed took me into her motherly heart. She wrestled with God day and night, interceding for me, and whenever I crossed her threshold, her lips overflowed with evangelical consolation for me. And God heard her supplications. At last I found peace in Christ. A bond of blessed fellowship in Christ embraced us, which nothing was able to tear asunder until her death." [3]

An even greater stabilizing factor in his spiritual life was the comfort and encouragement written Walther by Stephan. When no one was able to help him in his spiritual distress, pastors whose aid he had sought advised him to write to Stephan. This he did. When he received Stephan's reply, he did not open the letter until he had knelt in prayer and asked God to prevent his receiving false comfort should such be contained in Stephan's missive. But after reading it, he felt himself elevated from the depths of hell to the bliss of heaven. His tears of penitent grief changed to tears of joyful faith, for Stephan demonstrated to him that he had long experienced the contrition he sought in the Law and that he lacked nothing but faith. Walther says that he could not resist, he had to come to Jesus. And so the peace of God entered his heart.

Walther was deeply grateful to Stephan. When about a half year later Dr. Rudelbach informed him that he intended to propose him as tutor for a pious count provided that he would break off all relations with Stephan, Walther told him in detail what had led him to Stephan and asked: "Shall I forsake the man who by God's grace has saved my soul?" Deeply moved, Rudelbach replied, "No, my dear Walther, you must not forsake him; in God's name continue your relations with him, but beware of all worship of man." [4]

Ill health caused Walther to interrupt his studies during the winter of 1831—1832. While he was recuperating at home, he found the works of Dr. Luther in his father's library. His living conviction of the Scriptural character of the doctrine of the Lutheran Church and the necessity of its positive confession dates from that time.

His health having been restored, Walther returned to the university after the Easter season, 1832, and finished his theological course the following year. In 1834 he accepted a position as private tutor in the family of Attorney F. Loeber in Kahla, the brother of Pastor G. H. Loeber. Here he remained until 1836, when through Count Detlev von Einsiedel he was appointed to the congregation at Braeunsdorf.

Walther's steadfastness and faith were put to a severe test in his first charge. In addition to his unchristian, rationalistic superintendent, who despised him and hated him on account of his firm Lutheran stand, Walther had to contend with his unbelieving village schoolmaster, who opposed him wherever he could and stirred up enmity and strife against him.

When Stephan called upon his adherents to follow him to America, Walther heeded the call. However, he did not share Stephan's and the other emigrants' view that by leaving Germany they were saving the true Church of God. Koestering tells us: "We have often heard from the old emigrants that one of the pastors often testified before the other pastors and candidates that even though Stephan and the entire group would sink into the deepest depth of the sea, the Church would, for that reason, not perish, since there were some hidden believers in the corrupt State Church of Germany, whom the Lord was preserving as a holy seed among a faithless generation. He was not emigrating for Stephan's sake, but in order to help build the Kingdom of God in America." [5]

It would seem that Stephan did not trust Walther.

Koestering tells us that Stephan called Walther his Judas and tried to prevent his emigration to America. Hochstetter reports that while Walther was in St. Louis, Candidate Kluegel was assigned to him as roommate, with instructions to keep an eye on him.

After Stephan's removal from the colony, Walther remained in Perry County, assuming the pastorate of the congregations at Dresden and Johannisburg. He was much afflicted during the ensuing spiritual turmoil. Under date of May 4, 1840, he writes his brother Otto Hermann in St. Louis:

"The chief questions with which we are now concerned are these: are our congregations Christian Lutheran congregations, or are they sects? Have they the power to call and to excommunicate? Are we pastors, or are we not? Are our calls valid? Do we still belong to Germany, especially Pastor Loeber, who did not receive a governmental dismissal from office? Is it possible for us to have a divine call, since we have forsaken our divine call in Germany and run away, following our erring conscience? Ought not our congregations now depose us from office, since they realize with us what great offense we have given? Would it not be better if the congregations would at least dismiss us and then for a while endeavor to maintain themselves by the exercise of their spiritual priesthood, whereupon they might choose for themselves either the old pastors or new ones? It is impossible for me to give you all the various answers to all these questions as they have been given. Mr. Marbach has the strongest doubts that our congregations are Christian Lutheran congregations, that they may rightfully call and excommunicate, and that we are pastors; Mr. Sproede denies it most emphatically. Both advise a temporary dissolving of all ecclesiastical and congregational organization, hence, no longer visit the public service and confine themselves to worship in the home. In substantial agreement with their thinking is the former Candidate Kluegel and Tax Commissioner Barthel. Similar scruples have assailed Brohm, but more in his innermost soul; he attends public services and does not separate himself." [6]

During the spring of 1841 Walther was confined to the home of his brother-in-law, Pastor Keyl, with a stubborn illness. While convalescing, he used the opportunity to study the works of Luther and other sound Lutheran theologians and finally discovered the truth concerning the doctrine of the Church and the ministry.

At the suggestion of Pastor Buerger a public debate was arranged for April 15 and 20, 1841, in Altenburg. Pastor Walther, assisted by Pastors Loeber and Keyl, presented and defended the Scriptural views of the doctrine of the Church and the ministry, while Dr. Marbach and Pastor Buerger represented the opposing side.

In a manuscript prepared by Walther for the occasion and preserved for us by Koestering, he stated: "God removed a great oppressor from our midst, to whom we, contrary to the will of God, had entrusted ourselves as to a leader from heaven. What would have become of us if God had not continued to have compassion on us? But God did not yet weary of being merciful to us; He awakened men among us who gave public testimony of what they recognized as a remaining corruption. With deep gratitude I must here recall that document which, now almost a year and a half ago, Doctor Vehse, Mr. Fischer, and Mr. Jaeckel addressed to us. It was this document, in particular, which gave us a powerful impulse to recognize the remaining corruption more and more, and to endeavor to remove it. Without this document — I now confess it with a living conviction — we might have for a long time pursued our way of error, from which we now have made our escape. I confess this with an even greater sense of shame, because I at first appeared so ungrateful towards this precious gift of God. But although many with me handled with great unfaithfulness the light which was granted to us, yet God did not cease to cause ever more beams of truth to fall into our darkness; to tear us away from many a point which we, in our perverseness, sought to hold; to uncover to us great and perilous spiritual injuries, and to lead our hearts more and more in the way of truth." [7]

On the basis of eight prepared theses Walther demonstrated the Scriptural doctrine of the Church and the ministry so convincingly that Dr. Marbach after the first debate (April 15) declared himself in full agreement with the five paragraphs discussed and testified to this by subscribing to the record of the proceedings. After the second disputation (April 20), Marbach expressed himself as follows:

"1. I acknowledge that the Christian Church is present here.
2. I have been extricated from my fundamental error.
3. The true Lord's Supper is present here.
4. There remains for me only the question whether I can take part in it." [8]

Pastor Walther immediately instructed him with reference to Point Four, and Marbach graciously accepted the instruction.

The Altenburg Debate achieved its purpose. The hearts of the people were established, and the gloom and distress that had embraced them vanished. Years later, Pastor Geo. A. Schieferdecker, President of the Western District of the Missouri Synod, remarked regarding this disputation: "More was not needed to free the consciences from the heavy oppression, to restore faith in the hearts of many, and to revive them as from death. It was the Easter Morn of our sorely tried congregations when, like the disciples, they again beheld the Lord and in the light of His grace and in the power of His resurrection were filled with joy and hope. As important as was the Leipzig Debate (1519) for the Reformation, equally important was the Altenburg Debate for the progress and development of the Lutheran Church in the West."

The day after the Altenburg Debate, Walther embarked for St. Louis to succeed his brother as pastor of the local Lutheran church.

The Saxon immigrants remaining in St. Louis and several who had returned from Perry County had called Pastor O. H. Walther as their minister. He was inducted into office on the second Sunday after Trinity, June 9, 1839. Candidate C. L. Geyer, Walther's cousin, taught the school. Pastor O. H. Walther died on January 21, 1841, at the age of 31 years and four months. Funeral sermons were delivered by G. Wall, an Evangelical pastor in St. Louis, and by Candidate J. F. Buenger. A week later Candidate Geo. A. Schieferdecker preached a memorial sermon. By a strange coincidence all three sermons were based on Heb. 13:7. The elder Walther was buried in the City Cemetery, but later his remains were removed to the Lutheran Cemetery, where Holy Cross Church is now located. The congregation assumed the funeral expenses, which amounted to $27.95½, and paid the widow a pension of $5.00 a month until she married Pastor Ottomar Fuerbringer, October 18, 1842.

On February 8, 1841, the congregation called the younger Walther as its pastor. Walther appeared before the congregation on April 26, declaring that in view of the fact that his health had been restored, that the call was valid, that the sins which he had committed in the Saxon emigration were not of a nature to disqualify him for the ministry, and, finally, that the congregation was Christian and as such entitled to the rights and privileges of a Christian congregation, he would accept the call.

Henceforth Walther's place of labor was St. Louis. Not

Perry County, but St. Louis was to become the center of Lutheran orthodoxy.

The congregation as yet had neither name nor constitution. Past experiences had made the members wary and suspicious of all forms of church government. They dreaded the toils of priest rule and the loss of rights and privileges, which had been acquired after a long and bitter fight. For

First Lutheran Church in St. Louis

two years they discussed paragraph after paragraph of a proposed constitution until finally in the spring of 1843 it was adopted and signed by the members.

The congregation selected the name Trinity, purchased a building lot on Lombard Street, between Third and Fourth Streets, at a cost of $1,000, erected a church and dedicated it on December 4, 1842. The building, costing $4,120, housed a school in its basement. In later years three additional districts were established: Immanuel, Zion, and Concordia (now Holy Cross). The four districts with resident

Facsimile of the First Page of Vol. I, No. 1, of "Der Lutheraner"

pastors formed an organic unit, with Walther as senior pastor.

On September 7, 1844, Walther issued the first number of *Der Lutheraner*. The very first article announced the reason, purpose, and contents of the paper. Speaking of the origin of *Der Lutheraner*, Walther wrote 14 years later:

"These conditions, namely, the condition of the Lutheran Church in America, caused us to resolve together with several other Lutheran pastors who had emigrated with us to publish a little paper, which under the frank and honest name of *Der Lutheraner* was to serve our beloved Church according to local needs, as God would give us grace. The prospects of such a paper were dark indeed. Our immigrant congregations were still very poor and had to make almost impossible sacrifices to enjoy the benefits of properly organized and well supplied Evangelical Lutheran congregations. That they alone should secure the existence of the paper could hardly be expected, and otherwise we had no acquaintance and connection with the pastors and congregations. We dared send the paper only to two, both at present at the head of the so-called Saxon congregations as synodical officers, Wyneken and Sihler. Our expectations or, at least, our pretensions did not extend any further than to carry about as many papers into wider circles as were necessary to present an unmistakable public testimony as to what the Lutheran Church and its doctrine really is." [9]

It was *Der Lutheraner* which attracted the attention of other Lutherans. When Wyneken saw the first issue, he exclaimed, "Thank God, there are still Lutherans in America." Dr. Sihler, the other man to whom Walther sent a copy and who lived at Pomeroy, Ohio, at the time, writes in his biography: "It was a great joy to receive the first number of *Der Lutheraner*, and after I had read the succeeding issues, I did not hesitate to recommend the paper to any congregation, since the Lutherans needed such a periodical, for many of them did not know what Lutheranism was and why they called themselves Lutherans. Naturally, I soon entered into extended correspondence with the editor."

The names Wyneken and Sihler introduce us to the second contingent of the charter members of the Missouri Synod: the Loehe men.

4

FRIEDRICH CONRAD DIETRICH WYNEKEN

*N*ot a Loehe missionary, but responsible for Loehe's activities on behalf of the Lutheran Church in America was Friedrich Conrad Dietrich Wyneken.

Wyneken was born in a parsonage, May 13, 1810, in a small village near Verden, Hannover. His father died early, leaving the mother with nine children. Two of his brothers entered the ministry in Germany. Of his sisters, one was the mother of Justus Ruperti, pastor of St. Matthew's Lutheran Church in New York; another was the mother of Doctor H. C. Schwan, for many years President of the Missouri Synod.

Wyneken attended the village school, the *Gymnasium* at Verden, the universities of Goettingen and Halle. Though he had studied theology, he had acquired nothing to boast of, as he himself remarked. In fact, as a private tutor he would begin his course in Bible History with the Book of Maccabees. It was in the parsonage of Pastor von Hanfstengel in Hannover that Wyneken's real religious life — the life in Christ — began. From this time he devoted much time to the study of the Bible. As a private tutor in the family of a wealthy German he made a number of trips to France and to Italy. Later he became the head of the Bremervoerde Latin School.

In his search for sound Christian literature he found some missionary journals which described the miserable spiritual conditions of the German settlers in America. These reports so impressed him that he resolved to go to America at his own risk and expense to help these spiritually destitute people. It was not the lure of adventure or romance that attracted him to the New World, nor was it love for his Master or his Lutheran brethren that prompted him to leave kith and kin: He determined to go to America because his conscience drove him thither.

Five years later, in a letter to Candidate A. Biewend (November 29, 1842), he expressed himself as follows: "With deep regret I must confess that as far as I know myself, neither love for the Lord nor for the orphaned brethren drove me to America nor a natural desire. Rather I went contrary to my will and after great conflicts, from a sense of duty, driven in, and by, my conscience. As much as it saddens me that I did not have and still do not have more love for the Lord and that He had to drive me like a slave, still in times of spiritual trials and temptations, doubts and tribulations, which came over my soul during my ministry, this was my comfort that I could say: I had to come to America. Thou, O Lord, knowest how gladly I would have remained at home, but had I done this, I should not have been able to look up to Thee and pray to Thee; so I simply had to come." [1]

Shortly before he sailed, he passed his final examination for the ministry. His examiner was a consistorial councilor who was deeply steeped in rationalism. When the councilor adduced an unbelieving Jew like Spinoza as an authority on the subject of miracles, Wyneken replied: "What concern can it be to you or me what an unbelieving Jew philosophized on this subject? The Scriptures, sir, the Scriptures!" Although the examiner was very much displeased at Wyneken's firm attitude toward the Scriptures, the consistory, contrary to expectations, gave him a certificate of high merit.

In the early summer of 1838 Wyneken embarked with a certain Candidate C. W. Wolf for Baltimore, receiving free passage on the ship *Caroline* through the courtesy of the devout Captain Stuerje. He landed in July, a stranger in a strange country.

After having tramped the streets of Baltimore, Wyneken and Wolf finally met people who claimed to be Lutherans, but who later on proved to be Methodists (Otterbeinians). At last they found Pastor J. Haesbaert, a Lutheran clergyman, who looked upon them with mistrust, for there were many religious vagabonds and tramps abroad. Wyneken's candor, however, soon won the confidence of Haesbaert, and shortly after he supplied the pulpit of Haesbart's church for six weeks while the latter was ill.

Haesbaert, on Wyneken's request, communicated with the Mission Committee of the Pennsylvania Ministerium, with the result that Wyneken received instructions to proceed to Indiana, where he was to gather the "Protestants" into congregations.

Wyneken started on his western trip in the late summer of 1838, going by rail to Pittsburgh. Here he met Pastor F. Schmidt, editor of *Die Lutherische Kirchenzeitung*, which paper was to publish many of his articles and letters. From Pittsburgh to Zelienople he traveled on a canalboat. Continuing his journey on horseback, he traversed Allen and Putnam Counties, Ohio, finally reaching Decatur, Indiana, where he decided to make his headquarters.

At the home of "Father" Buuck he learned of the untimely death of the pastor of the Lutheran Church at Fort Wayne, Jesse Hoover, and immediately went to the village, which he reached the last week of September, 1838. In a letter addressed to Haesbaert, dated October 1, 1838, Wyneken wrote: "Eight days ago I arrived in Fort Wayne. Here as well as in two neighboring settlements I have already preached five times, baptized children, and read burial services. And now these people want me to stay — I advised the vestry of the church to write to the committee of their church body about this. Tomorrow I intend to continue my journey, and I expect to return in four weeks to receive the answer. I am ready to do the Lord's will, and I shall leave it to Him to direct the hearts of the members of the committee as He sees fit. I am satisfied with everything as long as I am certain that the Lord wants me to work here."

This letter indicates that Wyneken did not wait in Fort Wayne for further developments. He left the village October 2 for an extended missionary tour. Traversing the northwestern corner of Ohio, he entered Michigan and continued in a westerly direction to St. Joseph and Michigan City on the Lake. From here he turned back to South Bend and Elkhart, again entering Michigan and journeying from Mottville to Niles. Turning south, he went as far as Crawfordsville, Montgomery County, Indiana, and returned through Clinton County along the Wabash River to Fort Wayne on November 16.

In Fort Wayne, Wyneken found an answer from the East waiting for him, releasing him from his call as missionary and permitting him to take charge of the two congregations provided that he would minister also to the neighboring country and settlements.

The Lutheran congregation in Fort Wayne had been established largely through the efforts of Henry Rudisill, a German Lutheran from Pennsylvania who had come to Fort Wayne in 1829, when it was a village of 150 inhabitants. Through the German secular and religious press and through letters he induced other German Protestants to settle in and around Fort Wayne, so that by 1836 he could request a resident Lutheran pastor. Pastor Jesse Hoover of Woodstock, Virginia, who had visited Fort Wayne in July, 1836, for ten days, returned in the fall of the same year to become pastor of the German Protestants, organizing them into an Evangelical Lutheran congregation on October 14, 1837. On May 23, 1838, Pastor Hoover died at the age of 28.

Using Fort Wayne as his base of operations, Wyneken made numerous missionary journeys. The conditions he found were appalling. In a stirring appeal directed to the Lutherans in Germany, in 1841, he described the spiritual distress of the Lutherans of America. (Cf. Chapter 1.)

Realizing the magnitude of the task, Wyneken knew only too well that he could not cope with the situation alone. To Pastor Schmidt of *Die Lutherische Kirchenzeitung* he wrote on January 25, 1839: "I believe that the only way to accomplish anything worth while in the vineyard of the Lord is to call missionaries for smaller sections of the country. The General Synod ought to make an appeal to the Lutheran congregations. It certainly is not right that 2,000 churches, and perhaps more, cannot support more missionaries. If we have sufficient warriors in this country, then I am convinced that a strong appeal to the brethren in Germany, especially to the mission societies there, will bring us recruits enough to fill the ranks." In the summer of 1839 he did receive help in Johann Joseph Nuelsen, who was sent to Indiana by the Pennsylvania Ministerium. Wrote Nuelsen to Schmidt: "Wyneken wishes very much to return to Germany in order to secure more candidates, at least six of whom could be placed in the territory which he has visited."

Wyneken kept up a constant correspondence with individuals and with mission societies in Germany. His articles appeared in the *Zeitschrift fuer Protestantismus und Kirche*, edited in Erlangen by G. C. A. von Harless.

But the results were not forthcoming. True, he succeeded in inducing F. W. Husmann, a teacher in Bremen, to come to Fort Wayne in May, 1840; in May, 1841, Pastor Gossner of Berlin sent over Missionary A. F. Knape, who relieved Wyneken of his country congregation. The Stade Mission Society sent over two more missionaries in June, 1841, of whom G. Bartels went to Peoria, Illinois, and G. Jensen proceeded to Fort Wayne. But Wyneken was not satisfied. He was convinced that the solution of the problem among the Lutherans in America lay in a personal visit on his part to Germany, where he would have an opportunity to plead his cause face to face. Hence he wrote to Schmidt in 1841: "What I have in mind is the following: I desire with the help of God to have six or eight pastors come to America who are to parcel out a section of the country among themselves. A superintendent is to be at the head of all, who is to visit each circuit and who should be elected for a period of about four years. The preachers ought to visit their circuits first without attempting to organize the people into congregations. After some time, however, this ought to be done, but with such members only as have manifested their sincerity by Christian conduct. As a confessional basis the Augsburg Confession or, where the people are Reformed, a Reformed confession should serve. All congregations should be united together and, if possible, also become members of existing synods." It should be noted that Wyneken at this time did not take a firm stand against the unionistic practices, prevalent in almost all Lutheran synods of that day. In his own congregation Wyneken opened his pulpit to Reformed preachers and communed Reformed at his altar.

With the coming of Jensen to Fort Wayne the time seemed propitious to Wyneken to go to Germany. He had for some months past been suffering from a throat ailment, which was gradually becoming worse and making it practically impossible for him to preach. He communicated with the

FRIEDRICH CONRAD DIETRICH WYNEKEN

Mission Committee of the General Synod about the necessity of his going to Germany, both on account of his health and on account of the shortage of manpower. In May, 1841, this body resolved to send him to Germany as soon as possible in the interest of his work. Wyneken entrusted his parish to Jensen, and after having been married on August 11 to Marie Sophie Wilhelmine Buuck by Pastor A. F. Knape, he sailed from Philadelphia in October, 1841. He took with him letters of recommendation from Pastor Demme of Philadelphia, secretary of the Pennsylvania Ministerium, addressed to various mission societies in Germany.

Wyneken's trip to Germany had far-reaching results both for himself as well as for the Lutheran Church in America. The high esteem which his relatives enjoyed in church and governmental circles, especially in Hannover, opened many doors to him. Before he had fully recovered from his throat ailment, he corresponded extensively with religious leaders and undertook several journeys to various parts of Germany. He interviewed not only the clergy but also the laity. He delivered lectures on the conditions which he had found among the Lutheran settlers in America, giving vivid descriptions of camp meetings and revivals and other activities, especially of the Methodists, who were making deep inroads into Lutheranism. F. Lochner, who later came to America and served as pastor in Milwaukee and at Springfield, Illinois, gives a report of the lecture he heard Wyneken deliver at Fuerth, near Nuernberg. He wrote: "I hastened to Fuerth on the evening train. When I reached the school hall, I found it already crowded to the doors. At eight o'clock Wyneken appeared, escorted by the pastors of Fuerth. After Pastor Kraussold, now consistorial councilor, had recited a few lines which the entire audience sang, Wyneken began his lecture. All listened with rapt attention to his vivid descriptions of American church life and of his missionary work, to his original remarks on some Bible passages, either applying or explaining them or showing the difference in doctrine and practice between the true Church and the sects. He gave especial attention to the activities of the Methodists. The most brilliant part of his lecture was his description of a camp meeting. When he reached the moment when the individuals are invited to come to the mourners' bench, Wyneken suddenly approached those in the audience who were sitting or standing immediately in front of him, seized their hands, and asked them, 'Don't you, too, want to be converted?' I can still picture to my mind how some of them stared at the speaker in surprise and how others drew back, fearing that an actual Methodist conversion were to take place. — At the close of his address, as he pleaded for aid for the forsaken people of our faith, he assailed the numerous candidates of Germany who waited eight and ten years for a charge, while across the seas hungry souls were perishing in the wilderness. It was eleven o'clock when the mission hour came to a close. One hardly realized that it was so late." [2]

F. Lochner

In Erlangen, the university city, he gained the support of Prof. Karl von Raumer. In Dresden he was instrumental in organizing a mission society (*Verein zur kirchlichen Unterstuetzung der Deutschen in Nordamerika*). A similar organization was established by him in Leipzig. With the assistance of von Raumer and Loehe he published his famous pamphlet *The Distress of the German Lutherans in North America* (the American edition was printed in Pittsburgh, 1844), in which he showed not only the spiritual misery of the Lutheran immigrants, the dangers to which they were exposed, but also the decay of the Lutheran Church in America — increasingly manifest in unionism, revivalism, new methods — and the remedy. The contact, however, that had the most far-reaching results was his meeting with Pastor Wilhelm Loehe of Neuendettelsau, Bavaria, of whom we shall hear more in the next chapter.

Wyneken's visit to Germany was very beneficial also for his personal religious convictions. His fellowship with confessional leaders of the Lutheran Church overseas, especially with Loehe, undoubtedly strengthened his confessional position and stimulated in him a determination to oppose the doctrinal stand and practice of American Lutheranism.

Wyneken returned to America, arriving in New York on June 28, 1843, in the company of Candidate A. Biewend, whom the mission society of Stade had sent and who became pastor of the Lutheran church in Washington, D. C. The change in Wyneken became apparent when he returned to Fort Wayne. During his absence of nearly two years the congregation had split into two parties, one of them desiring to call Jensen as pastor. But H. Rudisill, together with Teacher Husmann, kept the congregation intact. When Jensen accepted a call to Pittsburgh, Husmann took care of the flock until Wyneken returned. The latter at once publicly emphasized the difference between the Lutheran and the Reformed Confessions and was persistent in his endeavor to establish a thoroughly Lutheran congregation. The result was that the Reformed element in his church left and founded a new congregation.

Wyneken, who was a member of the Synod of the West, which in turn was associated with the General Synod, in which unionism, revivalism, rationalism, and indifferentism were rampant, caused a sensation when he took such a decided stand for the Lutheran Confessions and opposed the Reformed and the Methodists so violently. Even members of his own church, including Rudisill, were disturbed and began to lose confidence in him. In order to make his position clear, he invited the Synod of the West to meet in his church in October, 1844, and prompted Rudisill to bring charges against him. He hoped thereby to have an opportunity to bear witness for the Lutheran Confessions and to demonstrate that he was a true Lutheran. He was successful. His congregation knew that it had a Lutheran pastor.

It was during this time that a copy of *Der Lutheraner*, published by C. F. W. Walther of St. Louis, came into his hands. This was his first contact with the Saxons of Missouri, of whom he had heard when in Germany.

In the same year (1844) he began to train two young men for the ministry, J. H. Jaebker and C. Frincke (Fricke), who were to be the first fruits of the new seminary in Fort Wayne, established in 1846 by Loehe.

When Haesbaert resigned his charge in Baltimore, Wyneken was called as his successor. He was installed on March 9, 1845, by Dr. Daniel Kurtz. Wyneken soon discovered that he was pastor of a congregation composed of Lutheran and Reformed elements. When he showed them the difference between the Lutheran and the Reformed Confessions and insisted that he was a Lutheran pastor, a vehement controversy followed, and more than 80 members left the church and organized another.

While in Germany, Wyneken, in the *Zeitschrift fuer Protestantismus und Kirche*, had attacked the General Synod, stating that this body was gradually assuming the form of a serpent seeking to destroy the Church; that it was "Methodistic" and was encouraging a union of Lutheran and Reformed churches in America. At the convention of the Synod of the West in 1844, Wyneken, together with three others, was elected a delegate to the convention of the General Synod at Philadelphia at the end of May, 1845.

Wyneken was not present at the first session of the General Synod. During his absence the General Synod resolved to contact the Lutheran brethren in Germany by way of correspondence in order to defend itself against the misrepresentation of its doctrine and practice circulated in Germany. (Wyneken's "Distress of the German Lutherans in North America" was meant!)

This was a challenge for Wyneken to defend the truth and his reputation. He proposed that the General Synod could clear itself of the accusations in a twofold manner. First, they should send books and periodicals which were rated as representing the doctrinal position of the General Synod, for instance, Dr. Schmucker's *Popular Theology, Portraiture of Lutheranism;* Dr. Kurtz's *On Infant Baptism, Why Are You a Lutheran? The Lutheran Observer* and *Die Hirtenstimme* to Dr. Rudelbach, Professor Harless, and other prominent editors of Lutheran periodicals in Germany for an opinion — whether the charges leveled against them were true or false; or, secondly, the General Synod should publicly renounce these books and periodicals and condemn the doctrine and practice contained therein. But the General Synod was not inclined to follow either suggestion. It could not accept the first proposal without meeting with a certain amount of disapproval, nor could it choose the second without either lying or undergoing a radical reformation in doctrine and practice.

When his proposals were rejected by the convention, Wyneken severed his connection with the General Synod. His congregation followed him. To Loehe he wrote: "I should have been happy if, by the acceptance of the second proposal, my character would have been branded in Germany as that of a liar and defamer. However, since the General Synod rejected both proposals, I again had to repeat publicly that she is harboring and nurturing false doctrine. As an honest man and a Christian, I wished to declare war against her, although it may seem silly to her, since I am only one insignificant individual. I desired to tell her in advance that I would do all in my power to oppose her influence, especially that I would warn against her, so that the few in Germany who are on the side of the truth do not bother with her." [3] Loehe remarked: "Wyneken is herewith beginning a war which he may carry on with the deepest peace of soul, a war in which all true children of the Lutheran Church will have to join him." [4]

Thus in 1845 Wyneken and his congregation at Baltimore were standing alone, unaffiliated with any Lutheran Synod, eager and ready to support any movement which would hold out the prospect of establishing a Lutheran body in which confessional Lutheranism would be upheld.

5

JOHANN KONRAD WILHELM LOEHE
AND HIS EFFORTS ON BEHALF
OF THE LUTHERAN CHURCH IN AMERICA

*T*HE name Loehe has been mentioned a number of times in the previous chapters of this book. The work which this man did for the Missouri Synod will always be remembered with deep gratitude.

Wilhelm Loehe was born February 21, 1808, in Fuerth, Bavaria, a few miles northwest of Nuernberg. He attended the *Gymnasium* at Nuernberg and studied theology at the universities of Erlangen (1826) and Berlin (1828). After completing his studies he served as vicar in Kirchenlamitz and at Nuernberg. In 1837 he became pastor of the village church at Neuendettelsau, Bavaria, which he served until his death. His missionary labors here made the village world-renowned.

Loehe was great as a preacher, crowding his church with strangers who often traveled from 20 to 30 miles to attend his services. Full of missionary zeal, he was stirred to action for the sake of the Lutherans in America by Wyneken's reports.

Towards the end of 1840 the mission society at Stade issued an "Appeal for Aid for the German Protestant Church in North America," basing its plea upon the statements of Pastor Wyneken of Fort Wayne, Indiana. This pamphlet revealed the spiritual distress of the German Lutheran immigrants in the United States. Loehe read the appeal and gave it wide publicity in the *Sonntagsblatt,* published by Pastor F. Wucherer of Noerdlingen. Number Two of the 1841 volume of the *Sonntagsblatt* contained Loehe's "Address to the Readers," in which, among other things, he said: "Thousands of families, your brethren in the faith, possibly your brothers and sisters according to the flesh, are hungry for the nourishing meat of the Gospel. They cry out and implore you: Oh, help us! Give us preachers to strengthen us with the Bread of Life, to edify us through the Word of the Lord, to instruct our children in the doctrine of Jesus. Oh, help us, or we are undone! Why do you not help us? Is that your love for Jesus? Is that keeping His Commandments? Consider the words: 'What ye have done unto one of the least of these My brethren, ye have done it unto Me.' —It is literally true that many of our German brethren in western North America plead with us in such terms. Besides, in many places a new danger has arisen. In no other country are there so many Christian sects as in North America. Even now some have directed their attention and efforts to the settlements of our German brethren and fellow Lutherans. Strangers wish to reap while the Lord is calling His own. Shall our brethren no longer worship in the Church of their fathers, filled with the breath of the Lord, but instead recline in the miserable shacks of sectarianism? Shall German piety decay in the new world under the influence of human propaganda? I beg of you, for Jesus' sake, take hold, organize speedily, do not waste time in consultations. Haste, haste, immortal souls are at stake." [1]

Loehe's appeal bore immediate fruit. In a short time the readers of the *Sonntagsblatt* contributed 600 gulden (a gulden was about 40 cents) to be used for work among the spiritually destitute brethren in America. While Loehe and Wucherer were debating how to use the fund, a solution for their problem presented itself to them in the person of Adam Ernst.

Adam Ernst, a cobbler's apprentice, read Loehe's appeal while living in Asch, Bohemia. He at once resolved to volunteer for church work in America and informed his friends of his decision. His friends communicated with the mission society at Dresden, which was preparing men for mission work in America. But Dresden informed them that there were opportunities in Bavaria to obtain the necessary training. Accordingly, about Pentecost, 1841, Ernst came to his former pastor, Wucherer, at Noerdlingen and revealed his desire to him. Wucherer sent Ernst to Loehe, who began to instruct him in July, 1841. Soon Ernst was joined by his friend George Burger. Wrote Loehe: "Now we had two students, and we had to consider ways and means to reach our objective. We must admit that our experience was like that of everyone who undertakes a new task without any training. We did not know what to do. So much we did realize that we could not make anything great out of our two students. Two schoolteachers who would work at their trade and support themselves — that was our objective."[2]

Adam Ernst

Loehe and Wucherer prepared a course of studies for their *Nothelfer* (emergency men). It included cursory reading of the Scriptures, the Book of Concord, church history, geography, English grammar, composition, penmanship, singing, piano, methods in reading and writing, Christian doctrine, pastoral theology, catechetics, liturgics, homiletics, participation in divine services and in congregational life.

When Wyneken visited Loehe in 1842, he encouraged him in his work and urged him to send Ernst and Burger to America. They arrived in New York, September 26, 1842. Ernst taught a German school at Columbus while working at his cobbler's trade at night to gain his livelihood; Burger attended the theological seminary at Columbus to complete his theological studies. Thus Ernst and Burger were the first emissaries (*Sendlinge*) of Loehe.

But more were to follow. Greatly stimulated by the personal visit of Wyneken, Loehe resolved to devote his time and energy to the upbuilding of the Lutheran Church in America. He published a monthly bulletin, called *Kirchliche Mitteilungen aus und ueber Nord-Amerika*, in 1843 for the support of the work in America. "We do not intend to withhold any aid from the heathen," he wrote in an early issue. "We shall do for them all that is in our power. Help the heathen, help them with all your resources, but do not forget the 'especially' of the Apostle which he accords to those of the household of faith. Do not forget that many North American Christians are actually lapsing into paganism unless they receive aid from the fatherland." [3]

To do more effective work, Loehe divided the Kingdom of Hannover into districts, placing a pastor at the head of each, whose duty it was to promote interest for the American cause in his parish and in the neighboring parishes. He secured the support of Dr. L. A. Petri, pastor of the city church in Hannover, who extended the hospitality of his home to many of Loehe's *Sendlinge* while en route to America and whose parish women supplied the emissaries with linens and other necessary personal equipment. In Mecklenburg Loehe found a zealous co-worker in Councilor Karl von Maltzan, whose influence gained for the American cause friends among the aristocracy of Mecklenburg, one of them the Grandduchess at Ludwigslust. Since no emissary from Mecklenburg had been sent to America before 1846, the Mecklenburgers provided the transportation and equipment of Aug. Craemer and Fr. Lochner in 1845, the amount necessary being 1,104 gulden.

Loehe's original purpose was to train teachers for parish schools among the Lutherans in America. But since the spiritual distress of the Lutheran immigrants was great, and since candidates of theology were slow in responding to his appeal, Loehe assumed the task of training workers himself. Most of the instruction of the young men was in his own hands. The afternoons were devoted to lecturing to these students. They would meet again for evening prayers at his parsonage, and at such times one of the students might be called upon to deliver a sermonet. They would catechize the children under his supervision, accompany him on his sick visits, and perform other pastoral duties under his direction. At stipulated times the students had to report on their pastoral activities, their reports forming the subject of class discussions. On Saturdays, Friedrich Hommel, assessor at Heilsbronn, a renowned liturgiologist, would instruct the students in the musical sections of the Lutheran liturgy. At the time of the organization of the Missouri Synod, Loehe had prepared and sent to America 23 emergency men. By 1853, the year in which Loehe and the Missourians parted, 82 candidates of theology, emergency men, and students for the Fort Wayne seminary had come to America through his efforts. Most of them joined the Missouri Synod after its organization.

When Loehe's *Sendlinge* left Germany, they carried with them "instructions" prepared by their sponsor. As a rule, these instructions contained, first of all, a statement that the *Sendling* was leaving his home country of his own free will to serve in the American mission field. There followed a pledge of allegiance to the Confessional Writings of the Lutheran Church and instructions how to perform the manifold duties of a missionary. The missioner, finally, was advised to join a synod, but only such a synod as was truly Lutheran.

After surveying the Lutheran Church in America, Loehe reached the conclusion that the Michigan and the Ohio Synod were the only orthodox Lutheran groups in the United States. He suggested to his missioners therefore that they associate themselves with either of these synods. Until the time of the organization of the Missouri Synod all of Loehe's men had been members of the Ohio Synod with the exception of Craemer, Hattstaedt, Lochner, and Trautmann, who had joined the Michigan Synod. Loehe was interested especially in the theological seminary of the Ohio Synod at Columbus, Ohio, and hoped that in some manner he could use this institution in the development of his American mission projects.

In 1845, however, Sihler and his companions broke with the Ohio Synod, as will be related in a later chapter, and thus cut their connections with the seminary at Columbus. The need of an orthodox Lutheran seminary for the training of missionaries and teachers was felt by Sihler and his friends. It was desirable that instead of receiving all their training in Germany, the young students would be given some of their education in America and thus become acclimated to local conditions. When Sihler declared himself willing to head such an institution, Loehe did not hesitate. On September 19, 1846, there arrived in Fort Wayne eleven young men, accompanied by Candidate K. Roebbelen, who was to serve as assistant to Dr. Sihler in the theological school. In November of the same year Candidate A. Wolter became Roebbelen's successor. The seminary, opened in October, 1846, was housed in rented quarters for two and one half years. It is today the Concordia Theological Seminary in Springfield, Illinois.

LOEHE AND THE LUTHERAN CHURCH IN AMERICA

One more phase of Loehe's activities for the Lutheran Church in America must be mentioned. Loehe had long cherished the wish to do mission work among the Indians of North America. In 1844 Loehe requested Pastor W. Hattstaedt of Monroe, Michigan, one of his emissaries, to investigate what could be done by the Lutheran Church for the Indians. Hattstaedt replied that the work of evangelizing the Indians might best be undertaken jointly with the Lutherans already settled in Michigan. Loehe's plan was to establish Lutheran congregations in the immediate vicinity of the Indian villages, the pastors of the congregations at the same time serving as missionaries to the Indians. He discussed his idea with Lorenz Loesel, one of his servants, who at once offered his services and who interested other young men in the vicinity of Rosstall, near Nuernberg, in the project. Seven young men and five young women volunteered to form the nucleus of the congregation.

The leader of the group was August Friedrich Craemer, a Franconian, born May 26, 1812, at Klein-Langheim. He studied theology at Erlangen 1830—1832, was involved in the Frankfurt Revolution of 1833, and served a prison term until 1839, when he was acquitted. He studied Old and Modern Greek, Old and Middle High German, French, English, and, at Munich, theology, at which time he found his Savior. In 1841 he was tutor in the home of the Saxon Count Carl von Einsiedel, through whose favor, in 1842, Craemer became the tutor of the children of Lord and Lady Lovelace of Devonshire, England. The latter was a daughter of Lord Byron. On the recommendation of Sir Henry Drummond, Craemer became instructor in the German language and literature at Oxford University. But Oxford at this time was involved in the so-called Tractarian Movement, an effort on the part of the later Cardinal Newman and others to Romanize the Anglican Church. Finding himself unsympathetic toward this movement, Craemer resigned. In the meantime, he had read the "Appeal" of Wyneken. Through his brother he learned of Loehe's missionary plan. Offering his services, he arrived at Neuendettelsau, where a small mission congregation was organized and Craemer chosen as pastor.

On the day before the departure of the group for the New World, April 4, 1845, Craemer was ordained to the ministry in the Lutheran cathedral at Schwerin, Dr. Kliefoth acting as ordinator. The installation of Craemer as pastor of the emigrant congregation took place in Bremen, the ceremony being performed by Pastor von Hanfstengel.

Aug. F. Craemer

The colonists — one couple, six men, and four young women (fiancées of four fellow voyagers) — sailed on the *Carolina* from Bremerhaven on April 20. They were en route to Michigan, where Pastor Friedrich Schmidt of Ann Arbor and Missionary J. Auch had selected for them a location on the Cass River, about 15 miles from Saginaw. On the same day Craemer united four couples in marriage. With them on the ship were four emissaries of Loehe: Friedrich Johann Carl Lochner, Philip Jakob Trautmann, Eduard Romanowski, and Adam Detzer.

After their arrival in New York on June 7, they were entertained by Pastor Theo. Brohm. On June 10, in St. Matthew's Church, Dr. Stohlmann performed the ceremony which united Craemer and Dorothea Benthien in matrimony. Craemer had learned to know her during the journey, on which she had nursed certain smallpox patients with tireless devotion.

By railroad, river, and lake steamers the group finally reached Monroe, Michigan, on June 17, where they visited friends and conferred with Pastors Hattstaedt and Schmidt. They returned to Detroit, whence they left on July 3, arriving a week later in Saginaw, where Missionary Auch had provided lodging for the colonists. Together with Auch and a land surveyor, the men trekked through the forests, and 15 miles from Saginaw founded the settlement of Frankenmuth on the Cass River. A company hut was built for the congregation members and another hut for the pastor, in which he conducted divine worship every morning and evening.

While the colonists were engaged in erecting log cabins, Craemer commenced his work among the Indians. Accompanied by Jim Gruett, an interpreter, he visited the Indian families living on the Kawkawlin, Swan, Chippewa, Pine, and Bell Rivers, shortly thereafter opening a school for their children. The first fruits of the Indian mission were realized on Christmas Day, 1846, when an Indian youth and his two sisters were baptized. In the following year nearly 100 new arrivals joined the colony of Frankenmuth, and by 1851 the colony consisted of more than 80 cabins and farmhouses, a sawmill, and a flour mill. There were also present a physician and three merchants. Because of Craemer's increasing duties in the German congregation, Missionary E. Baierlein, a graduate of the Mission House in Leipzig, was sent to Frankenmuth to assist Craemer in the Indian mission. He arrived in 1847.

The success of the Frankenmuth colony encouraged Loehe to establish other colonies. Thus Frankentrost was founded in 1847 under the leadership of Pastor John Philip Graebner, Frankenlust by Pastor Ferdinand Sievers (1848), and Frankenhilf under Pastor H. Kuehn (1850).

To summarize: Within the space of a decade Loehe sent into the American field more than 80 workers (pastors, candidates of theology, "emergency men," students of theology, and teachers); he established Concordia Theological Seminary at Fort Wayne; he founded the Franconian colonies in the Saginaw Valley; he was instrumental in obtaining comparatively large sums of money for the American cause; and, finally, he played no insignificant role in bringing about a meeting between his missioners and the Saxons for the purpose of organizing an orthodox, confessional Lutheran synod.

6

WILHELM SIHLER

*T*ogether with Wyneken and C. F. W. Walther, Wilhelm Sihler forms the triumvirate which exerted a tremendous influence on the Missouri Synod in its formative period. It is quite right, therefore, to devote a chapter to this remarkable man.

Wilhelm Sihler was born Nov. 12, 1801, near Breslau, Silesia. His father was a non-commissioned officer in the Prussian army, of the evangelical faith; his mother was a devout Catholic. Sihler was mentally exceptionally bright. He was able to read at the age of five, attended the *Gymnasium* before he was 10 and was graduated when only 15 years old. Choosing the military profession, he enrolled at the military academy of Breslau. After two and one half years he was transferred to the fortress at Neise, holding the rank of first lieutenant. In 1823 he entered the military school of Berlin, having as a classmate Helmut v. Moltke, the later hero of the Franco-Prussian war. This academy offered extension courses at the Berlin university, in which courses Sihler enrolled. After two years, however, Sihler abandoned his military career and spent a year in private study at Breslau. In 1825 he matriculated in the university of Berlin, majoring in philology and philosophy. In Berlin he attended the church services of Schleiermacher, the leader of current religious thought, who captivated him, but who did not bring him to a knowledge of his Savior. He finished his studies in 1829, when he also published his "Symbolik des Antlitzes" — a treatise on the manifestation of the inner man by the outer man — for which the university of Jena conferred upon him the degree of Doctor of Philosophy honoris causa.

After tutoring for one year at Breslau, he accepted a position at the Institute of Dr. Blochmann in Dresden, a school which prepared young men for entrance into the universities. Among his colleagues was Dr. Philippi, afterwards a noted theologian and professor at Rostock.

Sihler lived in Dresden eight years, 1830—1838. It was while at Dresden that his Damascus hour struck. Sihler was not a Christian; pharisaical self-righteousness was his religion. Sihler compares his conversion to that of St. Paul in that it was brought about suddenly, almost violently, without the instrumentality of a man or a book. After having given way to a violent fit of temper, he was struck to the floor and immediately became conscious of his wretched state. But just as instantly, Christ appeared in his heart with all His saving grace. Sihler was a changed man. The Spirit of God drove him into the Scriptures, so that the Bible was his constant companion. He lived in the Word, and the Word lived in him.

Desiring Christian fellowship, he often visited the home of the widowed Frau von Kuegelgen, where regular Bible study was conducted. A constant visitor at this house and a regular participant in the Bible hours was Louise Kuerbel, sister of Pastor M. Stephan's wife.

During the years 1830—1838, Pastor Stephan was the topic of the day in Dresden and vicinity. It seems somewhat strange that Sihler in his quest for Christian companionship did not meet Keyl or Loeber or some of the other Saxon fathers with whom he was to be so closely associated in America. Sihler tells us why he avoided Stephan. "There were two reasons for my not visiting his church. In the first place, it was a notorious fact that he often made evening excursions with some of his parishioners, men and women, young men and young women, to neighboring vineyards, extending them until early dawn. He declared that he was so occupied with his pastoral work during the day that he needed these nocturnal expeditions for recreation (although these meanderings gave much offense, as he well knew, he still persisted) and asserted that this was part of Christian liberty. Of the doctrine of Christian liberty I had no clear understanding at that time. Still I understood and felt in my conscience that this mode of living was an abuse of Christian liberty and contrary to Christian love. The other matter that repelled me from this man was his unkind attitude towards his wife and children . . . and his epicurean fondness for eating and drinking. Still I should have gone to his church, since he preached the Word of God. Then, too, I should have had the opportunity to ask him about his conduct and to reprimand him." [1]

E. G. W. Keyl

Through Pastor Wermelskirch, a former missionary to the Jews in London, Sihler was led to join the Dresden Mission Society whose president was Count Detlev von Einsiedel, one of the patrons of the Saxon fathers. Here he also met Dr. Rudelbach, a recognized leader of confessional Lutheranism, who created in Sihler the desire to study the Symbolical Books of the Lutheran Church. The study of the Book of Concord convinced Sihler that the Lutheran Church was the only true visible Church of God on earth, aroused in him an abiding opposition to the Roman Catholic Church, and filled him with contempt for the Reformed Church and abhorrence for any church unionism or religious compromise.

From 1838—1843, Sihler carried on his tutorial work in the Baltic provinces, especially at Riga and on the island of Oesel. While here, a strong desire to enter the ministry gripped him. On one of his trips to a friend near Riga, he found a copy of Wyneken's "Appeal." "Like a flash of lightning, it pierced my soul, as though God spoke with emphatic words to me, 'You must go!'" writes Sihler.[2] His whole nature revolted against going to America. He was not in sympathy with the democratic form of government prevalent in the United States, considering the American Revolution a wholesome punishment of proud and arrogant England, and believing the leaders of the American Revolution criminals in God's sight.

Urged by clergy friends, who did not know of his secret desire but who had also read the "Appeal," and requested by the Dresden Society, Sihler no longer conferred with flesh and blood, but followed the dictates of his conscience. From his northern friends he received 300 rubles and 10 ducats (a ruble was about 50 cents, a ducat $2.25); the mission society at Dresden gave him another 200 rubles. He visited Pastor Loehe at Neuendettelsau, who hoped to obtain for him a professorship at Columbus, Ohio. He was examined by Dr. Rudelbach and received his credentials from him. In Bremen he met Pastor Treviranus, v. Hanfstengel, and some of Wyneken's relatives. Together with Baumgart, an emissary of Loehe, he sailed on the *Caroline*, arriving in New York on November 1, 1843.

Sihler was not an academically trained theologian; yet he was a staunch, uncompromising Lutheran, who by the grace of God was able to cope with the problems and difficulties he encountered. The Lutheranism he found in the East as represented in the men whom he personally met, for instance, Doctors Stohlmann in New York, Demme in Philadelphia, Benj. Kurtz and Morris in Baltimore, was anything but reassuring. Nor was he slow to reprimand these men for their sympathetic attitude towards revivalism, unionism, Methodism. For the Lutheran Church he was ashamed that some of these men bore the Doctor of Divinity title.

Going by way of Philadelphia, Baltimore, and Zanesville, he arrived at Columbus, Ohio, where he met the two professors at the seminary, Winkler and Schaeffer, who were able to give him valuable data on the mission work in Ohio. At Lancaster his attention was directed by Pastor Lehman to a settlement of Rhenish Bavarians in and around Pomeroy who desired an Evangelical pastor. These people came from the unionistic Church of Germany, the smaller number being Lutheran, the rest Reformed. They requested Sihler to preach in the town courthouse and also in a country schoolhouse. Sihler acceded to their request, but, straightforward and uncompromising as he was, frankly informed them that he was a Lutheran and would preach nothing to them but the Lutheran doctrine according to the Confessions of the Lutheran Church. Still they called him, and on January 1, 1844, he preached his inaugural sermon on John 3:16.

A difficult future lay before the new pastor. His people resembled virgin timberland, which demanded resolute clearing and careful cultivation if there was to be a harvest. Sihler was no shirker. The harder he worked, the more he found he was able to accomplish. Judiciously studying the needs of his people, he applied himself with indefatigable vigor to teaching and preaching. Thus, by wise tact he gradually organized a town and a country congregation. After thorough instruction on the Lord's Supper and in other distinctive doctrines, the congregations were cleared of those who held to the Reformed teachings. On Sundays and once a week he preached to each of the churches, the farmers leaving their fields, even in the busiest seasons, and assembling to hear the Word of God. Sihler introduced personal announcement for Holy Communion; he taught school six days a week, three days in town and three in the country.

Despite all this labor he found time for private studies and even for writing. While he was at Pomeroy, he published in the *Lutherische Kirchenzeitung* the famous "Letters to the German Lutherans in America," in which he exhorted the readers to appreciate the glory of the Lutheran Church, with its pure Gospel and unadulterated Sacraments, in contrast to the Roman Catholic Church and the sectarians. As a result calls came from congregations in Boston, Milwaukee, Chicago, Allegheny City, and Dayton. Determined to complete his task at Pomeroy, Sihler turned down these calls. In Pomeroy he composed his tract *A Dialog of Two Lutherans on Methodism,* of which 12,000 copies were sold and which was translated into English, Norwegian, and Swedish.

Through the *Lutherische Kirchenzeitung* Sihler learned that the Western District of the Ohio Synod was soon to meet at Germantown, Ohio. Not wishing to be a separatist, he resolved to join this synod, especially since in its constitution it was pledged to the Lutheran Confessions. He applied for membership and ordination in 1844. In lieu of the obligatory examination, the credentials which he presented from Dr. Rudelbach were accepted as satisfactory. At his ordination, however, the synod at first demurred. At that time it was the practice of all synods first to license a candidate of theology to preach and perform ministerial acts for one or more years before granting him ordination. Sihler refused to be licensed. He maintained that by virtue of his call to the Pomeroy congregation he already was a pastor before God and the Church; ordination was merely a public recognition and confirmation of the fact that he was a called pastor. Rather than be licensed, he would withdraw his application for membership. His protestations were finally approved; he was ordained and received into membership in the Ohio Synod. This was early in 1844.

But Sihler was a disappointed man. To reach Germantown, he had to walk five miles from Miamisburg. He lugged a saddlebag which contained the Book of Concord and other tomes of Lutheran theology, hoping to refer to them in doctrinal discussions which he expected at the convention. To his dismay, he found the synod's work to be merely a business routine. There were other features in the Ohio Synod that depressed him. The pastor of the entertaining congregation, Andrew Henkel, was a Freemason, a fact that did not provoke any adverse comment from the synod. Most of the pastors did not require personal announcement for Holy Communion. The Communion liturgy of the synod contained the unionistic formula: "Christ says, This is My body," etc. In general he found that while the clergy had a historic regard for the Confessions of the Lutheran Church, very few of them were familiar with the contents of the Book of Concord and most of them indulged in church practices which savored of sectarianism.

July 1—5 a special meeting of the Ohio Synod was held at Zanesville to consider the problems confronting the seminary at Columbus. The constitution of the institution prescribed German as the sole medium of instruction, but an American party within the synod favored the use of the English language. It was feared that with the use of the English language the compromising principles so prevalent in the English theological literature of the General Synod would be introduced into the school. Sihler placed himself at the head of the German faction, which gained a temporary advantage by the passage of a resolution that "theological instruction should be given in the seminary only through the medium of the German language and that the

English language should be taught only as a literary study." [3] At this same convention Sihler, together with Candidates Ernst, Ferschner, and Burger, memorialized the synod to abolish the unionistic formula: "Christ says, This is My body," etc., at the distribution of the Lord's Supper. The synod resolved that "the petition be considered at the next regular convention and that the secretary submit this memorial to both editors for publication in order to prepare the absent brethren and the church at large for deliberation on this matter." [4]

In the fall of this year, 1844, Sihler received the first copy of *Der Lutheraner*, rejoiced at its confessional note, and was quick to place the new publication into the hands of his parish members.

The Ohio Synod met again in May, 1845, at Lancaster, Ohio. At this time the Zanesville resolutions concerning the language question at the Columbus seminary were rescinded. The memorial advocating a change in the distribution formula in the Communion service, submitted by Sihler at the previous convention, was rejected.

On July 15, 1845, Sihler arrived in Fort Wayne to become Wyneken's successor as pastor of St. Paul's Evangelical Lutheran Church.

In view of the action of the Ohio Synod at its convention at Lancaster, Sihler and his friends met in Cleveland and in a formal statement of September 18, 1845, severed their connection with this body. The document was signed by the following clergymen and candidates of theology: Fr. Winkler, W. Sihler, A. Schmidt, J. G. Burger, J. A. Ernst, Wm. Richmann, A. Saupert, Aug. Selle, and Teacher E. A. Scheuermann.

The same year which saw Wyneken and his congregation standing alone also found Sihler and his friends unattached to any Lutheran body and deliberating on the possibilities of establishing a confessional Lutheran synod in America.

7

PRELIMINARY MEETINGS LEADING TO THE ORGANIZATION OF THE MISSOURI SYNOD

*I*N 1845 the Saxon pastors and candidates of theology were disposed as follows: Walther was pastor in St. Louis; Loeber, Keyl, and Gruber were in Perry County; Buerger was in charge of the Silesians in Buffalo; Buenger was assistant pastor to Walther and teacher of the school; Fuerbringer was at Venedy, Illinois; Wege was in charge of the congregation in Benton County, Missouri; Geyer was ministering to a flock in Wisconsin; Goenner was teaching in the college at Perry County, Missouri; Brohm was pastor in New York, and Schieferdecker was working in Monroe County, Illinois. O. H. Walther had died in 1841; Stephan had been deposed and was now living in Horse Prairie, Illinois; Kluegel had separated from the Saxons and was serving a group in Wisconsin; Candidate Froehlich had departed this life in 1839 in Perry County, Missouri.

The Loehe men were working at the following places: Ernst at Neuendettelsau, Ohio; Burger at Zion, Van Wert County, Ohio; Baumgart, teacher at Columbus, Ohio; Sihler at Fort Wayne; Hattstaedt at Monroe, Michigan; Schuster, teacher at Pomeroy, Ohio; Zwerner, colporteur at Columbus, Ohio; G. Bartels at Zanesville, Ohio; Kornbausch, teacher at Sandy Creek, Michigan; Romanowski at Pomeroy, Ohio;

Lochner at Toledo, Ohio; Detzer, missionary at large, with headquarters at Fort Wayne; Trautmann at Danbury, Ohio; Saupert at Evansville, Indiana; Craemer at Frankenmuth, Michigan. Wyneken, although not a Loehe man, was closely associated with the Loehe men and was stationed at Baltimore.

The Saxons had kept aloof from all synodical groups. By correspondence and personal conferences they maintained a bond of fellowship among themselves and since September, 1844, were giving expression to their convictions through *Der Lutheraner*. The Loehe men were members of the Ohio or the Michigan Synod but were dissatisfied with their affiliations. *Der Lutheraner*, read and circulated by them, focused their attention upon the Saxons.

Loehe likewise was interested in the Saxons. When Hattstaedt sailed from Germany for America in 1844, he was given a set of instructions by Loehe, one of which stated that before he established himself permanently, he was to make an extended journey to the West. He was to visit the Saxons in Missouri, greet them from the fatherland, and request them to work together with the brethren in Ohio for the spreading of Christ's kingdom. In addition to these instructions, Hattstaedt received a number of questions which he was to present to the Saxons as points for discussion while visiting them.

Hattstaedt could not make the western journey. He was detained at Monroe, Michigan, to minister to the Lutherans of that community. Accordingly, he delivered the questions which he had received from Loehe to Sihler and to Ernst, with the request that they establish contact with the Saxons.

Thus it happened that early in December, 1844, Sihler and Ernst wrote to Walther in St. Louis, enclosing the questions submitted by Loehe, of which Number Six was: "Would it not be possible to establish a synod with our brethren in the East?" Walther answered on January 2, 1845: "I con-

MEETINGS LEADING TO ORGANIZATION OF SYNOD 85

sider this not only possible, but also very desirable and of great promise for the welfare of all; indeed, I consider it imperative for conscience' sake, if a union can be made possible in any manner. . . . I for my person am ready for any sacrifice necessary to effect a church union. For this reason I have dared in God's name to send forth a periodical such as *Der Lutheraner* into the world and submit it to the Church of God in America in order to do what I can to call the orthodox together." [1]

When the convention of the Ohio Synod at Lancaster, Ohio, May, 1845, refused to heed the request of Sihler and his companions regarding the use of the unionistic formula in the distribution of the Lord's Supper, the Loehe men resolved to leave this body and to organize a confessional Lutheran synod. They agreed to meet at Cleveland together with Wyneken, who was without synodical affiliation, and others to take the steps necessary for this purpose. Pastor Ernst informed Walther of the events at Lancaster and of the contemplated meeting at Cleveland and under date of August 21, 1845, received the following reply:

"Your letter of August 6 filled me with heartfelt joy. After perusing it with my dear colleague Pastor Buenger, I praised God fervently that He has strengthened you in faith and permitted you to grow in love to His holy Word, His Church, and to your brethren, and that, according to your letter, He is daily opening opportunities for the reviving of the Lutheran Church in the West at this late date. Oh, how such news quickens my heart! With great joy I extend to you the hand of fellowship and as your humble colleague offer this encouragement: let us ever hold firmer to that which we have, let us remain faithful in that which has been entrusted to us. Then we shall behold the glory of God.

"Much as it grieved me to hear that the errors of the synod of which you were until now a member are becoming heresies because they are retained and not corrected, it afforded me joy that you with your dear associates have testified so loyally and steadfastly. God bless you for this now and eternally! Your plan immediately to establish a new truly Lutheran synod in Ohio has my heartiest approval. I herewith implore the Lord of the Church that He would grant you, as God's architect, wisdom and loyalty to lay an immovable foundation for this new structure. No doubt, it will please you to learn that here the aversion to synodical organization is gradually waning and a sincere longing for a closer union with other true servants of the Church and their congregations is daily gaining ground.

"My desires concerning this matter are chiefly these: 1. That in addition to the Word of God the synod be founded on all the Confessions of our Church, including, if possible, the Saxon Articles of Visitation; 2. That a special paragraph of the constitution eliminate and exclude all syncretistic activities of members of the organization; 3. That the chief activity of the Synod be directed toward the preservation, nourishing, and supervision of the unity and purity of Lutheran doctrine; 4. That the synod exist not so much as a powerful court, but rather as an advisory body, to which a perplexed congregation may take recourse; it must particularly abstain from all encroachments upon the congregation's right to call; 5. That the lay delegates, yes, everyone who belongs to the Synod, be entitled to suffrage in the same manner as the pastors. The chairman, however, is to be elected from the latter (Acts 15:23). Finally, I think that in no matter decided by the synod should any individual be deprived of the right to appeal to the decision and vote of all the united congregations. For the moment these are my thoughts, which I submit to your brotherly love and consideration.

"God bless your deliberations with the most glorious results when you meet in Cleveland. You can be assured of our humble prayers. You have yourself anticipated that it will be impossible for me as well as my other brethren in the ministry here personally to take part in the announced conference. All the greater is our desire to have you with us after your meeting in Cleveland. I beg you that even though many obstacles are placed in your way, you do not permit yourself to be discouraged from carrying out your intention to come here with Dr. Sihler. (We most likely cannot count on the presence of dear Pastor Wyneken.) Think of the great, wholesome effects that would result from an alliance between the East and the West; how much more extensive your influence would be and how, perhaps, also our humble efforts could strengthen you spiritually. May the love of Christ to His bride and to us in the barren West tear asunder all bands woven by the devil which would restrain you from looking us up soon." [2]

The Loehe men and their associates met at Cleveland, September 13—18. Present were Wyneken, Sihler, Winkler, Ernst, Burger, Selle, Schmidt, Husmann, Richter, Detzer, Romanowski, Schuster, Hattstaedt, Baumgart, Lochner, Kornbausch, and two students: Wernle, Winkler's student, and Frincke (Fricke), Sihler's student. Craemer could not attend on account of illness, and Saupert was absent because of distance. Brohm, one of the Saxons, participated by means of correspondence from New York.

At this convention the Loehe men who were members of the Ohio Synod, in a document signed September 18, severed their connection with this body. Instead of organizing a new Ohio synod, as had been suggested by Ernst, the group decided to endeavor to include the Saxons in the new body, and delegates were appointed to visit the men in Missouri.

Lochner writes concerning this meeting: "Even though, while considering such important matters, the old man manifested himself here and there, the meeting was certainly of the utmost blessing. We strengthened ourselves with the Word of God, prayer, and the Sacrament. This was particularly true toward the close of the convention, when we younger brethren turned to the older brethren with all kinds of questions, especially pastoral questions, and received pastoral advice. I was deeply impressed by Wyneken, who is humble, charitable, and zealous; by Sihler, who has a penetrating intellect and a demeanor that inspires confidence and respect; and by Ernst, who is serene and openminded. Everyone realized and confessed: We must meet again. For our edification and for the edification of the Cleveland congregation sermons were preached by Wyneken, Sihler, Ernst, and Hattstaedt on the Lord's Supper, Baptism, Church, and justifying faith. More such sermons, also in other congregations, and spiritual life would soon be quickened. At the close of the convention Dr. Sihler ordained Burger, Schmidt, and Romanowski." [3]

At this conference, as has been stated, it was resolved to establish personal contact with the Saxons, Sihler and Ernst being delegated for this purpose. Lochner, who accompanied the two men at the invitation of Sihler and Walther "in order to gain something for the discussion of our Michigan Synod in June at Ann Arbor, and partly, following a sign from God, to seek a helpmeet in the home of Pastor Walther," writes as follows concerning this meeting:

"We (Sihler, Ernst, and I) rode down the Ohio to its mouth and then up the immense Mississippi. One evening we stopped at a settlement to take on passengers. The houses appeared to be German and likewise the new passengers; the black coats and white cravats of the men caused us to believe them to be clerics. We finally reached the conclusion that they were Methodist preachers. But who can describe our joy when we learned after a while that, though preachers, they were not Methodists, but Lutherans, namely, Pastors Loeber, Keyl, and Gruber, and that the landing place was the Saxon settlement Wittenberg, from which Alten-

MEETINGS LEADING TO ORGANIZATION OF SYNOD 89

burg is only seven miles distant. During the rest of the short journey of 100 miles we engaged in conversation with our new companions, and the result was the fear on our part that a complete union between us and the brethren in Missouri could not be reached without difficulties. It could not be denied that these brethren were filled with some distrust, for which we could not blame them, as they had been so grossly deceived by Stephan. Also the fact that we, except Dr. Sihler, had received no German university training caused them to hesitate. Furthermore, they doubted, especially Pastor Keyl, that we could divide the Word of God properly, since we had not thoroughly studied the works of Luther. I still vividly remember how troubled we were in our minds, Pastor Ernst and I, when we retired that night. We asked ourselves earnestly if we with our meager education could continue in office with a good conscience. They had also other scruples about this and that point in our 'instructions.' Thank God, however, our fears were in vain, as our three weeks' stay in St. Louis proved.

"Those were precious days and blessed, which I shall not forget as long as I live, and for me they were in more than one sense decisive for my whole life. We were welcomed in a most cordial and brotherly manner in St. Louis by Pastors Walther, Buenger, Fuerbringer, and Schieferdecker, who had been expecting us. Our 'instructions' were taken up first, and the unclear and doubtful points were ironed out orally and referred back to Pastor Loehe for explanation. When I today look back upon those instructions, I realize that the doubts of the Saxon brethren were justified, and I most gratefully confess that, although we — some more and some less — were very unclear in points of doctrine, especially regarding the Church and the ministry, yea, had weaknesses in us, yet we received very fine consideration from these brethren, who did not withdraw the hand of fellowship, because they saw that we were honest and upright in our attitude towards the Word of God and the Church. They began at once to confer with us on the draft of the present synodical constitution.

"We spent an entire week at this work, at the close of which we immediately made common copies and sent them to the other men who had left the Ohio Synod and to other friends, inviting them to a conference at Fort Wayne, beginning July 2, where the plan, we said, would be carefully discussed.

"At this time several meetings were held with the St. Louis congregation, in which their pastors presented the plan for consideration. I, being wholly inexperienced, occasionally opened my eyes wide in astonishment when I saw that the congregation did not at once acquiesce, but questioned this and that item; indeed, several members sharply disputed with the pastors. These men, however, entered into their doubts and objections with such calm and consideration, as if the congregation were made up of none but scholarly theologians.

"In this connection it should also be mentioned that we three were asked to preach as a testimony to the unity of faith. Though we went at this task unwillingly and with trembling, we could not on that account decline. Dr. Sihler preached in the afternoon of Rogate Sunday on Eph. 4:3-6, after Pastor Fuerbringer had preached on the day's Gospel lesson in the morning service; and on Ascension Day, Pastor Ernst preached in the morning on the Gospel lesson, and I, in the afternoon, on Matt. 28:20.

"Dr. Sihler and Pastor Ernst departed before Pentecost; but I remained a week longer, for on Pentecost Monday I was to marry Pastor Walther's sister-in-law, to whom I had become engaged on Sunday Exaudi." [4]

On June 25, 1846, Hattstaedt, Craemer, Lochner, and Trautmann severed their connection with the Michigan Synod. This synod had been organized by Pastor F. Schmidt

MEETINGS LEADING TO ORGANIZATION OF SYNOD 91

of Ann Arbor in 1840 and was known as the Missionary Synod, for Indian missions seemed to be its first object. As a matter of fact, three missionaries, among them J. F. Auch and F. Maier, began work among the Indians at Sibiwaing in 1845. Pastor Loehe put his newly established Indian missions under the care of the Missionary Synod upon Schmidt's pledge that confessional Lutheranism would prevail in his organization. Loehe's men, Hattstaedt, Craemer, Lochner, and Trautmann, joined this synod. Pastor Schmidt and his comrades, however, were not genuine Lutherans, most of them having been sent to America from Basel, which was contaminated by the Prussian Church Union and would make no distinction between Lutheran and Reformed congregations. A missionary by the name of Dumser, who had come from Basel and who steadfastly refused to subscribe to the confessional writings of the Lutheran Church, was received as a member of this synod during its convention at Ann Arbor, June, 1846, in spite of the protests of the Loehe men. Thereupon they could not do otherwise than declare their withdrawal from the Michigan Synod.

In July, 1846, the third preliminary meeting of the promoters of a confessional Lutheran synod took place at Fort Wayne for a further consideration of the draft of the constitution which had been signed at St. Louis by Walther, Loeber, Gruber, Keyl, Fuerbringer, Schieferdecker, Ernst, and Sihler. Sixteen pastors were present. Six clergymen who could not attend the meeting informed the conference of their hearty approval of the plan to organize an orthodox synod. The Saxons were represented by Walther, Loeber, and Mr. F. W. Barthel, who traveled down the Mississippi River to Cairo, Illinois, thence up the Ohio River to Cincinnati, thence north to the junction of the canal leading from Toledo to Indianapolis, and by Brohm, who came from New York. The Loehe men Craemer and Hattstaedt came by lake boat to Toledo, meeting Walther and Loeber at the junction. We have reports from both Loeber and Craemer regarding this meeting.

Writes Lochner, quoting Loeber: "While Walther was traveling together with Pastor G. H. Loeber and the latter's son (who was at that time still a student), to the conference which had been arranged, they spoke much of the synod which was formed on the basis of the proposed constitution. Walther could not conceal his concern about the success of the venture, since there was still no sufficient guarantee from all those invited of their doctrinal position or their attitude. Arriving at the junction of the Cincinnati Canal early in the morning, the travelers had the greater part of the day in which to wait for the canalboat from Toledo. Therefore they took advantage of the beautiful morning to walk in the forest and again discussed those problems which troubled their hearts. In the solitude of the forest they joined in the morning hymn: "Praise Be to God on High," suggested by the sainted Loeber, and when it had been sung to the end, Walther knelt down with his companions and poured out his heart in a moving prayer for the Church and for the realization of an orthodox synod in this land of freedom of conscience. After they had lingered a little longer in the forest, they repaired to the landing, because the Toledo canalboat would soon be due. Nor did they have to wait long. As it drew near, Walther called his companions' attention to the somberly dressed gentlemen standing on the deck, with their long pipes. It was Craemer, the Indian missionary and pastor at Frankenmuth, and some of his Franconian associates. Soon Walther and Loeber found themselves to be in complete doctrinal agreement." [5]

Craemer reports: "Since I had been prevented by fever from participating in the previous meeting at Cleveland, called by the sainted Dr. Sihler and others, I hastened all the more to attend the conference which had been invited to Fort Wayne in the following year, 1846, at which we pastors from Michigan, Ohio, and Indiana came together with our Saxon brethren from Missouri to deliberate about the constitution of the synod which came into being in 1847 at Chicago. At that time our Fort Wayne itinerary took us Northerners out of Toledo, on the Wabash Canal, which divides at the so-called junction into two branches. The one goes westward past Fort Wayne, through Indiana, and the other runs from Cincinnati to the junction. The Saxon brethren came by way of the latter, as they dreaded the inconvenient and tedious land route, rather traveling down the Mississippi to the mouth of the Ohio, then up the latter to Cincinnati, and from there via canal to Fort Wayne. The boat which brought them to the junction had already docked, awaiting only the local travelers to take its westbound passengers farther on. It was not very long before a slender man with a prominent nose and fiery eyes strode out of the door in the inn, followed by a serious, but milder looking, slightly built man and a young student, who boarded our boat. The first was, naturally, Walther, the others, the venerable Pastor Loeber and his son. The great joy at this fortunate encounter was mutual, and soon we all found ourselves engaged in a spirited conversation, while, undisturbed, we very smoothly slipped down the canal. Thus I was with Walther. It was very important to me personally to become more closely acquainted with the man whom I had already recognized from *Der Lutheraner* as a pillar of genuine Biblical, Lutheran truth. Walther, on the other hand, also wanted to know what sort of a man he might be whom Loehe had sent over to direct the colonization and mission affairs and to be a guide to his pupils. Soon we were in a serious discussion, absorbed in every detail, which lasted during the whole of the long trip." [6]

Sihler wrote concerning this conference: "The main purpose of this meeting was, in the presence of and with the participation of the Eastern brethren, to go over anew the basic articles of the draft of a truly faithful Lutheran synodical constitution, drawn up by Pastor Walther at St. Louis and to reach a conclusion — which occurred then, at the expiration of about a week, to the satisfaction of all in general. Naturally here, as in St. Louis, the Saxon brethren had to push the thing along, for we Easterners were pretty much novices for this ticklish and difficult work. Still we all had fresh courage and good confidence and finally resolved to meet at Chicago in the spring of 1847 with delegates from the congregations to form a small orthodox synod." [7]

In his report of this meeting to Loehe, Hattstaedt stated: "I doubt very much that the meeting at Fort Wayne would have achieved its purpose if the (Saxon) congregations had not sent those fine men (Walther, Loeber, and Barthel). The constitution of the future synod has taken a different shape from what you desired. According to the experience of all brethren who were assembled here and who have been in office for some length of time, a democratic form of synodical government is the only feasible one for the Lutheran Church in America. The Word of God is the only power with which to rule the people, and if this power does not accomplish the desired end, nothing else will. Your plan of granting greater powers to the President was rejected by all present. The congregations were given all rights in settling their own affairs. They may call their preachers, and they may dismiss them, provided that the pastor proves to be a wolf and preaches false doctrine or leads an ungodly life. If the congregations dismiss their pastors for other reasons, they cannot be members of Synod and must be regarded as non-Christians and as unorthodox."[8]

Loeber and Walther preached in Fort Wayne during the conference week in token of the unity of faith and doctrine.

The men who signed the draft of the constitution at Fort Wayne were:

1. G. H. Loeber, Altenburg, Perry Co., Mo.
2. Dr. W. Sihler, Fort Wayne, Ind.
3. A. Knape, Defiance, Henry Co., Ohio
4. A. Schmidt, Cleveland, Ohio
5. A. Ernst, Neuendettelsau, Ohio
6. C. F. W. Walther, St. Louis, Mo.
7. Th. Brohm, New York, N. Y.
8. J. E. Schneider, Marion, Ohio
9. C. Aug. Selle, Chicago, Ill.
10. F. W. Husmann, Marion Township, Allen Co., Ind.
11. A. F. Craemer, Frankenmuth, Mich.
12. J. Trautmann, Danbury, Ohio
13. W. Hattstaedt, Monroe, Mich.
14. A. Detzer, Williams Co., Ohio
15. J. G. Burger, Willshire, Ohio
16. G. H. Jaebker, Adams Co., Ind.

Those unable to attend but indicating their approval by letter were the following:

1. C. F. Gruber, Paitzdorf, Perry Co., Mo.
2. E. G. W. Keyl, Frohna, Perry Co., Mo.
3. Ottomar Fuerbringer, Elkhorn Prairie, Ill.
4. G. A. Schieferdecker, Monroe, Ill.
5. J. F. Buenger, St. Louis, Mo.
6. F. Lochner, Toledo, Ohio

The following candidates for the ministry were present: A. Lehmann, G. K. Schuster, Boehm, Wolf, C. F. W. Scholz.

The next step was to be the formal organization of the synod at Chicago in April of the next year. In the meantime due publicity was given to the movement. The Fort Wayne draft was printed in full in *Der Lutheraner* of September 5, 1846. Congregations were asked to study the constitution and, if in accord, to assist in the establishing of the new synod.

8

THE ORGANIZATION OF THE GERMAN EVANGELICAL LUTHERAN SYNOD OF MISSOURI, OHIO, AND OTHER STATES

*D*ER *Lutheraner* of February 9, 1847, contained the announcement: "The German Evangelical Lutheran Synod of Missouri, Ohio, and Other States will hold its first session on Monday after Jubilate Sunday, April 26, 1847, at Chicago, Illinois." In the issue of March 23 the periodical stated: "Those concerned are herewith again reminded that the organization and first session of the German Evangelical Lutheran Synod of Missouri, Ohio, and Other States will take place on Monday after Jubilate Sunday, April 26, 1847, at Chicago, Illinois."

Chicago, at this time, was a city of some 20,000 inhabitants. In 1843 the German Protestants of the place had built a Lutheran-Reformed church on the corner of Ohio and La Salle Streets. Pastor C. August T. Selle of Columbiana County, Ohio, had assumed the pastorate of the congregation and preached his first sermon (incidentally, the first Lutheran sermon in Chicago) on April 12, Easter Monday, 1846. This congregation split on April 9, 1848, only four members remaining with Selle. In this church the Missouri Synod was organized.

By Saturday, April 24, most of the pastors and delegates had arrived. There were no railroads leading to Chicago in

98   A CENTURY OF GRACE

those days. The Loehe men, as Dr. Sihler tells us in his autobiography, traveled for five days on horseback and in buggies, averaging 36 miles per day. The Saxons, Loeber, Walther, Fuerbringer, and the lay delegate from St. Louis, F. W. Barthel, evidently came via the Mississippi and the Illinois Rivers, making the last part of their journey either by stage or by canal.

On Jubilate Sunday, April 25, the opening service was held, Pastor G. H. Loeber preaching on the Gospel for the

Selle's Church in Chicago (1847)

day. Holy Communion was administered. In the evening the brethren gathered in the residence of Pastor Selle to establish the mode of procedure for the first session on the next day.

On Monday morning, April 26, 1847, the convention was solemnly opened with hymn and prayer. Thereupon Pastor Selle addressed the assembled delegates, dwelling upon the purpose of the convention. The men who had been present at the Fort Wayne meeting hereupon signed the constitution, and thus Synod was officially established. Temporary officers were elected, namely, C. F. W. Walther, President; F. W. Husmann, Secretary; W. Sihler, Treasurer.

The constitution which the Synod adopted was the result of thorough Bible study and diligent research in the confessional books of the Lutheran Church. Every word of the constitution had been examined and re-examined, not only by pastors, but also by congregations. Thus Walther's congregation in St. Louis had devoted ten meetings to the discussion of the new constitution. In this document are found the Scriptural principles governing synodical organizations. The reasons for the organization of a synod are stated as follows:

1. The example of the Apostolic Church (Acts 15:1-31);
2. The conservation and continuance of the unity of the true faith (Eph. 4:3-13; 1 Cor. 1:10) and a united effort to resist every form of schism and sectarianism (Rom. 16:17);
3. The protection of the pastors and congregations in the fulfillment of their duties and the maintenance of their rights;
4. The endeavor to bring about the largest possible uniformity in church practice, church customs, and, in general, in congregational affairs;
5. Our Lord's will that the diversities of gifts should be for the common profit (1 Cor. 12:4-31);
6. United effort to extend the Kingdom of God and to make possible and to promote special aims of the Synod (seminary, agenda, hymnbooks, Book of Concord, schoolbooks, distribution of the Bible, missionary activities within and without the Church, etc.).

As requisites for membership of pastors and congregations are stated:

"Acceptance of the Scriptures of the Old and New Testaments as the written Word of God and the only rule and norm of faith and practice. Acceptance of all the symbolical books of the Ev. Lutheran Church as a true and correct statement and exposition of the Word of God, to wit, the three Ecumenical Creeds (the Apostles' Creed, the Nicene Creed, the Athanasian Creed), the Unaltered Augsburg Confession, the Apology of the Augsburg Confession, the Smalcald Articles, the Large Catechism of Luther, the Small Catechism of Luther, and the Formula of Concord.

"Renunciation of unionism and syncretism of every description, such as serving union congregations composed of members of churches with different confessions as such; taking part in the services and sacramental rites of heterodox congregations or of such of mixed confession; joining the heterodox in missionary efforts or in the publishing and distribution of literature; exclusive use of doctrinally pure agendas, hymnbooks, and catechism in church and school; providing the children with a Christian school education."

The power of suffrage was recognized as an inalienable right of the congregation. In other words, only pastors whose congregations were voting members of Synod were entitled to a vote; pastors who joined without their congregations were designated advisory pastors, that is, pastors who, though members of Synod, have not the right of suffrage.

A number of changes in the constitution were proposed. The most important addition was submitted by Trinity Church of St. Louis, that Synod in its relation to the individual congregation is to be merely an advisory body; resolutions of Synod can have binding force only when the individual congregation has examined them and by formal resolution has voluntarily accepted and ratified them. If a congregation finds a resolution of Synod contrary to the Word of God or inexpedient as far as the condition of the congregation is concerned, it has the right to reject it. This addition was adopted by Synod.

The congregation at Frohna, Missouri (Pastor E. G. W. Keyl), memorialized Synod to change paragraph 14 of chapter 5, which permitted general confession and absolution, since it considered this institution un-Lutheran, offensive, superfluous, incautious, and insufficient. But Synod was not convinced and resolved to abide by its constitution, requesting the pastoral conference of Missouri to take up this matter with Pastor Keyl and his congregation.

Pastor E. Leonhardt of Lancaster, Ohio, had a number of criticisms to offer. One was directed against the paragraph which declares one of the purposes of Synod to be "the striving after the greatest possible uniformity of ceremonies"; another regarding the supervisory powers of the President. As to the first criticism, Synod ruled that no force or coercion should be used in introducing new customs and ceremonies; that under prevailing conditions uniform ceremonies would be salutary, but that new ceremonies should be introduced only after due instruction and in accord with the principle of Christian liberty. With reference to the second criticism, Synod declared that it did not share the fears of Pastor Leonhardt.

A more serious objection to the constitution was raised by Pastor C. L. Geyer and his delegate Mr. Hoekendorf of Watertown, Wisconsin. Geyer maintained that congregations had no right to enter synodical relations, since the Bible has neither a command nor any promise for this purpose and that the constitution erred in claiming that the convention of the churches at Jerusalem and Antioch was an example for the present organization. Synod replied that organizing a synod was a matter of Christian liberty, that a general command can be found in Eph. 4:3 and 1 Cor. 14:40; that the convention at Jerusalem was a pattern for us, inasmuch as those Christians held their convention in accordance with Christian liberty, and that what was permissible then cannot be forbidden now.

Synod deemed it advisable to obtain control of the two privately owned institutions for the training of pastors and teachers. Accordingly, it resolved to request Pastor Loehe to relinquish all rights to the institution of Fort Wayne and to support it financially and otherwise in the future. With reference to the institution at Altenburg, Missouri, it was resolved to appeal to Pastor Loehe, Dr. Delitzsch, and Pastor Karsten at Rostock, Dr. Petri in Hannover, and Dr. Harless in Leipzig for financial aid, with the promise to use this money solely for the support of this institution if the congregations now owning it would place it under the control of Synod. Elementary education was not slighted. The pastors were urged to establish parish schools and to teach such schools themselves if necessary.

Pastor Craemer and his companions arrived on April 30. They made the trip by lake steamer (Huron and Michigan) and had been detained by ice floes at Fort Mackinaw. Their arrival placed the subject of missions on the docket. Already in the first session Candidate Frincke (Fricke) volunteered to serve as missionary at large, and his offer was accepted. The mission work among the Indians, conducted by Craemer in Michigan, was under the control of Loehe. Synod resolved to request Loehe to place this mission under its care. Craemer reported that he had received a communication from the Central Mission Society of Nuernberg, Germany, with reference to mission work among the heathen. A committee was appointed to communicate with the society at Nuernberg.

Paragraph 4 of Section IV had reference to the publication and distribution of church periodicals. Pastor Walther offered Synod *Der Lutheraner*, which offer Synod gladly accepted. Beginning with Vol. IV, the masthead should read: "Published by the German Evangelical Lutheran Synod of Missouri, Ohio, and Other States, C. F. W. Walther, Editor." Synod urged Walther to comment even more than previously on church conditions in this country and instructed the treasurer of *Der Lutheraner* to insist that all subscriptions be prepaid. A committee was appointed for the publication of *Der Lutheraner*. Twelve pastors were appointed to read and comment on the twelve leading religious periodicals of the country.

Pastor Brohm reported to Synod that Mr. Ludwig of New York was contemplating a new edition of the Book of Concord and had printed Luther's Small Catechism (4½ cents each per 100). Synod declared its readiness to support Mr. Ludwig in his efforts to disseminate the Book of Concord and the new catechism.

A theological opinion was delivered in connection with the memorial of J. D. Bewersdorf of Milwaukee and F. Kauffung of Freystadt, Wisconsin, signed by 57 members of the two congregations, with reference to Pastor Krause.

Four pastors were colloquized: Fick, Streckfuss, Poeschke, Richmann.

Two men were ordained, Husmann and Poeschke.

Seven sermons were delivered. Besides the two on the opening day by Loeber and Sihler, sermons were preached by Walther, Fick, Husmann, Fuerbringer, and Wolter.

Eighteen public sessions were held, in the last of which officers and committees for the next three years were elected. They were: President, Pastor C. F. W. Walther; Vice-President, Dr. W. Sihler; Secretary, Pastor F. W. Husmann; Treasurer, Mr. F. W. Barthel. Examiners: Pastors G. H. Loeber and Wm. Sihler; correspondent for foreign countries, Pastor G. H. Loeber; chronologist: Pastor O. Fuerbringer; Mission Board: Pastors C. J. H. Fick, A. Craemer, and Mr. F. W. Barthel; committee for *Der Lutheraner:* Pastor J. F. Buenger and Mr. F. W. Barthel.

Synod was divided into six conference circuits: 1. St. Louis, Mo. 2. Chicago, Ill. 3. Fort Wayne, Ind.; 4. Monroe, Mich. 5. Fairfield, O. 6. New York, N. Y.

Candidate C. Frincke was solemnly commissioned as missionary at large. After having resolved to hold the next convention at St. Louis, to which Pastor Loehe was to be invited, Synod adjourned.

Charter members of the Missouri Synod as listed in the *Proceedings* of the first convention are:

A. Voting Members

Pastors	Congregations	Address
C. F. W. Walther	The German Ev. Luth. Congregation of the Unaltered Augsburg Confession, St. Louis, Mo.	St. Louis, Mo.
A. Ernst	St. John's German Ev. Luth. Congregation of the Unaltered Augsburg Confession, Neuendettelsau, Union Co., Ohio	Marysville, Ohio
Dr. W. Sihler	St. Paul's German Ev. Luth. Congregation, Fort Wayne, Ind.	Fort Wayne, Ind.
F. W. Poeschke	The German Ev. Luth. Congregation in Hassler settlement and the French Ev. Luth. Congregation on the Saminaque, Ill.	Peru, Ill.
F.A. (A.F.) Craemer	The German Ev. Luth. Congregation at Frankenmuth, Mich.	Frankenmuth, Mich.
F. W. Husmann	St. John's German Ev. Luth. Congregation in Allen and Adams Counties and the German Ev. Luth. Congregation at Fuelling, Adams Co.	Fort Wayne, Ind.

G. H. Jaebker	The German Ev. Luth. Congregation in Adams Co., Ind., on the left bank of the St. Mary's	Poughkeepsie, Ind.
G. K. Schuster	The German Ev. Luth. Congregation in Kosciusko and Marshall Co., Ind.	Mishawaka, Ind.
G. Streckfuss	Zion German Ev. Luth. Congregation in Van Wert Co., and St. Paul's German Ev. Luth. Congregation in Mercer Co., Ohio	Willshire, Ohio
C. J. H. Fick	The German Ev. Luth. Congregation in Neumelle, St. Charles Co., Mo.	Femme Osage, Mo.
E. Mor. Buerger	Trinity Ev. Luth. Congregation, Buffalo, N. Y.	Buffalo, N. Y.
W. Scholz	St. John's German Ev. Luth. Congregation at Minden, Washington Co., Ill.	Nashville, Ill.

B. Advisory Members

G. H. Loeber	Altenburg, Perry Co., Mo.	Apple Creek, Mo.
Ottom. Fuerbringer	Elkhorn Prairie, Washington Co., Ill.	St. Louis, Mo. (c/o Rev. C. F. W. Walther)
Ch. A. Selle	Chicago, Cook Co., Ill.	Chicago, Ill.
F. W. Richmann	Fairfield Co., Ohio	Lancaster, Ohio
J. Trautmann	Danbury, Ottawa Co., Ohio	Port Clinton, Ohio
C. L. A. Wolter	Fort Wayne, Ind.	Fort Wayne, Ind.
Th. Jul. Brohm	New York, N. Y.	New York, N. Y.
W. Hattstaedt	Monroe, Mich.	Monroe, Mich.
J. E. Schneider	Marion, Marion Co., Ohio	Marion, Ohio
A. Detzer	Williams Co., Ohio	Bryan, Ohio

C. Candidates of Theology

Carl Frincke	Missionary at large for Wisconsin	Fort Wayne, Ind.
J. Lor. Flessa	Frankenmuth, Mich.	Bridgeport, Mich.

D. Lay Delegates

Ernst Voss, delegate from Fort Wayne and the congregation in Allen and Adams Counties, Ind.

F. W. Barthel, delegate of Trinity Church, St. Louis, Mo.

J. L. Heinke, delegate of congregations in Kosciusko and Marshall Co., Ind.

J. L. Bernthal, delegate of Frankenmuth, Mich.

E. Guests

F. A. Hoffmann ("Hans Buschbauer"), Pastor at Addison, Ill.

Pastor C. L. Geyer and Mr. Hoekendorf, delegates of the congregation at Watertown, Wis.

J. D. Bewersdorf and F. Kauffung, delegates from Milwaukee and Freystadt, Wis.

C. Faude, delegate from Buffalo, N. Y.

Jul. Biltz, student of theology, Altenburg, Mo.

9

LENGTHENING THE CORDS
1847-1872

*T*HE Missouri Synod was established in a territory which was having a phenomenal increase in population. The Middle West was rapidly filling up with people, some of whom came from the East, the majority, however, being immigrants from Europe, particularly from Germany and the Scandinavian countries. Synod's first duty was to gather these Lutherans into congregations, but the lack of pastors was so great that many German Lutherans were absorbed by other denominations.

At its first convention, Synod appointed Candidate Frincke (Fricke) as a "visitor," whose duty was to travel to the new settlements and to organize them into congregations. Frincke traversed Wisconsin, Illinois, Indiana, and Ohio, but the settlements he found were not so promising as had been anticipated, and he soon accepted a call to an established parish on the White Creek, Bartholomew Co., Indiana. The following year (1848) Adam Ernst was asked to canvass Illinois, Missouri, and Iowa; F. Buenger, Cincinnati; and Pastor Frincke was requested to make another missionary journey, but none of the three could find the necessary time for the work. At the third convention (1849) Frincke was appointed to go to Cincinnati, and Pastor Johannes to Illinois,

Missouri, and Iowa. It was furthermore resolved at this convention to send a candidate to New Orleans to explore that city and the surrounding territory. But all these plans miscarried, although Pastor F. Sievers went to Cincinnati and Pastor J. P. Graebner made a number of mission journeys in the north.

Synod felt the need of missionaries at large, but it was not until 1865 that this office was established. In the meantime Synod used another agency to meet, in a measure, the mission opportunities: that of a colporteur. A colporteur was a layman whose duties Synod clearly defined in 1852. He was to look up settlements that had no preachers, sell Bibles, hymnbooks, catechisms, and other material of a devotional nature. He was to admonish the people to establish the office of the ministry, assist them in calling a suitable pastor, urge them to conduct private services in their homes, if no minister were available, and to instruct them how to conduct family devotions, teach the catechism to their children, and perform emergency Baptisms. The *Proceedings* of 1853 give a detailed report of the activities of Colporteur Gustav Pfau. Other men who served in this capacity were Fr. Lange and J. Umbach of St. Louis.

In 1857 Pastor Aug. Selle reported the resolution of the Western District requesting Synod to send out evangelists, who were to serve settlements until congregations had been organized and then move on to new communities. Synod, however, took no action in this matter.

Finally in 1860 Synod, on the basis of an essay delivered by Pastor Aug. Selle, resolved to call men as traveling missionaries (*Reiseprediger*). Dr. W. Sihler was appointed treasurer of the fund which was to defray the expenses of such men, and the Districts were requested to contribute liberally to this treasury. It was not until 1865, however, that the first missionary at large, Candidate Fr. Liebe, was sent out. Working under the Western District, Liebe made his first missionary journey on August 25, 1865, exploring Missouri.

The history of the expansion of the Missouri Synod is a story in itself. It is the story of missionaries who were self-sacrificing men, whose hearts throbbed with the love of Christ and His people, whose religious convictions were sincere and deep, who were staunch and sturdy in all sorts of weather. Day and night they were on their way, sometimes afoot through the pathless forests, sometimes on ponies or in their buggies, riding and driving across the trackless prairies. Using whatever means of transportation were available, they continued in season and out of season in their endeavor to bring the people the Bread of Life.

Wisconsin was brought into the orbit of Missouri under Pastor E. G. W. Keyl, the Saxon minister in Frohna, Mo. It will be recalled that at the first convention of Synod a delegation from Pastor Krause's congregations at Freystadt and Milwaukee requested a theological opinion regarding their relationship to Pastor Krause. Synod ruled in favor of the petitioners, and as a result these congregations called Pastor Keyl, who arrived in Milwaukee on October 7, 1847. He joined Synod in 1848.

The Northern District, convening at Detroit in 1856, commissioned Pastor Ferdinand Sievers of Frankenlust, Michigan, to explore the Minnesota country for its mission possibilities. He visited Minneapolis, Corcoran, St. Paul, Shakopee, Carver, Prairie Mount, St. Peter, Faribault, and Red Wing. At several places he was able to organize congregations. Candidate F. W. Kahmeyer, a graduate of the seminary at Fort Wayne, was ordained on August 19, 1857, at Coopers Grove, Illinois, and took up his work the same month in Carver County, Minnesota.

Pastor F. Lochner visited Iowa by authorization of Synod in the fall of 1848. He went to Keokuk, Fort Madison, Burlington, Davenport, Iowa City, and Dubuque. But the people at these places did not desire the Gospel, and for eight years no further missionary efforts were made. In 1856 Pastor H. Graetzel became the first resident of the Missouri Synod in Iowa, taking charge of a small congregation in Maxfield Township, Bremer County. He remained, however, only for one year. Pastor C. A. T. Selle of Rock Island, Illinois, began to preach in Iowa City and in Benton County, organizing a congregation in Iowa City, which Candidate F. Doescher served as pastor in November, 1859. It is reported that Doescher at one time had a circuit of 28 preaching stations.

Pastor J. A. Fritze of Adams County, Indiana, visited his relatives near Council Grove, Kansas, in 1860. On his way home he found a number of Lutherans at Lyons Creek and at Clarks Creek. He informed President Wyneken of the spiritual needs of the people in Kansas, and Candidate F. W. Lange was sent as the first missionary of the Missouri Synod in Kansas in August, 1861.

From Rock Creek, Cuming County, Nebraska, came a call for a pastor, addressed to Pastor J. F. Buenger. This was in 1867. Adolf Wilhelm Frese, after having been ordained by Buenger in St. Louis, organized the first Lutheran congregation of the Missouri Synod at Rock Creek, Nebraska, on February 16, 1868. He was joined the following year by his brother, Pastor E. J. Frese.

Although Synod's attention had been repeatedly called to California, whose inexhaustible gold fields were luring many people to that country, it was not until August 24, 1860, that the first pastor of the Missouri Synod, Jacob M. Buehler of Baltimore, after a journey of 24 days, came to San Francisco. On November 8, 1860, he organized a small congregation and dedicated a brick church on December 30, 1866. For 18 years Buehler worked alone in California, separated miles and miles from a neighboring minister, until he was joined in 1878 by Pastor Hoernicke, who took charge of the work at Placerville, California.

In the spring of 1852 a New Orleans daily paper, in its statistics of Protestant Churches, reported the existence of a congregation which called itself "Evangelical Lutheran." A member in St. Louis, seeing the copy of the paper, drew Walther's attention to it. Candidate George Volck was at once sent to New Orleans to investigate. The outcome of his visit was that the congregation asked him to procure for them a pastor from the Missouri Synod. Candidate Volck was called to New Orleans and was ordained and installed by Professor Walther on May 22, 1853.

In Texas a colony of Wends opened the door to that State for the Missouri Synod. Under the leadership of Pastor Johann Kilian more than 500 Lutheran Wends left Germany for America in September, 1854. Cholera claimed 73 victims before the group landed at Galveston on December 14. From Galveston the immigrants journeyed 200 miles inland, establishing themselves at Serbin. Pastor Kilian, who had been a fellow student of Professor Walther at Leipzig, joined the Missouri Synod in 1858, attending a convention of Synod for the first time in 1860

In Arkansas, Pastor M. Wyneken assumed the pastorate of the Lutheran congregation at Fort Smith in October, 1868, and Candidate J. H. Niemann was ordained and installed at Little Rock on August 15, 1869.

The congregation of Dr. G. M. Gotsch of Memphis, Tennessee, joined Synod on October 11, 1860.

A Lutheran pastor, Theodore Heischmann, came to Mobile, Alabama, from St. Louis and preached to a group of Lutherans at the Seamen's Bethel on October 6, 1867. Two weeks later a Lutheran congregation was organized with approximately 100 members. After two years Pastor Heischmann was succeeded by Pastor J. Dansing, who remained with the congregation only one year. The members heard about the good work which pastors of the Missouri Synod were doing in New Orleans, corresponded with Professor Walther, and received in H. G. Sauer its first Missouri Synod pastor. Sauer came to Mobile in 1870.

In the East Pastor Wyneken of Baltimore joined Synod in 1848. Massachusetts was entered by Missouri in 1862, when Pastor F. W. Foehlinger of Trinity Church, New York, received a call from Zion Church, Boston. Foehlinger, after visiting the congregation, declined the call but recommended Pastor C. J. Otto Hanser of Carondelet, Missouri. Hanser was installed in Boston on October 26, 1862. In 1866 Hanser made a missionary journey which took him north as far as Nova Scotia.

St. John's Evangelical Lutheran Church, Philadelphia, Pennsylvania, applied to Pastor Theo. J. Brohm, New York, for spiritual ministration. Brohm conducted services in a private home and advised the group to communicate with Pastor Wyneken of Baltimore. Wyneken referred the people to Missionary A. Hoyer, at that time working in Maryland, who organized the brethren into a congregation in 1848. For about one year Pastor G. Schaller ministered to this flock. He was succeeded by Pastor Hoyer, who became pastor of St. John's in 1851.

The oldest congregation of the Missouri Synod in Virginia is at Richmond, organized in 1852. The Lutherans at Alexandria, Virginia, were served first by Pastor P. Brand of Washington, D. C. In 1870 R. Bischoff moved to Alexandria to become the resident pastor of the congregation.

Lutherans in Washington, D. C., were ministered to as early as 1843 by Pastor A. F. Th. Biewend. When he went to the seminary at Fort Wayne, the congregation was cared for by Pastor Keyl until April 4, 1852, when Pastor Nordmann was installed.

Synod entered the States of Connecticut and Rhode Island through the missionary efforts of Pastor Hanser of Boston

LENGTHENING THE CORDS (1847 - 1872) 113

in 1866. The congregation at Egg Harbor, New Jersey, with its pastor, E. T. Richter, joined Synod in 1866.

Across the border Pastor A. Ernst of Eden, N. Y., preached in Canada and organized the Lutheran congregation at Middleton, Ontario, in 1854.

Thus by 1872, at the end of the first quarter of the century of its existence, the Missouri Synod had indeed "lengthened its cords and stretched the curtains of its habitation." The increase in membership is well illustrated in the following tables. Combining the voting and the advisory pastors into one group and keeping in mind that each pastor had at least one congregation, we find the following:

1847	22 pastors	1849	61 pastors
1848	50 pastors	1850	75 pastors
	1872	415 pastors	

The pastors were distributed as follows:

	1847	1848	1872		1847	1848	1872
Illinois	4	8	87	Minnesota	—	—	17
Missouri	3	12	51	Wisconsin	—	1	41
Kansas	—	—	7	Michigan	2	4	36
Iowa	—	—	17	Indiana	5	11	48
Nebraska	—	—	7	Ohio	6	11	24
Texas	—	—	7	New York	2	2	29
Alabama	—	—	1	Massachusetts	—	—	3
Louisiana	—	—	4	Maryland	—	2	8
Tennessee	—	—	1	Pennsylvania	—	—	7
California	—	—	1	Connecticut	—	—	3
Arkansas	—	—	2	Virginia	—	—	2
New Jersey	—	—	2	Rhode Island	—	—	1
Wash., D. C.	—	—	1	Canada	—	—	8

The rapid growth made it imperative to divide Synod into Districts. Already in 1848, at its second convention, expression was given to the thought of a possible division into branch synods. At the convention of 1849 the question was again discussed, and Pastor Craemer was requested to prepare a memorandum setting forth the disadvantages that might result from such action. While admitting that the vast distances and lack of funds would prevent many members, especially lay delegates, from attending the conventions, Craemer showed that a division at this time would nullify the purpose for organizing Synod. He said: "The word of the Lord: 'Endeavor to keep the unity of the Spirit' has moved us, living in all parts of the country, to band ourselves together on the basis of the one truth and the one pure confession. And God has blessed this our action. We on our part should, therefore, be all the more willing to be led in this matter by God's Holy Spirit. This willingness we have expressed in our constitution when stating the purpose of our organization: 'to preserve and promote the unity of pure confession among us, to provide a common defense against separatism and sectarianism, which is so prevalent in our country, and to use for this purpose the diversity of gifts for the common good.' Now, it cannot be denied that in such a short time and in a membership so diverse in age, gifts, experience, and knowledge we have not progressed to the stage 'that we all speak the same thing and are perfectly joined together in the same mind and in the same judgment.' — By establishing branch synods, we run the risk of losing much that would promote inner growth and a more lively and conscious unity in the faith. There is danger that in establishing different synods different theological tendencies will arise, and thus our purpose will be frustrated. Even if not all can attend the conventions regularly, the blessings resulting from such meetings will be received through the printed proceedings of the sessions." [1] At this convention, Synod resolved to continue as one group and added the resolution that members not attending synodical meetings shall be held to pay $5.00 into the seminary treasury provided they could afford to do so.

By 1852 it was felt that the existing unity of the Spirit

LENGTHENING THE CORDS (1847 - 1872)   115

was sufficiently strong to warrant dividing Synod into Districts. The St. Louis Pastoral Conference was appointed to frame a constitution governing the Districts and to submit it to the other conferences.

President Wyneken opened the 1853 convention with an address that dealt exclusively with the proposed reorganization of Synod. He closed with the words: "I remind you that our Synod has reached an important crisis and that the future of our Synod will largely depend upon our present action. God grant that every one of us, while deliberating on the subject, will keep in mind the purpose of our Synod, namely, the unity of the spirit, and that our resolutions be made with the knowledge of the great responsibility that rests upon us." [2] The delegates present declared that their congregations had consented to the dividing of Synod into four Districts. Since the St. Louis conference had not previously submitted the constitution governing the Districts, the definitive division did not take place until the following year.

Thus the meeting of 1854 was the last annual convention of the General Body. Henceforth it was to meet every three years. During the two intervening years the Districts were to have their conventions annually, but at different times. This rule continues until the present time, with this change, however, that after 1872 Synod has met every third year as a *Delegate* Convention.

The Districts organized in 1854 were the following:

1. The Western District: Missouri, Illinois, Louisiana (22 congregations, 46 pastors and professors, 11 teachers). First President: Pastor G. A. Schieferdecker.

2. The Central District: Indiana and Ohio (34 congregations, 45 pastors and professors, 6 teachers). First President: Dr. W. Sihler.

3. The Northern District: Michigan and Wisconsin

(12 congregations, 19 pastors, and 4 teachers). First President: Pastor O. Fuerbringer.

4. The Eastern District: New York, Maryland, Pennsylvania, District of Columbia (10 congregations, 11 pastors, 6 teachers). First President: Pastor E. G. W. Keyl.

Pastor Walther was President of the General Body from 1847 until 1850. In 1850 Wyneken, who had been called to Trinity Church, St. Louis, when Walther was appointed President of Concordia Seminary, was elected President of Synod. He was obligated as President to visit all congregations within three years, preach in every church, attend the pastoral conferences, and after 1854 also the District conventions. By 1857 it was found that the duties resting on the President were superhuman; hence Synod resolved that the stipulated visitations be made within a period of six years.

Wyneken received a salary from Synod, beginning with 1857. The financial report of 1860 shows that he was paid $2,400.00 for the triennium and $410.07 for traveling expenses. Although still pastor of Trinity Church, St. Louis, he moved to northern Indiana in 1859, making his home near Fort Wayne. In 1863 he requested Synod to relieve him of the general presidency, since his health was failing. Synod granted him his request in 1864, when Professor Walther was elected to succeed him, and Wyneken accepted a call to Cleveland, Ohio. From 1854 to 1864 Pastor G. Schaller was Wyneken's vicar at Trinity Church, St. Louis.

EDUCATIONAL INSTITUTIONS

When Synod was organized, two privately owned institutions for the training of pastors and teachers were existing in its midst, one at Altenburg, Missouri, established in 1839, the other at Fort Wayne, Indiana, opened in 1846. At its first convention, Synod instructed its Secretary to communicate with Pastor Loehe and with the congregations at Altenburg and St. Louis regarding a transfer of the seminaries and college to its body.

The document of transfer, issued by Pastor Loehe and dated September 7, 1847, stipulated that the seminary at Fort Wayne pass into full control of the German Evangelical Lutheran Synod of Missouri, Ohio, and other States under the following conditions:

1. "That it serve the Lutheran Church for all times and train pastors and shepherds for her only;

2. "That the German language be and remain the sole and only medium of instruction.

3. "That the seminary remain what it is, namely, an institution for the purpose of training, as rapidly but as thoroughly as possible, preachers and pastors for the innumerable orphaned German Lutherans and for the newly immigrating congregations of our race and confession. It should not be a theological institution in the usual German sense of the word, but a *"Pflanzschule"* of preachers and pastors, whose study would be a serious preparation for the holy office itself." [3]

It was the wish of the founder, Loehe, that the institution would also serve, if feasible, to train missionaries for work among the Indians.

Thus the first institution owned and controlled by Synod was the practical seminary at Fort Wayne, Indiana, which today is continuing its work at Springfield, Illinois.

The congregations at Altenburg and at St. Louis were likewise ready to transfer the Altenburg school to Synod, but agreement could not be reached with reference to the location of the institution. The Altenburg congregation desired to keep the school at Altenburg, while St. Louis considered its city the better place for the training of the students. A compromise was proposed by Altenburg to the effect that the college department remain at Altenburg, while the seminary section be transferred to St. Louis. At the request of Synod, Altenburg finally yielded and by a document of transfer, signed by Altenburg and St. Louis respectively on October 8, 1849, and June 4, 1850, the institution passed under the control of Synod.

The articles of transfer stipulated:

1. "That the institution serve the Lutheran Church for all time to come and to train pastors and teachers solely for her;

2. "That the German language be and remain the sole medium of instruction in the institution"; (It was conceded, however, that for certain courses in the seminary department the Latin language might be used according to the custom of German colleges and universities.)

3. "That the institution remain what it is, namely, a college offering courses preparatory for the study of theology and for the training of teachers of elementary and secondary schools, together with a seminary (theological) in which students receive a theoretical training in theology;

"Students not preparing for the ministry may attend the college but are to be excluded from all benefits derived from legacies and other donations given for the training of young men for the work in the Church;

"Should it be deemed advisable to expand the curriculum to include other courses of studies, the donors do not object provided that the present purpose ever remain the chief goal of the institution and that in no wise this purpose suffer." [4]

The faculty at Altenburg consisted originally of Pastor C. F. W. Walther and the candidates of theology Th. J. Brohm, O. Fuerbringer, and J. F. Buenger. When calls took these men away from Perry County, the task of instructing the students was taken up by Pastor Loeber, assisted for a short time by Pastor Keyl. In 1843 Candidate J. Goenner was called by the congregations of Altenburg and St. Louis as the first full-time professor of the institution. Carl Julius

Otto Nitschke of Altenburg was a part-time teacher from 1847 to 1849.

Pastor Loeber died on August 19, 1849. The Electoral Board for the synodical institutions placed Walther's name on the list of candidates for the theological professorship of the seminary, soon to be moved to St. Louis. On August 20, Trinity Church resolved to protest against his can-

First Section of Concordia Seminary (South Wing), 1850

didacy, not wishing to lose him as pastor, but Pastor J. F. Buenger, Walther's brother-in-law, convinced the congregation that Walther's outstanding gifts ought to be devoted to the benefit of Synod and the church at large. Walther was elected, accepted the call, but at the same time continued as pastor of Trinity.

On November 9, 1849, the cornerstone of the new seminary, which was built on the northwest corner of Jefferson and Winnebago Street, was laid. In December, 1849, Professor Goenner came up from Altenburg with nine students, most of whom were housed in the home of Mr. Roemer. The dedication of the building took place on June 11, 1850, on which occasion Pastor Wyneken delivered a German oration, Professor Walther one in Latin, and Pastor Schieferdecker closed with an address to the Young Men's Society, whose chief object was the support of indigent students.

Concordia Seminary, 1858
(North Wing Erected 1852)

Pastor Fick composed a hymn for the occasion: "Praise the Lord, Ye Nations All." On the next day an academic celebration was conducted, in which Professor Goenner spoke in Latin and Student Eissfeldt in German.

The north wing was erected in 1852, the center building connecting the two wings was built in 1857—58, and later, in 1871, a third story was added to the two wings. This building served until 1882.

Professor Walther began his instruction in January, 1850, in his parsonage on Lombard St. On June 4 he and his family and the students moved into the new college building. Prof. A. Biewend of Fort Wayne was added to the faculty in 1850.

In 1854 Synod appointed Professor Walther president of the two institutions at St. Louis, while Professor Biewend became principal of the college department. Pastor Geo. Schick of Chicago joined the faculty in 1856. About Easter, 1856, Professor Goenner requested a leave of absence from

Concordia Seminary, 1871

the institution in order to devote his time to the editing of the *Altenburger Bibelwerk*, published by the Bible Society of Trinity Church. His place was filled by Mr. A. Saxer, at first temporarily, later permanently. At the same time Dr. G. Seyffarth, formerly Professor of Archaeology at the university of Leipzig, gave his services to the college without compensation. The institution suffered a severe blow in the death of Professor Biewend on April 10, 1858. He was buried in the Lutheran Cemetery, now, in part, occupied by

Holy Cross Church. Professor Saxer succeeded him as director, while Pastor R. Lange was called as professor. Professor Goenner returned for a brief time to the classroom in 1859, but Dr. Seyffarth resigned in order to live in New York, where he wished to do literary work.

In 1859 Pastor Lauritz Larsen joined the St. Louis faculty as the Norwegian professor. The Norwegians in 1855 had chosen two representatives, J. A. Ottesen and Nils Brandt, to visit the various seminaries of the Lutherans in this country for the purpose of making arrangements for the training of their young men for the ministry. The tour of inspection was made in 1857. The committee visited the seminaries at St. Louis, at Columbus, Ohio (Ohio Synod), and at Buffalo, N. Y. (Buffalo Synod) and reported that among the Missourians they had found what they had been taught in their childhood concerning the nature and functions of a Lutheran free church. They recommended that their young men be sent to St. Louis, "where the name Lutheran not only because of old traditions was put into the letters of call and over church doors, but where well-nigh every adult member of the congregation knows his Augsburg Confession by heart and embraces the Lutheran faith and doctrine with a love and faithfulness which finds its honor and its joy in laboring for the preservation of the same." [5] At the convention of Synod in 1857 an agreement with the Norwegian brethren was reached with reference to a Norwegian professorship at St. Louis and the expenses for Norwegian students. Pursuant to this agreement Lauritz Larsen began his duties at St. Louis in the fall of 1859 and continued his work until 1861, when the Civil War made it necessary to withdraw both professor and students from the threatened city and to begin work in the newly founded Luther College at Halfway Creek, Wis.

At Fort Wayne Dr. Sihler, assisted by Candidate Roebbelen, had begun, in his study, to teach the eleven young men who had arrived in 1846. When Roebbelen accepted a call into the ministry, Candidate A. Wolter succeeded him (November, 1846). The institution occupied rented quarters until 1849, when the property of the widow Wines, consisting of 15 acres, was purchased for $2,500.00, contributed by the congregations in and around Fort Wayne. Wolter died on August 31, 1849, of the cholera. Sihler, writing his autobiography in 1880, remarked: "Even now at his memory a strong flow of tears breaks from my eyes." Professor Wolter was succeeded by Pastor A. Biewend of Washington, D. C., who ten months later accepted a call to the seminary at St. Louis. He was followed by Pastor A. Craemer of Frankenmuth, Michigan. Wrote Loehe concerning his election: "The Synod knows real well what it is doing by this election, and one must confess that it could hardly have chosen a more sincere representative of its convictions and practice than him." [6] In 1850 the so-called Wolter house was erected on the college property to accommodate the increasing number of students.

A pro-seminary was added to the Fort Wayne seminary in 1852. In the pro-seminary remedial courses were offered to students who were deficient in subjects deemed essential to the study of theology.

Another building, costing $7,000.00, was dedicated on October 26, 1857. It provided facilities for the normal department and the English academy which Synod resolved in 1857 to establish in Fort Wayne.

According to Loehe's plans the practical seminary was to serve also as a teacher-training institution. By 1855 it had graduated 15 teachers. Convinced that the available facilities were inadequate, Pastors Lochner, Fleischmann, Dulitz, and Teacher Dietz opened a normal school in Milwaukee in 1855. Swayed by the arguments of Dr. Sihler, Synod resolved to transfer the new institution to Fort Wayne, to which place Professor Fleischmann came on November 10, 1857, accompanied by six normal-school students. Pastor C. A. T. Selle joined him as a faculty member in 1861. The Teachers' Seminary remained in Fort Wayne until 1864, when it was relocated at Addison, Illinois.

Already at its 1852 and 1853 conventions Synod discussed the advisability of opening an English academy. Since the Fort Wayne seminary needed larger quarters, it was resolved to join the English academy project with the requirements of the German college. Mr. A. Sutermeister, a teacher of mathematics in a college at Boston, was chosen to head the new venture and began to work on November 11, 1857. The academy was closed after one year because of lack of students and funds.

Thus in 1861 Synod controlled five distinct institutions, housed in two buildings. The college and the theoretical seminary were in St. Louis; the pro-seminary, the practical seminary, and the normal school were in Fort Wayne.

For several years different groups in Synod had favored the combining of the two seminaries under one faculty. At the convention of 1860 seven reasons in favor of uniting the two theological institutions were discussed and adopted. Some of the reasons given were:

1. Through such a union more theological professors working at one place would promote the knowledge of the true doctrine and would be more of a guarantee against the development of different doctrinal tendencies.

2. The professors could specialize in their departments and thus do more effective work.

3. The older students (of the practical seminary) would exercise a wholesome influence upon the younger students who had gone through the college department in St. Louis.

Synod resolved in 1860 to unite the two seminaries, to inform Pastor Loehe of its action by sending him a copy of the printed *Proceedings,* to request the Fort Wayne congregation to permit the practical seminary to be transferred to St. Louis, and to extend a cordial welcome to the St. Louis college department, to notify the congregations in St. Louis of its action regarding the pre-theological section of the St. Louis institution and to obtain their consent in writing to the proposed changes.

The Civil War precipitated the projected union of the two institutions. Missouri was so close to the zone of battle as to render the conjunction of the college department with the theological department precarious. The college section, accordingly, with its six classes moved to Fort Wayne in Septemper, 1861, taking with it Professors Saxer, Schick, Lange, and the assistant, C. S. Kleppisch, while Professor Craemer came to St. Louis with his two departments, the pro-seminary and the practical seminary. Professor Walther was president of the entire institution at St. Louis; Dr. Sihler was president of the college and normal school at Fort Wayne. In the period of readjustment the teachers' seminary was obliged to move, first to a house in the city, then to a former tavern on the historic Piqua Road, two miles from the city limits.

At St. Louis, Walther and Craemer were joined in 1863 by Pastor E. A. Brauer. In 1864 H. Baumstark was called to teach in the pro-seminary department. Unhappily, he apostatized to the Roman Catholic Church in 1869. He was succeeded by Prof. E. Preuss, who assumed his duties in the fall of the same year and remained until 1871.

In Fort Wayne, Pastor W. Achenbach succeeded C. S. Kleppisch, who had to return to St. Louis to complete his studies. Synod in 1863 purchased five acres adjoining the college property for $2,400.00. R. Engel, a nephew of Professor Walther, joined the faculty in 1869. Professor Achenbach accepted a call into the ministry in 1871, and Professor Lange did the same in the following year. Professor Saxer, the principal of the institution, resigned his position to assume a professorship. In 1872 three new men were added to the faculty: Pastors R. Bischoff, H. W. Diederich, and C. J. Otto Hanser as director.

The normal school was moved from Fort Wayne to Addison, Illinois, in 1864, the dedication of the main building taking place on December 28. Professor Fleischmann, having returned to the ministry, was succeeded as principal by Pastor J. C. W. Lindemann. The local pastor, A. G. G. Francke, was president of the institution. Teacher K. Brauer came to the faculty as instructor of music in 1867, and Dr. H. Duemling joined the teaching staff in 1872.

Until 1852 Pastor Loehe sent young men for training to the two seminaries. After the break with him, Synod was on the lookout for another agency in Germany which would furnish a supply of students, since the members of Synod were slow to have their sons prepared for the ministry. In Steeden, Nassau, Pastor Frederick Brunn was holding his own against the State Church. After many conflicts he finally separated from it and with his congregation formed a free Church. Brunn was a born teacher. One of his students emigrated to America in 1851. After a few years he entered Concordia Seminary at Fort Wayne, and thus Professor Craemer became acquainted with Pastor Brunn's love for teaching. Craemer at once communicated with Brunn, requesting him to recruit students for America and in this way continue the work of Loehe. But Brunn wrote Craemer that he could not co-operate with him "unless unity in the spirit prevailed between the two." When Walther, in 1860, made his second trip to Germany in the interest of his health, he visited Brunn and persuaded him to open a preparatory school for boys or young men willing to work in America. Brunn did this and conducted his Steedener academy, subsidized by the Missouri Synod, until 1878. He furnished more than 200 students for the institutions at Fort Wayne and St. Louis.

LENGTHENING THE CORDS (1847 - 1872)

By 1872 the theoretical seminary at St. Louis had graduated 130 candidates for the ministry, while the practical seminary at Fort Wayne-St. Louis had prepared 298 men as missionaries and pastors.

MISSION WORK AMONG THE INDIANS

Synod's interest in the souls of the heathen in America was evident at its very first convention, when a Board for Missions, consisting of the pastors C. J. H. Fick, A. Craemer, and Mr. F. W. Barthel, was elected. In 1848 this Board submitted a plan to establish a mission in Oregon, proposing to place a candidate of theology at St. Louis, where he might get in touch with the Indian chiefs who came there to trade. The plan included the recruiting of a mission colony, composed of native Lutherans and Lutheran immigrants, which was to be the center of mission activities in Oregon. One of the reasons for choosing Oregon was the proximity of this territory to the Asiatic countries. The plan, however, was not carried out because of the unrest among the Indians in Oregon at that time. In 1852 the Board for Missions proposed to establish a colony of Lutherans in California with a view to having it serve as a center of missionary activity among the Chinese on the Pacific Coast. This plan, likewise, failed to materialize.

Thus Synod was limited in its missionary endeavors among the heathen in America to the Indians in Michigan. It will be recalled that Pastor Loehe had established the Frankenmuth colony for the express purpose of serving as a base of mission work among the Indians. In 1846 Pastor Craemer, assisted by Jim Gruett, a French-Canadian interpreter, began mission work among the Indians living on the Kawkawlin, Swan, Chippewa, Pine, and Bell Rivers. Owing to the rapid growth of the Frankenmuth colony, Craemer could not devote as much time as was necessary to heathen mission work, and so on June 10, 1847, Missionary Edward

R. Baierlein arrived to assist him. In 1848 Baierlein established a new mission among the Chippewas at St. Louis, Michigan, about 65 miles west of Frankenmuth, calling the station Bethany.

These two mission stations, Frankenmuth and Bethany, were placed under Synod's control in 1849, Synod resolving to regard June 1, 1849, as the date of taking possession of the stations. In the transfer document, Pastor Loehe and the Collegium of the Evangelical Lutheran Mission at Leipzig assured Synod that they would keep the mission in mind as heretofore and that they would supply the needs of Missionary Baierlein to the best of their ability.

The convention of Synod in 1850 rejoiced to hear that two stations among the Indians had been added to their mission project, namely, Sibiwaing, with Missionary J. F. Auch, and Shiboyank, conducted by Missionary F. Maier. Both men had been former members of the Michigan Synod. Missionary Maier lost his life in a storm on Lake Michigan September 15, 1850, and his station, Shiboyank, was taken over by Missionary Auch. Candidate J. E. Roeder was sent to assist Missionary Auch, and Henry Craemer, the 10-year-old stepson of Pastor Craemer, was sent to live with Auch in order to learn the Indian language, in the expectation that eventually he would prepare for work among the Indians.

In 1850 Pastor Craemer accepted a call as professor at the Seminary at Fort Wayne. The report of 1851 reads: "Since through the removal of Pastor Craemer the forces necessary to maintain a mission station were no longer available, we have recognized it as the Lord's will that we should no longer regard Frankenmuth as an independent station but add it to the other stations. Only the family of the Indian doctor, who together with his son and son-in-law, is living on the mission property, is being served with the preaching of the Gospel. Already during the time of Pastor Craemer the school grew smaller from month to month and can, therefore, well be closed. Within the near future an attempt will be made to assist the entire family to move to another station, and if this fails to materialize, the missionaries of the other stations are ready to serve the family with the preaching of the divine Word as often as possible. The land of the Frankenmuth mission is to be sold, and the proceeds are to be used to cover the extraordinary needs of the other stations, with this proviso that the Indian doctor retain his dwelling and field as long as he accepts the Word of God."[7] Thus ended the first mission among the Indians begun by the fathers of Synod. The church records of the St. Lawrence Church at Frankenmuth contain the names of 34 Indians who were received into the Kingdom by Baptism. Among them are three children of Jim Gruett, the interpreter, and one child of Peter Gruett of Bethany.

The second mission station to be abandoned was Sibiwaing. Here Missionary Auch had been laboring faithfully and with great zeal for a number of years. He was much harassed by the Methodists, who used all sorts of tricks and chicanery to undo the work of the Lutheran missionary. In spite of Missionary Auch's faithful labors the Indians continued in their heathen ways. In 1853 the station was discontinued, most of the Indians having moved away. Auch thereafter, devoting most of his time to the German Lutheran congregation at Sibiwaing, attended to the needs of the Indians at Shiboyank as well as he could, assisted by Roeder.

When Missionary Maier lost his life in Lake Michigan (1850), the Indians at Shiboyank were deeply grieved. Their love for the Gospel, however, did not die with the death of the young missionary, but broke forth all the more strongly. They appealed to the Mission Board that the preaching which had heretofore been heard among them might be brought to them also in the future. They expressed the cordial wish that Missionary Auch come to them. The

Mission Board regarded this wish as being virtually a call from these Christian Indians. In order to give them better facilities for hearing and learning the Gospel, the Mission Board proposed to them, in 1854, that they move to Bethany. However, in spite of the willingness of the Bethany Indians to receive their red brothers from Shiboyank and of the latter to make the move to Bethany, Satan succeeded in filling them with so much distrust and suspicion against

Bethany Chapel
Indian Mission Station at St. Louis, Mich.

their old faithful friend and teacher, Missionary Auch, that they not only refused to exchange their home at Shiboyank for one at Bethany, but rejected Christianity and reverted to their former heathenism in spite of the kindly and persistent exhortations of Missionaries Auch and Miessler. (Ernst Gustav Hermann Miessler had come to Bethany in 1851, sent by the Leipzig Mission Society as assistant to Baierlein.)

The most promising field was the station at Bethany. The report of 1850 states: "According to the latest information, a few of the men show a little inclination to become Christians. The small congregation, gathered through Baierlein, was increased through the Baptism of eleven Indians, among whom were six adults. One of these adults was a hundred-year-old blind woman. Working with Missionary Baierlein was Theodore Eissfeldt of Milwaukee, who intended to consecrate his life to the cause of missions among the Indians."

In 1852 Bethany Congregation built a log church and a mission home under one roof. A small bell, hanging in its tower, called the congregation to divine services on Sundays and to the daily prayer meetings. The congregation numbered about 60 souls, some of whom were soon to be admitted to Holy Communion. The Indians were abandoning their heathen customs, were following agricultural pursuits, and were filling the hearts of all lovers of the Indian mission with glowing hopes for the future.

Missionary Baierlein

The next year, however, Missionary Baierlein was recalled by the Leipzig Mission Society for work in India and left on May 19, 1853. Pastor Ferd. Sievers, chairman of the Mission Board, moved with his family to Bethany, which he served until June 26, 1853. At this time the former assistant to Baierlein, E. G. H. Miessler, was ordained and installed as missionary to the Indians in Bethany Chapel by President Wyneken, assisted by Pastor Sievers. The service was conducted in the English language, but since no English ordination and installation formulary was available, Wyneken, Sievers, and Miessler had to prepare an English order of service the night before the ceremony took place. In the same year, Synod purchased 400 acres of land on both banks of the Pine River to parcel out in plots of 30 acres for each Indian family, so that the Indians would not be crowded out by American settlers and thus be forced to migrate. J. F. Roeder, who had been helping Missionary Auch at Sibiwaing, came to Bethany in 1853 to assist Miessler.

In 1855 Roeder accepted a call to Canada, leaving Miessler alone with his assistant Henry Craemer. A new threat to Bethany was reported to Synod in 1857. The Government Bureau in charge of Indian Affairs at Washington was proposing to move the Indians to Isabella County, 25 miles north of Bethany, where an Indian reservation was being established. The Indians at Bethany were much affected by this proposal, for at Bethany they had only 30 acres of land, and the prospect of having 80 acres in Isabella County appealed to them. They were encouraged to make the exchange by the Methodists, who were selling their holdings in the vicinity of Bethany and who had been, and still were, making every effort to coax the Indians away, not only from Bethany, but from the Lutherans in general.

In order to enforce its new Indian policy immediately, instructions came from Washington that all Indians move to Isabella County unless they could point out other property in land which they had rightfully obtained. As yet the Indians at Bethany had not received title to the 30 acres which had been parceled out to each family. According to a written agreement the plot of land was to be their uncontested property for all times, provided they would annually make small payments in sugar or other products or in labor, according to their ability, until the purchase price of the land was refunded to Synod. At the time of the last payment they would receive a clear deed to their property.

Missionary Miessler hoped and prayed that his Indians would not leave Bethany, which had grown dear to his heart. But finally, in 1860, they all moved to Isabella County, where they were received with open arms by the Methodists.

LENGTHENING THE CORDS (1847 - 1872)

Henceforth Isabella County was their home, and only occasionally would they come to Bethany to visit friends. As a result the school at Bethany dwindled to almost nothing, and the services were attended but seldom by the Indians. And "all this just at the time when Missionary Miessler was able to offer them the preaching of the Word in their mother tongue." [8] (Until December, 1858, Miessler used an interpreter when preaching to the Indians.) The property at Bethany was valued at $4,000.00. At the convention of Synod in 1860 Missionary Miessler addressed the assembly in the Chippewa language, Henry Craemer serving as interpreter.

By 1863 Bethany was a mere farm. In Isabella County the Mission Board purchased 160 acres of land for a mission farm and built a school ten miles away at a cost of $100. Miessler began to teach in a public school on the reservation, having received permission from the authorities to teach the Catechism and Bible History to the Indians as part of the school curriculum. Finally, in 1869, the property at Bethany and in Isabella County was transferred to Concordia College, Fort Wayne, to be held in trust for Synod. Miessler's parting words were: "I leave the mission field of hard labor and anxiety with a broken heart and many tears, and with fervent prayers to the God of mercy for the true repentance on the part of our poor Indians."

Miessler went to Saginaw, where he served Holy Cross Church as teacher. Early in 1871 he resigned because of his wife's health and moved with his family to New Melle, Missouri. When his second wife died and his physician advised him to retire from the ministry, Miessler went to Chicago in the fall of 1871, where he studied and practiced medicine. He passed away on March 1, 1916.

Today only the cemetery of the former Indian mission at Bethany remains. It is located on the outskirts of St. Louis, Michigan. In 1931 the Saginaw churches spent much time in beautifying the half acre of land on the banks of the Pine River, so that now it resembles a well-kept park. A bronze tablet in the cemetery bears the names of Missionaries Craemer, Baierlein, and Miessler. Another plaque states that the names of the Indians buried there, with the exception of one, have been lost. Only two graves are marked, the inscriptions being:

SARAH MIKSIWE
Mother of the Chippewas
110 years old
Died in Christ 12. April, 1859

Gen. 49, 18 — "I have waited for thy salvation, O Lord."

JOHANNA MIESSLER, GEBORNE PINKAPONK
Geboren May 4, 1831
Gestorben July 22, 1867

Text: Offenbarung Johannis 14, 13.

"A white cross, ten feet tall, stands in the center of the cemetery. Hewn from wood, it stands as a reminder of the struggles, hardships, and sorrows of the missionaries who came from Germany to seek the conversion of the Indians in the timberlands. It was built by a white man to mark the grave of the young wife of a missionary, the only white woman buried in the cemetery."

Synod opened another mission among the Indians in Minnesota. In August, 1856, Missionary Miessler and the chairman of the Mission Board, Pastor Ferd. Sievers, explored the possibilities of starting a mission among the Chippewas of that State. Interpreter Jim Gruett accompanied them. The conditions seemed favorable, and a missionary was available in the person of Pastor Ottomar Cloeter of Saginaw, Michigan, who volunteered to work among the Indians.

Cloeter left Saginaw on May 28, 1857, arriving at Crow

Wing, Minnesota, on June 12 after having traveled by express, emigrant train, steamboat, wagon, and canoe. He was accompanied by his family and by Missionary Miessler, who was to introduce him to the Indians and help him in opening the mission. Henry Craemer also came along to serve as an interpreter.

West of the Mississippi River, between the river and the Mission Lakes, about 30 miles north of Crow Wing, Pastor Cloeter established himself. The station was called Gabitaweegama. In spite of many obstacles, Cloeter carried on the work, at first with the aid of Henry Craemer, but after 1859 alone. During the Indian uprising of 1862 he was more than once in peril of death. It was only through the aid of a friendly chief that Cloeter and his family saved their lives, having to flee from their home, leaving nearly all their earthly possessions behind. They had to wander for three days in the woods before they arrived at Fort Ripley, eight miles south of Crow Wing.

Ferd. Sievers, Sr.

After the outbreak, Missionary Cloeter did not return to Gabitaweegama, but continued his mission work from Crow Wing. Synod resolved that the mission among the Minnesota Chippewas should be continued until the Lord Himself would end it. Cloeter moved his residence in 1867 to Moose Water Lake, where he built a log house for himself and his family. In the same year the Indians were moved to the Red River and to White Oak Point, above Pokegama, and all hopes of success went with the Indians. In 1869 the mission was regarded as closed by the Mission Board. Cloeter, advised to work in a German congregation, was called to the Lutheran church at Afton, Minnesota, and was installed there on August 9, 1868.

IMMIGRANT MISSION

In the great stream of immigrants who came to America after the Civil War were many German Lutherans who, ignorant of the language and ways of our country, fell an easy prey to the money sharks and swindlers at that time infesting the harbors of New York and Baltimore. F. W. Foehlinger, pastor of Trinity Church, New York, in a memorial to the Eastern District in 1867, called attention to the sad fortune of so many immigrants and showed the aid, both spiritual and material, that could be accorded the new arrivals by the proper man. The convention was impressed by the need for action and resolved to urge the congregations to take suitable measures.

The New York Pastoral Conference took the matter in hand. They found in Pastor Stephanus Keyl, Walther's son-in-law, a man equipped in every way for this difficult post. In 1869 the secretary of the Immigrant Board reported to the convention of Synod regarding the work done by Keyl, with the result that Synod resolved, as of 1869, to make the work among the immigrants a missionary project of its own.

Keyl was to serve all Lutheran immigrants who came to New York. He was to see them immediately upon their arrival and provide them with suitable dwelling places where they could remain until they were forwarded to their destination in the West. He was to advise them as to the best places at which to locate and at the same time to direct them to the neighborhood of a Lutheran Church and proper educational facilities. He was, furthermore, to aid them in any way that was needful and especially to turn their attention toward their moral and spiritual interests. If they required financial aid, he was to provide it so far as actual needs were concerned.

Keyl's work was done in a wonderful manner. From 1870 to 1883 he cared for 27,000 immigrants. For years his correspondence was very extensive; for instance, in 1882 he received 5,376 letters and wrote 3,951.

In 1885 a five-story building was purchased by the Immigrant Board on State Street for $45,000. It was known as "Das Lutherische Pilgerhaus." A chapel was arranged in the building for services, conducted for the immigrants.

In Baltimore the Eastern District also opened an immigrant mission, for which Synod assumed responsibility in 1872.

THE CONTROVERSY WITH THE BUFFALO SYNOD

The Missouri Synod was organized as a confessional Lutheran synod. Confessional Lutheranism implies not only the teaching of the truth, but the rejection of every error. As a natural result of its confessional nature, the Missouri Synod soon became involved in religious controversies.

The first controversy Synod inherited from the Saxons. It was the controversy with the Buffalo Synod.

This synod was organized at Milwaukee in 1845 by Pastor J. A. A. Grabau, together with Pastors H. v. Rohr, L. F. E. Krause, and G. A. Kindermann. It was composed chiefly of Prussians, who under the leadership of Grabau had left their native country in 1839 in protest against the decree of the Prussian king to unite the Lutheran and the Reformed churches in his kingdom. These Lutherans settled in Buffalo, New York, and in southern Wisconsin. The official name of the synod originally was "The Synod of the Lutheran Church which Emigrated from Prussia," but it was commonly called the "Buffalo Synod," because it was directed from that city. It was hoped that this body would unite with the Loehe men and the Saxons, since all were confessional Lutherans.

While the Saxons were in spiritual turmoil regarding the doctrine of the ministry and the Church, there arrived in Perry County the *Hirtenbrief* (Pastoral Letter) of Pastor Grabau, dated Dec. 1, 1840. It covers more than 10 closely printed pages and was addressed to Pastor Loeber. In the *Hirtenbrief* Grabau first stated the reason for writing it. Some of his congregations, not being able to secure a pastor, had asked laymen to perform ministerial acts. Grabau considered this a violation of the doctrine of the ministry. He therefore felt compelled to warn the churches against receiving preachers who were not ordained according to the old church ordinances, maintaining that ordination was a divine and therefore necessary institution. Only properly called pastors could administer the Sacraments; their absolution alone was valid. To such rightfully called pastors the congregations owed obedience in all things not forbidden in God's Word. The question as to what was forbidden in Scriptures was to be answered not by individual Christians, but by the Church. Since these items concerned doctrines that were still perplexing the Saxon clergymen, they, for the time being, placed the *Hirtenbrief* into their files.

After the Altenburg Debate, 1841, Pastor Buerger, en route to Germany, stopped off at Buffalo and was prevailed upon by former members of Pastor Krause to become their pastor. Thus Grabau had a Saxon pastor in his own city. When Trinity in New York, considered by Grabau as one of his preaching stations, applied to Grabau in 1842 for a pastor, he, on the advice of Buerger, recommended Candidate Theo. Brohm. Krause as well as Grabau began to correspond with Loeber after the *Hirtenbrief* of 1840, expressing their desire for church union and suggesting the establishing of a seminary for the training of pastors in the Lutheran Church in America. Krause especially urged the Saxons to forward their opinion of the *Hirtenbrief*, indicating that Grabau was planning to come to St. Louis or Perry County early in 1844.

The *Hirtenbrief* had been discussed by the St. Louis and the Altenburg congregations, and in July, 1843, Loeber and Gruber journeyed to St. Louis to prepare an opinion of the document conjointly with Walther. The printed opinion covers 16 pages. It is a courteous, carefully worded reply. The gist of what they wrote is "that with respect to the so-much-emphasized church ordinances essentials and non-essentials have been confused and thereby Christian liberty has been curtailed; more has been ascribed to the ministerial office than belongs to it, and thus the spiritual priesthood of the believers has been forced into the background." The old church orders, they continued, do not exist by divine right; ordination is a wholesome ceremony, but has not been ordered by God and is therefore not essential to the ministry. To say that a congregation must obey its pastor in all things not contrary to God's Word goes beyond the word of the Savior: "Whosoever heareth you, heareth Me." Only when and inasmuch as the pastor proclaims the Word of God, can he demand obedience, and the decision whether or not he is proclaiming God's commands rests with the individual Christian. The efficacy of the means of grace does not depend on the office of the ministry, but on Christ's Word. The Saxons recognized in Grabau's position the same errors used by Stephan to gain control over his congregation.

G. H. Loeber

The representations of the Saxons were not well received. Grabau promptly charged the "Missourians"—he coined this term — with 17 errors, and the controversy was on. The Missouri Synod in 1849 supported the position taken by Walther, Loeber, and Gruber, especially since some of the

Missouri pastors felt bound to give pastoral care to such former members of Grabau as had been unjustly excommunicated by him. The Missouri Synod thus became involved in a controversy with the Buffalo Synod concerning the doctrines of the Church, the ministry, and the Office of the Keys, which continued until 1866.

Regarding the Church, Grabau taught "that the one holy Christian Church is a visible Church, that by it is not meant scattered believers, but those who gather about the Word and Sacrament, that members of the true Church are not found in communions that teach error, that communion with the invisible Church is not sufficient to obtain salvation, and that external fellowship with a visible orthodox Church is necessary for salvation." On the basis of Scripture the Missouri Synod maintained that the Church in its true sense is invisible (Luke 17:20; Acts 1:24; Col. 3:3-4); that even as in the days of Elijah God had preserved Himself a Church of 7,000, who were scattered and unknown even to the prophet, so today Christendom is scattered physically but united spiritually (1 Kings 19:18); that since the congregations at Galatia and Corinth, into which error had crept, were called churches by the Apostle, true believers necessarily must have been present, and so likewise today Christians are found in churches that hold false doctrine but do not deny the Word of God outright; that whoever makes salvation dependent on communion with any visible Church overthrows the article of justification of a poor sinner before God by faith only (Rom. 3:28; Gal. 3:26; Gal. 3:9; Rom. 11:2-4).

With reference to the ministry, Buffalo taught that it is not the congregation which gives or conveys the holy ministry, but the Son of God, together with the Father and the Holy Ghost; that a congregation has no right to call a pastor without the assistance and presence of a representative of the ministry; that the ministry forms a distinct rank, or class; that a congregation must obey its pastor in all things not contrary to God's Word; that not the congregation, but only the ministry has the right to judge doctrine, that ordination is a divine order and gives validity and efficacy to the work of the pastor.

The Missouri Synod held to the Scriptural truths that since the Christians are called a royal priesthood, they must have the power to elect ministers; that while the importance of having a qualified pastor should induce a congregation to consult with ministers before calling a pastor, yet its call is valid without the presence and co-operation of a clergyman; that the ministry does not form a distinct rank, since all Christians in the New Testament are called priests (1 Pet. 2:9; Rev. 1:6; Gal. 3:26); that a pastor is not a ruler of the church whom all members must obey (Matt. 20:25-26; 1 Pet. 5:1-3); that the laity has the right of judging doctrine (1 Cor. 10:15-16; 1 John 4:1; Acts 17:11); that it cannot be proved from Scripture that ordination is a divine institution and hence that the efficacy of the means of grace does not depend upon ordination.

Regarding the Office of the Keys, Buffalo taught that Christ did not give the keys of the Kingdom of Heaven to the Church and to every true believer, but solely and exclusively to the pastors; that a congregation dare not judge and declare that the sinner is to be held as an heathen and a publican, for the pastor alone has the power to excommunicate sinners. Missouri, on the contrary, taught on the basis of Matt. 18:17-20 that the Keys have been given to the whole Church originally and immediately, that is, not mediately, through the ordained pastor, but in such a way that they belong in like measure to every congregation, the smallest as well as the largest.

Repeated efforts were made to bring the opposing parties together in conference. In 1846 the Saxons invited Grabau to meet them in Fort Wayne. St. Matthew's in Detroit asked Grabau to meet Pastor Craemer for a doctrinal discussion in its church. The Leipzig Conference and the Breslau Synod urged Grabau to meet the Missourians in a colloquy. But Grabau refused all overtures. While Missouri as late as 1856, at the urging of the Ohio Synod, stood ready to establish closer relations with the Buffalo Synod (on the basis of doctrinal unity, of course), Grabau, in 1859, prevailed upon his synod to renounce all fraternal relations with Missouri and excommunicated the Missouri Synod *en masse* (over 200 congregations). In 1866 he excommunicated a number of his own Synod "for entertaining Missouri principles," in one instance an entire congregation.

As time went on, many of the pastors and congregations of the Buffalo Synod grew weary of Grabau's arbitrary rule, and the synod was divided into two factions, one headed by Grabau and the other by von Rohr. The latter party met with Missouri in a colloquy in November, 1866. Twelve pastors and a number of congregations agreed with Missouri, and in 1867 a formal recognition of doctrinal unity and church fellowship was sealed at a meeting of 12 pastors and five delegates of the Buffalo Synod and five representatives of the Missouri Synod.

THE BREAK WITH LOEHE
AND THE CONTROVERSY WITH THE IOWA SYNOD

Pastor Wilhelm Loehe of Neuendettelsau undoubtedly was one of the most farsighted churchmen of his generation. Beginning in 1842 and continuing until his death in 1872, he sent a constant stream of workers for the Church in America, most of whom, until 1853, joined the Missouri Synod. He projected plans for colonizing the forests of Michigan, which resulted in the establishing of Frankenmuth, Frankentrost, Frankenlust, and Frankenhilf. He opened the mission among the Chippewas in Michigan through Pastor Craemer. He was the founder of the Practical Seminary at Fort Wayne, Indiana, and later of a Teachers' Seminary at

Saginaw, Michigan. And when we consider his work in the interest of inner missions in his home village as it manifested itself in the building of a Deaconess Home (1854), a chapel for the same (1858), a House of Rescue (1862), a Home for Feeble-Minded (1864), a Home for Delinquent Girls (1865), a hospital for men (1867), and a hospital for women (1869), we can readily understand that through Loehe the obscure village of Neuendettelsau became known not only in America, but throughout Europe.

The relations between Synod and Loehe were most cordial at the time of its organization. The impulse to organize had emanated largely from the Loehe men at Loehe's urging, who realized that the Ohio and the Michigan Synod, to which he had directed his first men, were not synods standing unequivocally upon the Lutheran Confessions. He had proved to be the greatest benefactor of our Synod. It was, therefore, a matter of much regret that a break came between the two parties.

When the draft of the synodical constitution was made at St. Louis (1846) and discussed the same year at Fort Wayne, Loehe's men were present. The constitution was adopted the following year, when the Missouri Synod was organized. Writes Deindoerfer in his history of the Iowa Synod: "It is indeed strange that in such an important matter as the adoption of a synodical constitution, in which Walther's peculiar doctrine of the ministerial office was clearly stated, the pupils and friends of Loehe did not stop to ask those by whom they had been sent for their opinion and advice." [9]

Loehe was not well pleased with the constitution of the Missouri Synod. He was convinced that the congregations had been given too much power and that the prerogatives of the clergymen had been curtailed. Nevertheless, he was satisfied for the time being to let his men work under a constitution which did not in all respects have his approval.

At its first convention, Synod extended an invitation to Loehe to attend the meeting of 1848. The invitation was repeated in 1850. When Loehe could not come, Synod resolved to send a delegation composed of President Wyneken and Professor Walther to visit Loehe in person in the endeavor to remove whatever misgivings Loehe had about the doctrines of the Missouri Synod.

When Wyneken and Walther arrived in Hamburg in 1851, they met Pastor Deindoerfer, a Loehe emissary, who was en route to Frankenhilf, Michigan, an event which caused Loehe to rejoice. The American emissaries met with Loehe a number of times, and although the latter did not fully agree with Walther and Wyneken, he was hopeful as to the future. When the two Americans were about to leave Germany on their return home, Loehe published a special number of the *Kirchliche Mitteilungen aus und ueber Nordamerika* "to commemorate the presence of the venerable brethren Walther and Wyneken in Germany."

In 1853, however, Pastors Grabau and von Rohr toured Germany in the interest of their synod and also called on Loehe. The result was that the break with Loehe could no longer be averted.

The issue that separated Loehe and the Missouri Synod was that of the Church and the ministry. Like Grabau, Loehe did not believe that every Christian has all the rights and privileges of the Office of the Keys nor that the office of the ministry is derived from the spiritual priesthood of the believers. Only in exceptional instances may a congregation call a pastor without the presence of an advising pastor, for not through the local congregation, but through the Church, that is, the congregation and the clergy, the Lord calls and ordains men for the ministry. Loehe was not satisfied to admit that ordination is merely a church ceremony which publicly attests the validity of the call. He thought the Church to be a visible institution. He, however, did not, like Grabau, hold that church members must obey their pastor in all things which are not contrary to God's Word, nor did he approve of Grabau's papistic doctrine of excommunication.

When Walther and Wyneken were with Loehe, they discussed with him the problem of securing teachers for their parish schools and suggested to him the opening of a teacher-training institution in America. Loehe, agreeable to the proposal, considered Detroit a suitable place for such a college, for here one of his missioners, Pastor Johann Michael Gottlieb Schaller, for whom he had the highest regard, was stationed. However, in view of the large outlay of money required to open and maintain a college in Detroit, Loehe abandoned his original plan. Moreover, Gottlieb Schaller, Loehe's Timothy, after a prolonged debate with Walther, had frankly declared himself in favor of the latter's doctrine of the ministry in 1850. Previous to this, Loehe had thought of establishing a hostel for immigrants at Saginaw to provide temporary quarters for German Lutherans going to Michigan. It occurred to him now that the immigrant hostel could serve also as quarters for the teachers' seminary.

Inspector G. M. Grossmann arrived at Saginaw in July, 1852, with five students to open the normal school. The professor and the students of the seminary were members of Pastor Cloeter's church in Saginaw. Together with the other Missouri pastors, except Deindoerfer, Cloeter insisted that the Missouri doctrine of the Church and the ministry was that of the Bible. He threatened to discipline Grossmann if he abided by Loehe's doctrine. Grossmann withdrew from the congregation.

Deindoerfer, who joined the Missouri Synod in 1852, sided with Grossmann. When the tension between Grossmann, Deindoerfer, and the Michigan Missourians became unbearable, the former requested Loehe to permit them to relocate the seminary in Iowa. By the visit of Grabau and von Rohr in 1853 Loehe became strengthened in his conviction that he could no longer work with Missouri, and in a letter written on black-bordered paper, dated August 4, 1853, spoke his official farewells to the pastors and congregations in the Saginaw Valley. This ended the fraternal relations of Loehe and the Missouri Synod. On the twenty-fifth anniversary of his mission endeavors in America Loehe said: "Nothing has gone as we wanted it to go; still all has gone in such a way that success and blessing has attended our work down to the present hour."

Grossmann and Deindoerfer, having received permission from Loehe, migrated with about 20 souls in September, 1853, to Dubuque, Iowa. Of the original five students at the teachers' seminary at Saginaw three joined the Missouri Synod: Riedel, Simon, and Brater.

On August 24, 1854, Pastors G. M. Grossmann, J. Deindoerfer, S. Fritschel, and M. Schueller organized the Iowa Synod at St. Sebald, Iowa. The new synod did not adopt a constitution, but only certain guiding principles. The first of these reads: "Synod accepts all the Symbolical Books of the Evangelical Lutheran Church, because it believes that all their symbolical decisions of disputable questions which had arisen before or during the time of the Reformation were made in accordance with the Word of God. But because within the Lutheran Church there are different tendencies, Synod declares itself in favor of that tendency which, by means of the Confessions and on the basis of the Word of God, strives toward greater completeness." [10]

This paragraph reflected the views of Loehe, for Loehe believed that the Reformation of Dr. Luther was not definitive, but rather a progressive movement. In other words, Loehe believed that not all doctrines of Scripture had been fixed in the Confessions, and hence no branch of the Lutheran Church can claim to be in possession of the whole truth. Doctrinal completeness, indeed, should be desired and sought after, but it has not yet been attained, and hence, within limits, doctrinal differences and various theological tendencies, as represented by the different schools in the Lutheran Church, need not stand in the way of church fellowship. Absolute unity can never be attained and, therefore, should not be made the condition of church fellowship. Regarding church fellowship the Iowa Synod officially declared in 1879: "Our Synod was from the very beginning persuaded to make a distinction between such in the Confessions of the Ev. Lutheran Church as are necessary articles of faith (*Glaubenslehren*) and such other doctrines (*Lehrpunkte*) as are not doctrines necessary for salvation; and our Synod has considered it one of her duties very earnestly and emphatically to teach as an important truth that there are doctrines, even doctrines of the Scripture, concerning which members of our Church may hold different views and convictions without thereby being compelled to refuse each other church fellowship; and that these are the very doctrines for the sake of which the Missourians adjudge us to be heretical. In such matters unity should, indeed, be sought, but it is not absolutely required as in the doctrines of faith." [11]

Following the lead of Loehe, the Iowa Synod considered the doctrine of Sunday, the Antichrist, the millennium, the conversion of the Jews, and the resurrection of the martyrs open questions, that is, teachings or opinions not clearly stated in Scripture.

Missouri, on the other hand, taught and still teaches on the basis of Scripture that the New Testament Church has no command to set aside a special day for worship, that the Pope is the man of sin predicted in 2 Thess. 2, that there will be no 1,000 years of Christ's rule on earth before Judgment Day, that there will be no general conversion of the Jews, and that the only resurrection the Bible teaches is the resurrection on the Last Day. Hence it was inevitable that Missouri and Iowa became involved in doctrinal controversy.

At its convention at Toledo, 1867, the Iowa Synod resolved to meet Missouri in a colloquy. It was held at Milwaukee November 13—18. The points discussed were the attitude of the two bodies toward the Lutheran Confessions, the so-called "open questions," and items of eschatology. Time did not permit consideration of the doctrines of the Church and the ministry, on which the two synods had originally separated. No agreement was reached at Milwaukee, for Iowa would not admit that the doctrine of Sunday, the first resurrection (Rev. 20), and the Antichrist must be considered symbolically fixed by the Lutheran Church and classed as articles of faith. The representatives of the Iowa Synod were ready to substitute the term "problems" for that of "open questions," but could not agree with the Missouri men as to what is to be called a "problem." (Later, in 1873, Iowa defined "open questions" to mean "doctrines not divisive of church fellowship." Finally, in 1882, during the Predestinarian Controversy, Iowa charged Missouri with a fundamental error which was sufficient cause for separation.)

SYNOD AND SECRET SOCIETIES

Synod very early took a decided stand against anti-Christian societies. The position of Synod against lodges is all the more striking when one considers that at this time practically all Lutheran synods in America permitted not only laymen but also pastors to hold membership with the Freemasons, Odd Fellows, and other lodges. At its sixth convention, in 1853, Missouri declared its attitude toward secret societies. Basing its statement on Eph. 5:11; John 3:20; 2 Cor. 6:14; Matt. 5:33-37; Matt. 6:25-34, Synod declared: "These Scripture doctrines and others testify that whoever joins or retains membership in the Odd Fellows or other lodges, whether he attends their regular meetings or not, denies our blessed Savior and tramples God's Word underfoot. Therefore Synod warns all its members, all Christian people in general, particularly also our dear fellow believers who have just immigrated, against such secret societies. It considers it self-evident that proceedings according to the Lord's command (Matt. 18:15) shall be taken against those in Christian congregations who shall be found in the membership of the aforementioned secret organizations." [12]

SYNODICAL PRINTERY

Until 1870 Synod had no publication facilities of its own. *Der Lutheraner,* published by Trinity Church in St. Louis in 1844 and placed under the auspices of Synod in 1847, was printed by Weber and Olshausen and later by the firm of Wiebusch. In 1847 Trinity Church issued a German hymnal, which had been compiled by Walther and Loeber. It was printed in New York. The publication rights of the hymnal were transferred to Synod in 1863.

Already in 1849 Synod considered a number of proposals to establish its own publishing concern. Memorials to this effect were submitted by Pastors Keyl and Selle and by J. H. Tesch and F. H. Eilers. Pastor Theo. Brohm of New York likewise urged Synod to be concerned about having its own printery. The convention resolved that a stock company be formed for this purpose and set forth detailed regulations governing its activities.

In 1850 Synod learned that only 37 shares of the *"Verlagsgesellschaft"* had been sold and that the "Book Company" had a balance of $378.75. The shareholders, convinced that their business venture had no future, resolved to disband the company and to lend the shares to Synod for the establishing of a *"Verlagskasse"* (book concern).

Professor Walther, at the request of Synod, began, in 1855, to publish *Lehre und Wehre,* a professional theological journal. In 1865 President J. C. W. Lindemann of Addison issued the first number of *Ev.-Luth. Schulblatt,* a magazine for schoolteachers.

E. W. Leonhardt, C. Roemer, T. Schuricht, Louis Lange, and E. F. W. Meier, all of St. Louis, invested $3,000.00 in modest printing equipment in 1867 and set up the establishment in a room of the seminary.

Meanwhile the Northern District had become interested in a synodical printery. At its convention of 1867 it received a proposal from Trinity Church in Ottawa County, Michi-

Concordia Publishing House, 1870

gan, regarding printing facilities for Synod, and in 1868 the Northern District resolved to submit the suggestion to the convention of Synod in 1869.

At this convention the five men who had equipped the small printery in St. Louis in 1867 offered it to Synod, with the advice that it be financed through the sale of stock, which was to be retired in five years. Accordingly, a stock company was formed, the five directors being Louis Lange, Henry Kalbfleisch, H. Steinmeyer, E. F. W. Meier, and "Colporteur" F. Lange. The same convention assumed control of the *Schulblatt* and authorized the publishing of a *Kalen-*

der (an annual), Dr. E. Preuss, editor, the Dietrich Catechism, and a German reader for the middle grades.

On October 21, 1869, the cornerstone of the building which was to be the home of a publishing concern was laid. Its site was the campus of Concordia Seminary, the building fronting on Texas Avenue. The first press, purchased at a price of $3,800, was installed on February 6, 1870, power being provided by a seven horsepower steam engine. The first publication off the new press was *Das Schulblatt*.

Monday, February 28, marked the formal dedication of the new "*Synodaldruckerei*." A special service was conducted in Holy Cross Church, with a sermon by Walther. Music was furnished by the brass band of Immanuel Church and by the trumpeters of Carondelet and by the Seminary Chorus. The building was decorated with foliage, and over it flew the flag of the United States. Programs were presented in the afternoon and evening, Dr. Preuss delivering an oration on the subject of publishing Christian literature.

The venture thrived from the very beginning, the St. Louis convention of 1872 reporting a gross turnover of $145,953.02 for the period of August 1, 1869, to April 1, 1872. At this meeting of Synod it was resolved to accept the plant officially and to combine the book agency and the printery under one management. Louis Lange, publisher of *Die Abendschule*, supervised the new concern.

THE JUBILEE OF 1872

The year 1872 marked the twenty-fifth anniversary of Synod's organization. Pastor Theodore Harms, principal of the Missionary Institute in Hermannsburg, and Pastor F. Brunn, principal of the pro-seminary at Steeden, Hessen-Nassau, both of whom had sent many young men to the college and seminaries of Synod, were invited to attend the jubilee convention, the Eastern and the Central Districts guaranteeing their expenses. To Synod's regret both had to decline the invitation.

On April 26, the day of the founding of Synod, Professor Walther preached to the assembled group in Trinity Church, St. Louis, on Psalm 119:43: "Take not the Word of Truth utterly out of my mouth; for I have hoped in Thy judgments." The subject of his sermon was "The Preservation of Our Synod for Twenty-Five Years in the Word of Truth a Sufficient Cause for Our Jubilee This Day." In the evening all churches of Synod in St. Louis conducted anniversary services.

On April 27 Synod began its convention in the Mercantile Library Hall. Vice-President Brohm gave the address for the opening of the first business session. After showing the growth of Synod during the past twenty-five years, Brohm said: "At that time [1847] our Synod occupied a solitary and lonely position, was looked at askance, or even despised, by other church bodies; today we are in fraternal relationship with five, partly large, bodies. Immigration from Germany has in the last twenty-five years taken on such proportions as to have become a matter of world history. And our Synod has followed this immigration step by step as a true servant, ever seeking to bring the Bread of Life to the scattered brethren of the faith in the desert of this great western country."

Vice-President Brohm read an essay to the convention on the topic "What task have we to perform that the blessings which God in the past twenty-five years has showered upon us be not dissipated by us but rather be transmitted to our descendants?" He showed, first, the blessings received as they were manifest in the pure Lutheran doctrine, the continuous growth of Synod's membership, the prosperous condition of Synod's institutions, the blessed condition of the parish schools, the treasure of sound, orthodox books and religious peridicals, and the fraternal co-operation with five

LENGTHENING THE CORDS (1847 - 1872)

like-minded synods. Thereupon he set forth the dangers of losing these blessings; next, how these blessings might be preserved and transmitted to descendants; finally, the results which our endeavors to perform this task would have upon future generations. Of particular interest is Brohm's insistence upon Synod's making more generous provisions for the use of the English language in the parish schools as well as in the synodical institutions, so that its members might be the better equipped for their task as witnesses to the risen Savior also among the American people.

The first charter member of Synod to fall asleep in Jesus was Pastor G. H. Loeber of Altenburg, Missouri. Born at Kahla, Saxe-Altenburg, January 5, 1797, and educated at Jena, he tutored for five years and was then appointed pastor to the Loeber manor at Eichenberg in 1824. After Stephan's removal he was the oldest of the Saxon pastors. He was the leader in the controversy with Grabau. Dr. Vehse, who wrote an account of the Saxon emigration, characterizes Loeber in the following words: "All who have known Loeber in Germany will agree with me that he was one of the most excellent personalities. In Altenburg, his fatherland, he enjoyed universal respect. All slander was quieted when one observed his official and his family life. In America he won the hearts of everyone, not only of those of our company. His features and his figure were very much like those of St. John in the famous painting of Duerer. His dignified carriage, his soft and lovely voice, his entirely unassuming conduct, charmed everybody. I cannot think of his sermons without grateful emotions. Never will I forget the one that he preached in the auditorium of Christ Church, St. Louis, on Second Easter Day, from the text: "Simon, son of Jonas, lovest thou Me?" [13] His death on August 19, 1849, was mourned by all who knew him and cast a pall over Synod's convention in 1850.

10

THE EVANGELICAL LUTHERAN SYNODICAL CONFERENCE OF NORTH AMERICA
1872-1897

*T*HE founders of the Missouri Synod were not separatists. Wherever they perceived a quickening of confessional Lutheranism, they were quick to give it public recognition and support. It was their endeavor to establish unity in the spirit and to maintain such unity wherever possible.

Already at its second convention (1848) Synod delegated Dr. Sihler to the convention of the Tennessee Synod. In 1851 Professor Craemer and Pastor Fuerbringer were designated to represent the Missouri Synod at the meetings of the Indianapolis Synod. Walther and Wyneken were sent to Germany in the same year at Synod's expense in an effort to maintain friendly relations with Loehe. The Missouri Synod entered into lengthy negotiations with the Buffalo Synod in 1856, the object being eventual church fellowship. Beginning with 1857, Synod regularly sent delegates to the conventions of the Norwegian Synod.

In the foreword to *Lehre und Wehre,* January, 1856, Walther, briefly reviewing the state of the Lutheran Church in America, closes the account with an invitation to all Lutherans in America who unequivocally subscribe to the Augsburg Confession to meet in free conferences for the promotion and realization of a united Lutheran Church. For himself, his fellow theologians, and his laymen he promised to attend such free conferences wherever and whenever they might be held. Walther was prompted to issue this call by the appearance of the "Definite Platform," which had been published by a number of the leaders of the General Synod in the interest of "American Lutheranism." This "Definite Platform" was an endeavor to adapt the Lutheran Church to its American environment, and in order to do so, the document denied eight articles of the Augsburg Confession. The General Synod did not adopt the "Definite Platform," for at this time conservative Lutheranism was beginning to assert itself in too many quarters of the Lutheran Church. Walther saw in this a cause for rejoicing and for hope in the establishing of a united Lutheran Church.

Reporting on the reactions to this call for free conferences in the March issue of *Lehre und Wehre,* Walther informed his readers that the *Lutheran Standard* of the Ohio Synod had reprinted his invitation and that individuals had written him their approval. Accordingly, the July issue of *Lehre und Wehre* contained the following invitation for a general conference of all Lutherans who acknowledged the Augsburg Confession as the profession of their faith:

"The undersigned, clergymen of the Evangelical Lutheran Church in the United States, in the conviction that unity and the welfare of our Lutheran Zion may be effectively promoted through the free expression of views by brethren at one in the faith concerning the various interests of our Church in this country, herewith extend an invitation to all members of the Evangelical Lutheran Church in the United States who accept the Unaltered Augsburg Confession as a true presentation of the doctrines of the divine Word to meet with them for free and brotherly conferences concerning the present situation and needs of the Church in America on Wednesday, October 1, in the city of ———." [1]

The invitation was eventually signed by seventy-five clergymen and professors, among whom were the leaders of the Missouri and the Ohio Synods. The majority of signers preferred to meet in Columbus, Ohio. The first meeting was held from October 1 to 7. At Walther's suggestion the Augsburg Confession was discussed, article by article. Three further conferences were held, namely, at Pittsburgh, October 29 to November 4, 1857; at Cleveland, August 5 to 11, 1858; and at Fort Wayne, July 14 to 20, 1859. The discussion of the Augustana continued, and at the four conferences Articles 1—14 and 28 were accepted. Walther was not present at the fourth meeting because of impaired health. The conference expressed regret "that Professor Walther, who gave the first impulse to these conferences and through whom the Lord has blessed them so abundantly, was prevented this time from taking part in the proceedings" and added the wish "that it may please God soon to restore this noble instrument and long preserve it unto His Church."

Walther spent the greater part of 1860 in Germany in an effort to regain his health. By 1861 the country was embroiled in the Civil War.

After the Civil War the confessional trend which was growing in the older synods manifested itself in 1866 in a division of the General Synod, the more conservative groups forming the General Council in 1867. For a time it was hoped that the more orthodox Lutherans might all be united in this body, but this hope proved futile.

There were especially four points on which the synods could not agree: interchange of pulpits with pastors of other denominations; the inter-Communion with members of other churches; the right of members of secret societies to belong to Lutheran churches;. the doctrine of the millennium. Some of the largest and most influential of the western synods made it a condition of their entering the new body that it should take a definite and clear position on these important questions, and since this was not achieved, they did not join. Other synods, more hopeful in the beginning, withdrew when they realized that there was no prospect of settling these questions in the General Council in accordance with the Word of God.

It was only natural that the Missouri, Ohio, Wisconsin, Minnesota, Norwegian, and Illinois Synods, so much agreed among themselves, try to come to an understanding.

At its convention at Woodville, Ohio, 1866, the Ohio Synod resolved to appoint a committee which was to confer with a committee of the Missouri Synod to promote friendly relations. A colloquy was held at Columbus, March 4—6, 1868. While the Northern District of the Missouri Synod was in session at Milwaukee, the Wisconsin Synod requested that representatives of both bodies meet to establish doctrinal agreement. The meeting was held at Milwaukee, October 21—22, 1868. Pastor R. Knoll of Peoria, Illinois, President of the Illinois Synod, requested a colloquy between his and the Missouri Synod in a letter dated May 31, 1869, addressed to Walther. It was conducted on August 4 and 5, 1869.

At the convention of the Missouri Synod in 1869 the agreement between the Wisconsin and Missouri Synods was ratified as well as the arrangement whereby Synod was to place a professor at the Watertown college and Wisconsin a professor at St. Louis to train the respective students. With reference to the Ohio Synod the Missouri Synod was not prepared to accept the agreement of 1868, since it had become apparent that several members of this group did not share Missouri's doctrine of the office of the ministry. As to the Illinois Synod, Synod resolved that further conferences were necessary before fellowship could be declared.

At its convention at Dayton, Ohio, October, 1870, the Ohio Synod declared its acceptance of Missouri's doctrine of the office of the ministry and at the same time informed the Missouri Synod that "it had appointed a committee to confer with committees of other synods who were united with us in doctrine and practice regarding the possibility of co-operating in the maintenance of necessary institutions of learning and, if an agreement can be reached, to be ready to present to those synods taking part in the deliberations a plan whereby such co-operation would become possible." It requested Walther to appoint a committee to confer with the committees of other synods.

The meeting of the representatives of the Ohio, Norwegian, Missouri, and Wisconsin Synods took place at Chicago, January 11—13, 1871. Pastor Knoll of Peoria, Illinois, President of the Illinois Synod, also was present but took no active part in the discussion, since his group was still connected with the General Council. A draft of the constitution for a synodical conference was prepared. The committee met for a second time, November 14—16, at Fort Wayne to revise and give final form to the draft made in January. On this occasion President Sieker of the Minnesota Synod and delegates from the Illinois Synod were present at the invitation of Walther. At this meeting Prof. F. A. Schmidt read a paper setting forth the reasons for organizing the Synodical Conference. The prevailing tone of the conference was one of praise to God and of bright hopes for the future of the Lutheran Church. By resolution the synods concerned were called upon to meet for the organization and first convention of the Synodical Conference in St. John's Church, Milwaukee, June 10—16, 1872.

In the meantime the Minnesota and the Wisconsin Synods had established fraternal relations in 1871.

At the convention of the Missouri Synod in 1872 the past action of its committee was ratified. The Illinois Synod, which had severed its connection with the General Council, was recognized as being in fellowship with the Missouri Synod. A colloquy, conducted by the representatives of the Missouri and Minnesota Synods in June, 1872, had favorable results.

On July 10, 1872, the following clergymen representing their synods met at Milwaukee: Ohio Synod: Professors W. F. Lehmann and M. Loy; Pastors R. Herbst, H. Belser, J. C. Schulze, F. A. Herzberger, G. Trebel.

Missouri Synod: Prof. C. F. W. Walther; Pastors W. Sihler, F. J. Biltz, W. Bartling, A. Wagner, M. Tirmenstein, A. Crull, F. Lochner, C. A. Strasen, J. Herzer, Fr. Wyneken, H. C. Schwan, C. Gross, J. P. Beyer.

Wisconsin Synod: President J. Bading, Prof. A. F. Ernst, and Pastor A. Hoenecke.

Norwegian Lutheran Synod: President H. A. Preuss; Pastors U. V. Koren, P. A. Rasmussen, A. Mikkelsen, Prof. F. A. Schmidt.

Minnesota Synod: President J. H. Sieker, Pastor A. Kuhn.

Illinois Synod: President F. Erdman, Pastor F. Wolbrecht.

The name adopted for the new body was the Evangelical Lutheran Synodical Conference of North America.

Prof. C. F. W. Walther preached the opening sermon, using for his text 1 Tim. 4:16, from which he developed the thought: How important it is to make the saving of souls the one great object of our co-operative work in the kingdom of Christ. Two papers were read, the main one by Prof. F. A. Schmidt on "Justification," the other by Prof. M. Loy on "Our Duty to the English-Speaking Population of This Country," of which Thesis 5 reads: "Wherever there is the possibility, either of holding members who might otherwise fall to the sects or of gaining such as would otherwise remain without, our pastors, if at all possible, should preach the Gospel in English, until those of the English tongue can call a pastor of their own." Thesis 6: "Since in our times and country, people do very much reading, it would be disloyal to our Church not to do all in our power to acquaint the English-speaking population, by the spreading of periodicals and books, with the treasures of our Church, and therefore the achievement of this aim must always be considered as our main duty."

The constitution defined the purpose and object of the Conference as follows: "An expression of the unity of the spirit existing among the respective synods; mutual encouragement as to faith and confession; promotion of unity as to doctrine and practice and the removal of any threatening disturbance thereof; co-operation in matters of mutual interest; an effort to establish territorial boundaries for the synods, provided that the language used does not separate them; the uniting of all Lutheran synods of America into one orthodox American Lutheran Church."

With reference to the authority of the new federation, the constitution stated: "The Synodical Conference is only an advisory body with respect to all things concerning which the synods constituting it have not given it authoritative power. Only the totality of all synods represented in the Synodical Conference shall decide what church bodies cannot be received into membership thereof until all synods of the Synodical Conference have given their consent. The Synodical Conference shall see to it that conferences attended by pastors of the various synods be organized and held, the District Presidents taking the initiative. Without the consent of all the synods of the Synodical Conference none of its synods shall be permitted to enter into any church connection with other church bodies."

The officers elected at this first convention were Prof. C. F. W. Walther, President; Prof. W. F. Lehmann, Vice-President; Pastor J. P. Beyer, Secretary, Mr. J. Schmidt, Treasurer.

In 1876 a number of interesting resolutions were passed

by the Conference. Thus it was resolved that the minutes of all synods forming the Synodical Conference should be examined by a committee or committees, so that if some statements or opinions should be published that could not be approved by the other synods, these might be corrected. A plan was adopted to dissolve all synods belonging to the Synodical Conference and using the same language and to organize new synods, district synods, limiting the several bodies to the boundaries of one State. Consequently the Concordia Synod of Virginia, which had joined the Synodical Conference in 1876, became a District synod of the Ohio Synod in 1877; the Illinois Synod was absorbed by the Illinois District of the Missouri Synod in 1879, and the Missouri Synod organized the Districts of Illinois, Iowa, Nebraska, and Kansas to become eventually State synods of the Conference. At the meeting of 1876 it was furthermore resolved to suggest to the various groups to merge the existing theological seminaries into one school, with German, English, and Norwegian faculties. Definite proposals regarding both projects were submitted to the convention of 1879, but the development of the synodical boundary lines and the central seminary came to naught through the Predestinarian Controversy, which flared soon after 1879.

The Predestinarian Controversy caused the Ohio Synod to leave the Synodical Conference in 1881. The Norwegian Synod likewise withdrew in 1883, not because of doctrinal reasons, but in order to avoid the influence of nationalistic prejudices and antipathies and to fight the controversy in its own midst on purely religious grounds.

A number of clergymen and congregations withdrew from the Ohio Synod and organized the Concordia Synod of Pennsylvania and Other States. This group joined the Synodical Conference in 1882, but merged with the Missouri Synod in 1886.

In 1890 the English Synod of Missouri and Other States

was admitted to the Synodical Conference. The Wisconsin, Minnesota, and Michigan Synods in 1892 united into one body, bearing the name: The General Synod of Wisconsin, Minnesota, and Michigan. The union did not destroy the identity of these synods, but provided for joint use of their educational institutions. Thus the Michigan Synod became a member of the Synodical Conference. In 1896, however, a division took place within this group, and when the majority seceded from the larger federation, the remaining minority, reorganized as the District Synod of Michigan, was acknowledged as a member of the Synodical Conference.

Twenty-five years after its organization the Synodical Conference embraced the following bodies: The German Evangelical Lutheran Synod of Missouri, Ohio, and Other States; The General Synod of Wisconsin, Minnesota, Michigan, and Other States; The English Synod of Missouri and Other States. Presidents of the federation were: C. F. W. Walther, 1872—1873; W. F. Lehmann, 1873—1876; H. A. Preuss, 1876—1877; W. F. Lehmann, 1877—1880; L. Larsen, 1880—1882; J. Bading, 1882—(1912).

Already in 1877, at the convention in Fort Wayne, a plan had been placed before the Synodical Conference to begin a mission among the heathen. After much deliberation it was thought best to begin work among the Negroes in our country. A committee consisting of Pastors J. F. Buenger, G. F. H. Meiser, and Mr. J. G. Thieme was chosen to work out and submit plans for the beginning of this work. A Missionary Board was elected to supervise the mission, members of the board being Pastors J. F. Buenger, C. F. W. Sapper, and Mr. John Umbach.

The first man called by the Missionary Board for work among the Negroes was Pastor J. F. Doescher, an itinerant missionary in the Dakota Territory. He was commissioned for his work at the convention of the Western District of the Missouri Synod at Altenburg, Missouri, on October 16, 1877.

After working in Little Rock, Arkansas, from 1877 to 1878, Doescher traveled through Tennessee, Georgia, Florida, Alabama, Mississippi, and Louisiana, preaching to Negroes whenever and wherever he had an opportunity. In New Orleans he opened a Sunday school and continued his work among the colored people even after he had become pastor of St. John's Lutheran Church. His successor in New Orleans was Candidate N. J. Bakke, who arrived in 1880. The Missionary Board purchased an old church in 1882, converted it into a church and school, and dedicated it on December 3, 1882. The name of the congregation was Mount Zion Lutheran Church. Two other colored churches were opened in New Orleans, St. Paul's by Pastor Bakke and Bethlehem, established by Pastor Aug. Burgdorf (1887).

In Little Rock, Candidate F. Berg succeeded Doescher and organized St. Paul's Colored Lutheran Church on July 3, 1878. Pastor Berg had the first Baptism and the first funeral in our colored mission. On August 18, 1878, the Little Rock congregation dedicated its house of worship, and in the service Pastor Berg baptized 23 persons. Berg accepted a call to a white congregation in 1881. His successor was Pastor E. Mailaender.

Prof. H. Wyneken began to work among the colored people at Springfield, Illinois, in 1882. He was assisted by the seminary students, especially by H. S. Knabenschuh. The mission came under the control of the Missionary Board in 1887, and in 1888 Candidate Knabenschuh was called as the first pastor of the group.

In Virginia, Pastor W. R. Buehler, a former German missionary in Africa, began a mission among Negroes, which eventually was established at Meherrin. In 1890 Candidate D. H. Schoof became the resident pastor of this little flock.

Members of the Alpha Synod of the Evangelical Lutheran

Church of Freedom in America, organized in North Caroline in 1889, applied for assistance to President H. C. Schwan of the Missouri Synod (1891). The Missionary Board heeded the appeal and transferred Missionary N. J. Bakke from New Orleans to Concord, North Carolina, where he began his work in September, 1891.

Twenty years after mission work among the Negroes had been begun, the statistics showed 18 mission stations, served by nine missionaries and six teachers. The adherents numbered 1,400 souls, 610 communicants, 800 pupils attended the Christian day school and 1,152 the Sunday school.

In order to stimulate and sustain interest in the work among the colored people, the Synodical Conference in 1878 resolved to publish a missionary periodical. *Die Missionstaube* appeared in January, 1879, with Pastor F. Lochner of Springfield, Illinois, as editor in chief. For the benefit of the colored readers (Lutheran) the same convention of the Synodical Conference established *The Lutheran Pioneer*, which was edited by Prof. R. A. Bischoff for thirty-three years.

11

STRENGTHENING THE STAKES
1872-1897

$\mathcal{I}$N 1872 the Missouri Synod had 415 pastors, working in 26 States, including Washington, D. C., and in the province of Ontario, serving 543 congregations. By the end of the second quarter the *Statistical Yearbook* listed 1,564 pastors and professors on the roster of the Missouri Synod, who were serving 1,986 congregations and 693 preaching stations, totaling 687,334 souls.

The States added to the synodical territory were Florida, Kentucky, Mississippi, Montana, Nevada, New Hampshire, North Carolina, North Dakota, Oklahoma, Oregon, South Dakota, Washington, and Wyoming. Western Canada likewise was being opened to Synod, Pastor E. Rolf of St. Paul conducting the first German Lutheran service to be held in Western Canada at Poplar Point, Manitoba, in 1879. H. Buegel was the first resident pastor in Manitoba (1891). In 1884 the 11 Districts had 84 traveling missionaries, serving 531 congregations and preaching stations.

The tremendous expansion of Synod necessitated dividing two of the four original synodical Districts. The Eastern and the Central Districts remained unchanged, but the Northern and particularly the Western District were divided and redivided. From the Western District branched off

a. The Illinois District in 1875, Pastor H. Wunder, President;

b. The Iowa District in 1879, Pastor J. Lorenz Craemer, President;

c. The Southern District in 1882, Pastor Tim. Stiemke, President;

d. The Nebraska District in 1882, Pastor J. Hilgendorf, President;

e. The Kansas District in 1888, Pastor F. Pennekamp, President;

f. The California and Oregon District in 1887, Pastor J. M. Buehler, President.

The old Northern District changed as follows:

In 1875 Minnesota, the Dakotas, and Wisconsin left the Northern District to organize the Northwestern District, Pastor C. A. Strasen, President. But already in 1882 the Northwestern District lost its identity when it was divided into

a. The Minnesota and Dakota District, Pastor O. Cloeter, President;

b. The Wisconsin District, Pastor C. A. Strasen, President.

The original Northern District divided as follows in 1879:

a. The Canada District, Pastor J. A. Ernst, President;

b. The Michigan District, Pastor O. Fuerbringer, President. (Until 1882 the Michigan District was called the Northern District.)

The Mission Board appointed by the first convention in 1847 devoted its attention chiefly to work among the Indians. In 1860 Dr. Sihler was appointed custodian of the treasury established to provide for the needs of the itinerant missionaries. Later on, one Mission Board served for both Foreign and Home Missions. In 1878, however, a Board for

Home Missions was elected. It consisted of the Pastors A. Wagner, Ch. H. Loeber, and G. Link. At this convention it was resolved a) that the funds gathered in the Districts for Home Missions may be expended by the District boards for mission work in their District, b) that any funds not so expended are to be turned over to the Treasurer of Synod, c) that District Presidents requiring a subsidy for missions in their District are to inform the chairman of the General Home Mission Board immediately after the District convention of their needs, d) that a subcommittee composed of all District Presidents and Visitors meet under the chairmanship of someone appointed by the General President in order to allocate the funds in the treasury for Home Missions to the needs of the individual Districts.

At the convention in 1878 Walther asked to be relieved of his duties as President, which he had administered in addition to his professorship at St. Louis since 1864. Synod, recognizing the fact that Walther's duties at the seminary were of greater importance than his being President, acceded to his request.

His successor was Pastor H. C. Schwan of Cleveland, Ohio. Schwan was the nephew of Wyneken. He was born April 5, 1819, in Horneborg, Hannover, studied at Goettingen and Jena, and was ordained on September 13, 1843. After his ordination he lived for six years in Brazil, spending most of his time as private tutor in the home of a German coffee planter. Urged by Wyneken to come to America, he accepted a call to New Bielefeld, or Black Jack, Missouri, where he was installed September 15, 1850. In 1852 he was called to Zion Church in Cleveland, Ohio.

Synod realized that a pastor having charge of a congregation could not discharge the functions of a general President efficiently. Hence, in 1881, it resolved that the President of Synod should henceforth not be a full-time pastor of a congregation, but perform pastoral duties only in so far as they would not interfere with his presidential duties. The salary was $1,800 per annum. Schwan was president until 1899.

EDUCATIONAL INSTITUTIONS

The second quarter saw a marked emphasis placed upon the establishing of institutions preparatory for the course in St. Louis. The tremendous influx of German Lutheran immigrants compelled Synod to do its utmost to cope with the task of supplying pastors and teachers for the newly organized congregations, especially since towards the close of this period recruits for the ministry from Germany practically ceased.

For thirteen years, 1861 to 1874, the two seminaries had been housed under one roof in St. Louis and taught by the same faculty. Owing to the rapid increase in the student body, housing difficulties in St. Louis became acute by 1874.

At Springfield, Illinois, the Synod of North Illinois had established in 1852 the so-called Illinois State University. The building was erected on ground donated to the Synod by the Enos family of Springfield, with the proviso that unless it were used for educational purposes, the property would revert to the original donors or their heirs. In 1870 the property was purchased by the Pennsylvania Ministerium, and to safeguard it in view of the deed's stipulation, Dr. Passavant used the building for an orphanage. Actually, however, the Pennsylvania Ministerium had no use for the property and in 1873 offered it to our Synod. Since the committee which was approached in the matter felt that it had no power to act, nothing was done about it. Pastor Buenger of St. Louis, however, had long felt the need of a Lutheran girls' college. Hence he and several laymen from St. Louis met with Trinity Congregation in Springfield on October 12, 1873, to discuss the possibilities of using the institution for this purpose. An association was formed under the name of "The Evangelical Lutheran Female College and Normal School Association." It was resolved to buy the institution and to open a college for girls in 1874. However, neither the "Female College" nor the "Normal School" came to life because it lacked sufficient students and teachers.

The authorities of the seminary in St. Louis saw in the buildings at Springfield a solution to their problems. Accordingly, the pro-seminary of the practical seminary, under the leadership of Prof. G. Kroening, was provisionally transferred to Springfield on January 4, 1874. Twenty-nine students were housed in the original "Illinois State University" building.

The Delegate Synod of 1874 ratified the transfer of the academy section of the practical seminary to Springfield. Since there were not sufficient facilities to accommodate the remaining two schools in the building at St. Louis, the question arose whether to erect another building or move the practical seminary to Springfield. A long debate ensued. The arguments of 1861 were emphasized, but the opposing party contended that times had changed. Not only had the student body increased in number, but educational standards had risen. The students in the practical seminary were not sufficiently advanced to profit by the lectures which the students in the theoretical seminary required. Finally a vote was taken on the question whether or not the two seminaries ought to be "organically separated." "Organic separation" was defined to mean having separate faculties for the two seminaries. By a practically unanimous vote (only two or three dissenting) Synod resolved to separate the two departments organically. Thereupon the second question was debated, namely, the physical separation of the two schools. The advantages of keeping both institutions in St. Louis were exhaustively set forth; the congregational life in St. Louis, the opportunities for students to preach in the neighboring congregations, and many other arguments were adduced by the party upholding the negative side of the question. Finally two committees were appointed to present the arguments of both parties. The committee for the affirmative was composed of Prof. F. A. Schmidt and Pastors F. Koestering and E. A. Brauer; the committee for the negative consisted of Pastors J. F. Buenger and O. Cloeter and Prof. J. C. W. Lindemann.

While discussing the relocating of the practical seminary, two places were prominent in the mind of the affirmative debaters: Milwaukee and Springfield. Since facilities to house the institution were already available at Springfield, it was finally decided that in case Synod should resolve to relocate, the institution be moved to Springfield. After all: "Besser *ein* Sperling in der Hand, als ein Dutzend Tauben auf dem Dache" — "A bird in the hand is worth two in the bush."

When at last the basic question (the physical separation of the two institutions) was voted on, it was resolved by a vote of 117 to 21 to move the practical seminary to Springfield.

At this juncture Professor Craemer pleaded with Synod to be relieved of his professorship. He was now 62 years old, his physical powers had waned, and he felt that another man ought to undertake the laborious task of carrying out the transfer. But Synod resolved that it could not dispense with the services of the man who had been intimately connected with the practical seminary for twenty-five years. Accordingly, Craemer journeyed with his seminary in August, 1875, to Springfield, where lectures were begun in September of the same year. Including the 29 students in the pro-seminary division, 113 students were enrolled the first year at Springfield, of whom 53 came from the Missouri Synod, three from the Wisconsin Synod, three from the Illinois Synod, 19 from the Norwegian Synod,

STRENGTHENING THE STAKES (1872-1897)

33 were students sent from Germany, and two were from the English Conference. To accommodate the Norwegian students, Professor Asperheim was assigned to the institution by the Norwegian Synod. He remained, however, only one year.

Pastor Hy. Wyneken joined Craemer and Kroening on the faculty in January, 1876. In 1881 Teacher Johann Salomon Simon, one of the five students who had come with

Concordia Seminary, 1883
(Annex to the north added in 1907)

Grossmann in 1852 to study at the Saginaw Teachers' Seminary, came to Springfield. Prof. R. Pieper followed Professor Craemer in the presidency of the institution (1891), and in 1892 came Pastors J. Herzer, L. Wessel, and Fr. Streckfuss. The student body of the institution rose to 294 in 1893—94.

A particularly joyous event in St. Louis was the dedication of the new seminary building in 1883. The old seminary had been razed in 1882 and a magnificent building erected on the same campus at a cost of $140,000, more than $40,000 in excess of the original appropriation of Synod. On September 9 the building was dedicated in the presence of

15,000 people. Dr. Walther preached the sermon in the forenoon, Pastor C. Gross of Fort Wayne and Prof. A. Crull speaking in the afternoon service, the former in the German, the latter in the English language. The next day an academic service was held, in which Prof. F. Pieper and Pastor

F. Pieper

Geo. Stoeckhardt

A. L. Graebner

George Stoeckhardt delivered addresses in the Latin language. In the afternoon, orations were given by two students: A. W. Meyer of New Zealand and Otto Hattstaedt of Monroe, Michigan.

Prof. F. A. Schmidt was appointed Norwegian Synod professor in 1872, remaining in St. Louis until 1876, when he was transferred to Luther Seminary at Madison, Wisconsin. Pastor G. Schaller came to the faculty in 1872,

STRENGTHENING THE STAKES (1872 - 1897)

M. Guenther in 1873, and R. Lange and F. Pieper in 1878. After Walther's death, in 1887, Professor Pieper was elected president of the seminary. Added faculty members were George Stoeckhardt and A. L. Graebner (1887), L. Fuerbringer and F. Bente (1893), and George Mezger (1896).

At Fort Wayne, President Hanser served until 1879 and was succeeded in the presidency by Profs. F. Zucker and R. A. Bischoff. Prof. A. Baepler was made head of the institution in 1888, followed by Pastor J. Schmidt in 1894. Other members added to the faculty were A. Crull (1873), Dr. H. Duemling (1874), F. W. Stellhorn (1874), Dr. O. Siemon (1882).

At Addison, Director J. C. W. Lindemann died January 15, 1879. He was followed by the Rev. E. A. W. Krauss of Sperlingshof, Baden (1880). Other members of the faculty were E. Homann (1881), C. E. Haentzschel (1874), J. L. Backhaus (1884), F. Koenig (1891), F. Lindemann and F. Rechlin (1893), A. Kaeppel (1897).

L. Fuerbringer

A new institution was called into being at Milwaukee in 1881 under the auspices of the Northwestern and Illinois Districts. The prime movers of the new undertaking were Pastors H. Wunder and Chr. H. Loeber, both products of the seminary at Altenburg. The first instructor at the new college was Candidate C. Huth. The first college building was dedicated on January 2, 1883. For six years the school was owned and operated by the two Districts mentioned. Synod assumed control of it in 1887. The college developed into a junior college in 1891, sending its graduates directly to St. Louis for their theological training. The first president was Pastor Chr. H. Loeber (1885—1893), succeeded by Pastor Max Albrecht. Members of the faculty were E. Hamann (1882), G. W. Mueller (1883), O. Hattstaedt (1884), C. Ross (1890), Dr. E. G. Sihler (1891—1892), and G. Kroening (1892).

On June 7, 1881, the New York Pastoral Conference resolved to request St. Matthew's Church to open a *Progymnasium* in its academy. The congregation promptly acted upon the suggestion. Pastor Edmund Bohm was the first president, beginning with 12 students in September, 1881. In 1882 the institution was offered to the Eastern District, which assumed responsibility provisionally until 1883, when it definitely took charge of the college. By 1892 four classes were being taught. The college was removed to Hawthorne, New York, in 1894. In 1896 the Eastern District offered the school to Synod. Synod accepted the institution, but reduced the number of classes to three. Director Bohm died in 1895 and was succeeded in the presidency by Henry Feth, who had served as professor since 1888. Other members of the faculty were O. Hanser (1882—1884), H. Gerding (1885), Dr. Wagemann (1886), Hy. F. A. Stein (1892), R. W. Heintze (1894). The graduates of this institution completed their studies at Fort Wayne or at Milwaukee.

In Concordia, Missouri, St. Paul's College was opened in January, 1883, by Pastor Andrew Baepler. The founder of the institution was Pastor J. F. Biltz, a graduate of the Altenburg seminary. The congregations surrounding Concordia erected a building on the property purchased by the group, the day of dedication being Aug. 31, 1884. The Western

STRENGTHENING THE STAKES (1872 - 1897)

District assumed full control of the institution in 1885 and was assisted in financing it by the congregations in Kansas. In 1893 four classes were taught in St. Paul's. Having been offered the college free of debt in 1896, Synod placed it under its auspices, but reduced the number of classes to three. The second president of the institution was Pastor J. H. C. Kaeppel (1888). He was assisted by Profs. A. H. Schoede (1887) and E. A. Pankow (1891). The graduates of this institution likewise completed their studies at Fort Wayne or at Milwaukee before proceeding to St. Louis.

At the convention of Synod in St. Louis, in 1893, two memorials for the establishing of two institutions were presented, one from Nebraska, requesting the opening of another normal school, and the other from Minnesota, asking that a preparatory college be opened in its territory. This was the first time that Synod directly was asked to found a college.

The perennial shortage of teachers made it imperative that ways and means be found to supply the need. Addison could not do it, since transportation was not so available for all parts of the country as it is today. The Nebraska District considered its territory suitable for a second normal school. In Lincoln, Nebraska, a group of citizens had a plot of land comprising 20 acres and, in addition, 100 acres which could be parceled out in lots, the proceeds to go to the college. Synod resolved to open a second normal school and instructed its trustees at large to proceed to Lincoln and to investigate the proposition. The Nebraska District was permitted to collect in all synodical congregations for funds to erect suitable buildings, while Synod would assume the salary of a professor. In the meantime the members at Seward took action. When the committee to investigate appeared in Nebraska, twenty acres of land and $8,000 in cash were offered by a number of members in case Seward were chosen. The trustees chose Seward, and on November 18, 1894, the first building of Concordia Teachers College was dedicated and its first professor, Pastor G. Weller, installed. Until 1905 the institution was a feeder for Addison; then it became a fully organized normal school. The building erected in 1896 and 1897 was financed by the Nebraska District. Teacher F. W. Hackstedde was added to the faculty in 1895.

The Minnesota District supported its appeal for an institution in the North by referring to the tremendous task of meeting the challenge offered in the mission field. Its territory embraced, besides the States in the Northwest, all of Western Canada. On the average, each pastor was serving three congregations, and the majority were teaching school in addition to their pastoral duties. In Minnesota, the Dakotas, Montana, and Western Canada, 44 traveling missionaries, working at 247 places, had to be supported by the District. Hence the plea that Synod assume all responsibilities involved in the opening of their school. Dr. Pieper supported the appeal of the Minnesota brethren with all his force, and Synod appropriated $25,000 for an institution in Minnesota.

The school was opened in rented quarters in 1893 in St. Paul. In 1894 the buildings of a former State institution were purchased and dedicated to their new purpose on September 9. Pastor Theo. Buenger was the first president, opening the institution with 30 students. From 1893 to 1908 the college at St. Paul served also as a feeder for the Normal School at Addison. President Buenger received additional workers in C. A. Landeck (1894) and H. Juergensen (1895). In 1896 Pastor E. L. Arndt assumed his duties at the institution. The graduates of the college completed their preparatory studies for St. Louis at Milwauke or at Fort Wayne.

MISSION ACTIVITIES

Since 1869 Synod as such did no work among the heathen. Members of the Missouri Synod for decades supported European Lutheran mission societies, principally the Leipzig and the Hermannsburg missions. The desire to conduct mission work among the heathen grew stronger as the years passed on, Pastor F. Sievers of Frankenlust, Michigan, ever holding the matter of foreign missions before the eyes of Synod.

To the convention assembled in St. Louis in 1893 Sievers announced: "What for decades has been the longing of individuals and smaller groups, *viz.*, that we might again have our own foreign missions, seems to be in process of achievement. The Lord has warmed anew the hearts for foreign missions and not only shows us that the doors to the heathen are open wide throughout the world, He also has given us the means for new work among the heathen. — All synodical Districts, the majority with instructed delegates, have come to this convention to give a thorough consideration to a mission among the heathen. — Two candidates of our Springfield seminary, G. Blaess and J. W. Peters, have been called by the New Hermannsburg Synod as missionaries for New Zealand to assist Missionary H. Dierks of Maxwelltown in his work among the Maoris. There is at present a rather general desire on the part of our Christians, a desire supported by all conventions of the synodical Districts, that mission work be undertaken in some foreign country. The General Mission Board, in its report, submits this as a definite resolution to this convention." [1]

Synod reacted favorably and resolved to open a mission in some foreign field. Japan was the country resolved upon for the following reasons: 1. Japan had opened its doors to the world; 2. There was a strong movement in progress in Japan toward European culture and civilization; 3. Of the

40,000,000 people in Japan only 33,000 were Christians; 4. No Lutheran body was doing mission work in Japan. Another reason Japan received favorable consideration was that H. Midsuno, a young Japanese won for the Lutheran Church, was enrolled at Springfield, preparing to become a missionary.

A mission board was elected, namely, Professors F. Pieper, A. L. Graebner, Pastor O. Hanser, Messrs. L. Volkening and L. Lange (all of St. Louis), with Pastors F. Sievers, Sr., A. E. Frey, C. M. Zorn, C. F. W. Sapper, and Prof. F. Zucker as members at large, and instructed to call a Director of Missions and to open the mission in Japan according to its best judgment.

Before the new board could get down to work, two of the members were taken by death, Pastor F. Sievers and Mr. L. Lange. They were replaced by Pastor J. Schmidt and Mr. R. Leonhardt. Pastor J. Wefel returned the call as Director of Missions. Before the call was extended to Pastor F. Sievers, Jr., a turn of events had taken place which caused the board to direct its attention from Japan to India.

In India two missionaries, Theodore Naether and F. J. Mohn, in the employ of the Leipzig Mission Society, had severed their relations with said society because they could not subscribe to its views regarding the inspiration of Scriptures. From Germany the news had reached the board that these men, at home in Indian mission fields and conversant with the language of the country and in full agreement with the doctrinal position of our Synod, would welcome an opportunity to continue working in India under the auspices of the Missouri Synod.

The Board for Foreign Missions thereupon asked President Schwan to place the matter before the conventions of the District Synods and, if they were agreeable, to change from Japan to India, to extend an invitation to Missionaries

STRENGTHENING THE STAKES (1872-1897)

Naether and Mohn to come to America for a discussion with the board.

The Districts being agreeable, the two missionaries arrived in America, were examined orally, and were formally called by the Missouri Synod on October 13, 1894, at a meeting of the board in St. Charles, Missouri. On the same day the two missionaries became members of Synod by joining the Western District. Both were commissioned on October 14, by President Schwan.

T. Naether

F. J. Mohn

Missionary Naether arrived in India on January 20, 1895, and opened a mission station at Krishnagiri, a populous city in the Salem District of the Madras Presidency, among the Tamil-speaking people. A year later he was followed by Missionary Mohn, whose shattered health had to be restored before sailing. In 1896 the first mission compound was established. Mohn began to work at Ambur.

A third missionary, O. Kellerbauer, had been released by the Leipzig Mission Society. Offering his services to the Board for Foreign Missions of the Missouri Synod and satisfying it as to his orthodoxy, he was called on November 25,

1895, as the third missionary in India. In order to be able to learn the language better, he was assigned as assistant to Naether in Krishnagiri. The missionaries were paid a salary of $600 per annum. The statistical report of 1897 lists the following items regarding Foreign Missions: Receipts, $4,938.28; expenditures, $3,374.51. Two stations with three schools.

Already at the convention in 1881 mission work among the Jews was considered on the basis of a memorial from the Central Illinois District Conference. At this time Synod resolved to defer action until sufficient interest had been aroused in the congregations by articles in *Die Missionstaube* and in *Der Lutheraner*.

Immigrant missionary Pastor Stephanus Keyl had for some time been corresponding with Daniel Landsmann. Born in Russia and educated to be a teacher, Landsmann moved to Jerusalem, where he was converted to Christianity by Missionary Stern and changed his name from Eliezer Bassin to Daniel Landsmann. At Jerusalem, Landsmann suffered much for the sake of his faith; his wife divorced him, his children were taken from him, and he was tried in the fire of many and severe persecutions. Later he went to Constantinople as a Christian missionary. Having come to the United States, he was brought into contact with the Missouri Synod through Missionary Stephanus Keyl. The New York Pastoral Conference resolved to send Landsmann to the seminary at Springfield in order that he might become better acquainted with Lutheran doctrine and practice. After nine months of study Landsmann was called by the Commission for Mission Work Among the Jews and appointed by the New York Pastoral Conference as its missionary among the Jews. This was in July, 1883.

The work was attended by extreme difficulties. The Jews

who associated with Landsmann for religious purposes were ostracized and cursed by their fellow Jews. The Jewish catechumens had to be supported by the Mission; they were given shelter and allowed 25 cents a day for meals. By 1884 six Jews had been received by Baptism into our Church. Synod assumed control of this mission in 1894.

Missionary Landsmann annually delivered about 30 public lectures, which were attended by 25 to 30 Jews, distributed more than 200 Bibles and Testaments as well as 3,000 tracts and made about 200 personal calls on families and individuals.

Daniel Landsmann died on May 13, 1896. God, however, had provided a successor. Nathaniel Friedmann, converted through the instrumentality of Landsmann and desiring to serve his Master, studied at the Springfield seminary and later was employed by the Minnesota and Dakota District as missionary to the Jews in St. Paul and Minneapolis. In 1893 the brethren in Minnesota asked Synod to take over this work, but Synod postponed action until the following convention. After Landsmann's death Friedmann was called to New York, where he opened a Saturday and a Sunday school, attended by 50 to 150 children, and otherwise carried on the work in the spirit and manner of Landsmann.

G. Speckhard

In 1873 an association of Lutherans in Detroit, under the leadership of Pastor J. A. Huegli, founded an orphanage and called Pastor G. Speckhard from Sebewaing, Michigan, to be the superintendent. At that time Pastor Speckhard, who had been a teacher for the deaf in Germany before entering the ministry, was instructing two deaf girls from Frankenmuth, Michigan, for confirmation. When he left for Detroit, he took the two girls along to complete their course of instruction.

Aug. Reinke

Pastor Speckhard's reputation as an instructor of deaf children soon spread to other parts of the country, and before one year had elapsed, seventeen deaf children were under his care. Upon the advice of Professor Walther the association in Detroit converted its orphanage into the Evangelical Lutheran Institute for the Deaf in 1874.

In 1893 Mr. Ed. J. Pahl, a Lutheran of Michigan City, Indiana, who had been instructed and confirmed at the Detroit Lutheran School for the Deaf, wrote the following letter to his former teacher at the school, Director Uhlig: "Dear Director: Other church bodies are caring for their deaf in preaching to them in the sign language. Our Missouri Synod has no such mission. But Jesus has surely given the command 'Preach the Gospel to every creature' also to the Missouri Synod. But to us deaf-mutes, who are Lutheran and intend to remain Lutherans, no one of the Missouri Synod preaches. Why not? We are longing for it."

Director Uhlig transmitted this letter to Aug. Reinke, pastor of Bethlehem Lutheran Church, Chicago. Shortly after receiving this letter, Reinke met several deaf-mutes from his congregation on the occasion of a Baptism and discovered that they regularly attended services conducted by the

Methodists. They informed him that the Methodist clergyman was the only person in Chicago who preached to them by means of the sign language, the only language which they understood. Reinke, immediately sensing that the Lord was opening a new mission door to him, asked them to come to his church in two weeks, when he would preach to them in the sign language.

Although Reinke had a very large metropolitan congregation, he wrote a sermon and with the help of a trained deaf-mute learned the necessary signs to preach it in the language of the deaf-mutes. And two weeks later, on March 4, 1894, as he had promised, he preached the sermon in the sign language to a group of 16 deaf-mutes in his church.

The news of this venture spread, and in a short time deaf-mutes in other cities requested Reinke to conduct services for them. Soon Reinke was preaching in the sign language in Cincinnati, Louisville, Fort Wayne, Monroe, Elkhart, Peoria, Lincoln, Galesburg, Sheboygan, St. Louis, and in Milwaukee.

In 1896 he memorialized Synod to take over his mission among the deaf, since he no longer could do the work alone. He said among other things: "It is estimated that 40,000 deaf-mutes live in our country, of whom 300 are in St. Louis, 1,000 in Chicago, and 240 in Milwaukee. The majority of these people live without receiving any spiritual attention."

Synod at once resolved to place the mission among the deaf under its auspices and appointed a commission of five men for this purpose, one of the members being Pastor A. Reinke. The same year (1896) two candidates of theology were called into this new mission field, H. A. Bentrup for Louisville, Kentucky, and Tr. Wangerin for Milwaukee. In 1897 the First Evangelical Lutheran Deaf-Mute Congregation of Our Savior of Chicago, the first organized deaf-mute congregation in the Missouri Synod, numbering 65 souls and 32 communicants, called Candidate Arthur R. Reinke as its pastor.

In 1897 Synod had three missionaries to the deaf, who were preaching in the sign language at 14 places to an average attendance of 300.

TRANSOCEANIC RELATIONS

After the Saxon emigration of 1838 the state of religious affairs in Saxony continued to be bad. In the early forties of the last century a group of pious and devout laymen of Dresden organized the Evangelical Lutheran Society for Home and Inner Missions for the purpose of ministering to the sick and needy, not only materially, but also spiritually. To do this work properly, the society met at regular intervals for its own edification and growth in the knowledge of Lutheran doctrine.

Through Walther's visit to Germany in 1860 members of this society became acquainted with the Missouri Synod publications *Der Lutheraner* and *Lehre und Wehre,* which they read avidly. After Pastor Brunn opened his preparatory institution in 1861, he traveled to Dresden regularly and used the opportunity to further these brethren in Christian knowledge. The society supported Brunn's work and was diligent in spreading his periodical *Evangelisch-Lutherische Kirche und Mission.*

In an endeavor to confess the truth, this society in 1864 resolved to distribute tracts on religious subjects, being moved to do this also by the spirit of indifference and unionism prevalent in the Church.

On March 31, 1868, a group within the society organized the *Lutheraner-Verein* (Lutheran Society) for the specific purpose of spreading Lutheran literature.

The society soon attracted the attention of other people and in 1868 was joined by like-minded men in Zwickau and

STRENGTHENING THE STAKES (1872 - 1897)

in Planitz, who in turn organized similar societies in their home territory.

When in 1868 the abolition of the confessional oath and the substitution of an ambiguous oath was agitated in Saxony, the society protested vigorously; when in 1871 the change was effected, some of the members of the society in Dresden, Zwickau, and Planitz withdrew from the State Church ("it being no longer Lutheran") and formed independent congregations, calling themselves the Independent Evangelical Lutheran Church in Saxony.

When they appealed to Professor Walther for a pastor, he recommended Pastor H. Ruhland of Pleasant Ridge, Illinois. Ruhland arrived in Dresden on April 5, 1872, and was installed in the Dresden congregation in the presence of the elders of the congregation of Planitz on April 14 by Pastor J. Hein, who in 1853 had left the State Church and was now ministering to a "free" church at Wiesbaden. In 1873 Ruhland transferred to the congregation at Planitz, the Rev. E. Lenk becoming pastor of the Dresden congregation.

The testimony of Ruhland and Brunn bore much fruit. Other pastors and congregations joined them. In 1876 a preliminary meeting was held by the pastors and delegates for the purpose of organizing a synod. The draft was placed before the congregations in Nassau (Pastors Brunn and Hein) and five congregations in Saxony, and on November 6, 1876, the Synod of the Evangelical Lutheran Free Church of Saxony and Other States was organized. At its meeting at Planitz in 1877 there were present nine pastors (among them Pastor Geo. Stoeckhardt), one teacher, and six lay delegates. Through its official organ, *Die Ev.-Luth. Freikirche*, together with many tracts and books, which were distributed through *Colporteure*, the Saxon Free Church helped to spread the Gospel truth in Germany.

From its beginning the Saxon Free Church was in close relation with the Missouri Synod. Its greatest gift to our

Church was the scholarly Geo. Stoeckhardt, who came to St. Louis in 1878 as pastor of Holy Cross Church. In 1887 he was called as Professor of Old and New Testament interpretation at Concordia Seminary. The Free Church of Hermannsburg joined the Saxon brethren in 1896.

Teacher Ernst Rabe of Altenburg, Saxony, came to London in November, 1892. He accepted a position at the school of the Marienkirche on the condition that he need not become a member of the congregation, whose doctrinal position he could not endorse. At a restaurant he made the acquaintance of several members of the German-speaking division of the Y. M. C. A. Later he met with these young men for religious discussions, using the Gospel sermons of Walther for this purpose. In 1895 several of the group severed connections with the Y. M. C. A. because of religious convictions.

Rabe followed a call as teacher of the Saxon Free Church school at Planitz in 1894. From here he advised his friends in London to request a pastor from the Missouri Synod. The request was sent to Prof. Ludwig Fuerbringer, with whose name and doctrinal position the Londoners were familiar through the reading of *Der Lutheraner*. Professor Fuerbringer, after due inquiry, gave full support to the petition, and the Delegate Synod, in 1896, resolved to send a candidate to London, placing the matter into the hands of the Board for Home Missions. Candidate F. W. Schulze was given the call. Schulze preached his first sermon in London on August 30, 1896, and on December 5 of the same year he organized Immanuel Evangelical Lutheran Church of the Unaltered Augsburg Confession.

In November, 1838, Pastor August Ludwig Kavel landed at Pt. Adelaide, Australia, with his congregation. He had emigrated from Prussia in order to escape the intolerable religious oppression caused by his refusal to join the royally established union of Lutheran and Reformed Churches.

Other pastors and congregations followed; for instance, in 1841 Pastor G. D. Fritsche of Hamburg. The pastors and congregations united in a synod, which, however, was soon disrupted because of the chiliastic doctrines of Kavel. Fritsche became the leader of those contending for the truth.

Connection with Missouri was established in 1875 when President E. Homann, a reader of *Lehre und Wehre*, corresponded with Professor Walther, seeking his advice and counsel. A further step towards establishing fraternal relations was made in 1881 when at the request of the Australian brethren Candidate Caspar Dorsch, a St. Louis graduate, accepted a call as pastor of the congregation at Adelaide. Other candidates followed him, and Australian students came to Synod's institutions to prepare for the ministry in their native country. In 1891 a tract of land was purchased, and suitable buildings were erected at Murtoa for a college and seminary, to which J. Kunstmann, a graduate of St. Louis, went as professor in 1894.

THE SYNOD (ENGLISH) OF MISSOURI AND OTHER STATES

The original name of the Missouri Synod was *Die Deutsche Evangelisch-Lutherische Synode von Missouri, Ohio und andern Staaten*. The constitution provided for the exclusive use of the German language at the conventions of the Synod, making an exception in favor of such guests only as could not use the German language. The emphasis on the German language was quite natural. The founders of Synod, both clergy and lay members, with few exceptions had been born in Germany, had received their religious training in the German language, and, when they came to America, lived in German communities. The missionaries had to minister first of all to the members of the household of faith, and since there was a constant lack of workers, no attention could be given to the mission opportunities available through the medium of the English language. Besides, what the fathers saw and heard of the Lutheranism proclaimed in the English language was of such a nature as to fill them with suspicion and aversion.

The first English sermon by a member of the Missouri Synod was preached by Candidate Brohm in 1841 in Perry County. After the organization of the Missouri Synod we read of an English confirmation by Pastor G. Schaller of a lady in Baltimore who had received most of her religious instruction from Wyneken. In 1855 *Der Lutheraner* urged the younger generation in particular to become familiar with the English language for the sake of the Church and their English-speaking neighbors. The program of the Altenburg college and the Fort Wayne institution included a course in English. Already in 1852 Synod discussed the project of an English academy in Fort Wayne. About the same time four members of St. Paul's in Baltimore requested a release from the congregation to establish an English church. Not satisfied with the answer of the congregation, they organized St. Peter's in November, 1856. It was served by Pastor F. A. Schmidt until 1861. It disbanded in 1865 and was revived in 1875, when it became the mother of the Ohio Synod congregations in and around Baltimore. The organizing of this congregation was much misunderstood. The matter was brought before Synod in 1857, and a committee consisting of Professor Walther and Pastor Schwan was elected to go to Baltimore to compose the differences. At this convention Synod declared: "We account it our sacred duty to found English congregations as soon as it has become manifest that for the organization of a congregation there is a sufficient number of such as understand English better than German."

Professor Walther in particular was eager to promote English work. In 1859 he had Dr. S. L. Harkey of the Illinois State University of Springfield, Illinois, come to St. Louis for the purpose of conducting an English Lutheran service.

He rented a hall and announced the service in all German and English newspapers in the city. He called a meeting of those interested in establishing an English Lutheran congregation, but not enough people were interested. There were no hymnals, and the matter was dropped for the time being. His interest, however, continued, and in letters he urged Professor Crull to begin translating German hymns into the English language. At the Jubilee Synod in 1872 Pastor Theo. Brohm stressed the importance of using the English language in the work of our Church.

At the organization of the Synodical Conference Professor Loy presented theses on the work of our Church in the English language. Since the Ohio Synod conducted its services, to a large extent, in the English language, the Missouri pastors referred members who could no longer profit by the German services to Ohio Synod pastors.

The same year in which the Synodical Conference was organized witnessed the organization of the English Evangelical Lutheran Conference of Missouri at Gravelton, Wayne Co., Missouri. Members of the Tennessee and Holston Synods had migrated to Missouri before the coming of the Saxons. Eventually they were served by pastors of their synod. It was only natural that these men should seek closer union with the Missouri Synod, since for years it had been sending delegates to their mother synod in Tennessee. Invited by them, Professor Walther and Prof. F. A. Schmidt attended the meeting at Gravelton (1872). There were present "from the Tennessee Synod the Rev. Polycarp C. Henkel, Rev. Jonathan R. Moser, and six delegates; from the Holston Synod, Rev. Andrew Rader and three delegates. The Missouri Synod was represented by Professor Walther and the Rev. Ch. S. Kleppisch; the Norwegian Synod by Prof. F. A. Schmidt."[2] Besides the doctrinal discussion, led by Walther on the topic of the Holy Scriptures, "with a view of ascertaining, as well as giving expression to, our perfect

unity in the faith," the following matters were discussed:
1. What can we do for our scattered English Lutherans in the West, especially in regard to procuring faithful ministers for them? 2. The propriety or impropriety of forming some kind of organization among the English Lutherans of the West. 3. The establishment of parochial schools.

To these discussions the secretary, Prof. F. A. Schmidt, appends the note: "These three items as well as sundry other doctrinal and practical questions were discussed in private conferences at the residence of Rev. Moser, the public conferences being totally engaged with the discussion of the theses. It not having been made the duty of the secretary to take notes of these more free and social discussions, no official minutes concerning them can be published. Suffice it to say that the principles involved and the most profitable way of carrying them out were thoroughly discussed, and a firm and energetic purpose was formed to carry on the work of the Church in full earnest. May the Lord bless our endeavors." [3] During the sessions of the conference four divine services were held, Professor Walther preaching German; Professor Schmidt, Pastor Ch. S. Kleppisch, and Pastor A. Rader, English. A draft of a constitution was read and sanctioned and was to be submitted to the congregations and reported upon at the next meeting. The name adopted was "The English Evangelical Lutheran Conference of Missouri."

The little conference, consisting of only three pastors, each with a small congregation, managed under God's blessing not only to exist, but to grow, slowly indeed, but steadily. In 1879 it numbered seven pastors and seven congregations, one of them at Springdale, Arkansas.

An attempt to join the Synodical Conference in 1878 failed, the Synodical Conference recommending that the conference seek to unite with the Western District of the Missouri Synod. Delegates representing the Western District attended the meeting of the conference in 1879. They

STRENGTHENING THE STAKES (1872 - 1897)

met with the committee of the English Lutheran Conference appointed to confer regarding union with the Western District. The committee reported: "We, your committee, appointed to confer with the brethren of the Western District of the Missouri Synod concerning the subject of our union with the body, learned 1. That, as our conference was not represented in their last convention, no steps could be taken at that time toward a closer union with that body; 2. We consider it best for the cause of Christ among the English people for our conference to remain a separate organization; 3. We advise our conference to take steps now toward a closer union with said Western District and to that end appoint a delegate to represent us at the next convention of the same; 4. We kindly request the Western District to send a delegate to the future meetings of our conference, and, if agreeable with our congregations, we desire such delegates to become visitors to all our congregations convenient to the place of the meeting of the conference." [4]

Pastor A. Baepler of Mobile, Alabama, had been called by the Western District as English missionary in 1881. He was installed on March 26, 1882, at Frohna, Missouri, by Pastor C. L. Janzow. *The Lutheran Witness* stated on June 7, 1882: "The Western District of the Missouri Synod some time ago passed a resolution to aid the work among the English Lutherans in southern Missouri, Kansas, and Arkansas. The brethren of the English Conference lacked not only the funds to engage in this work, as they desired, but were restrained from it also by their pastoral labors. They, therefore, petitioned our Synod to make the necessary arrangements. Synod appointed a committee to take the matter in hand. The committee succeeded in securing the services of the Rev. Andrew Baepler of Mobile, Alabama, to take charge of the blessed work in this important field. After Easter, 1882, Rev. Baepler visited the several congregations constituting the English Conference of Missouri, the trip taking him through southern Missouri, southeastern Kansas, and northwest Arkansas."

In 1885 Candidate A. W. Meyer was called to Emmanuel, and in 1886 Candidate Wm. Dallmann to St. Paul's, both in Webster County, Missouri. Pastor C. L. Janzow of St. Louis was elected Visitor, and the Western District promised to pay all missionary expenses. The thirteenth convention of the English Conference, in 1886, resolved to join the German Missouri Synod as a District, but that body in 1887 advised the conference to organize as an independent English Synod. However, in 1887, the German Missouri Synod did take over the English work begun by the Western District, the Board being Pastor C. L. Janzow, Prof. M. Guenther, and Mr. C. F. Lange.

After the rupture in the Synodical Conference there remained in the East only one English congregation true to the old platform, but now without synodical affiliation, the old Coyner's Congregation, at Coyner's Store in Augusta County, Virginia, F. Kuegele, pastor. Prompted by the desire for a synodical home, it sent the following petition to the Synodical Conference, convening at Cleveland in 1884: "We, the Evangelical Lutheran Coyner's Congregation would submit the following to your consideration: In consequence of the late rupture in the Synodical Conference we are at present without synodical connection. This is not because we are not in agreement with the doctrine confessed by your venerable body nor because of a desire to stand independent, but because there is no synod in the boundary of the Synodical Conference making use of our language, and we do not see what advantage it would be for us to belong to a synod whose language we do not understand. We, therefore, submit to your consideration, whether the time has not come for the organizing of an English Synod or district synod, whichever might appear most advisable, within the limits of your body." [5] The Synodical Conference resolved "that the time has not yet come to proceed to the founding of an English Synod because of the lack both of English pastors and congregations." The petitioners, however, were encouraged to continue their efforts.

A few years later Pastor Kuegele's congregation corresponded with the English Evangelical Lutheran Conference of Missouri, and how the proposition was received is evident from the resolutions recorded in its minutes of 1886: "We hail with joy the idea of forming into one synodical body all genuine English Lutherans within bounds of the Synodical Conference." The congregation at Coyner's Store, Virginia, likewise appealed to the convention of the Missouri Synod at Fort Wayne in 1887 for permission to form an English District of the Missouri Synod, but the petition was denied, as already stated. The German Missouri Synod declared that it would be ready to aid the English work as far as its means would allow.

In the same year, 1887, an English mission was started in Baltimore, and English preaching was begun in New Orleans by Pastor T. Huegli. Encouraged by the report of the Missouri Synod, the English Conference appointed Pastors A. W. Meyer and Wm. Dallmann, the latter having gone to Baltimore in 1888, to draft a constitution for a synod. This draft, endorsed by Pastor Kuegele, appeared in the *Lutheran Witness* of August 7, 1888.

On October 18, 1888, the pastors with their delegates interested in the organizing of an English Lutheran confessional synod met at Bethlehem Lutheran Church, St. Louis, Missouri. An opening sermon was preached by Pastor Kuegele on Ps. 20:5. Pastor C. L. Janzow, chairman of the Board for English Missions of the Missouri Synod, was elected to preside over the preliminary discussions. On October 22 the organization was effected and the constitution signed. The following congregations united: Coyner's Congregation, Augusta County, Virginia; Immanuel Mission, Baltimore,

Maryland; Immanuel and St. Paul's, Webster County, Missouri; Zion, Gravelton, Missouri; St. James, Barton County, Missouri; St. Peter's, Neutral, Kansas; Salem, Springdale, Arkansas. The pastors signing were A. S. Bartholomew, Springdale, Arkansas, W. Dallmann, Baltimore, Maryland; R. L. Goodmann, Milford, Missouri; H. S. Knabenschuh, Springfield, Illinois; F. Kroeger, Pendleton County, West Virginia; F. Kuegele, Augusta County, Virginia; A. W. Meyer, Rader, Missouri; C. F. W. Meyer and A. Rader, Marshfield, Missouri; R. E. Rader, Springdale, Missouri. Pastor T. Huegli New Orleans, Louisiana, was prevented from attending but was received at his request. The first president was Pastor F. Kuegele.

The name adopted by the new body was "The General English Evangelical Lutheran Conference of Missouri and Other States," but in 1890 the name was changed to "The English Evangelical Lutheran Synod of Missouri and Other States."

Two valuable gifts were given to the synod at its first convention. *The Lutheran Witness*, then in its seventh volume, was presented by its editor, Pastor C. A. Frank of Zanesville, Ohio, and was made the official organ of the body. *The Lutheran Witness* had been started by the Cleveland Pastoral Conference in 1882, at the time of the Predestinarian Controversy. Its purpose was to supply English readers with an orthodox English Lutheran periodical. The first number was dated May 21, 1882. When the Cleveland Conference was no longer willing to support the paper financially, Pastor Frank assumed all responsibility and risk. Through his energy and tact *The Lutheran Witness* had become a well-established paper.

The other gift was a manuscript for an English Lutheran hymnal, compiled by Prof. A. Crull and containing more than 200 hymns. The first edition of this book was published in 1889.

Pastors Dallmann and Kuegele, together with Mr. Philip C. Treide, were elected the Publication Board.

The organization of this synod, under God's blessing, caused the rapid spread of English mission work in the Synodical Conference. In quick succession missions sprang up in St. Paul, St. Louis, Buffalo, Albany, Chicago, Pittsburgh, Fort Wayne, Milwaukee, and at other places. When the English Synod met for its second convention at St. Louis (1890), it had the pleasure of meeting in Grace English Lutheran Church.

At the close of 1891 the Board of Trustees of Conover, North Carolina, offered its institution through Pastor Kuegele to the English Synod. Pastors Dallmann and Kuegele investigated the proposition in December, 1891. "The institution did not need money, but teachers." The offer was provisionally accepted, and Pastor W. H. T. Dau of Memphis, Tennessee, was called to the presidency of the college in 1892. Candidate Geo. Romoser in 1892 and Candidate L. Buchheimer in 1893 joined the faculty. The procedure was ratified by the English Synod at its convention in Chicago, 1893. The college at Conover was founded by Pastor P. C. Henkel in 1877. It belonged to an association, and for several years the school had been under the fostering care of the Tennessee Synod, of which Henkel was a member. In 1896 Pastors Geo. Luecke and C. A. Weiss joined the Conover staff of teachers.

The hope that doctrinal agreement could be reached with the Tennessee Synod failed, but several pastors in and around Conover affiliated with the English Synod.

In 1893 Mr. J. P. Baden of Winfield, Kansas, appropriated $50,000 toward the establishing of a college in the West. The school was located at Winfield and built in 1893. When the English Synod met at Chicago in 1893, the college was offered to it as "St. John's English Lutheran College." Synod accepted the institution and called Pastor Henry Sieck, Candidate J. H. Stoeppelwerth (1893), Prof. Chas. Scaer (1894), and Pastor L. Steiner (1895) as faculty. In 1895 Pastor A. W. Meyer assumed the presidency of the institution.

In 1890 Pastor Dallmann became editor of *The Lutheran Witness*. The Publication Board got out Dallmann's *Ten Commandments*, and numerous *Lutheran Witness* tracts. The business of the Publication Board was transferred in 1895 to the American Lutheran Publication Board at Chicago. In 1897 it was moved to Pittsburgh, with Pastor H. B. Hemmeter as chairman. A *Sunday-School Hymnal* was prepared by Pastor Dallmann, Dr. E. Miller, and Mr. Fred Miller, all of Baltimore, and a hymnbook, music and word edition, by Pastors Dallmann, Morhart, Hemmeter, Kaiser, Dr. E. Miller, and Mr. Fred Miller.

THE PREDESTINARIAN CONTROVERSY

The organization of the Synodical Conference in 1872 was the occasion of great joy among the confessional Lutheran synods in America. Although the Conference was not an organic union of the constituent groups, hopes were cherished that eventually synodical lines would be dropped and one united Lutheran Church established composed of State synods.

As evidence of existing fraternal relations the Ohio Synod on January 28, 1878, conferred upon Walther the title of Doctor of Divinity. In the same year Missouri in convention assembled proffered the chair of English theology at the St. Louis seminary to Dr. M. Loy, professor at Columbus, Ohio (Ohio Synod). Loy, however, did not accept the call. Pastor C. A. Frank of the Missouri Synod was a professor at the Ohio seminary (1878).

Before a decade had passed, after the organizing of the Synodical Conference, all hopes of achieving a large united Evangelical Lutheran Church in North America were shattered through the Predestinarian Controversy.

This controversy was begun by Prof. F. A. Schmidt of the Norwegian Seminary at Madison, Wisconsin. Schmidt, a German by birth, was reared in St. Louis and was confirmed by Walther. After his graduation from the seminary (St. Louis, 1857), he held pastorates in the Missouri Synod at Eden, New York, and at Baltimore, Maryland. Having mastered the Norwegian language, he was called as teacher at the Norwegian Luther College, Halfway Creek, Wisconsin (1861). When the Norwegian Synod again established a Norwegian chair at St. Louis, Schmidt was appointed to the position. In 1876 he was transferred to the Norwegian Seminary at Madison, Wisconsin.

Schmidt had given every token of being in harmony with the doctrinal position of the Missouri Synod. He was a member of the St. Louis faculty when Walther, in 1872, refuted the charges of Crypto-Calvinism made against him by Dr. G. Fritschel of the Iowa Synod. In the foreword of *Lehre und Wehre* of 1874 Schmidt rejected Fritschel's theory of human co-operation in the process of man's conversion. When Missouri was contemplating calling an understudy for Walther and a professor for the English chair of theology at St. Louis, Schmidt indicated his willingness to serve as Walther's colleague on a card addressed to Pastor Wunder (May 7, 1878).[6]

For a number of years Walther had been reading essays before the conventions of the Western District of the Missouri Synod on the general topic: "The Doctrine of the Lutheran Church Alone Gives All Glory to God — an Irrefutable Proof That Its Doctrine Is the Only True Doctrine." At the Altenburg, Missouri, convention, 1877, he discussed the doctrine of predestination on the basis of the Formula of Concord. The third thesis reads: "The Lutheran Church teaches that it is false and wrong to teach that not the mercy of God and the most holy merit of Christ alone, but that also in us there is a cause of the election of God, for the sake of which God has elected us unto eternal life." In elaborating this thesis, Walther declared: "God foresaw nothing, absolutely nothing, in those whom He resolved to save which might be worthy of salvation, and even if it be admitted that He foresaw some good in them, this, nevertheless, could not have determined Him to elect them for that reason, for, as the Scriptures teach, all good in man originates in Him." [7] At the same time Walther rejected the unfortunate terminology of some of the Lutheran theologians of the 17th century that God elected "in view of faith," that is, that God foresaw that a person would believe in Christ and for that reason elected him to salvation.

It was this discussion and these statements that precipitated the controversy. The *Proceedings* of the Western District, containing Walther's essay, were on the market in December, 1877, and in the convention of the Synodical Conference in 1878 official approval of the doctrinal contents of the Western District Report was given.

Schmidt, on January 2, 1879, presented to Walther his objections to the Report of 1877, stating at the same time: "I can no longer go with you. . . . I dare no longer keep silence." To Walther's answer of February 8, Schmidt replied: "Your silence indeed pained me very much, not because I thought I had therewith received a testimony of heterodoxy — that I received sufficiently at the convention of the Delegate Synod." He notified President Schwan of his intention to make public his *dissensus* if conditions remained as they were. At the convention of the Northwestern District in 1879 he began to agitate against the Altenburg Report and was admonished by Schwan. Schwan furthermore invited Schmidt and his brother-in-law Allwardt to a conference with President Fuerbringer of Frankenmuth, Michigan, at the same time referring him to the agreement of the Synodical Conference which pledged its members to make no public attacks (in periodicals) against each other until every means of adjusting doctrinal differences had been exhausted. But all was in vain. In January, 1880, Schmidt published *Altes und Neues,* a monthly periodical, in which he violently attacked Dr. Walther.[8]

The Missourians thereupon appealed to Professor Lehmann, the President of the Synodical Conference, to call a special convention of that body in order to avert a public controversy. However, Professor Lehmann, already at that time sick unto death, thought he was not authorized to do so. To strengthen the Missourians, a special pastoral conference was convened by the Missouri Synod at Chicago,

W. F. Lehmann

L. Larsen

September 29 to October 5, 1880, in which the matter under controversy was discussed. It was attended by more than 500 pastors.

After Professor Lehmann's death, December 1, 1880, Prof L. Larsen, the Vice-President of the Synodical Conference, arranged a meeting of all the faculties of that body at Milwaukee, January 5, 1881. No agreement was reached, the Ohio representatives leaving after five days. A proposal to meet again within the year and in the meantime to refrain from carrying on the controversy publicly was rejected, Schmidt maintaining that he had been commanded by God to carry on this war. Walther thereupon replied: "Be it so! You want war; you shall have war!" The Ohio Synod publicly aligned itself with Schmidt in February, 1881, by publishing *The Columbus Theological Magazine*, containing articles on predestination opposing the doctrinal position of Missouri.

At the Delegate Convention of the Missouri Synod, May 11—21, 1881, Fort Wayne, thirteen theses on the doctrines in question, prepared by Dr. Walther, were adopted as the official statement of our Synod. The same convention gave the following instructions to its delegates to the Synodical Conference meeting: "You are not to sit together and deliberate about church affairs with such as have publicly decried us as Calvinists." "You recognize no synod as a member of the Synodical Conference which as a synod has accused us of Calvinism."

Immediately after this convention a pastoral conference of the Missouri pastors met at Fort Wayne, May 23—24, 1881, and it was resolved that our pastors no longer could recognize the opponents as co-workers in the Kingdom.

(The opposition party later organized at Blue Island, Illinois, as the "Evangelical Lutheran Conference" seceded from the Missouri Synod, and joined the Ohio Synod in 1882 as the Northwestern District.)

Professor Stellhorn, who was married to Walther's niece, left the Fort Wayne institution, after having attacked Walther and Missouri in *The Columbus Theological Magazine*, February, 1881, and accepted a call to the Ohio Synod seminary at Columbus, Ohio. The Ohio Synod, in September, 1881, resolved to withdraw from the Synodical Conference. Fourteen pastors, among them C. A. Frank, who had been a professor at Columbus, left the Ohio Synod to organize the Concordia Synod of Pennsylvania and Other States (1882), which later was absorbed by the Missouri Synod.

At the convention of the Synodical Conference, Chicago, October 4, 1881, Prof. F. A. Schmidt appeared as a lay delegate of a conference of the Norwegian Synod. The delegates of the Missouri, Wisconsin, and Minnesota Synods protested his being seated as a member of the convention so long as he did not admit that he, in person and without proper preliminary negotiations, had accused the Synodical Conference of Calvinism and broken into its congregations, causing divisions and offenses. Upon his failure to give a specific answer to the question whether he came as friend or foe of the conference, the assembled delegates refused him official recognition as a delegate. The Norwegian Synod was divided in its attitude towards Schmidt.

The controversy raged with unabated bitterness and violence from 1880 to 1884, but the effects of the conflict were felt for many decades. The leading protagonists for the Missouri Synod were Professor Walther, Prof. F. Pieper, and Pastor G. Stoeckhardt; for the opposition: Dr. Loy, Professors Schmidt and Stellhorn; Pastors Allwardt, Eirich, and Ernst; the last five were former members of the Missouri Synod.

The basic questions involved in the controversy were these: What moved God to elect certain people to salvation? Was it purely His grace and Christ's merit, or did God foresee some good in man that prompted Him to choose him? Is a Christian's faith the result of his election, or is his election the result of man's persevering faith? Can I as a Christian be certain of my salvation? The thirteen theses adopted by Synod in 1881 give the answer to these questions. They read:

1. "We believe, teach, and confess that God has loved the whole world from eternity, has created all men for salvation and none for damnation, and earnestly desires the salvation of all men; and hence we reject and condemn the contrary Calvinistic doctrine with all our heart.

2. "We believe, teach, and confess that the Son of God has come into the world for all men, has borne, and atoned for, the sins of all men, has perfectly redeemed all men,

none excepted; and hence we reject and condemn the contrary Calvinistic doctrine with all our heart.

3. "We believe, teach, and confess that God earnestly calls all men through the means of grace, that is, with the intention of bringing them through these means unto repentance and unto faith, and of preserving them therein to the end, and of thus finally saving them; wherefore God offers them through these means of grace the salvation purchased by Christ's atonement and the power of accepting this salvation by faith; and hence we reject and condemn the contrary Calvinistic doctrine with all our heart.

4. "We believe, teach, and confess that no man is lost because God with His grace passed him by or because He did not offer the grace or perseverance to him also and would not bestow it upon him; but that all men who are lost perish by their own fault, namely, on account of their unbelief and because they have obstinately resisted the Word and grace of God to the end — and hence we reject and condemn the contrary Calvinistic doctrine with all our heart.

5. "We believe, teach, and confess that the persons concerned in election, or predestination, are only true believers who believe to the end or who come to faith at the end of their lives; and hence we reject and condemn the error of Huber, that election is not particular, but universal, and concerns all men.

6. "We believe, teach, and confess that divine election is immutable and hence that not one of the elect can become reprobate and be lost, but that every one of the elect is surely saved; and hence we reject and condemn the contrary Huberian error with all our heart.

7. "We believe, teach, and confess that it is folly and dangerous to souls, leading either to fleshly security or to despair, when men attempt to become or to be certain of their election or their future salvation by searching out the

eternal mysterious decree of God; and hence with all our heart we reject and condemn the contrary doctrine as a piece of pernicious fanaticism.

8. "We believe, teach, and confess that a believing Christian should try from the revealed Word of God to become sure of his election; and hence with all our heart we reject and condemn the contrary papistic error that a man can become and be certain of his election only through a new and immediate revelation.

9. "We believe, teach, and confess 1) that election does not consist of the mere foreknowledge of God as to which men will be saved; 2) also that election is not the mere purpose of God to redeem and save mankind, for which reason it might be termed universal, embracing all men generally; 3) that election does not concern temporary believers (Luke 8:13); 4) that election is not the mere decree of God to save all those who believe to the end; and hence with all our heart we reject and condemn the contrary errors of the rationalists, Huberites, and Arminians.

10. "We believe, teach, and confess that the cause which moved God to choose the elect is His grace and the merit of Jesus Christ alone, and not any good thing God has foreseen in the elect, even the faith forseen of God in them, and hence we reject and condemn the contrary doctrines of the Pelagians, Semi-Pelagians, and synergists as blasphemous, frightful, subversive of the Gospel, and therefore of the entire Christian religion.

11. "We believe, teach, and confess that election is not the mere foresight or foreknowledge of the salvation of the elect, but also a cause of their salvation and what pertains thereto, and hence with all our heart we reject and condemn the contrary doctrine of the Arminians, the Socinians, and of all synergists.

12. "We believe, teach, and confess that God has 'still

kept secret and concealed much concerning this mystery and reserved it alone for His wisdom and knowledge,' which no man can or should search out, and hence we reject the attempt to penetrate into what is not revealed and to harmonize with reason those things that seem to contradict our reason, whether this is done in the Calvinistic or in the Pelagian-synergistic doctrine.

13. "We believe, teach, and confess that it is not only neither useless nor even dangerous, but rather necessary and wholesome, to present publicly also to our Christian people the mysterious doctrine of predestination as far as it is clearly revealed in God's Word, and hence we do not agree with those who think that this doctrine must either be entirely concealed or must be reserved only for the disputations of the learned."

One error seldom marches alone. It was only natural that when Schmidt and the Ohio Synod made faith the cause of man's election to salvation, they would err also in the doctrine of conversion. Said Schmidt: "When only one of two ungodly men is converted, there must have been a difference in their resistance; for if not, they would both have been converted."[9] Again: "I believe and teach now as before that it is not synergistic error, but a clear teaching of God's Word and our Lutheran Confession that 'salvation in a certain sense does not depend on God alone.'"[10] The same thought was expressed by the Ohio Synod in its *Zeitblaetter*, 1887, p. 325: "It is undeniable that in a certain respect conversion and final salvation are dependent upon man and not upon God alone." Hence, since the expression "elected in view of faith," which had been employed by the theologians in the 17th century without any thought of implying human co-operation in the process of conversion and which term some of our synodical fathers employed in articles dealing with election in *Lehre und Wehre*, was being used to cloak synergistic doctrines, Dr. Walther corrected said articles in

Lehre und Wehre, and the Missouri Synod has ever since avoided the formula "elected in view of faith" when treating of the doctrine of election.

From May, 1881, to December, 1882, Prof. R. Lange edited the *St. Louis Theological Monthly* in defense of the truth as confessed by the Missouri Synod.

GUARDING THE CHRISTIAN DAY SCHOOL

Christian day schools were always very much cherished by the Missouri Synod The Saxons as well as the Loehe men opened Christian day schools almost immediately upon their arrival in America. Whenever danger threatened these highly prized institutions, Synod was quick to take the necessary steps to protect them. In the late eighties and early nineties there was considerable agitation to make attendance at the public schools compulsory for all children. This was true especially in Illinois, where the Edwards Law was passed in 1889, and in Wisconsin, where a similar bill called the Bennett Law was introduced, both of which were directed against the existence of private elementary schools.

Synod took cognizance of these events at its convention in 1890, when it resolved the following:

1. "Whereas the Word of God, our rule of life, enjoins upon all Christian parents the duty of bringing up their children in the nurture and admonition of the Lord; therefore all Christians who educate their children in schools are in duty bound to entrust their children who are not yet confirmed in Christian truth to such schools only as secure the education of children in the nurture and admonition of the Lord, while at the same time it is with us self-understood that we are willing to make good citizens of our children, to the utmost of our ability, and that we endeavor to give them the best possible schooling in the use of the English language.

2. "Whereas in the non-religious public schools, wherever they are conducted in the sense of the non-religious state, not only Christian education is excluded, but also, as a rule, things not in harmony with the Word of God are by way of instruction and discipline inculcated in the children, and the spiritual life of Christian children is thus endangered and impaired; therefore we as Christians are in conscience bound to submit to no law of the State which is directed or may be used toward forcing our children into such public schools.

3. "In accordance with our daily prayer 'Thy Kingdom come' it is our duty to preserve and extend the orthodox Evangelical Lutheran Church in this our country, and we are, therefore, in conscience bound to combat each and every law which is directed or may be used to the detriment and damage of extending and perpetuating the Kingdom of God.

4. "Forasmuch as our Lord Jesus Christ says: 'My kingdom is not of this world' and 'Render unto Caesar the things which are Caesar's and unto God the things that are God's,' the separation of Church and State is for all times to be acknowledged as in accordance with the Word of God; and since God has in this country vouchsafed unto us the precious boon of religious liberty, we may not as faithful stewards approve of any legislation which tends toward a confusion of spiritual and secular affairs and endangers our religious liberty, and we most cordially approve of combating with legitimate means such laws as have to the detriment and damage of our parochial schools been enacted in the States of Wisconsin and Illinois during the past year, while on the other hand we, for the same reason, condemn all demands upon the public funds for the erection or maintenance of parochial schools.

5. "For all the reasons stated we must, as Lutheran Chris-

tians, grant our cordial approval to the fact that our brethren in the States of Wisconsin and Illinois have, whether in courts of law or at the ballot box, taken up and hitherto carried on the contest forced upon them against such laws, and we are, furthermore, determined to give most energetic opposition wherever in other States such or similar legislation may be attempted." [11]

CONCORDIA PUBLISHING HOUSE AND ITS PUBLICATIONS

The publication plant dedicated in 1870 soon became too small to handle the business of the rapidly growing Missouri Synod. In 1874, therefore, a new plant, 40 by 90 feet and four stories high, was erected on Indiana Avenue and Miami Street at a cost of $20,964.13. Mr. M. C. Barthel, who for several years had served as "Book Agent" for Synod, was made "General Agent" in charge of both the manufacturing and the selling end of the firm.

In 1877 a new periodical, *Das Magazin fuer Ev.-Luth. Homiletik*, a professional journal for pastors, was authorized by Synod. Prof. M. Guenther was the editor. In 1878 the concern became officially known as the "Concordia-Verlag." A two-story annex, 16 by 80 feet, fronting on Indiana Avenue, was added to the 1874 plant in 1882. In 1889 appeared *Kinder- und Jugendblatt*, a magazine for the Lutheran youth.

Martin Tirmenstein replaced Mr. Barthel as manager in 1891, and two years later a new building was erected on the corner of Jefferson and Miami Streets, at a cost of $23,570.00. It served chiefly as an office building.

The twenty-fifth anniversary of the Publishing House was observed with appropriate ceremonies in 1895. Pastor E. A. Brauer, the sole surviving member of the St. Louis faculty of 1870, preached the sermon. In the same year the *Concordia Magazine* was started, which in 1902 was changed to the *Young Lutherans' Magazine*. Finally, in 1897, an English professional theological magazine was founded under the editorship of Prof. A. L. Graebner. It was called *The Theological Quarterly*.

THE WALTHER LEAGUE

In 1893 the Walther League was organized at Buffalo, New York. Prior to this, Synod had no organized religious youth program. This is not to say that no youth work was done in our congregations or that pastors were indifferent to the spiritual needs of the young. Already at the convention of 1850 a resolution was passed authorizing Pastor J. F. Buenger to write an article describing the activities of Trinity Young Men's Society in St. Louis. This society had been organized on May 7, 1848, and in 1851 numbered more than 70 young men. By 1852 young men's societies were started in Chicago, New York, Cleveland, Cincinnati, Fort Wayne, and Monroe, Michigan. Young ladies' groups also were organized. In 1853 there were at least 23 young people's societies within the Missouri Synod. In 1856 M. P. Estel, president of the Trinity Young Men's Society of St. Louis, endeavored to organize the various groups into a federation, but was unsuccessful.

In 1891 Trinity Society of Buffalo, N. Y., issued a circular to all youth societies within Synod, encouraging the formation of a Synod-wide organization of young people. On receipt of sufficient responses, a convention was held at Buffalo, May 20—23, 1893, with representatives of twelve societies. Thus the Walther League came into being. The name chosen reflected the work of Walther among the young people, his society being the first to be organized in the congregations later forming the Missouri Synod. The first president was Herman Gahwe of Buffalo, followed by H. F. Landeck (1898—1900).

STRENGTHENING THE STAKES (1872 - 1897)

At the end of the first half century of Synod's existence nearly all of the fathers and founders had gone to their eternal rest. The first was Pastor E. G. W. Keyl. After serving the congregations at Frohna, Milwaukee, Baltimore, and Willshire, Ohio, he retired to Monroe, Michigan, where he died July 28, 1872. He was an indefatigable student of Luther, and of his books the best known is his *Katechismusauslegung*.

President Wyneken departed this life May 4, 1876. After being relieved of the presidency of Synod in 1864, he was called to Trinity Lutheran Church in Cleveland, Ohio. In October, 1875, he journeyed to San Francisco in quest of health, living with his son-in-law, Pastor J. M. Buehler. There he died. His body was brought East and lay in state in St. Louis and Fort Wayne, where memorial services were held, and in Cleveland, where it was buried. Walther characterized him in the following words: "He was a highly gifted man, a truly evangelical preacher; eloquent and mighty in the Scriptures; thoroughly experienced in the school of spiritual trials; a fearless witness to the pure and unadulterated truth and its valiant defender; a faithful watchman in his Church; a man without guile, whose life bore the marks of uprightness and singleness of mind; a foe of all falsehood and hypocrisy, a true Nathanael; in short, an upright Christian and faithful servant of the Lord, who, however, in true humility knew only his weakness and not his strength. To a host of pastors and laymen he was an example, to thousands a spiritual father, an apostle to a large section of America, beloved and honored by all who knew him, one of the finest men who graced our Lutheran Zion and one of her mightiest champions, whose name will never be forgotten, but will remain blessed as long as the Lutheran Church in our country remains true to her name." [12]

Theo. Jul. Brohm was called home while living with his son, Prof. Th. Brohm, at Addison, Illinois, on September 24,

1881. Having taught at the college at Altenburg, 1839 to 1843, he was pastor of Trinity Church, New York, 1843 to 1858, and after that in charge of Concordia District (later Holy Cross Church), St. Louis, until his retirement in 1878. While pastor in St. Louis, he taught in the seminary, chiefly Old Testament Interpretation. He was Vice-President of Synod 1851—1857; 1860—1864; 1869—1874.

On January 23, 1882, Pastor J. F. Buenger departed this life. After coming to America, he spent his entire life in St. Louis, first as Walther's assistant and later as pastor of the Immanuel District of the *Gesamtgemeinde*. He was interested especially in mission work — Home Missions, Negro Missions, Chinese Missions — and was particularly active in welfare work. He established the first Lutheran hospital in our Synod (St. Louis, 1858), and the Orphans' Home at Des Peres, Missouri (1865). He was contemplating the founding of a mental asylum and a foundling home when death overtook him.

Dr. William Sihler, after Loeber the Nestor of the Missouri Synod, fell asleep on October 27, 1885. After serving the Lutheran congregation at Pomeroy, Ohio, 1844—45, he spent the rest of his life as pastor of St. Paul's Church, Fort Wayne, Indiana. Through him it grew to be "a congregation thoroughly indoctrinated, full of living faith, and rich in good works." Sihler was "a zealous champion of confessional Lutheranism and a keen-eyed, warmhearted promoter of Synod's practical work, advocating these things with all the force of his sturdy Christian character and of his blunt and vigorous pen. He put a lasting mark upon Synod." [13]

While the 1887 Delegate Synod was in convention at Fort Wayne, news reached it of Dr. C. F. W. Walther's departure. Already at the synodical convention of the Western District in St. Louis, October 13—16, 1886, he was very feeble, but he finished his assigned essay and said: "Thus we are at the end with our theses which we have been discussing during the past thirteen years and in which we showed that our Lutheran Church in all of these doctrines gives all glory to God and never ascribes to any creature the glory which alone belongs to the great God. Now may the dear Lord grant that we not only rejoice at belonging to such a Church, but that we give Him all glory also through our faith, confession, life, suffering, and death. The motto of our life must be: *Soli Deo Gloria.*" Although physically very weak, he continued his lectures, celebrating his 75th birthday on October 25. On November 3, urged by the Board of Control, he discontinued his lectures. On January 16, 1887, he observed the fiftieth anniversary of his ordination. Synod had contemplated an appropriate celebration, but in view of his weakened condition, the day passed quietly. The student body gathered before his home to congratulate him with fitting hymns and words. Representatives of Synod, of the faculty, and of the St. Louis congregations waited on him. The local churches heard sermons appropriate to the occasion; letters and telegrams of felicitation came from every part of the country, and *Der Lutheraner* appeared in a jubilee issue. Growing weaker, he quietly and peacefully fell asleep on Saturday, May 7, 1887. At Synod's request, funeral services were postponed until May 17. On May 13 the body of Walther was carried by eight students to the seminary, where it lay in state until May 15, when it was taken to Trinity Church. At the funeral, President Schwan preached on the 90th Psalm, Professor Craemer of Concordia Seminary, Springfield, Illinois, on 2 Kings 2:12. At the grave, Pastor O. Hanser and Professor Larsen, representing the Norwegian Synod, spoke. Pastor H. Birkner conducted an English service on May 14 in the chapel of the seminary for the benefit of Walther's American friends. All synods belonging to the Synodical Conference were represented. Walther was buried in Concordia Cemetery. The congregations of St. Louis erected an imposing mausoleum over his and his wife's graves in 1892. This was in accordance with the last resolution of the *Gesamtgemeinde* (1889), which after Walther's death was divided into four individual congregations.

Friends and foes alike acclaimed the wonderful achievements wrought by Walther through the grace of God. He was the soul of the Missouri Synod during his lifetime, and his influence persisted throughout the next generation. Indeed, to this day streams of living waters continue to flow from his many articles and books. May his memory ever remain fresh!

Prof. Aug. F. Craemer of Springfield, Illinois, had also grown feeble and worn in His Master's service. An indefatigable worker, he at times had given twenty-three lectures a week besides performing the duties connected with the presidency of the seminary. During the vacation months he frequently managed to put in his time preparing emergency classes. Besides, he had a congregation at Chatham, Illinois. On April 8, 1891, he installed Prof. R. Pieper in the chapel of the new, but as yet undedicated, building which Synod, in 1890, had resolved to erect. He collapsed immediately after the ceremony and was carried to his home by students. Here he lingered until May 3, 1891, when his soul was released and borne to the heavenly mansions, a few weeks before his 79th birthday. Funeral services were conducted on Ascension Day, May 7. Prof. R. Pieper addressed the gathering in the chapel of the seminary; in the church service Prof. A. L. Graebner preached on Matt. 6:13, the last words spoken by the deceased, and his pastor, the Rev. G. Link, based his remarks on the words: "Er hat getragen Christi Joch, ist gestorben und lebet noch." He was buried in Oak Ridge Cemetery. His funeral was the largest that Springfield witnessed since the funeral of President Abraham Lincoln.

Pastor Ottomar Fuerbringer passed away on July 12, 1892. Together with Brohm, Buenger, and C. F. W. Walther he had founded Concordia College in Perry County, Missouri. In 1840 he became pastor at Venedy, Illinois. In 1851 he moved to Freistadt, Wisconsin, where he served this congregation and one at Kirchhayn. He was president of the Northern District from 1854 to 1872 and again from 1874 to 1882. In 1858 he became pastor of St. Lawrence Church, Frankenmuth, Michigan. During the Civil War he called together all the unmarried men in his parish and persuaded them voluntarily to fill the quota of men demanded by their country in order that fathers of families might be exempted. Dr. A. L. Graebner characterized him as "the profoundest thinker among the fathers of the Missouri Synod."

Johann Adam Ernst, one of the first two *Sendlinge* of Loehe, who came to America in 1842 and who was very active in the movement leading to the founding of our Synod, held pastorates at Marysville, Ohio, and Eden, New York. From Eden, New York, he served Lutherans living in Canada, eventually taking up his residence at Elmira, Ontario. He was the first President of the Canada District (1879). He died at Euclid, Ohio, January 20, 1895.

12

STEADILY FORWARD
1897-1922

*T*HE Missouri Synod in 1897 numbered 687,334 souls in 1,986 congregations and 683 preaching stations, ministered to by 1,564 pastors and professors. Twenty-five years later the figures had risen to 3,073 pastors (including retired ministers and pastors serving as field secretaries and professors) and 1,041,514 souls. Synod was represented in all the States of the Union except Arizona, Georgia, and South Carolina. Its missionaries had penetrated into the Province of Quebec, had established themselves in British Columbia, and were laboring in India, South America, and in China.

The tremendous growth of Synod necessitated a further division of the existing synodical Districts, and the following new Districts were organized:

The Oregon and Washington District (including Idaho), 1899. First President: H. A. C. Paul.

(The former California and Oregon District was now called the California and Nevada District.)

The Brazil District, 1904. First President: William Mahler.

The Texas District, 1906. First President: A. W. Kramer.

The Atlantic District, 1906. First President: E. C. Louis Schulze.

The South Dakota District, 1906. First President: A. F. Breihan.

The Northern Illinois District, 1907. First President: H. Engelbrecht.
The Central Illinois District, 1909. First President: F. Brand.
The Southern Illinois District, 1907. First President: F. W. Brockmann.
The North Dakota and Montana District, 1910. First President: T. Hinck.
The South Wisconsin District, 1916. First President: Ed. Albrecht.
The North Wisconsin District, 1916. First President: J. G. Schliepsiek.
The Colorado District, 1921. First President: O. Luessenhop.
The Alberta and British Columbia District, 1921. First President: Aug. J. Mueller.
The Manitoba and Saskatchewan District, 1922. First President: Paul Wiegner.
The Southern Nebraska District, 1922. First President: C. F. Brommer.
The Northern Nebraska District, 1922. First President: W. Harms.

Pastor H. C. Schwan, President of Synod since 1878, requested to be relieved of the office in 1899. In his farewell address he said: May the Lord keep Synod in the truth and give her courage to confess the truth at all times fearlessly." Synod voted the retiring President an annual pension of $1,000.00.

Francis Pieper, president of Concordia Seminary, St. Louis, was elected to the presidency of Synod. Thus, as in the days of Walther, one man again had to bear the burden and responsibilities of two important offices. Synod endeavored to adjust the duties of the new president in such a manner as would enable him to perform them efficiently without neglecting his work at the seminary. The burden, however, proved too great, and Dr. Pieper's health began to fail. Synod relieved him of the office of President of Synod in

H. C. Schwan

F. Pfotenhauer

1911, sent him to Europe for recovery, and chose Pastor Frederick Pfotenhauer of Hamburg, Minnesota, as his successor. President Pfotenhauer established his office in Chicago, which has since been the home of Synod's President.

A Board of Directors was created in 1917, which was made responsible for all business matters of Synod as well as for the supervision of its real estate. The Board of Directors replaced the General Board of Supervision, which Synod had appointed in 1905 and which was concerned only with the educational institutions of Synod. The first Board of Directors was composed of the President, the Secretary, and the Treasurer of Synod; Pastor W. Hagen, Detroit, Michigan; Benjamin Bosse, Evansville, Indiana; Henry Horst, Rock Island, Illinois; Fred. Pritzlaff, Milwaukee, Wisconsin.

Synod adopted a revised constitution in 1917, in which the word *German* was dropped from its name. Henceforth, Synod's name was "The Evangelical Lutheran Synod of Missouri, Ohio, and Other States."

To improve the collecting of the necessary funds to carry

on Synod's work, the so-called Budget System was introduced by the convention of 1917. Synod resolved in 1920 to employ a financial secretary, whose duty would be "to prepare the financial budget each year and give it proper publicity through our church periodicals and otherwise, so that each congregation of Synod is properly informed regarding the budget for the following year and to keep in touch with the various Districts, circuits, and congregations in such a manner as decided by the Board of Directors, under whose direction, supervision, and approval his work is to be performed." Mr. Theo. W. Eckhart was appointed to this office and continues to serve as Financial Secretary at this writing.

EDUCATIONAL INSTITUTIONS

The educational institutions of Synod were the subject of many and long discussions during this period. Attention was given to the opening of new colleges to meet the still increasing demand for pastors and teachers, the relocating of three of Synod's institutions, and the raising of the educational standards.

The St. Louis seminary suffered a severe loss in the deaths of Dr. A. L. Graebner (1904) and Dr. Geo. Stoeckhardt (1912). Dr. Graebner's successor was Pastor W. H. T. Dau; Dr. Stoeckhardt's, Prof. E. Pardieck. Prof. E. A. W. Krauss was added to the faculty in 1905. Pastor Theo. Graebner joined the teaching staff in 1913, Pastors J. T. Mueller, J. H. C. Fritz (as Dean), and M. S. Sommer in 1920. Prof. Wm. Arndt came in 1921, and Pastor W. A. Maier in 1922.

Because the number of students overtaxed the capacity of the beautiful and large building dedicated in 1883, a suitable annex was added in the years 1906—07. By 1920, however, and for some time previous to this, the seminary buildings were overcrowded, some 300 students living in quarters designed for 200. A large dwelling was being used to take care of the overflow. There were only three classrooms and many other untoward features. Wrote Dr. Fuerbringer (1920): "Our present buildings are, indeed, not in a condition that they would have to be condemned. The present location, however, is no longer suitable for a boarding school with a large number of students. Seventy years ago our seminary stood on the outskirts of St. Louis; today it is surrounded by many buildings in the midst of the city. Available building space can no longer be found. Within three blocks there are four different car lines, one of these passing directly in front of the seminary. The din and the noise of the large city and the continuous heavy traffic on the city streets very much interfere with the work of the professors and the students in the lecture room and with the work of the individual student at his desk; in fact, these disturbing factors very much annoy and distract. Close by there are business houses, and not far away a few factories. When the students leave the seminary buildings, they are out on the street. The present ground space is almost entirely occupied by the seminary buildings, and there is no free space upon which the students can take a little bodily exercise except a small space between the buildings, which is hardly worth mentioning. If additional buildings would be erected on the present site, several professors' dwellings would have to be torn down, and the new seminary buildings, erected on that ground, would be adjacent to a large school, which in the daytime is attended by several hundred children and at night is used by various societies. The objectionable features mentioned before would remain."[1]

At the Delegate Synod at Detroit, 1920, Synod unanimously voted (after only five minutes' discussion) one million dollars for a new Concordia Seminary at St. Louis. At the same time Mr. A. G. Brauer of St. Louis announced that the St. Louis congregations had gathered pledges to the amount of $75,000 for the purchase of a site. Building operations, however, were not begun until after 1923.

At the Springfield seminary Prof. J. S. Simon retired in 1904 and was replaced by Pastor Theo. Schlueter (1905). When Schlueter left in 1908, Pastor O. C. A. Boecler was called to fill the vacancy. President Pieper and Prof. J. Herzer resigned in 1914, their successors being Pastors R. Biedermann and Theo. Engelder. Professor Boecler, accepting a call into the ministry in 1918, was followed by Pastor R. C.

Craemer Hall, Springfield

Neitzel. Pastor C. J. Hoffmann was added to the faculty in 1921. President R. Biedermann passed to his eternal reward on March 8, 1921, and Pastor H. A. Klein was called to the presidency in 1922.

A new service building was erected in 1917 at a cost of $24,054.39, the Southern Illinois and Central Illinois Districts contributing $23,475.28 towards this amount. The curriculum of the institution was expanded to include educational subjects, enabling the graduates to pass State examinations for teachers.

The Normal School at Addison, Illinois, likewise added to

Addison Normal School

its faculty. President E. A. W. Krauss, accepting a call to the St. Louis seminary in 1905, received a successor in Theo. Brohm (1905—1913), who in turn was followed by Pastor W. C. Kohn (1913). Others who joined the faculty during this period were: Alb. Miller and F. H. Schmitt (1906), Ed. Koehler (1909), G. Eifrig (1909), M. Lochner (1912), E. H. Engelbrecht (1915), O. F. Rusch (1916), H. C. Gaertner (1921), A. Schmieding (1922).

The institution at Addison was the subject of a lengthy consideration at Synod's convention in 1911. The buildings had become dilapidated; the village lacked the amenities of the city. The Lutheran Education Society of Chicago offered a plot of 36 acres in one of the Chicago suburbs on which to build a new normal school. After the question of relocating the institution was debated for several days, Synod resolved by a very small majority vote to accept the offer of the Lutheran Education Society and to request the Northern Illinois District to apply the sum of $30,000 which had been collected for a new building at Addison to the new buildings to be erected at River Forest. Synod appropriated $100,000 for the new plant.

On November 12, 1912, ground was broken, and on December 15 the cornerstone was laid in the presence of 7,000 to 8,000 people. On October 12, 1913, some 40,000 members of Synod attended the dedication ceremonies of the new Teachers' College at River Forest. Three services were held simultaneously at different places on the campus. The speakers were Dr. F. Pieper and Prof. F. Bente; President Max Albrecht and Pastor Wm. Koepchen; President M. Luecke and President G. Weller. In 1914 fire destroyed the administration building, but it was rebuilt the following year through the generous gifts of the congregations of Synod.

At Fort Wayne, President J. Schmidt relinquished the presidency of the institution in 1903 and was succeeded by

Pastor M. Luecke of Springfield, Illinois. Military training was introduced in 1906. Members added to the staff of teachers were L. Dorn (1900); W. H. Kruse (1903); W. L. Moll (1904); J. G. Sohn (1912); Geo. V. Schick (1914); W. C. Burhop (1917); J. G. Kunstmann (1918); E. Schnedler (1920); Paul F. Bente (1920); M. H. Bertram (1920); W. A. Hansen (1921); M. Stoeppelwerth (1921); Geo. P. Schmidt (1921).

Teachers College, River Forest, Ill.

At the Milwaukee institution Pastor G. Christian Barth of St. Louis followed Max Albrecht as head of the school in 1921. Professors joining the faculty were C. Gaenssle (1904); A. E. Bergmann (1911); M. Graebner (1922).

The following men served our college at St. Paul as teachers: Dr. C. Abbetmeyer (1902); Dr. H. W. F. Wollaeger (1904); Wm. Moenkemoeller (1905); C. J. Heuer (1906); E. Lussky (1909); P. E. Kretzmann (1911); A. Schlueter (1916); S. C. Ylvisaker (1919); O. B. Overn (1920); L. Blankenbuehler (1921); F. Wahlers (1922).

The Normal School at Seward had a change in the presidency when Pastor F. C. W. Jesse succeeded President Weller in 1914. New members on the staff were G. Ritzmann (1902); F. Strieter (1903); H. B. Fehner (1906); Karl Haase (1906); Aug. Schuelke (1906); J. T. Link (1908); P. Reuter (1908); H. L. Hardt (1921).

Pastor A. Baepler joined the teaching staff at Concordia, Missouri, in 1899 and was followed by E. Pardieck (1902); H. Lobeck (1905); W. Schaller (1906); W. Arndt (1912);

Seward Teachers College

Ad. Haentzschel (1917); O. W. Wismar (1921); O. Krueger (1921).

Through the amalgamation of the English Missouri Synod with the German Synod the institution at Conover was added to Synod's system of ministerial schools. In 1899 Professor Dau was succeeded in the presidency by Prof. G. A. Romoser. Other members added to the staff were H. B. Hemmeter (1902—1905); Ad. Haentzschel (1907); C. O. Smith (1911); W. O. Bischoff (1912); M. H. Coyner (1913). Pastor H. B. Hemmeter returned to Conover in 1914 as president, which office he relinquished in 1918 to

Pastor O. W. Kreinheder. C. F. Fredericks joined the faculty in 1919.

Pastor M. Walker became a member of the faculty at Hawthorne (1902), but returned to the ministry in 1906, Prof. J. Schwoy being his successor. In 1907 L. Schmidtke and L. Heinrichsmeyer were added to the staff of teachers. At the convention of Synod in 1908 the Board of Control presented a memorial asking for a relocating of the whole school to Bronxville, 16 miles from the Grand Central Station in New York City. The conditions at Hawthorne were unfavorable for the development of the institution. Besides, repairs in the amount of $26,400 were necessary in order to keep the plant serviceable. The Lutheran Education Society offered Synod a plot of land, comprising 16 acres, at Bronxville, purchased for $57,000, and the brethren in the East promised further financial assistance provided the institution were built upon the offered tract. Synod accepted the offer of the Lutheran Education Society and appropriated $40,000 towards the erection of new buildings.

The college property at Hawthorne was sold in 1918, and until facilities were available at Bronxville, the classes were taught in classrooms of St. Matthew's and St. Luke's Churches, New York City. On November 29, 1909, the newly built institution at Bronxville was dedicated to the service of the Lord. The property was valued at $214,000.00, toward which Synod had contributed only $40,000. The following were called as professors: H. Kuehn (1913); Dr. J. N. H. Jahn (1914); G. A. Romoser (1915); O. Prokopy (1916); H. J. Rippe (1918); Theo. W. Hausmann (1919); E. C. Hassold (1921); H. C. Engelbrecht (1922). Professor Romoser followed Professor Feth in the presidency in 1918.

St. John's College, Winfield, Kansas, and Concordia College at Conover, N. C., the property of the English Synod, were given an annual grant of $3,000 in 1902. In spite of this, the English Synod in 1905 offered its institution at Winfield to our Synod, but Synod declined the offer, stating it had no need of an institution in that territory. In 1907 the English Synod again proffered the school to our Synod as a free gift. Synod accepted it in 1908, placing it under the fostering care of the Kansas District and appropriated $1,500 per annum toward its support. In 1910 Prof. I. J. Kloster was called to open the commercial school. Other instructors were M. Graebner (1910); J. W. Werling (1918); A. E. Kunzmann (1920); W. H. Wente (1922).

Already in 1903 the brethren living in Oregon and Washington were discussing the question of opening a preparatory college on the Pacific Coast. When informed that California was contemplating the same thing, they considered the matter jointly with their California brethren. Learning that California required an institution in its own territory, the District Conference of the Oregon and Washington District asked the President of Synod, Dr. F. Pieper, for advice. He said: "My personal opinion is that the Pacific Districts from the very start should plan to establish two schools. The distances are too great for one school only. The Districts will develop more quickly if each has its own college."

A canvass of the congregations revealed that a college should be opened, and so on September 10, 1905, F. W. J. Sylwester was inducted into his office as the first professor of the institution, in Trinity Church, Portland, Oregon. The school was opened on September 11 the same year. For two years the students were lodged in private homes, while classes were conducted in the basement of Trinity Church. A permanent home was provided for the college in a building dedicated on December 15, 1907. Candidate L. Blankenbuehler was called as the second professor in 1911, after having served as assistant professor for two years (1907 to 1909) prior to his graduation from St. Louis. The institution was offered to Synod in 1911, but Synod deemed it wiser only to pay the salaries of the teachers, while the Oregon and Washington District assumed the upkeep of the property. Pastor E. H. Brandt joined the faculty in 1921.

By 1904 the agitation for opening a college in California had crystallized sufficiently to be given into the hands of a committee for action. Synod in 1905 approved the proposal of the brethren on the Pacific Coast to establish an institution and pledged itself to underwrite the salaries of the faculty members provided the California and Nevada District furnished and maintained the physical plant. Concordia College in East Oakland was dedicated on July 15, 1906. For one year the institution was served by pastors until H. Jonas accepted the call as the first professor in May, 1907. Pastor Theo. Brohm of Detroit, Michigan, came to Oakland in 1909 as the second professor and first president. Pastor R. Eifert joined the faculty in 1918.

In Western Canada the question of having a Canadian preparatory school was discussed in Saskatchewan as early as 1912. Towards the end of the second decade of the current century the need of a native ministry was keenly felt by reason of the continuous turnover of missionaries. Accordingly, in 1919, Pastor W. A. Baepler was delegated by the Manitoba-Saskatchewan Pastoral and Laymen's Conference to attend a similar conference at Stony Plain, Alberta, with a view to obtaining the support of said conference for a memorial to Synod to open an institution in Western Canada. Due to the energetic efforts of Pastor (now Professor) A. M. Rehwinkel, the Alberta and British Columbia constituents joined the proposal of their neighboring brethren. Synod at Detroit, in 1920, resolved to open an institution in Western Canada, leaving the decision of its location to the Board of Directors. The Board of Directors chose Edmonton, Alberta. The institution was opened in rented quarters on October 31, 1921, Pastor A. H. Schwermann having been called as president. In 1922 Pastor A. M. Rehwinkel was added to the faculty.

Synod resolved in 1905 to add two classes to the college at Bronxville, Concordia, and St. Paul, thus making them Junior Colleges. Henceforth the graduates of these institutions would go directly to the seminary at St. Louis instead of completing their preparatory training either at Fort Wayne or at Milwaukee.

A General Board of Control was created in 1908, composed of Pastor C. F. Obermeyer, Mr. Benjamin Bosse, and Mr. F. G. Walker. The duties of the Board pertained chiefly to the physical plants of the institutions. An unusual number of overtures with reference to the curriculum having been submitted to the convention of 1917, Synod resolved to have the President appoint a Committee on Educational Survey, which was to make a complete survey of all of Synod's educational institutions with respect to the educational standards and the courses of instruction offered. The members of the Survey Committee were Pastors L. Hoelter, P. Roesener, F. Tresselt, W. Dallmann, and President C. F. Brommer.

MISSIONS

At the beginning of the third quarter of the century four workers were laboring in the mission fields of India: Naether, Mohn, Kellerbauer, and Freche. At the end of this period 27 missionaries (21 in the religious field, two in the educational, and four in the medical field) were serving 90 stations and out-stations. They were assisted by 225 native helpers, of whom 159 were either Lutherans or professed Christians. Synod was operating 67 day and night schools, 4,166 pupils, three boarding schools for girls, and three for boys. The mission numbered 2,695 baptized members, 661 communicant members, and 1,888 catechumens. Synod owned 15 bungalows, 28 churches, 25 pandals, 29 permanent schools, 35 houses for Indian workers, one hospital, and a missionary summer home and day school for missionary children at Kodaikanal. Institutes for the training of native workers were being operated at Ambur, Nagercoil, and at Trivandrum.

On February 13, 1904, the pioneer missionary Theo. Naether passed to his eternal rest. While serving members of his flock stricken with the bubonic plague, he was infected by the deadly disease. From a distance, in order not to expose them to infection, he spoke words of farewell to members of his congregation as well as to the heathen and thus entered into the joy of his Lord.

In 1907 a new field was opened 500 miles south of the northern field. Prompted by an appeal to our missionaries in behalf of an independent Christian congregation at Vadasari, near Nagercoil, by G. Jesudason, Secretary to the British Resident at Trivandrum, Missionary A. Huebener investigated the field and found a group of 140 people, some of them Christians and others willing to receive religious instruction. As soon as possible, Synod began to work in this southern field, finding many doors open. From Nagercoil, Missionary H. Nau in 1912 opened a new field among the Malayalams at Trivandrum.

Up to World War I the following missionaries had entered the mission field of India besides Theo. Naether, Franz Mohn, Geo. Kellerbauer, and R. Freche: Albert Huebener (1900); Geo. Naumann and F. Forster (1902); H. Nau (1905); Theo. Gutknecht (1907); G. Huebener (1909); F. R. Zucker (1910); Geo. Kuechle (1919); J. Harms, A. J. Lutz (1912); A. Ehlers, J. Williems, R. W. Goerss (1913); H. Stallmann (1911); H. Hamann and Eric Ludwig (1915).

World War I severely crippled our work in India. British war measures removed three missionaries (A. Huebener, Williems, and Stallmann) from their fields, prevented three from returning from a home furlough (Freche, Naumann, Harms), and barred new men from re-inforcing the depleted ranks. When on March 31, 1919, Missionary Ludwig was called home by God, only five men remained in the field: Zucker, Ehlers, Goerss, Hamann, and Lutz.

When finally the barriers caused by the war were removed, the work was resumed with renewed vigor. Kuechle and Harms returned to India, accompanied by Candidates P. Heckel and P. Kauffeld (1921), and in 1922 Candidate A. Fritze joined the ranks of missionaries. Others were L. Boriack, R. Jank, H. Levihn, G. Oberheu, Geo. Schroeder,

Bergheim, India

and Bernard Strasen. From Australia E. A. Noffke accepted a call to India. In 1921 G. Jesudason, the man instrumental in bringing our Church to the southern field, was ordained to the ministry and became the first native missionary serving a mission station.

In order to gain access to the heathen more readily and to overcome barriers of prejudice and suspicion, limited medical mission work was begun in 1913, when Miss Lula Ellermann, a registered nurse, opened a dispensary at Bargur. In 1921 she was joined by Miss A. Georgi and in the following year by Miss Etta Herold and Miss Angela Rehwinkel, and by a teacher, Miss Henrietta Ziegfeld. The same year Dr. Theodore Doederlein of Chicago volunteered to spend a few years in India to supervise the establishing of a hospital and the organizing of the medical mission field.

Midway between the northern and the southern mission fields a mountain retreat was erected at Kodaikanal in 1913 by the women and the ladies' aids of our Synod. This home serves the missionaries as a vacation resort during the hot periods of the year, and the school erected there is attended by the children of the missionaries. On March 10, 1922, Teacher Paul Bachmann sailed for India to become manager of the *Bergheim* and to serve the school as teacher.

Under date of September 2, 1917, President Pfotenhauer made the following announcement: "The China Mission, having been duly offered us by the Commission of the Evangelical Lutheran Society for Foreign Missions in China, has been taken over by the Missouri Synod and placed under the direction of the Foreign Mission Board. Pastor A. Rehwaldt, of the former Commission, has been added as nonresident member to our Foreign Mission Board. For the present the treasuries for missions in India and in China will be kept separate; as soon as possible, a member of our Board shall visit the field in China. The call issued by the former Commission to Cand. L. Meyer has been ratified by our Board, and Pastor Meyer is now in China." [2]

The mission in China was begun by Prof. E. L. Arndt of St. Paul, Minnesota. When he resigned his professorship in 1910, he became enthusiastic about opening a mission in China. He published two volumes of sermons, using the proceeds of the sales to raise funds for his China mission propaganda. Through mission letters he was able to organize a society, The Evangelical Lutheran Mission for China, at Gaylord, Minnesota, on May 1, 1912. This society chose central China as the place for initial Lutheran mission work and on July 14, 1912, commissioned Arndt as its first missionary.

Arndt arrived in China in 1913. He was then nearly 49 years old. Three months after his arrival in Hankow he preached his first Chinese sermon. The first Baptism was performed on March 29, 1914, and the first Communion administered on April 9 of the same year.

E. L. Arndt

The society sent out Erhard Riedel and wife in 1915. In 1917 Candidate L. Meyer was called. In the same year the society offered the mission to Synod, which accepted it.

The force of mission workers was augmented in 1920 by A. H. Gebhardt, H. Gihring, and Walter Arndt, who soon resigned in order to prepare as medical missionary, H. Bentrup, and L. Schwartzkopf. In 1921 Geo. Lillegard, a member of the Norwegian Synod and who had been in China before, entered the work. In the same year Herman Klein, Arno Scholz, Max Zschiegner, and H. W. Theiss sailed as missionaries for China. The first woman worker in the China mission was Miss Olive Gruen, who went over in 1921. By 1922 the missionaries had established three stations: Hankow, Ichang, Shinanfu. Arndt established a seminary at Hankow in 1922 for the training of native workers.

The statistics for 1922 show: 14 missionaries and one woman teacher; native helpers — nine evangelists and 42 teachers and other helpers; 11 chapels; 12 schools, also a seminary, higher primary and language schools. The mission comprised 239 communicant members, 381 baptized members, 132 catechumens, and 1,073 pupils. A plot of land had been bought at Kuling for a missionary retreat.

To expedite the Foreign Mission work, the Board for Foreign Missions, on instructions from Synod (1893), appointed a mission director. Prof. F. Zucker of Fort Wayne, a former missionary in India, filled the office 1894 to 1912, when he was succeeded by Pastor J. A. Friedrich of St. Charles, Missouri. Pastor Friedrich made an inspection trip of the India field in 1912. When he retired in 1915, Pastor R. Kretzschmar was appointed his successor until Synod in 1920 resolved to elect a director who would devote all his time to this office. Pastor F. Brand of Springfield, Illinois, Vice-President of Synod, was elected to this position in 1920 and established his office in St. Louis.

F. Brand

Since 1899 the Missouri Synod had a Board for Foreign Tongue Missions, which supervised mission work among such Lutherans as could not be ministered to through the medium of the German or the English language.

The first of these missions was begun among the Letts and the Esthonians by Pastor A. Biewend in Boston in 1892. Two years later, Pastor H. Rebane, who had arrived in America as a candidate for the ministry, continued the work of Biewend and soon organized small congregations of his fellow nationals in Newport, Philadelphia, and Baltimore. In 1897 he made his first missionary journey, which took him to Cleveland, Chicago, South Dakota, and Saskatchewan, Canada. At all places visited he was able to establish preaching stations and to arrange for reading services. He received invitations from Letts and Esthonians living in Ontario, Minnesota, North Dakota, Oregon, and San Francisco.

In 1899 Synod assumed charge of this mission and called Pastor J. Sillak (1901) to take over the western field. Pastor J. Ballod entered the work in 1907 and organized the Pacific territory. In 1910 Pastor E. Yurawitz joined the ranks of missionaries, making Chicago his headquarters.

The work among the Letts and the Esthonians was attended by great and many difficulties. In 1922 there were only two missionaries, Pastor C. F. Buchroth in Boston and Pastor Alb. Zetzer in Chicago, serving 13 congregations and preaching stations, totaling 766 souls.

A second mission among foreign-tongue Lutherans was the Lithuanian mission, taken over by Synod in 1908. Work among these people was begun by H. S. Brustat, who already as a student at Concordia Seminary, Springfield, Illinois, made extended journeys to serve his countrymen. After his graduation in 1903, he ministered to Lithuanians in Boston, Brooklyn, Philadelphia, Baltimore, and Pittsburgh. In 1894 the Eastern District took this mission under its wings, calling Pastor Peter Drignat for Philadelphia, Scranton, Pennsylvania, and Baltimore, thereby enabling Brustat to make Brooklyn his center of activity. Pastor J. J. D. Razokas was added to the Lithuanian workers in 1912, followed by Pastor Geo. Matzat (1914), Pastor E. Kories (1915), and by Pastor G. Jurksaitis (1919), the latter translating the synodical Catechism into the Lithuanian language. In 1922 four pastors were serving eight Lithuanian congregations, with more than 1,000 souls and seven preaching stations.

In 1908 Synod took control of the mission work among the

Polish Lutherans. This work was begun by Pastor F. Sattelmeier and placed under the auspices of the Eastern District in 1894. In 1894 Pastor C. Mikulski was called as missionary among his fellow nationals, and soon he had established preaching stations at Baltimore, New York, Philadelphia, Trenton, Buffalo, Pittsburgh, Detroit, and Saginaw, Michigan. In 1911 Pastor Sattelmeier and Candidate B. Hein entered the work, the latter serving three groups in Western Canada. Other workers followed, so that in 1922 it was reported that five missionaries were attending to the spiritual needs of Polish Lutherans in 15 congregations and preaching stations and numbering 1,628 souls.

Of short duration was the mission among the Persians, begun by Missionary J. Pascha, supported by the New York Pastoral Conference and adopted by Synod in 1911. Pascha served about 1,500 souls at eight preaching stations. He reported that 5,000 Persians in Chicago and in Pittsburgh were urging him to preach to them. When Pascha died in 1911, his son, Philip Pascha, was called as his successor. Although he worked faithfully, the number of Persians attending his services decreased constantly, so that in 1913 he resigned. For a while Pastor A. von Schlichten of Yonkers ministered to the Persians in his locality through an interpreter. Pastor Lazarus Jaure canvassed Chicago in 1917, but failed to establish a preaching station. Accordingly, the *Proceedings* of 1920 remark: "Mission work among the Persians has not been resumed."

In 1911 Synod placed the work among the Finns under the auspices of its Board for Foreign-Tongue Missions. It had been reported by the Mission Board of the California and Nevada District that more than 500 Finnish families were working in the copper mines of Arizona, many of whom desired the service of a Finnish Lutheran pastor. A graduate of the Springfield Seminary by the name of Conrad Klemmer, an Esthonian, who also was conversant with the Finnish language, was prepared to preach to the Finns in their native language.

Synod called Klemmer into its service, who, after working for one and a half years in Arizona, moved to the East, where he served six Finnish preaching stations. Pastor J. Sillak for a time served a number of families in Alberta, Canada. The report of 1922 showed one Finnish missionary, serving five preaching stations, with about 200 souls.

Although the Slovak Evangelical Lutheran Synod was organized in 1902, it was unable to meet all missionary opportunities and therefore requested our Synod to establish a mission among the Slovak Lutherans. Synod complied with the request in 1914, and called as its first Slovak missionary Pastor Joseph Kolarik, who was serving a small mission in Detroit. When Kolarik accepted a call into the Slovak Synod, Candidate J. Marcis was placed at Detroit. From Detroit the mission work extended to Pontiac and Indianapolis. Under Pastor Andrew Daniel, stations were opened in Toledo and Lima, Ohio. In 1922 two pastors were working among the Slovaks at eight preaching stations.

Pastor Andrea Bongarzone, a former Roman Catholic priest, opened a Lutheran mission among the Italians in West Hoboken, New Jersey. Having passed an oral examination in 1916, he joined our Synod, and his mission work was placed under the supervision of our Board for Foreign-Tongue Missions. In 1922 he was serving Italians in West Hoboken and in Jersey City, about 92 souls.

The Immigrant Mission of Synod continued to do effective work as a handmaiden for its Home Mission program. Outposts had been established in Bremen and in Hamburg, which were placed under the supervision of the Saxon Free Church in 1899. Pastor Stephanus Keyl died December 15, 1905, and was succeeded by Pastor O. H. Restin.

When the North German Lloyd and the Hamburg-American steamship lines began to run their ships into Philadelphia (1910), a third immigrant station was established there under the direction of Pastor A. H. Winter (1911), and later, under Pastor E. J. Totzke, a seamen's mission.

During World War I the *Pilgerhaus* in New York and the services of the immigrant missionary were very much in demand. From the far Western States, as well as from Mexico, Guatemala, Brazil, and Africa, travelers came in an effort to secure passage to Europe. Some succeeded, but many never left port. Many of those remaining in New York, particularly seamen, cut off from their native country, appealed for aid to our Mission. With the help of Western brethren, relief was afforded, and work was found for about 3,000 reservists, seamen, and travelers.

After the war, immigration greatly decreased, owing to the quota applied by the United States. The *Pilgerhaus*, no longer serving its purpose, was sold, and Pastor Restin opened an office at 234 East 62d Street, from which he carried on his work as opportunity presented itself. In 1922 New York had the only immigrant missionary in Synod. The Seamen's Mission, begun in 1918 by Pastor Max Pinkert, was placed under the Immigrant Mission Board by Synod in 1920.

The Jewish Mission in New York was in charge of Nathaniel Friedmann. Constant opposition on the part of Jewish mobs, which occasionally culminated in violent persecution of Friedmann, necessitated relocating the mission several times, until it was at last established in the Mission Hall at 250 E. 101st Street.

Officials of Synod who inspected the work of Friedmann at different periods suggested moving the mission to another city, where less Jewish opposition might be expected. The Board for Jewish Missions, however, considered New York the proper place in view of the millions of Jews living there. While the number of converts remained small, nevertheless, the work was not in vain. Missionary Friedmann prepared a number of items of Christian literature in the Yiddish tongue for use in his work, among them a translation of the Catechism.

In 1922 it was reported that Friedmann had preached 48 sermons to a total attendance of 1,375. He had given 375 talks on religion in Jewish families, had made 598 calls in various sections of the city, had received 1,023 calls, and had distributed gratis 666 tracts, 450 Catechisms, and 185 copies of the New Testament.

In 1856 a group of Stockbridge Indians, descendants of the Mohicans, settled on the Indian reservation six miles north of Shawano, Wisconsin. The Presbyterian Church worked among them for some time, but later abandoned its work. They requested Pastor Th. Nickel of Shawano in 1898 to preach to them and to instruct their children.

Pastor Nickel, having served these Indians for about one year, offered the mission to Synod in 1899. Synod commissioned Candidate D. Larsen as missionary among the Indians, but he soon had to resign on account of impaired health. After Student E. Biegener had supplied at the reservation for one year, Pastor R. Kretzmann of Rhineland, Ontario, took over the mission station. In 1907 he was succeeded by Pastor D. Larsen, who was followed by Candidate Otis Lang and by Pastor H. M. Tjernagel in 1918. A church was built at Red Springs in 1901, a day school established in 1902, and a boarding school erected in 1920. In 1922 Missionary Tjernagel was preaching at Red Springs, Morgan Siding, and at Neopit.

In 1920 Synod resolved to open a mission on the White Earth Reservation in Minnesota. Pastor E. Yurawitz was called for this purpose. After a careful survey of the field, it developed that a mission could be opened only if Synod would begin an Indian institute. Since no money had been appropriated for this purpose, the project was abandoned.

TRANSOCEANIC RELATIONS AND SOUTH AMERICA

Relations with the Saxon Free Church continued to be very fraternal. Students from Germany attended the seminary at St. Louis for a longer or shorter period of time and thereafter entered parishes in their native country. World War I disorganized the work in Germany to some extent, but when peace was declared, Synod sent over a number of commissions, not only for the purpose of alleviating physical distress, but especially with a view to studying the religious conditions in Germany and other European countries. Thus Pastor W. Hagen and Mr. W. Schlake went over in 1919, and in 1921 Prof. H. W. T. Dau spent a number of months overseas. In 1922 several American friends purchased a piece of property at Berlin-Zehlendorf, in which a seminary was opened, thus eliminating the necessity of sending German students to America.

In 1911 the Free Church of Denmark joined the Saxon Free Church. This Church was established by Pastor N. P. Grunnet of Copenhagen, who in 1855 had severed his connection with the Danish State Church. Approached by many people from the surrounding neighborhood for divine services, Grunnet selected a number of men, trained them as lay preachers, and then sent them out. These lay preachers, however, in the course of time developed into independents and destroyed much of the work done by Grunnet. Having established connections with the Missouri Synod through the Saxon Free Church, he finally succeeded in obtaining a pastor, J. M. Michael, who had been stationed in Hamburg since 1896. Pastor Michael went to Denmark in 1900.

At the request of the brethren in Australia, Prof. A. L. Graebner paid them a visit in 1902. Through his visit the bonds of fellowship were strengthened, and by his suggestions the work in Australia began to prosper. Pastors C. F. Graebner, M. Winkler, G. Koch, and E. Wm. Zschech, all from America, were called in the course of time to the seminary at Adelaide, which henceforth was able to supply the needed pastors. When the Australian brethren requested assistance for their mission work in West Australia and among the natives in South Australia, Synod gladly acceded to their request by formal resolutions in 1905.

Fourteen hundred miles east of Australia lies New Zealand. Here the Hermannsburg Free Church was conducting a mission among the Maoris through Pastor G. Blaess. While on his Australian journey, Dr. Graebner also called on the Lutherans in New Zealand. Through his efforts a number of Missouri Synod workers went to the country under the Southern Cross. A Maori, Hamuera Te Punga, studied at the Springfield seminary and after his graduation entered the work among his kinsmen. Since 1914 the New Zealand Lutherans, formerly affiliated with the Missouri Synod, have been a part of the Evangelical Lutheran Synod in Australia.

The brethren in the lands under the Southern Cross suffered much during World War I. All parish schools were closed by government decree in 1916, and it was not until 1925 that some of them were opened again. The official publication, *The Australian Lutheran,* has been issued since 1913.

Pastor F. W. Schulze in London was joined in 1899 by Teacher J. Vornsand, who opened a Christian day school in South Tottenham. In 1899 Bruno Poch was installed as second pastor of the Kentish Town congregation, preaching also at South Tottenham, where a congregation was organized in 1903. It was known as the Holy Trinity Lutheran Church of the Unaltered Augsburg Confession. When Schulze left in 1904, Poch served both congregations until he returned to America in 1909. A mission station established at Silverton in 1901 was discontinued in 1908 because of lack of means and men. Pastor K. Knippenberg took over the work in London in 1910 and was joined by W. M. H.

Holls in 1911. In 1911 the two London congregations affiliated with the Missouri Synod by joining the Atlantic District. Pastor Holls, in 1914, accepted a call to the United States, leaving Pastor Knippenberg to bear the burdens caused by World War I. During the war many of the members were interned and some deported, so that the membership in both congregations decreased from 300 to 100 souls. Knippenberg, who returned to the States in 1920, was succeeded by Oscar H. Battenberg, who took up his residence in London in 1921.

About the same time that the tide of immigration began to bring thousands of people to the shores of the United States, ambitious European colonial agencies, subsidized by South American governments, sought to divert the migration southward. Glowing reports of fertile uninhabited pampas and virgin forests drew thousands of Germans to Latin America, particularly to Brazil, Argentina, Chile, and Paraguay. Between 1823 and 1858 large colonies of Germans, especially from various parts of Russia, established themselves in the cities or (the majority) founded purely German colonies in the vast untracked sections.

It was in Brazil that Synod's work first began. By 1898 its 18,000,000 inhabitants included 500,000 to 600,000 Germans, and in the three southern states the Teutons formed one fourth of the population. The Prussian State Church and several German mission societies supplied these people with pastors and teachers, but because of the vastness of the project and the primitive conditions could not even begin to cope with the task. Furthermore, none of these religious emissaries was very mission-minded. Satisfied with a leisurely life, they permitted thousands of their compatriots to die in the hinterland without spiritual care.

For a long time Prof. Ludwig Fuerbringer had championed the cause of the neglected South American Lutherans through the medium of *Der Lutheraner*. In 1899 Dr. Francis

Pieper placed the matter before the Delegate Synod which met in Holy Cross Church, St. Louis, Missouri.

An appeal to Synod for a pastor to take over a large congregation in Estancia Velha, Rio Grande do Sul, Brazil, had come from Pastor Fr. Brutschin. A graduate of St. Crischona Anstalt in Basel, Switzerland, he had for many years served his church and conducted a private school in his home. Through correspondence with Pastor Emil Duerr of Wayside, Wisconsin, and reading our periodicals he found Synod to be grounded on the Word of God. Leaving the united *Riograndenser Synode*, he applied for membership in the Missouri Synod. However, because of poor health, he decided to return to Germany as soon as an orthodox pastor could succeed him.

The appeal to Synod was answered by a resolution authorizing the Home Mission Board to take action. It reads as follows: "Resolved that the petition that our Synod be now willing to begin Home Mission work also in South America, particularly in Brazil and Argentina, since the circumstances there are very favorable, be placed into the hands of the General Commission for Home Missions with the charge that it — the General Commission — give this matter its special attention and in whatever way the circumstances prove, act according to their best judgment. Should the commission, upon the advice of the General President, come to the conviction that this is the time to begin Home Mission work in South America, it should then bring it to the attention of our congregations and at the same time ask for the necessary resources, but keep the latter sharply separated from moneys in the established treasury."

The Committee, composed of Pastor Louis Lochner (chairman), Pastor Karl Schmidt (later chairman), and Mr. C. Esemann, published an appeal in *Der Lutheraner*. The response was gratifying, the first gift being $2,000 from an anonymous donor.

STEADILY FORWARD (1897 - 1922) 245

Pastor J. C. Broders of Scranton, Mississippi, was sent to Brazil to survey the new mission field. He left on March 1, 1900, arriving at Novo Hamburgo four weeks later. He received a very favorable impression of Pastor Brutschin, whom he described as a "serious son of Luther, who not only knows our writings, but also studies them diligently and is at home in the latter."

Aided by Brutschin, Broders quickly orientated himself. Sadly he learned that a worldly attitude prevailed among the Germans, who as a whole had fallen prey to religious indifference, Freemasonry, and personal lust. Sunday dances, which usually ended in brawls and knifings, had long since superseded weekly divine worship, because the straw of human knowledge was fed the people instead of the Bread of Life. Schools were in an abominable condition, children being subjected to licentious teachers, vagabonds from Germany.

This he personally found out during his first missionary journey to the St. Jeronymo territory, near Porto Alegre. He reported: "What the fathers have acquired by the sweat of their brows, the second and third generations are rapidly squandering." They wanted nothing of Broders or his mission. The influence of the rationalistic *Riograndenser Synode* covered the largest and most important territories of the state; so he quickly decided against this state as focal point of mission work.

Broders, however, decided on a visit to Pelotas and Sao Lourenco, in the southern part of the state when he heard that there were some 10,000 settlers, ignored by the *Riograndenser Synode* and among whom existed about 30 schools with a religious aspect. He was disappointed again, for the teachers were nothing but men who had failed in former pursuits and really cared little for the Gospel. But in the little out-of-the-way village of Sao Pedro he happened to find a group of 17 poor families who had retained their faith by home devotions. Broders was the answer to their prayer. Under his leadership they organized a congregation and school, which on October 8, 1900, numbered 22 pupils. A request for a pastor resulted in the arrival of Pastor Wm. Mahler in March, 1901.

The trip to Sao Lourenco likewise was successful. Broders had become known, and two congregations gladly requested the services of the Missouri Synod, and a host of friends in various places offered bright mission prospects. Since Broders was only acting as Synod's "surveyor," he returned home to report on his activities, but before the end of 1901 Candidates A. Vogel, H. Stiemke, and J. Hartmeister went to assist Pastor Mahler in a promising field.

In 1902 four more congregations associated themselves with us, and in that year the Delegate Synod encouraged the formation of a Brazil District. This took place June 24, 1904, at a conference in Rincao Sao Pedro, at which Pastor Lochner of the Mission Board was present. Fourteen pastors and 10 congregations constituted the District. Pastor Mahler was the first President.

That same year the Macedonian cry "Come over and help us!" was sounded by Pastor von Matthesius of Entre Rios, Argentina. A missionary of the Prussian State Church, he had applied for membership in the La Plata Synod (Lutheran-Reformed). Sent to Entre Rios on probation, he proved to be a zealous pastor, who soon gathered a large congregation. Shortly before he and his flock were to be received into the La Plata Synod, he discovered its true nature and for a long time remained independent. Desiring to lay down his office and learning of the Missouri Synod's doctrinal stand, he wrote to President Mahler. Upon investigation by the latter, work was soon begun there, and in three years the number of preaching stations had so increased that another man was called. Argentina became an integral part of the Brazil District.

Immigration swelled the membership of the congregations, and the Gospel preaching spread to other states in Brazil and Argentina. By 1922 there were 13 pastors, serving 57 stations in the latter country, and in Brazil 37 pastors served parishes that included 131 preaching places. (One parish numbering 675 souls in three congregations was vacant.) The Lord had bountifully blessed the missionaries' labors despite their bitter hardships under primitive conditions.

From the very outset Christian day schools were established as an integral part of the parish, and they flourished, because the schools of South America, for the most part, were unable to care for the thousands of children in the hinterland.

Nor was the training of pastors and teachers neglected. At a conference at Bom Jesus, Brazil, the second week after Easter, 1903, the first four missionaries decided to open a seminary. Shortly thereafter, on October 27, a two-room primitive hut was opened to three students and their instructor, Pastor J. Hartmeister. Later, two more arrived. In 1944 three of these students were still active in the Kingdom.

Mornings the students worked the Bom Jesus parish farm to provide their food, because Pastor Hartmeister had to teach his parish school at that time. Instructions lasted from 2:30 P. M. until 5. Between 1905 and 1907 the seminary was closed because the District could not grant Pastor Hartmeister an assistant, and the pressure of his parish duties did not permit his further teaching the theological students. However, in 1907 Pastor Mahler reopened the institution as Director, with Pastor E. C. Wegehaupt serving as *Hausvater*. In 1908 the latter became Director, and the institution with an enrollment of 10 students bore the proud name: *Seminario Concordia.*

As the number of students increased, the faculty was enlarged. Among the men who served as professors were J. Kunstmann (président), 1915; L. C. Rehfeldt, 1917; Paul Schelp, 1919. President Kunstmann, sad to say, resigned in 1921 and severed his connection with Synod.

The physical plant gradually was increased to care for the larger enrollment. In 1909 buildings were rented in Porto Alegre, and, after a personal appeal of President Wegehaupt to Synod in 1911, $5,000 were granted to erect

Seminario Concordia at Porto Alegre

a near frame building. Five contos ($5,000) were raised for this purpose by the Brazil District. Dedication took place on September 29, 1912. Finally, in 1921, the present site on Mount Serrat was purchased, and, in addition to the buildings standing on the property, a new edifice and five professors' homes were erected.

THE CHURCH EXTENSION BOARD

Not until 1902 did Synod establish a General Church Extension Fund. An appeal for a loan of $6,000 from the brethren in London was the immediate occasion for the founding of this new venture. A proposed plan was adopted whereby congregations would contribute regularly to a general fund, from which non-interest bearing loans would be made to needy congregations for the building of schools or churches, said loans to be repaid in ten annual installments.

From 1902 to 1908 only $400 were paid into this fund. From 1909 to 1911 $4,000 more were added. The memorial collection at the time of the Walther Centennial in 1911, amounting to $40,000, increased the fund to $44,400. The quadricentenary of the Reformation in 1917 provided the occasion for a thankoffering in the amount of $344,895.24, which was collected for this treasury. The surplus of the Army and Navy Board, after its dissolution, amounting to $313,747.14, was also placed by Synod into this treasury. On December 31, 1922, the Church Extension Board was in possession of $834,445.58, of which amount $737,913.48 had been loaned to needy congregations.

ELEMENTARY EDUCATION

The Delegate Synod of 1914 created a new Commission on Schools, composed of F. Pfotenhauer, W. C. Kohn, F. W. C. Jesse, W. E. Moll, O. Kolb, F. Ruenzel, O. F. Rusch. At the same time all Districts were urged to appoint District Commissions. By this action the parish-school question became very live in all parts of Synod. The report of 1917 contained this observation: "Every congregation should provide a good school, a suitable building, all necessary teaching equipment, and capable instructors in sufficient numbers. District Commissions and Mission Boards should put forth efforts to have new schools established or classes added to existing schools. Our fathers knew no other, no better way for founding and building up Christian congregations. Therefore they simply began with Christian day schools wherever they settled; and the results fully justify their procedure. Let not their example put us to shame! Nor is it a favorable indication that so many of our pastors must still teach school. Our congregations should be taught that they owe it to their schools as well as to their pastors to engage teachers who have been especially trained for this work. — A serious evil is the poor salary paid to many teachers. This has compelled not a few to give up their calling. It, furthermore, harms the school in that the teacher is virtually compelled, for the sake of income, to devote time and strength to outside work. And thus is lost the leisure and the love for personal preparation, advanced study, and for making visits." It was reported that the Commission on Schools was preparing a model teaching schedule, and it was urged that uniform textbooks be used in the schools of Synod.

The convention of 1920 created the office of a Secretary of Schools. Mr. A. C. Stellhorn was later appointed to this position. With reference to the school fight in Michigan, Synod resolved: "We heartily endorse the protests of our Michigan District in behalf of their parochial schools; we wish the brethren Godspeed in their efforts to save these schools, and we assure them of our moral and financial support in this campaign for civil and religious rights." [3]

THE LUTHERAN UNION MOVEMENT

In an effort to settle the doctrinal disputes occasioned by the Predestinarian Controversy, five meetings were held by representatives of the Ohio and Iowa Synods and the Synodical Conference (1903—1906). The doctrinal discussions, however, did not serve to bring the opposing parties closer together.

Beginning in 1915, pastors of the Minnesota, Iowa, Ohio, and Missouri Synods in the Northwest met for doctrinal discussions. In 1917 the Intersynodical Conference, assembled at St. Paul, requested Synod to appoint a committee to examine the results of the deliberations on controverted doctrines as they were documented by the Conference or to take any other feasible steps to achieve complete unity of doctrine in the several synods. Prof. Geo. Mezger and Pastors J. G. F. Kleinhans and O. L. Hohenstein were elected a Committee on Lutheran Union.

This committee met with similar committees of the Joint Synod of Wisconsin, Minnesota, Michigan, and Other States, the Iowa Synod, and the Joint Synod of Ohio from 1918 to 1920, discussing the doctrines of conversion and election. On the basis of these discussions, 10 theses were prepared concerning the doctrine of conversion which were submitted to Synod in 1920. Synod resolved to present these theses to the District conferences for study and encouraged its Committee on Lutheran Union to continue its efforts on behalf of doctrinal unity in the Lutheran Church of America.

THE LUTHERAN LAYMEN'S LEAGUE

At the convention of the Delegate Synod at Milwaukee in 1917 Mr. Benjamin Bosse and Mr. John Boehne, Sr., both of Evansville, Indiana, announced the formation of a Lutheran Laymen's League, which proposed to raise $100,000 during the course of the year to cancel the debt in the various synodical treasuries.

The men who originated this League were A. H. Ahlbrand, J. W. Boehne, Sr., H. W. Horst, Theo. H. Lamprecht, Benjamin Bosse, A. G. Brauer, J. A. Leschen, H. A. Luedtke, Fred C. Pritzlaff, and Edmund Seuel. These men had been invited to the home of Mr. Pritzlaff in Milwaukee during the convention of 1917, where the subject of Synod's deficits was discussed. Sensing an opportunity for serving the Church in a special way, they formed a temporary organization, with the immediate purpose of soliciting funds from prosperous members of Synod to liquidate its debts.

At a meeting in Chicago, October 1, 1917, it was proposed to establish a permanent organization. After the $100,000 had been gathered and Synod's accounts balanced, a permanent organization was effected on December 3, 1917. The constitution of the organization states as one of its purposes: "to aid Synod with word and deed in business and financial matters."

At this meeting the Lutheran Laymen's League proposed as its next project the raising of $250,000 as a permanent fund for the support of superannuated pastors, teachers, and their widows and orphans. While engaged in raising this amount, World War I ended by an armistice. A month later, on December 15, 1918, the Lutheran Laymen's League resolved, out of gratitude to God for having made the war to cease, to raise the project to $3,000,000 and to initiate a Synod-wide campaign to gather this amount for the proposed Endowment Fund.

The Lutheran Laymen's League, believing that endorsement and co-operation of the synodical officers and District Presidents to be essential to the success of its undertaking, met with these men at Chicago on January 22, 1919. The College of Presidents approved the plan, and the Lutheran Laymen's League appointed a Campaign Executive Committee, with power to act. At the Delegate Synod of 1920 the Lutheran Laymen's League was happy to give Synod the sum of $2,050,095.25 as an Endowment Fund, whose proceeds were to be used for the support of the Veterans of the Cross. In 1946 this fund had grown to $2,697,730.43.

THE BOARD OF SUPPORT

Synod very early realized its obligations to the aged servants of the Church and to their widows and orphans. Before Synod was organized, the widow of Pastor O. H. Walther received a pension of $5.00 per month from Trinity Church in St. Louis. *Der Lutheraner* of September 8, 1847, reports a gift of $40.00 for the widow of the sainted Pastor Geo. Burger, one of Loehe's first *Sendlinge*. While Synod in the years following endeavored to support the Veterans of the Cross and their widows, it was not until 1872 that Synod elected a Board of Support, the first board consisting of Pastors J. F. Buenger, Th. J. Brohm, and Treasurer J. F. Schuricht.

Until 1905 the pastors in the employ of Synod, such as the professors and Presidents of Synod, received a pension from Synod on retirement from office. This was changed in 1905 when a board was appointed to support such cases according to need and not by a pension system. In 1917 Synod created a General Board of Support and Pensions, which was to provide support for Synod's invalid and incapacitated professors, their dependents, and also for retired pastors, parish schoolteachers and their dependents.

For the triennium 1920—1922 the Board of Support received $491,016.31 and disbursed $413,500.00.

THE UNION
OF THE SYNOD OF MISSOURI AND OTHER STATES AND THE GERMAN EVANGELICAL LUTHERAN SYNOD OF MISSOURI, OHIO, AND OTHER STATES

Difficulties between the English and the German Missouri Synods, growing out of the affiliation of an English congregation with the Western District of the German Missouri Synod, induced Synod to send Pastors P. Brand and G. Spiegel and Prof. F. Pieper to the convention of the English Synod in 1899 to confer with the English brethren. The outgrowth of the conference was the agreement that German congregations should seek German and that English congregations should seek English synodical connections.

In 1905 Synod's Board for English Missions, established in 1887, was dissolved, because practically all Districts were engaged in English mission work, 400 pastors preaching in that language. It was resolved that henceforth all English mission work of Synod be conducted by the District Mission Boards. It was furthermore resolved to receive English-speaking congregations and pastors as members of the German Synod.

President A. W. Meyer of the English Synod appeared before the same convention, asking whether Synod could not find ways and means to remove the barriers which in 1887 had made it impossible for the English brethren to join the German Missouri Synod as an English District. Accordingly, Professors F. Bente and J. Herzer and Pastor C. F. Obermeyer attended the convention of the English Synod (1905) and reported that Synod had resolved 1) that the official language on the floor of Synod remain, as heretofore, the German; 2) that the German Synod, however, is now ready and willing to receive into its membership English-speaking congregations and pastors.

In 1908 the Missouri Synod resolved that a union with the English Synod was desirable and appointed Pastor J. W. Miller, Prof. F. Bente, and Mr. W. C. Schuetz to confer with the English brethren and to report their findings to the convention of 1911. During the convention of the English Synod at Cleveland, July 7—13, 1909, the above-mentioned men met with a committee of said body, with the result that the English Synod resolved to effect a union with the German Synod either through amalgamation or through reception as a District on the basis of the so-called Cleveland Articles of Union. They are:

1. "That the English Synod transfer its publishing business and its book trade to the German Synod, but that a committee, the majority of its members being members of the English District, shall be elected in order that such a committee may have such literature as hymnbooks, Sunday-school literature, tracts, etc., prepared for the special needs of the English District.

2. "That the *Lutheran Witness* be made the official English church paper for the entire Synod, but that the editor be elected from the English District or that the English District be at least equally represented on the editorial committee. The same rule shall hold good also for the *Lutheran Guide*.

3. "That the English language may be used by the members of the English District at the meetings of Synod and that at least a brief summary of the minutes be read and printed in the English language.

4. "That the Mission Board of the English District be permitted to open English missions wherever it thinks such be necessary, provided that it properly respect the divine principles of congregational rights (church membership) and the law of Christian charity.

5. "That, as a rule, entire English congregations affiliate with the English District but that finally every congregation may decide for itself which District it will join, provided that Christian charity be not offended against and that congregations shall not be blamed if for special reasons they do not follow this rule.

6. "That the Concordia College at Conover, N. C., be transferred to the Synod.

7. "That the question when and how often the English District shall meet shall be decided by the District itself." [4]

In 1911 both Synods met in St. Louis, the German Synod at Holy Cross Church, the English Synod at Redeemer Church. At the English Synod convention it was reported that in a canvass of the congregations 53 votes had been cast, the result being 39½ in favor of District union, one in favor of amalgamation, 12½ opposed to any union.

The German Synod likewise adopted the resolutions of the English Synod (the Cleveland Articles of Union) with the following understanding:

"As regards Point 1: The publications in question are subject to revision by the theological faculty at St. Louis, and the English District is to assume the financial responsibility of such publications in the same manner as is now done in similar instances by our German Districts.

"As regards Point 4: The phrase: 'With due regard to the principles of Christian love,' embraces the following, viz., that new English congregations shall not be organized without previous conference with the congregations affected. (The committee of the German Synod expressly declared that the English word *conference* and the German word *Auseinandersetzung* do not imply that the permission of German congregations must be received.)

"As regards Point 5: We hold that also such of our congregations as have become entirely English should remain in affiliation with the respective Districts, and we shall advise such congregations accordingly.

"As regards Point 6: The [English] District, however, is to have due regard to chapter III, par. 4, of our Constitution. ('The Delegate Synod holds triennial conventions. The District Synods hold annual conventions in the interval; however, each District meets at a different time. There are no conventions of District Synods every third year.')

"As regards Point 7: Charter and deed are to be examined. The Delegate Synod is to determine the future status of the institution." [5]

The resolutions of the German Synod were brought to the English brethren by a special committee consisting of Profs. W. H. T. Dau and A. W. Meyer, Pastor H. B. Hemmeter, Mr. Th. F. Lamprecht, and Mr. H. Thiemeyer, who expressed the cordial feelings of their body and the hope that the union would be realized, and stated that the vote favoring union was practically unanimous. Thereupon the English Synod resolved that since the Cleveland Articles of Union had not been essentially changed, the German Synod be notified officially of the vote in favor of District union.

The union of the two synods was formally consummated on Monday, May 15, at 4:30 P. M. The English Synod marched in a body to Holy Cross Church and was received at the door by a special committee, which escorted the English brethren to seats of honor in the front of the church, the members of the German Synod having risen from their seats. It was a most impressive sight and gave all present a thrill which will never be forgotten. Pastor Adolph Biewend welcomed the new group as follows:

"We thank God, our heavenly Father, that He has fulfilled our hopes. You, dear brethren, have come back to your mother; you have come back to your brethren. You, indeed, ever were our brethren, but you did not dwell in the same house with us. Now you come to live under our roof. This has not come to pass by our wisdom and power, but by the hand of God, our heavenly Father. Yea, the angels of heaven rejoice. We have no doubt but that our dear Savior will say: 'Well done!'"

President H. P. Eckhardt of the English Synod responded in the following words:

"The honor has been conferred on me to represent the English Synod of Missouri, acting as its first spokesman on this momentous and significant occasion. It is an honor of which I am not worthy. In the name of our body I heartily thank the preceding speaker for his kind words and hearty welcome extended to us in behalf of your venerable body. We feel certain that we are finding a cordial reception and welcome among you.

"Our final vote on this union proposition was not unanimous. A few votes were recorded in the negative. But these were cast by delegates who felt that they must refer the matter back to their congregations. And such were their final declarations that we have every reason to hope and trust that not one of our congregations will be lost to us. Mr. President, I have the honor and pleasure to formally announce the final decision of our Synod as being favorable to District union.

"Such has been the spirit that has manifested itself in our deliberations and yours that we are convinced it was none other than the Holy Spirit of God who ruled and led both bodies. Therefore we see in this result the hand of God pointing out to us the way in which we should go. And this fact is also our hope for the future.

"It is significant that this union is being consummated in this city of St. Louis, Missouri. For it was in this place that our fathers wrote the early chapters of your venerable German Synod's history. It was in this city, twenty-three years ago, that our English Synod was organized and its opening chapters written. It is in this same place that this new chapter is now being written, telling of the union of the two Missouri Synod bodies. May our God in heaven close this chapter with an approving 'Amen.' And we add to it the old motto of Missouri: *Soli Deo Gloria!*

"It is fitting that we are able to make the consummation of this union a part of our Walther Centennial celebration. Most of the pastors in both bodies have received their theological training either under the sainted Dr. Walther or under his pupils in the same alma mater. We all are enjoying the fruits of his labors. We are all contending for the same sound Lutheranism for which he so unflinchingly stood. It is befitting that we all should unite into one body at this time and under the shadow of this alma mater.

"We come into this closer union with your venerable body fully and sincerely trusting you as brethren, and you, we know, are coming with us in the same trust. We are persuaded that our mutual confidence shall never prove to have been in vain. We come here to join ranks with you and march with you, hand in hand, shoulder to shoulder, bearing farther and farther into the world of lost sinners the one saving Gospel, whether it be by means of the German language, or the English, or any tongue, just so it be the old Gospel. We have been one in faith. Now we are one in organization. May we ever be one and inseparable! God bless this union! I close with a word taken from Solomon's prayer at the dedication of the Temple. I know no more appropriate one. It is: 'The Lord, our God, be with us, as He was with our fathers! Let Him not leave us nor forsake us!'"

After this Pastor F. Kuegele, the Nestor of the English Synod, gave expression to his joy in the following words in German: "It is thirty-two years that our heavenly Father led me out of the Synod of Missouri. This took place when I accepted a call to an English congregation of the Ohio Synod. Heavy conflicts have passed over our American Lutheran Zion in these thirty-two years. This is well known by our older pastors, especially by all those who took a stand in the midst of the struggle. Our Great Shepherd, the Lord Jesus Christ, frustrated the purpose of the Evil Foe, and the true Lutheran Church came forth from the Election Controversy strengthened and rejuvenated.

"After the waters had calmed somewhat, at the advice of the German Delegate Synod, about a dozen pastors not connected with the Missouri Synod met in Bethlehem Church, St. Louis, and founded the present English Synod of Missouri. It was done at the direction and with the help of the English Mission Board of the German Synod. Of the original founders there are three remaining in our body. They are, besides myself, Pastors W. Dallmann and L. M. Wagner.

"God's blessing rested upon the organization. The time had come that God wanted English work to be conducted on a greater scale than hitherto. It is needless for me to dwell upon the past. In regard to what is taking place today, permit me to say only what that man whose centenary we commemorated yesterday advised, namely, that an English

District be created. He expressed this shortly before his end. What, then, would have been a small mission District has become an imposing body. I, indeed, welcome this day with hearty joy, and I believe the worthy fathers and brethren will join me when I say: 'My soul rejoiceth in my God, for He hath done great things.' His blessing rest upon our union! May He speak His great 'Amen' thereto!"

In conclusion, President Pfotenhauer of the German Synod spoke the following words in German: "This day is a day of great joy for the English and the German Missouri Synods, not in this respect that we today for the first time greet each other and sit together as brethren. We have always been brethren, children of one Church. But in this respect is this day a great day of great joy, that from today on we would walk together hand in hand in the same way which we regard as most advantageous for the work of our dear Church in this glorious land, which is our and our children's earthly fatherland. Now let us give all glory to Him to whom alone it is due and unite in the singing of the *Te Deum*." [6]

Thereupon Dr. Luther's version of the *Te Deum* was sung responsively by the teachers' choir and those present. The solemn exercise concluded with the Lord's Prayer and the benediction.

In 1911 the English District was working in 19 States. The *Lutheran Witness* was edited by Prof. Geo. A. Romoser of Conover, North Carolina. The fact that the publishing house was in one city and the editor in chief in another, far-distant city frequently delayed matters and caused difficulties. The Delegate Synod of 1914, therefore, resolved that an editorial committee consisting of Pastor M. S. Sommer and a member of the St. Louis faculty, designated by the faculty, edit the periodical. Since that time M. S. Sommer and Theo. Graebner have been the editors of the *Lutheran Witness*.

THE WALTHER LEAGUE

The growth of the Walther League, organized in 1893, was relatively slow. By 1917 the number of societies was under 300. Its headquarters were in Milwaukee, Wisconsin. World War I gave impetus to the growth of the League. An appeal for funds to supply the boys of the Missouri Synod in the armed forces with suitable literature resulted in the gathering of approximately $25,000 for this purpose. The League sent out more than 400,000 pieces of reading material.

From 1918 to 1923 the number of societies rose from 310 to 1,182. The project of this period was the "Monument of Gratitude," the sanatorium for tuberculosis patients, erected at Wheat Ridge, Colorado, in 1921. For this purpose the Walther League societies contributed $200,000. This hospital has been and still is the favorite charity endeavor of the Leaguers, who at Christmastime through the sale of Christmas seals raise sufficient funds for free treatment to needy persons.

The presidents during this period were: H. F. Landeck (1898—1900); L. Hohnsbehn (1900—1904); F. A. Klein (1904—1909); E. A. Ehlert (1909—1914); O. Kotsch (1914 to 1918); Prof. E. H. Engelbrecht (1918—1921); A. A. Grossmann (1921—1928).

Pastor W. A. Maier served as the first executive secretary of the organization, 1920—1922. In 1922 appeared the *Bible Student*, edited by Prof. Theo. Graebner. The *Walther League Messenger* was edited by Dr. W. A. Maier 1920 to 1945.

CONCORDIA PUBLISHING HOUSE AND ITS PUBLICATIONS

Concordia Publishing House in St. Louis kept pace with the growth of Synod. At the World's Fair in St. Louis, 1904, it received the highest prize and award for excellence of material and workmanship.

In 1907 Mr. M. Tirmenstein resigned his position as manager and was succeeded by Mr. E. Seuel, who served in this capacity until 1944, when he became manager emeritus. In 1910 the most ambitious project of the Publishing House, the publishing of Luther's works in the German language in 25 volumes, was completed. Work on this venture had begun in 1879 under the editorship of the Revs. G. Stoeckhardt and E. W. Kaehler. From 1886 to 1910, Pastor A. F. Hoppe devoted all his time to this task. The first number of the *Lutheran Annual* appeared in 1910.

E. Seuel

A new unit, costing $60,000, was added in 1911 to the office building fronting Jefferson Avenue. In 1912, following the merger of the English Missouri Synod with the German Synod, the *Lutheran Witness*, as well as the *Lutheran Guide*, was printed at Concordia.

The *Concordia Triglotta*, the confessional writings of our Church in German, Latin, and English, edited by Professors F. Bente and W. H. T. Dau, came off the press in 1917, and in 1921 appeared the first volume of the *Popular Commentary* by Dr. P. E. Kretzmann. The *Theological Quarterly* was changed to the *Theological Monthly* in 1920.

A Juvenile Literature Board was appointed in 1914 to examine the literature adapted to young people in German and English in order to sift the good from the bad, and to assist the Church in watching over the reading of its young people. The members of the first Board were Prof. Th. Graebner, Pastors A. G. Merz, R. Jesse, W. H. Behrens, and Teacher L. H. Becker.

At its convention in 1920 Synod resolved to create a General Literature Board for the purpose of surveying the needs of Synod as a whole, studying the available literature and planning new publications. The first Board was composed of Mr. E. Seuel, Pastor M. S. Sommer, and Teacher H. F. Bade.

In 1911 Concordia Publishing House began to publish English and German Sunday school literature as a private venture, appointing its own editors and committees. Synod, in 1920, instructed its President to appoint a Sunday School Committee. The committee was composed of Prof. Geo. Mezger, Dr. P. E. Kretzmann, and Superintendent Theo. Kuehnert. At the same convention Concordia Publishing House was directed to discontinue publishing Sunday school material in the German language.

WORLD WAR I

On April 6, 1917, Congress declared war on Germany, and thus our country became involved in World War I. The Delegate Synod, meeting at Detroit, June 16—25, the same year, at once passed the resolution: "That a committee be appointed to consist of five members, to be named by the President, to provide for the religious welfare of all members of the Lutheran Church of the Evangelical Lutheran Synod of Missouri, Ohio, and Other States, with full power and authority necessary or convenient to act in the premises and as official representatives of our Church." The men appointed were Pastors C. Eissfeldt, F. C. Streufert, F. J. Wenchel, D. H. Steffens, and Mr. F. Wolff. In 1918 Mr. H. F. Rohrmann was added to the Board, and Prof. W. C. Kohn was made chairman, succeeding Pastor C. Eissfeldt. The Walther League in the same year appointed a similar committee for the purpose of supplying literature to our members in the armed forces. It consisted of A. A. Grossmann, Pastor W. G. Polack, and Mr. E. C. Rakow.

In its report to Synod (1920) the Army and Navy Board stated: "The greatest difficulty, however, was caused by the fact that other denominations, and also Lutheran bodies not affiliated with the Synodical Conference, looking to the spiritual welfare of the men with the colors, sought the co-operation of this [our] committee, they deeming it unnecessary to duplicate the work carried on in the various camps and on the battlefield. They were trying moments indeed, but the Committee could not believe that the principles as laid down by the Word of God for times of peace could be any other for times of war and distress and, therefore, for conscience' sake, demanded that we ourselves look after the spiritual needs of our men with the colors whenever and wherever this were possible, at the same time offering to co-operate with them along external lines, whenever and wherever this would be expedient. Being unable to co-operate in full and along all lines with the bodies mentioned, it was indeed a source of great pleasure and gratification to join hand with the War Committee of the Joint Synod of Wisconsin, Minnesota, Michigan, and Other States, with the Rev. J. Brenner, the Rev. O. Hagedorn, and Mr. E. von Briesen as members. Early in the war said War Committee met with your Committee, and by agreement your Committee took over their work also with full charge and responsibility; the Wisconsin Synod, however, paying their proportionate share of all expenses incurred, this being one fifth of the total amount expended."[7]

The work of the Board growing rapidly, a subsidiary department was created, called the Eastern Department, and consisting of the Pastors Arthur Brunn, Wm. Schoenfeld, Paul Lindemann, J. Geo. Spilman, and O. H. Restin. To facilitate necessary negotiations with the Government, the War Department, and the Federal Council of Churches, which was charged by the Federal authorities to assist in the selection of chaplains for the Army and Navy, Pastor

D. H. Steffens and Pastor J. F. Wenchel were designated by the Board as the Washington Bureau of the Committee. A Finance Committee was appointed, of which Pastors J. M. Bailey, E. T. Lams, K. G. Schlerf, and Mr. Theo. W. Eckhart were members. The Army and Navy Board published a periodical entitled *The Soldiers' and Sailors' Bulletin,* which was edited by Pastor K. G. Schlerf. Two field secretaries, Pastor P. Matuschka and Pastor Geo. F. Schmidt, were engaged to carry on the work in the various camps in a uniform manner.

At the camps and cantonments of the United States Army the Board purchased parcels of land and erected buildings as "Centers" for the Lutheran members of the service, where they could attend divine services with regularity and also find a place of recreation. Seventy pastors were engaged by the Board as "camp pastors," who devoted their whole time to serve the boys in the camps, while 124 pastors were in the service of the Board as "Camp Missionaries," who worked in camps adjacent to their home charges or in camps where there were not so many boys of our Church.

Although more than 500 pastors offered their services to their country, our Government did not see fit to appoint more than thirteen chaplains in the Army and Navy and to assign but five for overseas service.

37,582 of our boys served our country in the Army and Navy; besides these were 249 other war workers and 101 women workers. 10,692 were with the American Expeditionary Forces; 472 died in the A. E. F., and 352 died in the United States. The Board distributed 80,000 hymnals, 12,000 Bibles and Testaments, 425,000 sermons, 260,000 tracts, and an endless number of periodicals. When the Board for Army and Navy finally wound up its business, it was able to turn over to Synod a balance of $313,747.24, which was transferred by Synod to its Church Extension Fund.

During the World War a number of our congregations and pastors were harassed by overzealous Americans. In some territories local authorities forbade the use of the German language in church and school in the vain delusion that we were adherents of the "Kaiser's Church." The Missouri Synod, however, at no time had anything in common with the State Church of Prussia, the Church of the German Emperor. The loyalty of the members of Missouri Synod to its Government was manifested externally by the purchasing of more than $94,000,000 of Liberty Bonds and Stamps and by liberal contributions to the Red Cross.

SYNODICAL CONFERENCE

The Slovak Evangelical Lutheran Synod affiliated with the Synodical Conference in 1908. Fifteen congregations, represented by 10 pastors and 4 laymen, organized this group at Connelsville, Pennsylvania, September 2—4, 1902. Since the group had no theological institutions of its own, it sent its students to the colleges and seminaries of the Missouri Synod.

The Delegate Synod was memorialized in 1914 by the Wisconsin District to endeavor to effect a closer union of the synods comprising the Synodical Conference by amalgamating them into one body. The committees of the groups constituting the Synodical Conference reached the conclusion that a closer union of the synods was desirable and could be effected on the following basis:

1. All synods forming the Synodical Conference shall disband.

2. The proposed new body shall be known as "The Evangelical Lutheran Synodical Conference of North America."

3. The thus organized Synodical Conference shall take charge of and administer all general missions.

4. This Synodical Conference shall take over the administration and maintenance of the publication concerns.

5. This Synodical Conference shall take over the administration and maintenance of the theological seminaries.

6. If a District or Districts in whose territory there is a preparatory school should desire to take over the administration and maintenance of such school, the General Body shall give the control of that school over to such District or Districts.

7. All property of the present synods shall be transferred to the new body.

8 The General Body shall be divided into State or District Synods.

The proposal, however, did not find favor with the Wisconsin Synod, for at its convention in July, 1916, it adopted the following resolution: "Inasmuch as our Synod is already divided into Districts, and the union in our General Body has prospered and the plan for the consolidation or amalgamation of all synods within the Synodical Conference tends toward general confusion, this plan is not acceptable to us." Later this resolution was amended to read: "That our General Body consider the matter after a reorganization shall have taken place."

In view of this, Synod made no further effort to work toward an amalgamation with the other synods of the Synodical Conference, but a committee was appointed which was to be ready to act further as soon as this were agreeable to the Wisconsin Synod.

In 1920 the Norwegian Synod of the American Lutheran Church was added as a member of the Synodical Conference. This body was organized in June, 1918. Its members had, for doctrinal reasons, seceded from the large Norwegian

Synod when the latter merged with the Hauge Synod and the United Norwegian Lutheran Church, forming the Norwegian Lutheran Church of America, in 1917. The Norwegian Synod, like the Slovak Synod, made use of the institutions of the Missouri Synod for the training of its pastors.

The work among the Negroes of our country, the project of the Synodical Conference, prospered to such an extent that at the end of 1922 the Negro Missions had 49 organized congregations and 8 preaching places. 95 workers were in the service of the Mission, of whom 72 were colored and 23 white. The Mission numbered 3,705 souls, 2,105 communicant members. 38 mission schools were attended by 2,684 pupils and 52 Sunday schools by 2,729 children and adults. Three institutions for the training of colored workers were being maintained: Immanuel Lutheran College at Greensboro, North Carolina, with an enrollment of 160 students; Luther College at New Orleans, Louisiana, enrollment, 49 students, and the Teachers' Training School at Selma, Alabama, with six students (all girls).

In 1916 the mission among the Negroes was extended to Alabama. Pastor C. F. Drewes on October 29, 1915, received a letter from Rosa Young of Rosebud, Alabama, in which she offered to place her school, established in 1912, under the control of the Board for Colored Missions. Booker T. Washington, head of Tuskegee Institute, had advised her to communicate with our Board, when she was no longer able to maintain her school owing to the difficult times. Pastor Nils J. Bakke was immediately dispatched to Rosebud, and on Palm Sunday and Easter Sunday, 1916, 58 persons were baptized, and 70 were confirmed. On Easter Day, 1916, a congregation was organized with 117 baptized members, and in less than a year the congregation had grown to 187. Pastor Bakke was made superintendent of the Alabama field, which position he held until 1920, when he was succeeded by Pastor G. A. Schmidt.

For years, in fact from 1882 to 1904, colored workers for the Negro Mission were trained in institutions of the Missouri Synod. Thus Pastors J. McDavid, W. H. Lash, James Doswell, L. Thalley, and others were prepared for their work at the seminary in Springfield, while Teacher Napoleon Seeberry received his education at Addison, Illinois.

In order to expedite the training of colored boys and girls for work among their fellow men, Immanuel Lutheran College was opened at Concord, North Carolina, on March 2, 1903. The school was organized in three departments: a high school, a normal school, and a theological seminary. The institution was moved to Greensboro, North Carolina, in 1905. Luther College was opened in New Orleans, Louisiana, in September, 1903, the first teacher and principal being Pastor F. J. Lankenau. It was organized along the line of the school at Concord. A normal school was opened at Selma, Alabama, on November 13, 1922.

THE WALTHER CENTENNIAL

The high spot of the 1911 Synodical Convention in St. Louis was the anniversary of the 100th birthday of Dr. C. F. W. Walther. The celebration was held on Sunday afternoon, May 14, at 3 o'clock in the Coliseum. More than 20,000 people attended the services. The students' chorus, a mixed choir of 600 voices, and a children's choir of 3,000 voices sang appropriate selections. Prof. F. Bente spoke in the German language and Prof. H. W. T. Dau in English. Prof. H. G. Stub, D. D., represented the Norwegian Lutheran Synod, and Prof. J. Schaller spoke for the Synod of Wisconsin, Minnesota, Michigan, and Other States. The services were concluded by the recitation of the Apostles' Creed and the Lord's Prayer, the huge audience being led by the newly elected President, F. Pfotenhauer. The collection of $2,772 was for the General Church Extension Fund.

Said Professor Dau: "Walther's age, like ours, was char-

Immanuel Lutheran College, Greensboro, N. C.

acterized by indifferentism. The unionist, the church federator, the advocate of peace at any price, the gentleman who proposes to you: We agree to disagree — was very busy. I know of no man in the Lutheran Church of America between 1845 and 1887 who approached this momentous subject of the essential unity of the entire Christian brotherhood of believers with as great reverence as Walther and who labored as enthusiastically for the true unification of divided sections of the Church. His writings in this matter will remain Christian classics. But in these labors Walther proved a quickener of the confessional concepts. On Scriptural grounds he declined union without unity and was not greatly agitated over the absence of organic union between bodies with whom he knew himself one at heart as regards teaching and practice.

"The firm position occupied by our body on this question was secured by Walther's conscientious application of two sets of Scripture texts: those which issue urgent appeals for brotherly fellowship and those which issue emphatic warnings against false union. Walther bowed to the authority of both these sayings of the Lord: 'Be ye one!' and 'Be ye separate!' In whatever form time and the changing conditions of men may compel us to apply these sacred rules, we propose to apply either religiously, and we call for no revision at this point." [8]

Another event observed throughout Synod was the Quadricentennial of the Reformation in 1917. Services were held in all congregations, and in the larger cities mass celebrations were arranged. The amount collected in these services was $344,895.24, which flowed into the General Church Extension Fund. Synod published two books to commemorate the 400th anniversary of the Reformation: *Unser Erbteil* and *Four Hundred Years*.

This period saw the passing of the only remaining man who had attended both the Cleveland meeting of 1845 and the preliminary meeting at St. Louis (1846), Pastor Friedrich Lochner. He had come to America as a Loehe *Sendling* in 1845, becoming pastor of the Lutheran-Reformed Salem Church of Toledo, Ohio. Upon its refusal to be a Lutheran church, he resigned in 1846. After serving Lutheran congregations at Pleasant Ridge and Collinsville, Illinois, he accepted the call to Trinity Church in Milwaukee, Wisconsin, where he remained until 1876. From 1876 to 1887 he was pastor of Trinity Church, Springfield, Illinois, serving at the same time as professor of liturgics at the seminary. Returning to Milwaukee in 1887, he became assistant pastor of Trinity Church, dying on February 14, 1902. He was an outstanding liturgiologist.

President H. C. Schwan died on May 29, 1905, at Cleveland. Since 1851 he had been pastor of Zion Church at Cleveland, Ohio, serving it until 1899, during the last decades as assistant pastor. From 1878 to 1899 he served as President of the Missouri Synod. In 1890 Synod asked him to write a catechism, which, known as Schwan's Catechism, was used in our circles for more than 40 years.

On December 4, 1904, Dr. August L. Graebner went to his eternal rest. Born at Frankentrost, Michigan, July 10, 1849, he received his training at Fort Wayne and St. Louis. While still a student at the Seminary (1872), he became a teacher at the *Lutherische Hochschule* (Walther College) in St. Louis. Three years later he accepted a professorship at Northwestern College, a Wisconsin Synod institution at Watertown. In 1878 the Wisconsin Synod elected him to a chair of theology at its newly established seminary at Milwaukee. He succeeded his father-in-law, Prof. G. Schaller, as instructor of church history at the St. Louis seminary in 1887. He was generally recognized as a scholar of universal learning. In 1902 he visited the churches of Australia, New Zealand, and Germany. Dr. Graebner died at the early age of 55 years.

Another outstanding scholar called home during this period was Dr. George Stoeckhardt. Born February 17, 1842, at Chemnitz, Saxony, he studied theology at Erlangen and Leipzig. Thereupon he was tutor at a ladies' seminary at Tharandt (1866—1870), assistant pastor of a German Lutheran Church in Paris (1870), and for three months chaplain at the Sedan hospitals (1871). From 1871 to 1873 Stoeckhardt was an instructor in Old and New Testament Interpretation at Erlangen. He was sent to Planitz, Saxony, as pastor of the State Church in 1873, but becoming acquainted with Ruhland and the literature of the Missouri Synod, he resigned his office after his suspension from the ministry by the consistory. With part of his congregation he joined the Saxon Free Church and was associated with Ruhland as assistant pastor of the Free Church congregation at Planitz. He went to the United States in 1878 to take charge of Holy Cross Church, St. Louis. In addition to his pastoral duties he lectured from 1879 on Old and New Testament Exegesis at Concordia Seminary. In 1887 he became a member of the seminary staff. Stoeckhardt died suddenly on January 9, 1913. His exegetical learning and his devotion to the Scriptures made him one of the leaders of the Missouri Synod with Walther and Pieper in the controversies of the Church.

13

ABOUNDING MORE AND MORE
1922–1947

The last quarter of the first century of Synod's existence saw its missionaries in all States of the Union, congregations being organized at Atlanta, Georgia (1922), Irmo, South Carolina (1932), and at Yuma, Arizona (1939). During the same period Synod established itself in Mexico (1922), Alaska (1926), Paraguay (1926), Africa (1936), Uruguay (1942), and Honolulu (1945).

The statistics for 1944 read: Pastors serving congregations—3,508; congregations and preaching stations—5,240; baptized members—1,501,314; communicant members—1,033,875.

To conduct the work of so large a body more efficiently the following new Districts were organized:

Oklahoma District, 1924. First President: Pastor Hy. Mueller.

Argentina District, 1927. First President: Pastor A. T. Kramer.

Southern California District, 1930. First President: Pastor G. H. Smukal.

Iowa East District, 1936. First President: Pastor H. Harms.

Iowa West District, 1936. First President: Pastor Ad. Schwidder.

Southeastern District, 1939. First President: Pastor J. Geo. Spilman.

Montana District, 1945. First President: Pastor P. Freiburger.

The Canada District in 1923 changed its name to Ontario District to conform to the nomenclature of the other two Canadian Districts.

During this period the transition from the German to the English language was practically completed in Synod's congregations, at the meetings of its Districts, and at the conventions of the General Body. Since 1917 the proceedings of the Delegate Synods appeared in the English language. Synod, in 1926, appointed an assistant secretary for its English minutes. At the convention of 1929 an English sermon was preached in the opening service in addition to the German sermon. In 1938 the German minutes were discontinued. Only an English sermon was given at the opening of the convention at Fort Wayne in 1941.

The Fort Wayne Convention in 1923 instructed President Pfotenhauer to appoint a committee to consider the spiritual needs of Missouri Synod students at non-Lutheran institutions of higher learning. The committee recommended to Synod in 1926 to call a field secretary who was to devote his full time to general student work under the supervision of a Student Welfare Committee. It was not until 1940, however, that this resolution of Synod was carried out by calling Pastor R. H. Hahn to this office. Under the direction of the Student Service Commission 13 pastors are devoting all their time to student welfare, while 674 pastors give some of their time to this work. State the *Proceedings* of 1944: "Through an intensified program of action at these schools it pleased God to grant a fine yield of visible fruit, although the grand total of souls influenced, conserved, reclaimed, or won only eternity will fully reveal."

A Press Committee was created by Synod in 1926. Its

duty is to correct any misleading and erroneous statements appearing in the newspapers and magazines, to assure our Church a voice in the press, and to arrange for news coverage of Synod's regular conventions. At the same time Synod recommended that all District Presidents appoint or have the Districts elect press committees of their own, who are to collaborate with the synodical Press Committee in representing Lutheranism in the various communities and throughout the nation.

In order to keep its greatly enlarged program before the eyes of its constituents, Synod in 1929 resolved to appoint a Director of Publicity. Pastor Lawrence Meyer, who had worked in the China mission field for several years, was called to this position and established his office at St. Louis.

When the Board of Assignment of Calls met at St. Louis, May 27 and 28, 1930, it found to its dismay that only 124 calls were available for 136 ministerial graduates. By 1932 there was a surplus of 110 candidates of theology. When Synod met at Cleveland in 1935, the candidate situation was ventilated at length. At this time approximately 300 graduates from the seminaries had not been permanently called into the service of the Church. Synod resolved to establish a "Candidate Fund" out of which to subsidize candidates who were to be placed temporarily into good-sized congregations to assist pastors or mission boards, to canvass given territories, to survey new fields, and to perform such other pastoral duties as the pastor in charge or the mission board would assign them. Up to December 1, 1936, the Board for Home Missions had granted subsidy for the temporary placement of 80 candidates at $60.00 per month. By March, 1941, there still were 233 candidates who were not permanently placed. Owing to the large number of pastors entering the armed forces as chaplains, the expansion of mission work, and the earlier retirement of pastors, the candidate situation was eased, so that when the calls were assigned to the graduates in January and July, 1945, there were not sufficient men to supply the demand.

In order that Synod's missions might be conducted more efficiently, Pastor F. C. Streufert was appointed Secretary of Missions in August, 1932, with the duty to gather and furnish to the Board of Directors, the Mission Boards, the Fiscal Conference, and the Church Extension Board information on all missions operated by Synod. In 1935 the Secretary of Missions was made Executive Secretary of the Board for Home Missions in North America and also advisory member of the Board of European Missions, the Board of South American Missions, the Board for Foreign Missions, the Board to the Deaf and Blind, and the General Church Extension Board. In this way the Secretary acts as co-ordinator of all of Synod's missions.

At the Cleveland Convention, 1935, Dr. J. W. Behnken was elected to succeed Dr. F. Pfotenhauer as President of Synod. By a rising vote the following resolution was adopted:

"This Convention, assembled at Cleveland, Ohio, June 21, 1935, recognizes with gratitude toward the Lord of the Church the blessings which have come to our Synod and affiliated bodies through the ministrations of Dr. Frederick Pfotenhauer during his many years of executive service, first in the field of the Minnesota District and since 1911 as General President of our body. Endowed with talents requisite for leadership, a firm grasp of the details of administration, an amiable disposition, and an ability to conciliate those of differing opinions, so that these many years our Synod has been characterized by a harmony of purpose and co-operation of forces which is the wonder of other church bodies — all this, but more than that: blessed by the Lord God, who has been his constant Refuge in every difficulty, with love of evangelical truth and a profound comprehension of it, a fearless witness-bearing in the face of the unionistic and divisive tendencies of our day, Dr. Pfotenhauer has been a tower of strength for the promotion and preservation of sound Lutheranism in this and foreign lands. For these manifestations of divine favor upon our revered Doctor and upon the Church by his twenty-four years in office, we address our thanks to Jesus, our Lord, and acknowledge His bountiful mercies. At the same time we extend hearty greetings to our incoming President, the Rev. J. W. Behnken, and bespeak for him the same blessings of God, as we also pledge him the same loyal support throughout the thirty Districts of Synod as his predecessor in office enjoyed." [1]

Synod conferred upon Dr. Pfotenhauer the title of Honorary President as an expression of the great esteem in which it held the man who for 24 years had served it so efficiently.

J. W. Behnken

Dr. John William Behnken, the son of Pastor G. W. Behnken, was born March 19, 1884, at Cypress, Texas. He received his pretheological training at St. John's College, Winfield, Kansas, and was graduated from the seminary at St. Louis in 1906. Called as pastor of Trinity Lutheran Church, Houston, Texas, he was active especially in missionary endeavors and was instrumental in establishing six daughter congregations in the city of Houston. He was President of the Texas District, 1926 to 1929, and Vice-President of Synod, 1929—1935. In 1934 the faculty of Concordia Seminary, St. Louis, conferred upon him the degree of Doctor of Divinity. Dr. Behnken is the first American-born President of the Missouri Synod. His office is at Chicago (Oak Park), Illinois.

Synod created a Board of Appeals in 1941, at the same

time resolving that each District elect a similar board for the purpose of considering and adjudicating appeals by individual members or congregations from the decisions of an officer or a committee of a District or of Synod. The rules of procedure for this Board are found in the *Proceedings* of 1941 and 1944.

In accordance with Synod's resolution of 1941 the Lutheran Women's Missionary League was organized in St. Stephen's Church, Chicago, on July 7, 1942, with twelve District Leagues as charter members. The objectives of this organization are:

"a. To develop and maintain a greater mission consciousness among the women of Synod: Missionary Education — Missionary Inspiration — Missionary Service.

"b. To gather funds for mission projects sponsored by Synod, especially such for which no adequate provision has been made in the budget."

The first regular convention of the Lutheran Women's Missionary League was held at Concordia College, Fort Wayne, August 31 and September 1, 1943. Nineteen districts with 36,890 active members were represented by 73 delegates. The motto of the League is Ps. 100:2: "Serve the Lord with gladness."

Dr. E. Seuel, having served Synod as treasurer for twenty-eight years, resigned his office on March 24, 1942. Mr. W. H. Schlueter was appointed his successor.

At the Saginaw Convention, 1944, Mr. Henry W. Horst of Rock Island, Illinois, who had faithfully served Synod since 1917 on its General Board of Control and later on the Board of Directors, and Mr. A. H. Ahlbrand of Seymour, Indiana, who had been a member of the Board of Directors since 1923, were made honorary members of this Board.

At the same convention Synod resolved to adopt as its name: "The Lutheran Church, Missouri Synod." The change, however, was unpopular and failed to obtain ratification in a Synod-wide referendum.

EDUCATIONAL INSTITUTIONS

Synod's institutions of higher learning came in for many and long discussions during the years 1922—1945. One new academy was opened, one junior college was discontinued, three modern plants were built, and the curriculum in the existing schools was adjusted to conform to present-day standards of higher education.

The million dollars appropriated by the convention of 1920 for a new seminary at St. Louis were found to be insufficient for the needs of the institution. The firm of architects, Day and Klauder, submitted to the Delegate Synod of 1923 two plans of buildings for St. Louis. After a debate of four days, Synod adopted the more expensive group and voted an additional million and a half dollars to build it.

At the same convention the Texas District requested Synod to establish a preparatory school in its territory, so that native sons might be trained for the ministry and the frequent changes in the pastorates of its congregations eliminated. The brethren in Texas had subscribed $30,000 toward the building of an academy, and Synod granted an additional $50,000 for this purpose.

At Edmonton, Alberta, the college, opened in 1921, was still conducting its work in rented quarters. Synod, recognizing the need for permanent quarters, resolved to erect the necessary buildings as soon as the question of location was decided.

From practically all other institutions requests for dormitories, administration buildings, and professors' houses, had been presented to Synod, so that the total sum granted to the institutions by the convention of 1923 amounted to $3,850,000.

A Ways and Means Committee, consisting of Dean J. H. C. Fritz, Pastor J. C. Baur, and Mr. Theo. W. Eckhart, was appointed to raise the funds required for carrying out Synod's building program. Under the direction of this

Concordia Seminary, 1926

committee a house-to-house canvass was made throughout Synod on November 25, 1923, with the result that $4,824,-368.40 were pledged and paid by the end of 1924.

Just outside St. Louis a plot of 71.215 acres was purchased for $185,387.31, the St. Louis congregations contributing $75,000 of this amount. The cornerstone of the group of new buildings was laid on October 26, 1924, the service being broadcast by Radio Station KFUO. The new seminary was dedicated during the convention of 1926, on June 13. The chief speakers were Dr. F. Pfotenhauer in the German language and President J. W. Behnken in English. It was estimated that nearly 75,000 people attended the dedication ceremonies.

The Board of Directors, after hearing the arguments advanced by the two Western Canada Districts, fixed Edmonton, Alberta, as the permanent location for the Canadian Concordia. A new plant was erected at a cost of $146,875.76 and dedicated on January 10, 1926.

The location of the academy in Texas presenting no difficulties, the first unit of the school was erected at Austin at a cost of $83,489.48 and dedicated on October 17, 1926. The institution was opened with 26 students on October 26, with Pastor H. Studtmann as principal.

The work of survey committees, begun in 1917 for the purpose of raising the educational standards in Synod's schools of higher learning, was continued. In 1932 the Board of Directors was instructed to appoint a committee of thirteen to present recommendations to the convention of 1935 with reference to the whole field of Synod's educational system.

The Committee of Thirteen advised Synod in 1935 to close the seminary at Springfield. After a long debate the convention by a vote of 266 to 265 resolved to discontinue the institution which had been serving since 1846. But the chairman of the floor committee proposed further consideration of the question. When this was done a few days later, the vote was 283 to 256 in favor of retaining the practical seminary. The Committee of Thirteen advised also the closing of the junior colleges at Concordia, Missouri, and at Conover, North Carolina, and the academy at Portland, Oregon. Synod resolved to retain Concordia and Portland but to eliminate Conover.

The same convention (1935) instructed the President and the Vice-Presidents of Synod to appoint a Committee on Higher Education, which in turn was to select a Committee on Curriculum to decide on all matters pertaining to the courses both in the junior colleges and in the seminaries at St. Louis and Springfield. A special curriculum committee was appointed for the normal schools.

The courses of study suggested by the Committee on Curriculum were introduced in the pretheological schools in 1938. At the same time a fourth year was added to the seminary at St. Louis, in which certain pretheological courses, including Hebrew, are featured. The normal schools were expanded to senior colleges, and the colleges at Bronxville and at Oakland were granted co-education and a program for general education as experiments in these fields of education.

The Board for Higher Education again in 1941 proposed the closing of Springfield, Concordia, and Portland, but Synod postponed action until a complete institutional survey had been made. Prof. Theo. W. Hausmann of Bronxville, New York, was employed as Survey Director, beginning his work in October, 1941. His report to the convention of 1944 covered more than 125 closely printed pages. The convention resolved to retain all existing institutions in its educational system. Prof. M. J. Neeb was appointed Executive Secretary for the Board for Higher Education in 1945.

Dr. F. Pieper, who had been president of the seminary at St. Louis since May, 1887, departed this life June 3, 1931.

ABOUNDING MORE AND MORE (1922 - 1947)

He was succeeded in the presidency by Dr. L. Fuerbringer. When Dr. Fuerbringer retired in 1943, Dr. L. J. Sieck was called to head the seminary. In 1932 Synod made field work after two years of theological study obligatory for all St. Louis students. A mission department was added to the seminary's program of studies in 1941. The following men were added to the faculty: P. E. Kretzmann (1923); O. C. A. Boecler (1925); W. G. Polack (1925); R. W. Heintze (1926); Theodore Engelder (1926); Theodore Laetsch (1927); E. J. Friedrich (1930); Theodore Hoyer (1930); A. M. Rehwinkel (1936); F. E. Mayer (1937); George V. Schick (1938); R. A. Jesse (Dean, 1940); R. Caemmerer (1940); P. Bretscher (1941); A. W. C. Guebert (1943); W. R. Roehrs (1944); A. C. Repp (1945); M. H. Franzmann (1946); Lewis W. Spitz (1946).

The enrollment limit of 175 students placed upon the Springfield seminary in 1896 was raised by the convention of 1926. Synod in 1929 declined the memorial advocating combining the theological department of the practical seminary with that of St. Louis. The courses at Springfield were recast from time to time in accordance with the instructions of Synod and of Synod's Board for Higher Education. After 1941 the two high-school years were discontinued, and graduation from a high school or its equivalent was fixed as requisite for enrolling at the institution. On December 21, 1935, President H. A. Klein was fatally injured in an automobile accident. He was followed in the presidency by Dr. H. B. Hemmeter, who served in this capacity until June 1, 1945. Other members added to the faculty were F. Wenger (1923); W. H. Behrens (1924); F. E. Mayer (1926); O. P. Kretzmann (1927); W. Albrecht (1927); M. H. Coyner (1928); W. A. Baepler (1936); C. W. Spiegel (1938); F. L. Precht (1944); M. J. Steege (1946). Pastor G. Chr. Barth assumed the presidency of the seminary on December 16, 1945.

At the Teachers College at River Forest, Dr. W. C. Kohn was succeeded in the presidency by Dr. A. Klinck in 1939. Other members added to the faculty were A. Beck (1923); P. Bretscher (1923); A. E. Diesing (1923); R. T. Rohlfing (1925); T. C. Appelt (1926); W. O. Kraeft (1926); Theo. Kuehnert (1927); W. F. Kruse (1938); A. V. Maurer (1939); H. H. Gross (1940); R. A. Lange (1941); E. J. Wibracht (1941); W. R. Roehrs (1941); C. S. Scaer (1943); H. O. A. Keinath (1943); G. H. Reifschneider (1943); V. Hildner (1944); A. G. Huegli (1944); J. W. Klotz (1945); E. H. Deffner (1945); W. E. Buszin (1946).

At Seward, Director F. Jesse re-entered the ministry in October, 1923, Pastor C. F. Brommer becoming his successor in 1924. The faculty was enlarged by the following men: H. A. Koenig (1923); H. O. A. Keinath (1926); Theo. Stelzer (1926); W. Kruse (1927); W. Hellwege (1928); L. G. Bickel (1929); W. H. Beck (1937); C. T. Brandhorst (1938); H. Meyer (1941); W. G. Loesel (1944); W. F. Wolbrecht (1945); H. F. Werling (1945); L. C. Wuerffel (1946); P. Rosel (1946). Since 1941 Pastor A. O. Fuerbringer is president of the institution.

President W. C. Burhop of the Fort Wayne college returned to the ministry in 1937 and was followed in the presidency by Prof. O. Krueger, who served in this office until 1945. The staff of teachers had the following additions: E. C. Lewerenz (1923); H. D. Mensing (1923); K. H. Henrichs (1926); W. G. Herrling (1927); E. E. Foelber (1928); E. L. Meyer (1931); H. G. Bredemeier (1937); P. Huchthausen (1938); W. E. Buszin (1939); W. G. Kitzerow (1942); A. W. Reese (1946); Wilbert H. Rusch (1946). Prof. H. G. Bredemeier became president in 1946.

When President Barth left Milwaukee in 1934, he was succeeded by Prof. L. C. Rincker, who had been teaching at the institution since 1927. Additional faculty members were P. F. Koehneke (1923); P. Zanow (1924); V. Bartling

ABOUNDING MORE AND MORE (1922 - 1947)   287

(1926); A. C. Rehwaldt (1926); C. A. Hardt (1927); E. Hattstaedt (1927); A. Dede (1928); J. H. Gienapp (1930); J. E. R. Schmidt (1930); E. A. Jenne (1930); E. M. Plass (1936); O. E. Rupprecht (1937); J. Sullivan (1945).

In 1927 Prof. M. Graebner succeeded Director Theo. Buenger in the presidency of the college at St. Paul. Professors added to the staff were W. A. Dobberfuhl (1923); E. G. R. Siebert (1926); A. C. Streufert (1929); J. Berger (1931); E. J. Otto (1943). Pastor W. A. Poehler became president in 1946.

Director J. H. C. Kaeppel, the president of St. Paul's College at Concordia since 1888, departed this life in 1925. He was followed by Prof. O. Krueger, who, in turn, was succeeded by Pastor A. J. C. Moeller in 1938. Professors called to this institution since 1922 are L. W. Spitz (1925); (1930); O. T. Walle (1940); L. C. Otto (1942); L. F. Wahlers (1942); N. Gienapp (1944); Dr. E. L. Lueker (1946). napp (1944); Dr. E. L. Lueker (1946).

A. W. Meyer, President of St. John's College, Winfield, retired in 1928. Prof. A. M. Rehwinkel was his successor, and in 1937 he was followed by Pastor C. Mundinger. Members of the faculty during this period were C. A. Gieseler (1924); Geo. C. Schroedel (1924); G. A. Kuhlmann (1926); Theo. Hoyer (1927); F. C. Lankenau (1927); E. A. Wolfram (1930); L. C. Wunderlich (1939); O. Kruger (1940).

In 1936 Dr. Geo. A. Romoser, president of our institution at Bronxville, was unexpectedly called home. Pastor A. Doege entered upon his duties as president in 1937. Faculty members added were R. Hope (1926); E. T. Schroeder (1926); E. W. Luecke (1927); H. Grunau (1928); W. H. Luecke (1929); P. Woy (1931); Dr. H. Koch (1936); A. Meyer (1938); E. Manning (1940); O. Hoffmann (1941); H. E. Proehl (1945).

The college at Oakland passed under the control of Synod in 1923. The teaching force was increased by the following:

B. Lange (1923); E. Scaer (1926); O. H. Theiss (1928); A. Wessling (1930); H. Glock (1939); P. Huchthausen (1942).

The academy at Portland, likewise, was taken over by Synod in 1923, and Pastor K. Lorenz was added to the faculty. Pastor Thomas Coates became president in June, 1946.

The institution in Texas was opened in 1926 under the presidency of Pastor H. Studtmann, who was joined by the following professors: G. Viehweg (1928); M. J. Neeb (1930); G. F. Beto (1942); E. Huebschmann (1946).

Pastor O. W. H. Lindemeyer began to teach at Conover in 1928. Dr. H. B. Hemmeter returned as president of the institution the same year. The college was discontinued by Synod in 1935.

The faculty at our Canadian Concordia, Edmonton, Alberta, had the following additions: W. A. Baepler (1923); J. H. Herreilers (1924); M. W. Riedel (1926); A. Guebert (1928); A. R. Riep (1942); H. G. Witte (1945).

MISSIONS

During this period the missionary forces in India were augmented by the following missionaries:

1922: Teacher Paul Bachmann; F. J. H. Blaess; E. H. Meinzen.

1923: A. A. Brux; Miss Gertrude Strieter; M. G. Kuolt.

1925: R. H. Brauer; H. A. Schulz.

1926: Miss Anena Christensen; P. G. Eckert; W. W. Gnuse; S. G. Lang; Miss Louise Rathke; G. R. Stelter; D. S. Stevenson; A. R. Rasch.

1927: G. C. Hattendorf; E. H. Knoernschild; Miss Elsie Mahler, R. N.; H. J. E. Meyer; A. A. J. Mueller; Miss Clara Mueller, R. N.; A. von Schlichten; Miss Meta Schrader, R. N.; K. M. Zorn.

1928: A. J. Buehner; R. J. Burow; W. G. Landgraf; W. A.

Luedtke; H. T. Manns; H. E. Miller; C. L. Rittmann; M. L. Wyneken.

1929: D. S. Chuvala; J. G. P. Naumann; Miss Gertrude Oberheu, R. N.; H. F. Peckman; L. M. Wetzel; R. M. Zorn; Dr. Eleanor M. Bohnsack.

1930: W. C. Dukewitz; B. P. Hahn; W. E. Kraemer; M. L. Kretzmann.

1931: W. E. Bertram; N. W. Kline; W. E. Reiser.

1932: Miss Amelia Docter, R. N.; Miss Esther Feddersen; M. H. Grumm; E. H. Prange.

1935: Miss Margarete Lutz, R. N.; M. J. Lutz.

1936: H. Lachmann; Dr. N. F. Leckband.

1937: Teacher K. Mueller; R. P. Sieving; J. G. Steinhoff.

1945: A. Graf; E. E. Griesse; Theo. Michalk.

For various reasons some of the missionaries could serve in India only a few years and then had to return to the States.

In 1922 Bethesda Hospital was founded at Ambur by Dr. Theo. Doederlein of Chicago and generously endowed by him and his wife. Miss Angela Rehwinkel, R. N., has served as superintendent of this institution since its founding. In 1924 a theological seminary was established at Nagercoil, Travancore, for the purpose of training an indigenous ministry.

Besides the missionaries, deaconesses, and nurses, Synod employs teacher-catechists, evangelists, and Bible women in its missionary work. A teacher-catechist is a person trained to teach not only the common secular subjects, but also the Christian truths to young and old in the villages. He reads a sermon to the village flock in the Sunday services if there is no evangelist in the village and if it is impossible for the missionary to be present. An evangelist is a graduate of our Nagercoil seminary who passed his first examination, but must submit to a final examination before he is recommended to a pastorate. These men work for a number of years in the village congregations under the supervision of a missionary and, when they have approved themselves, are admitted to the final examination for the ministerial office. Bible women are native female workers who are trained to meet the Indian women in their homes and to teach them the Word of God. They work under the supervision of the wives of our missionaries, nurses, and

Bethesda Hospital, Ambur, India

deaconesses in the so-called zenana missions, that is, missions to the female population of India.

In 1923 A. A. Brux, Ph. D., was called for work among the Mohammedans in India. Later R. J. Burow joined him. Although a few converts were won, no congregation could be founded.

The mission field in India was visited by Dr. F. Brand, Director and General Secretary of Foreign Missions, in 1921 and in 1926; by M. S. Sommer and Pastor H. M. Zorn in 1930, and by Pastor O. H. Schmidt in 1943.

Our Chapel at Vaniyambadi, India

Mission School with Native Teachers, India

Synod supports the following mission stations in India: Madras Presidency: Krishnagiri, Salem District (1895); Ambur, North Arcot District (1896); Bargur, Salem District (1898); Vaniyambadi, North Arcot District (1898); Pernambut, North Arcot District (1923); Vadakangulam, Tinnevelley District (1928); South India Evangelical Lutheran Church (1923).

Close of Service in Kollegal, India

Travancore: Nagercoil (1907); Trivandrum (1911); Kattakal (1914); Balaramapuram (1922); Ponvilla (1924); Nilamel (1925); Alleppey (1927).
Mysore State: Kolar Gold Fields (1914).
Ceylon: Colombo (1929).

As of July 1, 1945, 36 male and 4 female missionaries were engaged in the work. Of Indian Mission helpers there were 20 pastors, 17 evangelists, 152 catechists, 10 Bible women, 264 teachers, 2 Indian doctors, 5 male nurses, and 5 female nurses. Work was being carried on in 210 congregations and at 66 teaching and preaching places. 19,503 souls, 16,034 of them baptized and 5,211 communicant members, were shepherded by Synod's mission force.

The following workers were sent to China since 1922:

1922: C. D. Nagel; C. F. Schmidt; A. H. Ziegler.

Preaching at a Village Market at Krishnagiri, India

1923: Miss Frieda Oelschlaeger; Miss Marie Oelschlaeger, R. N.; J. W. Fischer.

1924: Miss Martha Baden, R. N.; Dr. Peter Kleid.

1926: A. E. Cloeter; A. F. Meyer; Miss Gertrude Simon, R. N.; M. P. Simon; H. O. Theiss; E. H. Thode.

1928: W. A. McLaughlin; E. C. Zimmermann.

1929: R. J. Mueller; E. N. Seltz.

1930: L. A. Buuck; W. H. Werling.

1931: A. C. Diers; H. C. Meyer; R. J. Muehl; Teacher N. Nero; Miss Clara Rodenbeck, R. N.; A. Koehler.

1932: G. K. Wenger.

1934: Teacher T. Breihan.
1936: P. W. Frillman.
1939: P. R. Martens; K. E. Voss.
1940: C. E. Dohrman.
1943: H. A. Hinz; R. C. Egolf.

After Dr. Brand's visits to China in 1921 and in 1926, additional stations were established in four large cities, all lying on the Yangtse River and accessible by steamer from Hankow. These were Ichang, 370 miles from Hankow; Shasi, 287 miles from Hankow; Wanhsien, 600 miles from Hankow, and Kweifu, lying between Ichang and Wanhsien. Shinan (Enshih) had been opened in 1919.

In 1933 Missionary M. Zschiegner explored part of the Hopei Province, 1,000 miles north of Hankow, where Evangelist Bee had been working for several years. A permanent station was opened in this territory. Another station was opened at Simakow, in the Han River district.

Christian day schools were opened as well as two middle schools, one for boys and one for girls, in Hankow. A school for evangelists in Hankow prepared teachers and evangelists. Concordia Theological Seminary at Hankow was founded in 1921. Dispensaries were opened at Shinan and at Hankow, likewise an orphanage at Shinan.

By the liberality of the Walther League and by the special efforts of Mrs. Blair, the former Agnes Arndt, a number of residences were built at Kuling, about 190 miles below Hankow. The hill station is called the Walther League Mountain Retreat and serves as a vacation resort for our missionaries.

After sixteen years of untiring work, the pioneer of Missouri Synod missions in China, Missionary E. L. Arndt, died on April 18, 1929. He had been an indefatigable translator of Christian literature into the Chinese language, having translated Walther's *Evangelienpostille*, parts of the *Book of Concord*, Pieper's *Christliche Dogmatik*, over 900 sermons of Dr. Walther, Stoeckhardt, and others, and many other theological books and Lutheran literature into Chinese.

The report for October 31, 1937, listed 16 organized congregations, 36 preaching stations, 17 male and 2 women missionaries, 53 native mission workers, 2,589 souls, 2,273 baptized members, 859 communicant members.

The sudden death of Missionary Max Zschiegner was a stunning blow to his co-workers in China and a shock to

Baptismal and Confirmation Class Received into Membership with Trinity Congregation, Hanyang, China, by Missionary A. H. Ziegler, May 30, 1937

his many friends in America. He died at Wanhsien January 23, 1940, at the age of 42 years.

Mission work in China has been very much hampered and disorganized through internal political troubles and war. In the political uprisings of 1927 all missionaries except E. L. Arndt were forced to flee from their stations and to retire to the coast for safety. Then came the Chinese-Japanese War, beginning in 1937. As the Japanese soldiers spread out in occupied China, the missionaries had to move westward. The seminary at Hankow was moved to Wanhsien in 1938 and finally had to be closed because of lack of students. When America became involved in war with Japan, Missionaries H. Klein, E. H. Thode, L. A. Buuck, E. C. Zimmermann, and Mrs. A. H. Ziegler and their families were made prisoners of war. They were repatriated in 1942, arriving at New York on the *Gripsholm*, August 25.

Baptismal Group, Shasi, China

By October, 1945, only four American workers were left in China; Wenger at Enshih, Martens at Kunming, Voss and Hinz at Wanhsien. They were assisted by seven Chinese pastors, twelve evangelists, and about two dozen natives.

A new day for missions in China is dawning, however. Immediately after the conclusion of the present war Missionaries Martens and Wenger cabled the Board for Foreign Missions: "15 missionaries, one doctor, two nurses urgently needed for rehabilitation." In the fall of 1945 Missionary A. H. Ziegler returned to China and was followed in November of the same year by Candidate W. Hoeltje.

Since 1940 Pastor O. H. Schmidt is serving as Executive Secretary to the Board for Foreign Missions.

The Board of Missions to the Deaf widened its program in 1927 by including mission work among the blind. Pastor A. H. Kuntz was called for this purpose and after learning to read and write Braille, published Luther's Catechism and a monthly periodical, the *Lutheran Messenger for the Blind*. At first it was intended to provide Synod's blind people with Christian literature. But when other blind people heard of the *Messenger*, the missionary soon was swamped with inquiries and requests. More books were published: a Bible History, a hymnal with tunes, a prayer book, and a biography of Luther.

A second missionary, Pastor O. C. Schroeder, was called to publish a quarterly in Moon type, the *Lutheran Herald*. Missionary Schroeder edited also *Der Lutherische Bote* in German Braille and tracts in the Spanish language.

The *Lutheran Messenger*, in Braille, is being mailed monthly to about 1,200 addresses, reaching approximately 2,000 readers through libraries and other agencies. The *Lutheran Herald*, in Moon type, is sent to 770 addresses quarterly, reaching about 1,200 blind. Spanish Braille tracts were mailed quarterly to 50 addresses, reaching several hundred blind. Owing to the war, the Braille *Bote*, which had been serving 2,000 blind, was discontinued for the duration.

In 1943 a home was purchased in Chicago, which serves in part as a library for the literature for the blind. The library contains more than 600 volumes of religious books in Braille, Moon Type, and New York Point. About 60 volumes are added each year by volunteer transcribers. The books are sent as a free loan to the blind in America and many foreign countries. No postage is required for this in our country.

In its work among the deaf and blind Synod has at present twenty full-time workers, one part-time worker, and three interns. At three stations also colored deaf receive the Gospel. In 1943 the missionaries were serving 258 stations with 4,980 souls and 2,648 communicant members.

The official organ of the mission among the deaf is the *Deaf Lutheran.* The missionaries meet annually as the Ephphatha Conference. Pastor J. L. Salvner, D. D., is the Secretary of Missions for the Deaf.

Bethlehem Lutheran Church for the Deaf and Parsonage at Omaha, Nebr.

At its convention in 1932, Synod eliminated the boards for Foreign-tongue Missions, Jewish Missions, Indian Missions, Seamen's Mission, and Immigrant Missions and transferred these missions to the District or Districts in which the work was being done. The status of the various missions at this time was:

    a. Jewish missions: Nathaniel Friedmann, New York; Kenneth Frankenstein, St. Louis; and Isidore Schwartz, Chicago.

    b. Indian Missions: O. W. C. Boettcher was stationed at Red Springs, Wisconsin, C. Aaron, a native Indian, at

Oneida, Wisconsin, L. Dau at Neopit and Morgan Siding, Wisconsin; C. C. Gutekunst was serving a station at Tomah, Wisconsin, and F. Geisweiler was stationed on the Yakima Reservation in Washington.

c. Polish Mission: Jose Olszar was working in Colgate, Maryland, John Olszar in Inglis, Manitoba, Theo. Engel in Chicago, and S. Martell in Trenton, New Jersey.

d. Lithuanian Mission: J. Rozak was stationed in Chicago; H. S. Brustat in Naugatuck, Connecticut.

e. Latvian Mission: J. Graudin, stationed in Boston; F. C. Pudsell in Philadelphia; W. V. Kuhlberg in Chicago.

f. Slovak Mission: M. M. Hevlir, stationed in Northampton and West Hatfield, Massachusetts; Geo. Pankuch in Hudson, New York.

g. Italian Mission: A. Bongarzone, stationed in Union City, New Jersey; A. Messina in Englewood, New Jersey; P. D. Maida in Hoboken, New Jersey.

h. Finnish Mission: A. E. Kokkonen, stationed in Jersey City.

i. Persian Mission: L. Pera, stationed in Chicago.

j. Spanish (Mexican) Mission: Jose Fernandez, stationed in Chicago; B. Martinelli in Los Angeles.

k. The Immigrant Mission in New York was in charge of Pastor C. Gallman, and Pastor M. Pinkert was engaged in mission work among the seamen. Pastor John E. Herzer was working in Winnipeg, Manitoba, as immigrant missionary.

In 1922 Pastor C. Frieling began to explore mission possibilities among the German-speaking people in Mexico. For one year he was at Monterrey and after that in Mexico City. Here he was able to gather a flock of 65 souls and 30 communicants. He conducted services also at Tampico and at Gonzales. His successor was Pastor J. H. Gaertner, who arrived in Mexico City in 1931, but who had to discontinue his work because of ill health. The depression in the United States and the nationalistic movement in Mexico combined to close down the mission work in Mexico.

The Texas District began work among the Spanish-speaking people in Texas early in 1926. At the present time such missions are established at San Antonio, Three Rivers, Brownsville, Corpus Christi, Houston, and Austin

In 1940 the Texas District opened a mission among the natives in Mexico City through Pastor C. A. Lazos, a native Mexican. Pastor F. Segovia is in charge of the Mexican mission at Monterrey. In order to train a native ministry, Synod resolved to open a theological Seminary in Mexico City. Prof. A. W. Reese of Concordia, Missouri, was called for this purpose in 1945.

Noticiero Luterano, an eight-page monthly, is the official paper for all our Spanish work in Texas and in Mexico.

In 1912 John E. Herzer, Vernon, British Columbia, was dispatched by the mission board of the Minnesota District to make an exploration trip to Alaska. He canvassed Ketchikan, Wrangell, Petersburg, Treadwell, Douglas, and Juneau, finding twenty resident Lutherans and many transient Lutherans, chiefly of Scandinavian origin.

Pastor H. Kuring, missionary at large of the Alberta-British Columbia District, made a thorough canvass of the Alaskan centers in 1926, and in 1927 took up his abode at Anchorage as the first resident pastor of our Synod in Alaska. The mission work was extremely difficult, but a small band was very faithful in attending services and the little flock gradually increased. By means of the radio, Station KFQD, the missionary was able to bring the Gospel to the people of Alaska every Friday evening. Other places served by Pastor Kuring were Wasilla, Eklunta, Fairbanks, Matanuska, Tanana, and Seward.

Pastor Kuring was succeeded in 1930 by Candidate R. M. Frieling, whose work was discontinued at the end of 1932, when owing to the depression and lack of funds the Alberta-British Columbia District had to close its mission work in Alaska.

When the Federal Emergency Relief Administration settled some 200 families in the Matanuska Valley, 160 miles north of Seward, the Board for Home Missions of our Synod in 1935 requested Pastor Frieling, who had remained in Alaska, to minister to the needs of the Lutherans in the Matanuska colony.

After the officials of the Mission Board of the Oregon and Washington District had thoroughly investigated the conditions and prospects of the Valley, a call was extended to Pastor Frieling. On July 18, 1937, a church-parsonage was dedicated at Palmer, and on the same evening a congregation numbering 75 communicants was organized. Pastor Frieling resigned as pastor the same year and was succeeded in January, 1939, by Candidate Martin Zschoche. During the interval Pastor W. F. Georg served the flock at Anchorage and at Palmer. Pastor Zschoche was followed in 1941 by Candidate W. Kurth. In 1944 Pastor G. E. Nitz of Pocatello, Idaho, took up his residence at Anchorage to serve as missionary at large in Alaska. Candidate W. L. Zeile went to Palmer in 1945.

Synod in 1941 instructed the Board of Home Missions to make a thorough survey of the mission opportunities in the Hawaiian Islands and gave it authority to begin work there, if in its estimation such action was warranted. In November of the same year Pastor F. C. Streufert, Executive Secretary of Missions, and Pastor Aug. Hansen, the field secretary of the California and Nevada District, went to Honolulu, where, on December 3, a joint meeting of civilians and men in the armed forces was held to discuss the possibility of opening a mission station in that city. The war delayed the mission project. The Board of Home Missions turned over the spiritual care of our Lutheran civilians to the Army and Navy

Commission, which had purchased a service center in a centrally located spot in Honolulu. Pastor Virtus Gloe was called to take care of the spiritual needs of servicemen and civilians.

In 1945 Pastor Adolph R. Meyer of Augusta, Georgia, was sent as missionary to the Hawaiian Islands by the California and Nevada District. On August 12, 1945, he organized a congregation in Honolulu under the name "Our Redeemer Ev. Lutheran Church of Hawaii." The congregation resolved to open a Christian day school as soon as possible.

In the year 1940, Pastor O. H. Schmidt and Candidate Alvaro Carino, a Filipino, educated at Concordia, Mo., and at St. Louis, made an extensive survey of the Philippine Islands, interviewing most of the church leaders in the commonwealth of the Philippines and many leaders in education, industry, and public life. Although the Board for Foreign Missions resolved in March, 1941, to open a mission in the Philippines, the invasion of the Japanese forces brought all plans to nought. In 1945 Candidate Herman Mayer was designated as missionary for the Philippine Islands.

TRANSOCEANIC RELATIONS AND SOUTH AMERICA

Dr. Geo. Mezger of the St. Louis seminary was sent to Germany in 1923 to act as the representative of the Missouri Synod in Europe and to teach at the theological institution at Zehlendorf. He continued in this position until his death, November 3, 1931. Statistics of the Saxon Evangelical Lutheran Free Church as of 1938 were: 40 pastors, 62 congregations, 12,662 souls, 9,362 communicants. Services were being conducted in 190 towns and cities. Eighteen of the congregations were self-supporting.

The four pastors working in Alsace organized the Evangelical Lutheran Free Church in Alsace, France, in 1928. The statistics for 1938 were: five pastors, fourteen congregations and preaching stations, 552 souls, and 393 communicant members. Pastor F. C. Kreiss was serving a Lutheran congregation in Paris, France.

In Finland the Evangelical Lutheran Free Church of Finland was established in 1928 by four pastors who had left the state church. In 1938 this group numbered 3 pastors, 56 preaching stations, 429 souls, 259 communicant members.

Since 1928 Synod has been supporting the Lutheran congregation at Arensburg on the island of Oesel, in Estonia, the pastor, the Rev. N. Baeuerle, and his flock having separated from the state church. The congregation numbered 105 communicant members in 1938.

The convention of 1941 granted these churches in Europe an annual subsidy of $30,000.

World War II ruined the congregations in East Prussia, West Prussia, and Pomerania. Of the four buildings at Zehlendorf two cannot be repaired, and the other two only at heavy cost. The churches in Berlin and Dresden were completely destroyed. Of the 52 pastors appearing in the roster of the Saxon Free Church prepared by President P. H. Petersen in August, 1945, fifteen had been drafted into army service, four were dead, and no information was available concerning four other pastors.

At an emergency meeting of the German Synod, held at Gross-Oesingen, August 13, 1945, the name of the body was changed to the Evangelical Lutheran Free Church of Germany. This convention resolved urgently to request the Missouri Synod:

1. "To send to the Evangelical Lutheran Free Church all available German theological and devotional literature gratis, especially the works of Dr. C. F. W. Walter and Dr. F. Pieper and some standard English theological literature, also German Bibles and catechisms.

2. "To send to Europe and especially to Germany a commission consisting of the foremost theological and spiritual leaders.

3. "To lose no time, but for Jesus' sake and for the succor of souls to act at once."

Fraternal relations with the brethren in Australia were strengthened by the visit of Dr. John H. C. Fritz in 1938. During his stay of 4½ months, during which time he visited most of the Australian congregations, he preached and lectured more than 90 times.

Marked strides forward were made in the South American work. As a result of personal visits by men such as President

College and Normal School at Crespo

Pfotenhauer, Pastor Aug. Burgdorf, Pastor L. Schmidke, Mr. Henry W. Horst, Dr. Paul Schulz, and Dr. F. C. Streufert, the congregations are assuming year after year a larger measure of self-support and self-government.

The work in Brazil has been hampered to some extent by the "Nationalization Program," effective since the beginning of the present decade, under which Synod can no longer send North American missionaries to that country. To help relieve the crying need for men, the faculty of the seminary at Porto Alegre has intensified the curriculum of the institution, making it possible to graduate more ministerial candidates. After Brazil entered the war, the use of the German language was forbidden; the language of the country, Portuguese, is the only language permitted in church and in school. The Brazilian school laws present another difficulty. Only native-born Brazilians can be heads of schools. Since this law is rigidly enforced, a number of Synod's schools have been closed. The missionaries, preaching in the Portuguese language, are branching out in their work to reach the natives of Brazil.

In 1923 the Casa Publicadora Concordia, Synod's Brazilian Publishing House, was established at Porto Alegre, in which the necessary schoolbooks, hymnbooks, church papers, and other literature are printed.

The statistics covering the work in Brazil are: 88 pastors, 6 professors, 71 teachers, 41,040 souls, 72 congregations members of Synod and 156 congregations not yet members, 135 preaching stations. Of the 92 pastors and professors now active in the Brazil District only 18 were trained in North America.

Argentina branched off as a District from Brazil in 1927. The nationalization program and the language situation are not so grave here as in Brazil. Missionaries from North America can still be sent to Argentina. The laws of the country, however, make it impossible to have parochial schools. The missionaries are doing much work by means of the Spanish language, not only among Lutherans, but especially among the natives, thereby opening an unlimited field for our work.

In order to stimulate the development of a native ministry, an institution was opened at Crespo in 1926, serving both as a normal school and as a pre-theological college for the seminary at Porto Alegre. However, since the language of Argentina is Spanish and that of Brazil Portuguese, Synod deemed it wise to open a seminary in Argentina. This was done in 1942, when Prof. A. Lehenbauer opened the Argentina theological institution at Buenos Aires.

The statistics for Argentina (1944) are: 27 pastors, 3 professors, 19 congregations belonging to Synod, 47 congregations not yet members of Synod, 55 preaching stations, 12,700 souls, including Paraguay and Uruguay. Less than 12 of the pastors and professors working in the Argentine District received their training in North America.

Concórdia Seminary, Buenos Aires

Since 1936 Synod has a mission station in Paraguay, at Hohenau, in the midst of a large German colony. The parish is served by Pastor Vernon Harley.

Pastor E. Jauck, a native of Argentina, but trained at St. Louis, is working at Montevideo, Uruguay, since 1942. He has gathered two different groups, one speaking the German, the other the Spanish language. In the latter group we have 70 families, in the other 12.

In both Brazil and Argentina the radio is being used for broadcasting Lutheran services in the language of the countries.

SYNOD AND ITS FINANCES

In order to adjust Synod's finances, the Board of Directors through the Financial Secretary, Theo. W. Eckhart, called a meeting of the fiscal officers of each District at Holy Cross School, St. Louis, June 7 and 8, 1926. Synod, realizing the wisdom and benefit of such deliberations, resolved at its convention the same year that "a meeting of the fiscal officers of the Districts, each District to be represented by its President and one of its financial officers, be held annually for the purpose of reviewing and discussing the financial situation of Synod and making such recommendations to the various Districts as will help them to solve their financial problems." Thus the annual Fiscal Conference of Synod came into being.

To provide for a continuous audit of its finances, Synod in 1929 appointed Mr. A. W. Huge as its auditor, a position which he still holds.

The depression years of the early thirties made themselves felt also in Synod's work. Deficits in the various treasuries began to accumulate, so that at the convention of 1932 it was reported that as of May 31, 1932, Synod's debt stood at $856,520.65, of which $591,000 had been borrowed from banks and other sources. The Board of Directors was instructed to make a special effort during the current year and the following years to bring the receipts up to the budget requirements and to collect a Synod-wide self-denial offering. The suggestion of the lay delegates that every communicant member of Synod be urged to contribute at least five cents a week for one year, and that every child of school age be requested to pay two cents a week for one year in order to liquidate Synod's debt and to balance the budget was adopted at this time.

The Board of Directors at once took drastic measures to stabilize Synod's finances. A cut in the salaries of all employees of synod (professors, secretaries, etc.) amounting to 25 per cent, saved Synod $99,000 as compared with 1931. A further considerable saving was effected by transferring expense items in connection with the house service at the institutions to the students, thereby relieving Synod of an outlay of $103,994.79 as compared with 1931. In spite of these measures, Synod's debt as of October 31, 1932, stood at $1,130,797.77.

The self-denial collection helped materially to balance the budget of 1932. No special effort of this kind having been made in 1933, Synod closed the year with a deficit in its operating accounts. The banks' refusing to lend Synod money without acceptable collateral moved the Board of Directors on April 25, 1933, to appeal to the members for loans for which Synod's treasurer was ready to pay four per cent interest. In 1934 the Open Bible Thankoffering brought in sufficient funds (about $400,000) not only to balance the budget, but to pay off some of the debts remaining from previous years. The liberality of Louis H. Waltke made it possible for all Visitors of the Districts to attend the Fiscal Conference at River Forest in 1936, when these important officials were given a helpful insight into the finances of Synod and the making of the budget. A similar meeting was arranged by Mr. Waltke in 1937 for the members of the District Centennial Committees. In 1938 a pre-convention debt collection was inaugurated by the Board of Directors under the direction of Pastor G. Chr. Barth. At this time Synod's debt stood at $614,687.19.

Synod in 1938 resolved to gather a nation-wide Centennial Thankoffering in the amount of one million dollars, which sum was practically collected in 1939, thereby liquidating all of Synod's debts, although the operating budget was short in the amount of $38,362.85 at the close of the fiscal year.

The Call-of-the-Cross movement, introduced in 1939 and

ABOUNDING MORE AND MORE (1922 - 1947)   309

carried on under the direction of the President of Synod and the Publicity Department and which involved about 80 meetings in various parts of Synod did much to advance the laity to a consciousness of the work of their Church and of their own personal mission obligations.

Since 1940 Synod was able not only to meet its annual budget, but to lay aside a handsome amount for the lean years to come. The per-capita contribution of Synod's members which in 1930 amounted to $21.19 rose in 1944 to $30.83. The budget for 1946 has been fixed at $2,750,000.00.

At its meeting in September, 1944, the Fiscal Conference resolved "that the Board of Directors be authorized to inaugurate a Five Million Dollar Peace Thankoffering," in order to supply Synod with funds to carry out its building program at the various institutions, rehabilitate its missions at home and abroad, and to assist in the reconstruction work in Europe after World War II. April 22, 1945, was fixed as the beginning of the ingathering of the Thankoffering and Pentecost Sunday as the termination of the time for receiving pledges. The total amount received and pledged as of August 31, 1945, was $5,661,700.

PREACHING THE GOSPEL OVER THE AIR

On February 19, 1923, the Board of Control of Concordia Seminary, St. Louis, by request of its chairman, Pastor R. Kretzschmar, discussed the possibilities of erecting a radio station at the seminary. At a joint meeting of the Lutheran Laymen's League and the building committee of the new Concordia Seminary February 28, 1923, it was reported that the Seminary Board had reached the decision to install a powerful radio station for the purpose of spreading the truth of God's Word to counteract the error, deception, and unbelief which were being broadcast daily throughout the country. The Lutheran Laymen's League immediately resolved to support the project and pledged $2,285 at the meeting. On May 21 the St. Louis Lutheran Publicity Association appropriated $1,000 for the maintenance and upkeep of a radio station, and the students of the seminary at the suggestion of Dean Fritz solicited donations in the amount of $1,500 from their relatives and friends for this purpose, at the same time donating $1,000 from the Students' Treasury to this project. At its convention at St. Paul, Minnesota, in July, 1924, the Walther League resolved to appropriate $7,000 toward the proposed radio station.

On October 26, 1924, at 2:45 P. M., Station KFUO went on the air for the first time, broadcasting by remote control the cornerstone-laying service of the new seminary. After a soundproof studio had been built and equipped and the control room completed (in the old Seminary), the station was dedicated to the service of the Triune God on December 14, 1924.

The removal of the seminary to its new location involved the transfer of Station KFUO. The Lutheran Laymen's League resolved to rebuild and maintain the station at the new seminary site with the understanding that $50,000 would be required for the new station and an annual sum of $20,000 to $25,000 to operate it effectively. Synod, having taken over the station in 1926, expressed its gratitude to the Lutheran Laymen's League in appropriate terms. On May 29, 1927, the new home of KFUO was dedicated.

The Federal Communications Commission on July 1, 1940, assigned a new frequency to KFUO, namely, 830 kilocycles instead of 550. On March 29, 1941, the frequency was changed to 850 kilocycles. At the same time the Government authorized KFUO to broadcast continuously throughout the day from sunrise at St. Louis to sunset at Denver, Colorado. A new 5,000-watt transmitter went into operation on September 14, 1941. The station was enlarged in 1942 at an expense of $100,000, contributed by freewill offerings.

Since 1924 Pastor H. H. Hohenstein has been director of the station. He is assisted by a staff of approximately 25. The monthly sum of nearly $6,500 required to operate the station is made up by contributions from our congregations, listeners, Synod — $10,000 annually since 1941 — and the Lutheran Laymen's League. The station has remained noncommercial since its beginning and has in every sense of the word proved to be the "Gospel Voice."

On October 2, 1930, the Lutheran Hour was launched by the Lutheran Laymen's League. The religious program was conducted on Thursday evenings over a coast-to-coast network of thirty-eight stations. On June 11, 1931, the last Lutheran Hour broadcast was sent over the air. It was not until early in 1935 that the Lutheran Hour was resumed over WXYZ in Detroit and WLW in Cincinnati. Since that time it has been a regular weekly feature on the radio.

Three significant and far-reaching steps of progress were taken in 1939: the number of stations was increased to 99, the use of electrical transcriptions was introduced, and the radio system was extended into fields outside the United States.

The broadcast year 1944—1945 numbered 682 stations. The number of letters received at headquarters was more than 500,000. In 1944 broadcasts were introduced into Australia.

The Thirteenth Lutheran Hour (1945—1946) is heard in English, Spanish, and Portuguese, either by voice or by electrical transcription, over a total of 682 stations. In the United States 438 outlets carry the Lutheran Hour in English and 38 in Spanish. Outside the United States 70 stations carry the Lutheran Hour in English, 130 in Spanish, and 6 in Portuguese in the following countries: Alaska, Argentina, Australia, Bolivia, Brazil, British Guiana, British West Indies, Canada, Chile, Colombia, Costa Rica, Cuba, the Dominican Republic, Dutch Guiana, Ecuador, Haiti, Hawaii,

Honduras, Mozambique, Nicaragua, Panama, Paraguay, Peru, Puerto Rico, Uruguay, and Venezuela. 36 outlets are used throughout Australia and the neighboring Island of Tasmania.

Dr. W. A. Maier of Concordia Seminary, St. Louis, has been the speaker on the Lutheran Hour since its beginning in 1930.

THE BOARD OF SUPPORT AND PENSIONS

For years the support of superannuated pastors and teachers and pastors' and teachers' widows and orphans was a vexing problem. Synod annually spent relatively large sums in the discharge of its obligations towards these servants — the 1946 budget has an item of $400,000 for this purpose — but the amounts paid to the beneficiaries were a mere pittance.

Already in 1917 Synod instructed its Board of Support to submit a plan for a synodical pension system which was eventually to supersede the current system of assisting the "Veterans of the Cross," but it was not until 1937 that Synod ordered the Board of Directors to introduce a system of pension that would be equitable to all concerned. Acting on the instructions of the Board of Directors, the Board of Support, together with five advisory members appointed by the Board of Directors, completed the plan which had been submitted to Synod in 1935 and with the help of expert counsel and after most careful deliberation and consultation instituted the present pension system on October 1, 1937.

When the plan was introduced, more than 600 workers and 350 congregations had registered, practically all District boards had voted to participate, and the Fiscal Conference had included the necessary funds in its 1938 budget for the workers salaried by the synodical boards.

As of August 31, 1945, 5,052 workers and 2,914 congregations were enrolled in Synod's pension plan. The assets of the fund amounted to $3,092,973.87.

SUNDAY SCHOOLS AND ELEMENTARY EDUCATION

Synod in 1920 resolved to appoint a Sunday School Board which was to assist congregations in preserving and improving the Sunday schools in a truly Lutheran spirit. The Board was charged to provide for the publication of the necessary lessons and pertinent literature in general and to see to it that Concordia Publishing House offered appropriate Sunday school supplies. In 1923 the Board was made a permanent institution. It consisted of Pastor P. Koenig, Dr. P. E. Kretzmann, and Th. Kuehnert, Superintendent of Schools of the Western District.

The Board not only emphasized the use of proper material in the Sunday schools, but advocated in particular the thorough training of Sunday school teachers. It urged all pastors and congregations to have regular meetings for the Sunday school teachers, preferably weekly. For the sake of such teachers as had no opportunity to receive the necessary instruction it instituted a Correspondence Course, which from the very beginning was self-sustaining.

In 1927 Pastor Wm. H. Luke of Calgary, Alberta, was called to the position of editor of the Sunday school literature, director of the Correspondence School, and acting secretary of the Sunday School Board.

The Board of Christian Education and the Sunday School Board amalgamated in 1932 to form the Board of Christian Education. Since that time additional areas have been assigned to this Board, including the supervision of high schools controlled by congregations and adult education. This led Synod in 1944 to change the name of the Board to the Board for Parish Education.

Pastor Luke having died in 1933, Pastor A. C. Mueller was called as his successor. In 1943 Pastor A. C. Repp assumed the duties as Executive Secretary for the Board for Parish Education.

The work of the staff of the Board for Parish Education is divided into three departments. Mr. A. C. Stellhorn, Secretary of Schools, assisted by Mr. Wm. A. Kramer, looks after the interest of our Christian day schools. Pastor A. C. Mueller, assisted by Dr. J. Weidenschilling and Mr. A. W. Gross, prepares the material for use in our Sunday schools, Junior Bible classes, and vacation Bible schools. Pastor Oscar Feucht is in charge of the department of adult education. Mr. A. L. Miller is the Executive Secretary.

Since 1944 Lutheran Education Week has been observed annually in Synod. Its purpose is to make the congregations more conscious of their educational obligations and opportunities and to help them carry out the program of the Board for Parish Education.

YOUNG PEOPLE'S WORK

At its convention in 1920 Synod elected a Board for Young People's Work, consisting of Prof. Theo. Graebner, Pastors R. Jesse, A. Merz, Teacher L. H. Becker, and Mr. Theo. F. Lange. On recommendation of this Board Synod in 1923 adopted the following resolutions:

1. "We fear that in our circles not enough work has been done among our confirmed youth and, when carried on, has frequently been done unsystematically, with little definite aim, and with but insufficient energy. Where, for example, young people's societies were organized, these often were of short duration or frequently degenerated into mere societies for entertainment. The young people were not really familiarized with the Bible and were not systematically encouraged and educated to take an active part in the work of the Lord and to offer and give active service.

2. "We recommend that sound helps be provided for work among our young Christians, especially for promoting Bible knowledge. We would advise the Board for Young People's work to acquaint itself with the entire work of the

Walther League and repeatedly to report on it in our church papers.

3. "We call attention to the fact that in young people's societies entertainment is easily overstressed while church history and church work are not sufficiently emphasized; that entertainments may degenerate and be carried on in a worldly spirit. At times no real co-operation exists between the pastor and the society.

4. "Young people's societies and organizations of such are to be told that they must not of their own accord take up any work that encroaches upon the rights and privileges of congregations or synods. If properly aroused, much desire for work will show itself among our young people, and they are able to render great help. But they must remember that they are merely to assist, not to rule."

Synod resolved to continue the Board for Young People's Work and encouraged it to remain in close touch with the Walther League and to this end approved the following agreement made between the officials of the Walther League and Synod's Board, April 30, 1923:

a. "That there be mutual co-operation between Synod's official Board for Young People's Work and representatives of the Walther League. This is to be brought about by joint meetings and exchange of reports of the committees on the activities in the interest of young people's work.

b. "All larger matters pertaining to young people's work and affecting the congregations of Synod shall be undertaken only after the approval of the Board for Young People's Work has been obtained."

Synod likewise endorsed the following guiding principles for young people's work submitted by the Western District in 1922:

a. "That the Bible be studied more by our young people. We, therefore, urge that every young people's society be a Bible society.

b. "That particular stress be laid upon educational work among our young people in order that in future our Church may have well-informed and intelligent workers.

c. "That the congregations provide libraries for their young people, selecting books recommended by our Publishing House. We feel that in this way the reading of our young people will receive the proper supervision.

d. "That young people's societies of our Districts be advised to affiliate with the Walther League, since the things mentioned are fostered most effectively by the Walther League.

e. "That congregations having no young people's societies be advised to organize their young people.

f. "That congregations organizing their young people be advised to co-operate with the Walther League." [2]

At its convention in 1929 Synod urged the Districts to elect Boards for Young People's Work which were to cooperate with Synod's Board for Young People's Work and in 1932 again reaffirmed its endorsement of the Walther League and its worthy aims. It furthermore recommended the close and wholehearted co-operation between the synodical District Committee for Young People's Work and the respective Walther League District boards. At this convention it also commended the sponsoring of a Synod-wide roll call.

The Walther League enjoyed a prosperous growth during this period. Pastor W. A. Maier, executive secretary since 1920, was followed by Pastor P. G. Prokopy, who in turn was succeeded by Pastor E. Umbach. In 1935 Prof. O. P. Kretzmann was called to fill this position, relinquishing his office to Prof. O. H. Theiss in 1940.

Prof. E. H. Engelbrecht served the organization as field secretary from 1920 to 1941, during which period the League grew from approximately 1,100 to 2,500 societies.

In 1922 the Walther League office was moved from Mil-

ABOUNDING MORE AND MORE (1922 - 1947)

waukee to Chicago and was established at 6438 Eggleston Ave. On September 20, 1942, the League dedicated its beautiful Lutheran Youth Building, erected at a cost of $100,000 and located at 875 North Dearborn Street.

The League accepted a grant of land at Arcadia, Michigan, in 1922, for the purpose of a summer camp. Since 1923 the camp has been conducted every summer under the leadership of W. F. Weiherman.

Forty districts comprise the League, which numbers nearly 3,000 societies with 56,502 members. Presidents during the present period have been: E. J. Gallmeyer, 1928 to 1933; W. E. Helmke, 1933—1939; Henry W. Buck, since 1939—1946; William J. Zeiter, since 1946.

Besides the *Walther League Messenger*, the Walther League publishes *The Cresset* and other periodicals.

CONCORDIA PUBLISHING HOUSE AND ITS PUBLICATIONS

The largest single expansion in the history of Concordia Publishing House was the construction of a complete factory in 1925, at a cost of $260,000. In 1941 a one-story enlargement of the pressroom and pamphlet bindery was added.

Mr. O. A. Dorn, who entered the firm as assistant general manager in 1941, succeeded Dr. E. Seuel as general manager in 1944. Dr. F. Rupprecht, who had served as house editor since 1900, was succeeded by Prof. L. Blankenbuehler in 1941.

Of the many publications issuing from Concordia Publishing House during this period we shall mention only a few. In 1927 the *Concordia Cyclopedia*, an 850-page reference book on the Lutheran Church, was published. The professional magazines for our clergymen were merged into the *Concordia Theological Monthly* in 1930. The largest venture, the publishing of the *Lutheran Hymnal*, was completed in 1941, the total output reaching approximately 1,500,000

O. A. Dorn

copies. Twenty-five Districts are issuing District Supplements to the *Lutheran Witness,* raising the subscription list of this periodical to about 280,000. *Der Lutheraner* still is printed in more than 30,000 copies per issue. And in 1944 the devotional booklets, begun in 1937, were being printed in editions of over 400,000 copies. The *Lutheran Woman's Quarterly,* official organ of the Lutheran Women's Missionary League, numbers 63,000 copies.

In the course of years Concordia Publishing House has become the largest denominational publishing concern in the world. It employs approximately 250 people. For the triennium of May 1, 1941, to April 30, 1944, its sales amounted to $4,098,070.89. For years it has been contributing more than $100,000 per annum to Synod's treasury.

Synod resolved in 1929 that the President appoint a committee of eleven men to make a thorough study of the Schwan Catechism with a view to its eventual revision as well as to the grading of the catechism material. The Cate-

Concordia Publishing House, 1941

chism Committee in 1938 was composed of Prof. R. C. Neitzel, Dr. H. O. A. Keinath, Dr. E. A. Koehler, and Mr. A. C. Stellhorn. The work of the committee, under the chief authorship of Professor Neitzel, was accepted by Synod in 1941, and the new catechism came off the press in 1943.

The Delegate Synod of 1929 also authorized President Pfotenhauer to name a Committee on Hymnology and Liturgics which was to revise the English hymnbook used by Synod since 1911. Members of this committee were Prof. W. G. Polack, Dr. L. Fuerbringer, Prof. L. Blankenbuehler, Pastor O. Kaiser, Pastor O. H. Schmidt, and Mr. B. Schumacher. Similar committees of the other synods of the Synodical Conference co-operated with our committee in preparing a hymnal for all the churches of this federation. The *Lutheran Hymnal,* referred to above, appeared in 1941.

THE LUTHERAN UNION MOVEMENT

Between the years 1920 and 1923 Synod's Committee on Lutheran Union met three to four times annually with representatives of the Wisconsin, Iowa, Ohio, and Buffalo Synods. Theses and antitheses on the doctrines of conversion and election were adopted. In 1923 Synod appointed Profs. R. C. Neitzel, Th. Engelder, and Pastor Paul Schulz to examine these theses, resolving at the same time to continue the doctrinal discussions.

The committee appointed to examine the so-called Intersynodical Theses published its criticism in 1926, but since members of Synod did not have sufficient time to study the report of the examining committee, Synod resolved to suspend final action until the following convention. In 1929 the Intersynodical Theses were rejected by the Missouri Synod as being insufficient and incomplete to serve as a basis of doctrinal agreement. A new committee was elected to draw up the doctrinal statement of the Missouri Synod. Its report was adopted by Synod in 1932 and is known as the

Brief Statement of the Doctrinal Position of the Missouri Synod. (The reader will find this on page 371 ff.)

In the meanwhile the Ohio, Iowa, and Buffalo Synods had merged in 1930 to organize the American Lutheran Church, and this group in the same year established with the Norwegian Lutheran Church, the Swedish Augustana Synod, the Lutheran Free Church, and the United Danish Lutheran Church the federation known as The American Lutheran Conference.

At the Cleveland convention in 1935 a communication was presented to Synod from the American Lutheran Church seeking to establish with Missouri pulpit and altar fellowship, whereupon Synod took the following action:

"WHEREAS, Our Synod has always recognized the duty and desirability of 'the conservation and promotion of the unity of the true faith (Eph. 4:3-6; 1 Cor. 1:10)' and a united defense against schism and sectarianism (*Handbook,* p. 1); and

"WHEREAS, God-pleasing Scriptural external union and co-operation is based upon internal unity, oneness in faith, confession, doctrine, and practice; therefore be it

"*Resolved,* That we declare our willingness to confer with other Lutheran bodies on problems of Lutheran union with a view towards effecting true unity on the basis of the Word of God and the Lutheran Confessions.

"*Resolved,* That a standing committee of five, to be known as the Committee on Lutheran Church Union, be appointed by the Chair to conduct these conferences.

"*Resolved,* That the terms of the members of this committee be three years, successors being appointed by the Chair on the expiration of each term, at least two members succeeding themselves.

"*Resolved,* That this committee confer with the other members of the Synodical Conference and keep them informed in this matter." [3]

The Committee on Lutheran Church Union consisted of Drs. Wm. Arndt, Th. Engelder, C. F. Brommer, and the Pastors K. Kretzmann and F. H. Brunn.

At the St. Louis convention, 1938, the committee reported that it had held six meetings with the representatives of the American Lutheran Church, the discussions being based on the Brief Statement of the Doctrinal Position of the Missouri Synod. The commissioners of the American Lutheran Church did not unqualifiedly accept the Brief Statement, but in a lengthy Declaration of their own summarized their convictions. This Declaration was presented to our Synod. The reviewing committee, known as Committee 16, reported to Synod that it found "first of all an agreement in the doctrinal statements concerning teachings disputed in the past or still in debate in some sections of the Lutheran Church in America, notably in the doctrine of inspiration, predestination and conversion, Sunday, and the office of the public administration of the means of grace." The committee furthermore reported that "in some nonfundamental points concerning the doctrine of the last things the Declaration of the American Lutheran Church representatives asks tolerance for certain teachings and interpretations which have been rejected in our circles." The committee also referred to the fact that the Declaration speaks of "a visible side of the Church."

The recommendations of Committee 16 adopted by Synod were among others:

"That Synod declare that the Brief Statement of the Missouri Synod together with the Declaration of the representatives of the American Lutheran Church and the provisions of this entire report of Committee No. 16, now being read, and with Synod's action thereupon be regarded as the doctrinal basis for future fellowship between the Missouri Synod and the American Lutheran Church.

"That in regard to the points of nonfundamental doctrines

mentioned in the Declaration of the American Lutheran Church representatives (Antichrist, the conversion of the Jews, the physical resurrection of the martyrs, the fulfillment of the thousand years), we endeavor to establish full agreement and that our Committee on Lutheran Union be instructed to devise ways and means of reaching this end.

"That in regard to the propriety of speaking of the 'visible side of the Church' we ask our Committee on Lutheran Union to work to this end that uniform and Scripturally acceptable terminology and teaching be attained.

"That since for true unity we need not only this doctrinal agreement, but also agreement in practice, we state with our synodical fathers that according to the Scriptures and the Lutheran confessional writings, Christian practice must harmonize with Christian doctrine and that, where there is a divergence from Biblical, confessional practice, strenuous efforts must be made to correct such deviation. We refer particularly to the attitude toward the antichristian lodge, anti-Scriptural pulpit and altar fellowship, and all other forms of unionism.

"That regarding the establishment of church fellowship between the two bodies on this basis, Synod recognize the following points, which embody and augment the four recommendations of Synod's Committee on Lutheran Union:

a. "The establishing of church fellowship between the American Lutheran Church and the Missouri Synod will depend on the action taken by each body with reference to the Brief Statement, the Declaration of the representatives of the American Lutheran Church, and the report of this committee as adopted by Synod.

b. "The establishing of church fellowship between the American Lutheran Church and the Missouri Synod will depend also on the establishing on the part of the American Lutheran Church of doctrinal agreement with those church bodies with which the American Lutheran Church is in fellowship.

c. "As far as the Missouri Synod is concerned, this whole matter must be submitted for approval to the other synods constituting the Synodical Conference.

d. "Until church fellowship has been officially established, the pastors of both church bodies are encouraged to meet in smaller circles wherever and as often as possible in order to discuss both the doctrinal basis for union and the questions of church practice.

e. "That if by the grace of God fellowship can be established, this fact is to be announced officially by the President of Synod. Until then no action is to be taken by any of our pastors or conrgegations which would overlook the fact that we are not yet united." [4]

Synod's committee had the intention of discussing with the American Lutheran Church commissioners the five points mentioned in the report of Committee No. 16, concerning which there still existed a difference between some members of the American Lutheran Church and Missouri. But the discussion was diverted into different channels by the resolutions of the American Lutheran Church at its Sandusky convention in October, 1938. The items that caused apprehension to Synod's committee were the statements made by this body:

1. That it is neither possible nor necessary to agree in all nonfundamental doctrines.

2. That the American Lutheran Church will not give up its membership in the American Lutheran Conference.

3. The phrase "in the light of," occurring in the sentence: "We believe that the Brief Statement viewed in the light of our Declaration is not in contradiction to the Minneapolis Theses."

Moreover, many members of Synod expressed doubt as to the correctness of the sentence in the Declaration that God "purposes to justify those who have come to faith."

With reference to the attitude of the American Lutheran Church to the Brief Statement, its commissioners stated that "their assertion of agreement with the Brief Statement did not imply endorsement in every case of the exegetical or other lines of argumentation and the feeling of obligation to use the same phraseology." It became apparent, however, that with reference to prayer fellowship the difference was more than mere phraseology. Likewise, the reference to objective and subjective justification and to fundamental and nonfundamental doctrines required further clarification.

When in 1939 it became known that the Fellowship Commission of the American Lutheran Church and the United Lutheran Church in America had adopted the Pittsburgh Agreement, including an article on inspiration which was unsatisfactory to Missouri, Synod's committee was disturbed, for it thought that it was in full harmony with the American Lutheran Church on this doctrine, while the United Lutheran Church commission had definitely refused to endorse what the Brief Statement states on this subject.

At the meeting of the two committees on March 26 and 27, 1940, the American Lutheran Church commissioners asked for a formal statement enumerating the obstacles preventing the establishing of fellowship between their body and Missouri. The Committee on Lutheran Union summarized its objections as follows:

a. "The membership of the American Lutheran Church in the American Lutheran Conference, inasmuch as we cannot unite with the American Lutheran Church unless its sister synods in the American Lutheran Conference occupy the same position as the American Lutheran Church and the Missouri Synod.

b. "Our membership in the Synodical Conference, inasmuch as we cannot enter into fellowship with a church body if our sister synods cannot share the new relationship.

c. "The points in the Sandusky Resolutions and the one sentence in the Declaration, *viz.*, that God "purposes to justify those who have come to faith."

d. "The apparent approach between the American Lutheran Church and the United Lutheran Church in America, inasmuch as the American Lutheran Church would make it impossible for us to enter into fellowship with it if it established fellowship with the United Lutheran Church in America, which as a body does not share our common doctrinal position.

e. "The matter of church practice, inasmuch as there does not seem to exist at present sufficient uniformity in this respect to assure wholesome relations if we should acknowledge each other as brethren." [5]

At the Detroit convention of the American Lutheran Church, October, 1940, to which two commissioners were sent by Missouri's committee, the points mentioned above were discussed, but satisfaction was not reached with reference to all of them.

Synod's committee was furthermore dismayed when at the meeting of the American Lutheran Conference at Minneapolis, November, 1940, no attempt was made on the part of the American Lutheran Church to bring about the occupying of the same doctrinal position by the other synods within that body as that of the American Lutheran Church. On the contrary, the American Lutheran Conference was assured by the American Lutheran Church that it had no intention of leaving that body. Synod's committee, therefore, reported in 1941: "The question arises whether there is not a fundamental difference between the American Lutheran Church and our Synod on the meaning of confessional loyalty."

In a meeting with the sister synods of the Synodical Conference on January 3 and 4, 1941, the Norwegian and the Wisconsin Synods were of the opinion that for the present negotiations with the American Lutheran Church should be discontinued. The Synodical Conference, however, at its meeting in Chicago, 1940, took no such action, but resolved "that the Synodical Conference ask the Missouri Synod not to enter into fellowship with the American Lutheran Church until matters now objected to by members of the Synodical Conference have been clarified and until the whole matter has once more been presented to another meeting of the Synodical Conference."

It was furthermore resolved at this convention, "that we ask the Missouri committee earnestly to consider the framing of one document of agreement."

To the convention of Synod in 1941 six printed and 46 unprinted memorials were addressed, all referring to Lutheran church union. No memorial was presented which petitioned Synod completely to discontinue negotiations with the American Lutheran Church. Memorials from 27 individual pastors, 27 congregations, 11 pastoral conferences, the English District, one men's club, one circuit, and the Lutheran Laymen's League urged Synod to continue negotiations with the American Lutheran Church.

Synod resolved:

"That we express our willingness to continue our efforts toward bringing about true unity in the Lutheran Church of this country both in doctrine and practice, but that we are determined to do so only on the basis of the Word of God and the Lutheran Confessions, lest we be unthankful to the Lord for our Lutheran heritage, unfaithful to the trust which the Lord has committed to us, and unworthy of the Lord's continued blessings.

"That we acknowledge with joy and gratitude to God that, according to reports which we have received, many individuals and groups within the American Lutheran Church have made efforts to establish doctrinal unity with us; but we regret that the American Lutheran Church as a body has not taken as firm an attitude in reference to establishing doctrinal unity as under the circumstances we had reason to hope for.

"That we continue our negotiations with the American Lutheran Church in an effort to establish doctrinal unity, because

a. "They have requested us to strive together with them to attain doctrinal unity for which the need exists, and it is in accordance with the Lord's will that Christians should strive for doctrinal unity (1 Pet. 3:15; 1 Cor. 1:10).

b. "The efforts between our Synod and the American Lutheran Church have not been barren of good results, and we have the Lord's promise that the testimony of His truth will not be in vain (Is. 55:10-11).

"That to this end a committee, henceforth to be known as 'The Committee on Doctrinal Unity in the Lutheran Church of America,' be again appointed, in accordance with the resolutions of the Cleveland convention of 1935.

"That our sister synods in the Synodical Conference be asked to send their representatives to the joint meetings of this committee.

"That further procedure be governed by the following instructions: that

a. "The immediate objective be not organic union, but doctrinal unity;

b. "Since the Synodical Conference has asked us 'earnestly to consider the advisability of bringing about the framing of one document of agreement,' and since it has become quite evident that it is not only desirable, but necessary to have one document, our committee be instructed to make every possible effort that such one document be prepared;

c. "In preparing this one document, our committee prayerfully and carefully consider all the misgivings and objections that have been expressed in memorials presented to this convention or otherwise; and that this document be so clearly written that there can be no misunderstanding in reference to the meaning which the words are to convey;

d. "In calling for one document, we do not mean to dispense with any doctrinal statement made in our Brief Statement — for we believe that it correctly expresses the doctrinal position of our Synod — but we concede that, for the sake of clarification under the present circumstances, some statements may need to be more sharply defined or amplified;

e. "It be understood that the term 'nonfundamental doctrines,' which has been used, should not be made to convey the idea that anything clearly revealed in Scripture, although not absolutely necessary for salvation, may be denied;

f. "In addition to any controversial doctrines that may need further study and clarification, the teachings concerning Antichrist, the conversion of the Jews, the physical resurrection of the martyrs, and the fulfillment of the thousand years be given careful study by the committee and pastoral conferences on the basis of Scripture and our Confessions, and that also in reference to these teachings we endeavor to establish full agreement;

g. "The pastors of both church bodies be encouraged to continue to meet in smaller circles wherever — and as often as — possible, in order to discuss both the doctrinal basis of unity and the questions of church practice;

h. "The pastoral conferences receive information from our committee and report the results of their joint meetings to the secretary of Synod's committee;

i. "After one doctrinal document has been agreed on, such document be submitted to the various pastoral conferences for study and any suggestions in reference thereto be sent to the secretary of the synodical committee;

j. "Beyond this procedure, as it has been outlined in the previous paragraphs, no further official action be taken until our Synod and the American Lutheran Church have officially ratified the doctrinal agreement prepared by the joint official committees.

"That after favorable action has been taken by our Synod and the American Lutheran Church in reference to the one doctrinal agreement presented, our Synod take no further action with the American Lutheran Church until our Synod has submitted the entire matter to our sister synods in the Synodical Conference and the American Lutheran Church has submitted the entire matter to its sister synods in the American Lutheran Conference and all this has resulted in favorable action; in the meantime discussions by joint pastoral conferences may continue.

"That we reaffirm our declaration made at the St. Louis convention in reference to 'agreement in practice.' . . .

"That in the meantime it be understood that no pulpit, altar, or prayer fellowship has been established between us and the American Lutheran Church; and until such fellowship has been officially declared by the synods concerned, no action is to be taken by any of our pastors or congregations which ignores the fact that we are not yet united." [6]

The report of the Committee on Doctrinal Unity to the convention of 1944 stated that of the synods comprising the Synodical Conference only the Slovak Evangelical Lutheran Church had declared its willingness to co-operate in the endeavor to formulate one document as a basis for church fellowship. It also gave the resolutions of the American Lutheran Church adopted at its convention at Mendota, Illinois, October, 1942, in which this body declared its readiness to establish pulpit and altar fellowship with either the Missouri Synod or the United Lutheran Church in America, or with both, on the basis of the Pittsburgh Agreement, the Brief Statement in the light of the Declaration, and its own Declaration, in the hope that any existing obstacles might be removed. Synod's committee stated further that it had held a very brief meeting with the commissioners of the American Lutheran Church on February 12, 1943, and that arrangements had been made for subcommittees of the two commissions (A. L. C. and Missouri Synod) to meet for the framing of the one doctrinal agreement. It finally mentioned the fact that many joint conferences of American Lutheran Church and Missouri Synod pastors had been conducted and stated its conviction that such conferences point the way to the reaching of the goal which we have in view.

Eighteen printed and nine unprinted memorials dealing with Lutheran union and kindred subjects lay before the convention of 1944. The Norwegian Synod and a number of individuals requested Synod to rescind its 1938 resolutions. The Wisconsin Synod appealed to Synod to discontinue further negotiations for establishing church fellowship with the American Lutheran Church for the time being.

The reviewing committee in judging the material presented to it was guided by the following principles, which together with the recommendations of this committee were accepted by Synod:

"In the first place, Scripture on the one hand encourages every endeavor to recognize and promote a unity actually existing (Eph. 4:3; Acts 2:42), but just as definitely warns against every kind of false union (Rom. 16:17-18; 2 Thess. 3:14-15; 1 Tim. 6:3-5; Tit. 3:10-11; 2 John 10-11). As to the truth of any of its statements, Scripture makes no distinction between fundamental and nonfundamental, more important or less important truths. The organic foundation must remain inviolate, its authority and inviolability unimpaired and unassailable. (Is. 34:16.) We cannot entertain a motion recently presented that statements made in Scripture apply only to historical situations, since the principles involved are definitely intended by God to be applied to similar situations until the end of time. Hence not expediency, not a false philosophy, but only the truth of Holy

Writ is to be our guide, and every aberration which destroys the organic foundation is divisive of church fellowship.

"In the second place, we must squarely face the issue that no matter how acceptable the confessional stand of a church body may be, it must be accompanied by supervision of teaching and by doctrinal discipline, so that no public teaching will be tolerated for any length of time which is contrary to the Word of God and the Lutheran Confessions. (2 Thess. 3:14; 2 Tim. 4:10; 1 Cor. 5:13 b.)

"In the third place, in connection with the preceding paragraph, we must keep in mind that the autonomous character of the Christian congregation does not absolve it from synodical allegiance. The congregation is indeed autonomous, as the constitution of our Synod states. On the other hand, Synod is not a mere informal group, and, therefore, one of the factors involved in the present situation is the right of the corporate group to determine the character of its membership and to protect itself, by disciplinary action if necessary, from disintegration through the refusal of an individual congregation to conform to the standards of doctrine and practice. While Scripture does not prescribe a synodical organization or synodical authority, the implication of the duties of fellowship as found in Holy Scripture cannot be set aside by those who are ready to follow both precept and example of Holy Writ. (Acts 8:14; 11:30; 1 Cor. 16:1.) For example, the letters of transfer in Apostolic times were recognized and respected by the various congregations that regarded themselves in fellowship with other groups of the Apostolic age. A congregation belonging to Synod, for example, is bound by the law of love to make every effort indicated in Holy Scripture to remove any objectionable doctrinal situations not in keeping with the spirit of Matthew 18 before threatening to withdraw from membership.

"In the fourth place, the insistence upon one doctrinal

declaration or confessional affirmation is in keeping with the usage of the Church through the centuries, as the history of the Christian Confessions shows. The simple confession of the Ethiopian eunuch was shortly afterward followed by the larger confession referred to by Paul in a number of places, for example, Rom. 6:17. In the same way the Athanasian Confession came into existence at the instigation of the Arian Controversy. In the 16th century also the various confessions of the Lutheran groups and of other Protestants were written to meet the actual situations in the Church.

"With regard to the report of the Committee on Lutheran Unity and the overtures pertaining thereto, the entire picture has been changed due to the fact that our Committee on Lutheran Unity has succeeded in taking the first steps in preparing the document which was ordered by resolution of the Synod at Fort Wayne. This document, or Doctrinal Affirmation, as agreed upon by our committee and a subcommittee of the American Lutheran Church Commission, has already been submitted in a preliminary way to the entire group of the American Lutheran Church commissioners, and we have the promise that the document will be presented to the convention of the American Lutheran Church in the fall of this year.

"We recommend that our Committee on Doctrinal Unity be instructed, as soon as the document is in shape to be presented, to make it accessible to all members of our Synod, not only pastors and teachers, but also to our congregations, in order that all members of our Synod everywhere may have an opportunity to study the document carefully and be ready for the final vote in the convention of 1947. This document will, therefore, after acceptance by the respective bodies, clearly supersede all previous doctrinal documents and resolutions as accepted by Synod in 1938 and 1941." [7]

SYNOD AND SECRET SOCIETIES

Secret societies with religious principles, doctrines, or rites came under consideration at the convention of 1926. The following resolutions were adopted concerning the lodge:

"WHEREAS, Present-day conditions demand a reaffirmation of our position on the lodge question, therefore be it

"*Resolved,* That Synod go on record as being as firmly as ever opposed to lodgery because of its unchristian and antichristian character; and be it further

"*Resolved,* That we hold it to be the solemn, sacred, and God-given duty of every pastor properly to instruct his people on the sinfulness of lodgery in denying the Holy Trinity, the deity of Christ, the vicarious atonement, and other Scriptural doctrines and to induce his congregation or congregations to take action against all members who after thorough instruction refuse to leave the lodge; and be it further

"*Resolved,* That we deem it the duty of every fellow Christian, fellow pastor, and especially of the officials of Synod to admonish all pastors who neglect their duty in this respect; and if Christian admonition has been administered in the spirit of Matthew 18 without the proper results, the officials of Synod shall bring such cases to the attention of the synodical District for further action; and be it further

"*Resolved,* That, if congregations, after having received due instruction, refuse to take action against lodge members, Synod shall deal with them and eventually refuse the Christian fellowship; and be it further

"*Resolved,* That Synod earnestly request the various synodical Districts to carry out the above resolutions and faithfully to assist their congregations in eradicating the lodge evil." [8]

The same convention resolved to appoint a committee of nine men to make a further study of questions in connection with lodges submitted in a number of memorials to Synod. This committee requested Prof. Theo. Graebner and the Rev. O. F. Engelbrecht to serve as a Lodge Information Bureau, which appointment the 1929 convention ratified. The 1929 convention adopted the following additional resolutions:

"*Resolved,* That our Synod hereby declare that it is, and shall be, the practice of our Synod not to administer Holy Communion to members of lodges; and be it further

"*Resolved,* That Synod, in agreement with the resolutions of 1926, instruct its officers to exercise vigilant care and urge all pastors and congregations to admonish such congregations and pastors as permit the lodge evil to exist in their churches without counter-testimony and decisive action. If, after due investigation, it becomes evident that such congregations and pastors refuse to remove the offense, they are to be suspended and eventually expelled from synodical connection.

"*Resolved,* That we do not deny that a conscientious pastor may under certain conditions administer Holy Communion to a person who is still outwardly connected with a lodge. But in such a case the pastor shall earnestly beware of procrastinating and giving offense, and to this end he shall freely and conscientiously consult with his vestry and congregation, his brethren in the ministry, and with officials of Synod, as the case may require." [9]

WORLD WAR II

The convention at Cleveland (1935) instructed the President and the Vice-Presidents to appoint a committee which should investigate thoroughly the question of calling men into the service of chaplaincies in the Army and Navy and, if this could be done without violating Scriptural principles, to appoint also an Army and Navy Commission for Chaplains. The committee, consisting of Dr. Geo. A. Romoser and the Pastors J. F. Wenchel, H. D. Mensing, A. G. Dick, and F. C. Proehl, made the following declaration to Synod in 1938:

"Pursuant to the resolution of Synod, your Committee has carefully studied the official documents regarding the office and functions of the chaplaincy in the Army and Navy. The Committee also heard reliable testimony from several of our pastors who have been chaplains in the Army; furthermore, the Committee received interpretations personally from the Chief of Chaplains on some of the paragraphs and wording of the regulations which were indefinite and might be variously interpreted. The Committee was impressed with the fact that again and again it is emphasized in these documents that the chaplains are to function 'according to their respective creeds or conscientious practice in each case.' (A. R. 60 — 5, p. 3.) And although they are under the authority of the commanding officers, this provision does not imply any dictation as to their spiritual ministry; consequently the conscientious Lutheran chaplain can avoid all unionistic practices. This has been corroborated by pastors who have been chaplains in the Army. The Committee is also convinced that in offering our men for the chaplaincy there is no departure from the accepted Scriptural position of our Synod on the separation of State and Church. The Government is interested in the moral welfare of the Army and Navy and presents, through the chaplaincy, opportunities for service to those who desire the ministrations of the chaplains; and while it contributes towards the maintenance of the chaplains a stipulated allowance, this does not conflict with the doctrine of the separation of Church and State, especially since he must perform his duties 'in conformity with the teachings of denominational beliefs.' (*Chaplain: His Place*, p. 13.) And again: 'The chaplain will naturally give such religious ministrations as the rites and practices of his Church may warrant, provided it be seen that such are desired by the patient.' (*Chaplain: His Place,* p. 23.) Furthermore, the Church commissions or calls these men and, even though appointed by the Government, they represent us only as long as they conform to the principles and practices of our Synod as members in good standing. Therefore we hold that the President should carry out the resolution of the Cleveland convention and forthwith appoint an Army and Navy Board." [10]

The men appointed to the commission were Pastors H. D. Mensing, O. A. Sauer, F. C. Proehl, and K. W. F. Schleede. Pastor O. Sohn replaced Pastor Mensing, who died December 17, 1940. Pastor P. L. Dannenfeldt was appointed chairman of the commission, and later the commission was increased by the addition of Mr. Theo. Schlake and Mr. O. C. Rentner. Dr. Paul Schulz represented the Board of Directors on this commission.

When the Selective Service Act was introduced in the summer of 1940, the Army and Navy Commission served in the interest of the trainees from the Missouri Synod. It sent to all chaplains a small magazine, entitled *The Lutheran Chaplain,* once a month and to every trainee a nicely gotten-up folder called *Loyalty* (monthly). Tracts were prepared for free distribution, such as 1) Farewell; 2) Your Service Record; 3) The Call to Worship; 4) A Soldier's Prayer. A special service prayer book for men in the armed forces was prepared and furnished gratis to the selectees.

A chaplains' training conference was held at Fort Wayne, January 21—23, 1941, attended by fifty men and some visitors. Lutheran centers were built at some places; at other places property was rented for this purpose. In order to avoid duplication of effort and waste of funds, the following Articles of Agreement with the National Lutheran Council were made:

A. "That it be the general policy that only one Lutheran Center be built wherever necessary.

B. "That the administrative committee of the Service Men's Division of the National Lutheran Council and the Army and Navy Commission of the Missouri Synod determine in consultation with each other, in the vicinity of which camp the one or the other group build and maintain a Lutheran center, in order to avoid duplication.

C. "That in all cases where the one group establishes a center, the other group will contribute an agreed sum toward the maintenance of the center.

D. "That the Army and Navy Commission of the Missouri Synod and the Service Men's Division of the National Lutheran Council instruct directors and staff members in charge of Lutheran centers to respect the confessional position of the Missouri Synod and the National Lutheran Council.

E. "That the spiritual welfare work in the interest of members of the Missouri Synod be done by pastors of the Missouri Synod and the spiritual welfare work in the interest of members of the National Lutheran Council be done by pastors of the National Lutheran Council." [11]

In June, 1941, the Army and Navy Commission reported 43 chaplains on active duty, 22 reserve chaplains not on active duty, 9 civilian Lutheran service pastors on active duty, 123 contact keymen, and 5 Lutheran service centers in operation.

And then came Pearl Harbor.

It is too early to record the full account of the activity of the Army and Navy Commission. Statistics as of October 2, 1945, are as follows:

Men and women in service 115,000; men and women overseas 77,000; dead 3,250; chaplains on active duty 236; chaplains serving overseas 126; service and parish centers 83. Overseas service centers were established at Kunming, China; Manila, Philippine Islands; Anchorage, Alaska; Balboa, Panama Canal Zone; London, England; Paris, France; and Frankfurt, Germany. Contact key pastors 657. Total number of prayer books mailed 285,000.

The cost of the program for the men in the service was about $13.00 per serviceman, the expenditures for the whole project averaging between $50,000 and $60,000 per month. By freewill offerings Synod raised for the Army and Navy Commission more than $2,000,000 during the years 1941—1946.

Following the outbreak of the war, President Behnken, in 1942, appointed a National Advisory Emergency Planning Council to meet the needs and problems arising out of the conditions incident to the war. Chief among these problems were: providing for "shifting America," the spiritual ministry to the German prisoners of war, and postwar emergency work in Europe.

It is estimated that about 23,000,000 people changed their places of residence during the duration. This shifting of population affected many of Synod's congregations; it also opened new mission opportunities, especially in war-production areas. The Emergency Planning Council aided the Board of Home Missions by granting subsidies out of its funds to carry on the necessary work, much of which developed into permanent District work with the promise of becoming self-supporting. Of particular interest are the trailer missions, of which seven were in action during 1945. A complete unit consists of a car, trailer, tent, chairs, visual equipment, charts, loud-speakers, etc. The trailer missions were located in the following Districts: Oregon-Washington, California-Nevada, Southern California, Montana, Texas, Central, and Atlantic. For a while a trailer mission was operated on the Alaskan Highway.

German prisoners of war were interned in approximately 165 base camps, plus 600 branch camps. About 105 civilian pastors and 23 chaplains gave part or full time to the spiritual ministry of these men. Through the work more than 70 German pastors among the prisoners learned to know and appreciate the Missouri Synod. At one time more than 45 theological students among interned Germans were enrolled in the correspondence course especially arranged for them by Dr. P. E. Kretzmann of the St. Louis seminary.

For the work in Europe plans are being made. Early in 1945 Dr. Lawrence Meyer visited England, France, Germany, Sweden, Finland, and Switzerland to confer with European and American leaders regarding postwar work in Europe. In October, 1945, Dr. J. W. Behnken and Dr. Lawrence Meyer proceeded to Europe for further conferences. Pastor Herman Mayer of Bay City, Michigan, and Pastor L. Buchheimer of New York were given leaves of absence by their congregations to act as representatives of Synod in Europe, as soon as conditions are stabilized enough to permit them to begin their work and our Government gives permission for a longer sojourn in occupied territory.

ANNIVERSARIES

This period marked the observance of numerous anniversaries. Said President Pfotenhauer in his opening address at the convention of 1929: "With this session our Church enters into a triennial period rich in days commemorative of mighty deeds wrought by God in our dear Lutheran Church, deeds which vividly set before our eyes the glorious treasures our Church possesses and exhort us: 'Hold that fast which thou hast that no man take thy crown.'

"Four hundred years ago, in 1529, Luther gave to our Church his two Catechisms. In the same year he held his epochal colloquy with Zwingli and his followers at Marburg. Next year, on June 25, we shall celebrate the quadricentennial of the presentation of the Augsburg Confession to the Emperor and his empire, as well as the 350th anniversary of the first publication of the whole book of confessional writings of our Church known as the *Book of Concord.*" [12]

These anniversaries were fittingly commemorated throughout Synod.

Likewise three anniversaries of Synod were observed: in 1938 at St. Louis the Saxon Immigration Centennial, in 1941 at Fort Wayne the Wyneken Centennial, and in 1944 at Saginaw the Franconian Centennial.

THE SYNODICAL CONFERENCE

In 1932 the Missouri Synod again took the initiative in effecting an organic union of the synods constituting the Synodical Conference, its efforts being motivated by one of the stated purposes of the Synodical Conference, *viz.:* "the uniting of all Lutheran synods of America into one orthodox American Lutheran Church." The Committee on Organic Union reported in 1935 that the Slovak and Norwegian brethren felt that the present language conditions did not permit organic union on their part and that the Wisconsin brethren were to decide the matter at their convention in August, 1935. The Joint Synod of Wisconsin tabled the report of its Committee on Amalgamation of the synods within the Synodical Conference until its next convention in 1937. For various reasons no further action was taken in the matter, and Synod's Committee on Organic Union was dismissed.

At the request of Pastor K. E. Salonen, President of the Finnish Ev. Lutheran National Church in America, a committee of the Missouri Synod met with a committee of the Finnish Synod at Ironwood, Michigan, February 20, 1923. The report of Synod's committee as given in 1923 reads:

1. "The discussion which took place at the pastoral conference at Ironwood, Michigan, on June 2, 1923, showed that we are agreed in the principal doctrines.

2. "However, we also found that in a practical question,

namely, in regard to woman suffrage in the Church, there was a divergent policy in the two conferring synods, and that the question relates to the correct understanding and strict application of certain Bible texts.

3. "Inasmuch as both parties bow to the Word of God, it is our opinion that the discussion of this question as well as the deliberation regarding official fraternal recognition of each other by the conferring parties and regarding an eventual union should be continued, and that the Finnish National Church should appoint a committee for this purpose, which is to continue the conference with the committees of the Missouri Synod.

"As regards the statement in the official letter of President Salonen to our President, Dr. F. Pfotenhauer, concerning the training of Finnish students, we declare that, if requested, we as a committee are ready to recommend to our Synod to make the necessary arrangements at one of our schools for admitting students from the Finnish National Church under the same conditions as with our own students." [13]

Because of language difficulties further negotiations were carried on by correspondence. In 1929 Synod voted the Finnish Synod an annual subsidy of $1,200 for the support of Finnish pastors. At the request of the Rev. G. A. Aho, the President of the Finnish Ev. Lutheran National Church, an instructor in the Finnish language was placed at the seminary at Springfield in 1938 in the person of Alex. A. Monto, who has since been taking care of the needs of the Finnish students. While the Finnish Ev. Lutheran National Church (now called the National Evangelical Lutheran Church) is not a member of the Synodical Conference, it is in fellowship with Missouri.

Pastor C. Gausewitz was succeeded in the presidency of the Synodical Conference by Dr. L. Fuerbringer in 1927. Since 1944 Pastor E. Benj. Schlueter is President of this federation of synods.

The co-operative efforts of the constituent synods of the Synodical Conference are still confined to mission work among the Negroes in our country and since 1936 to the Ibibios in Nigeria. Luther College in New Orleans, which had been opened in 1903, was discontinued in 1925 because of lack of necessary buildings and teaching facilities. For a short time it was reopened in the following years, but permanently closed when the depression in the early thirties compelled greater economy in the entire field.

C. *Gausewitz*

In order to have an institution for the training of mission teachers and helpers in Alabama, Alabama Luther College was established at Selma, Alabama, on November 13, 1922. Since the enrollment at this college increased rapidly, the Missionary Board in 1925 purchased 13 acres of land and erected suitable buildings at a cost of $40,000. During the depression the curriculum of this college was reduced so that today under the name of Alabama Lutheran Academy the institution serves as a preparatory school for Immanuel Lutheran College, Greensboro, North Carolina.

Twenty miles from Jackson, Mississippi, Lawrence C. Jones, in 1909, established Piney Woods Country Life School for Negro young people who were too poor to obtain an education in any other school. Founded "on a pine stump with three illiterate pupils and $1.65 cash," the institution now has a $250,000 plant, 1,700 acres of land, and an enrollment of 440 students, ranging in age from six to forty and drawn from more than 15 States. The students of this school have been under the spiritual care of Lutheran pastors since 1930,

ABOUNDING MORE AND MORE (1922 - 1947)

when Pastor G. A. Schmidt took charge of the work. He was followed in 1936 by Pastor Wm. Wedig of Pascagoula, Mississippi. Over 250 students of this school have been gained for the Lutheran Church.

Three superintendents under the Missionary Board supervise the work among the colored people: Pastor G. M. Kramer in the Louisiana field, Pastor E. A. Westcott in the Alabama field (until 1945), succeeded by Pastor W. H. Ellwanger in 1946, and Pastor Wm. H. Gehrke in the Eastern and Northern field. Pastor L. A. Wisler, who served as Executive Secretary of the Missionary Board, died in 1944. He was followed by Pastor K. Kurth, who assumed his duties in July, 1946.

Increased migration of the colored race to Northern cities induced Synod's pastors and congregations in the metropolitan areas to do mission work among the newcomers from the South. In Chicago, New York, Detroit, Pittsburgh, and in other large centers the work of colored missions is being sponsored, and congregations are being established.

Benj. J. Schlueter

At the present writing the Colored Mission numbers 53 pastors working in 21 States, serving 79 congregations and 12 preaching stations with 11,905 souls and 6,815 communicants. Forty-two Christian day schools are being maintained with an enrollment of 2,648 children. The report for 1944 states that ten congregations have assumed the entire responsibility for their pastor's salary. The total contributions for all purposes in 1944 amounted to $110,055.

In 1928 a young man, Jonathan Udo Ekong, was sent from distant Africa to this country by his clan, the Ibibios in Ibesikpo, to train for the Gospel ministry. Although the

Ibibios had the Bible in their own language, the Efik, they had no one competent to assume the duties of a Christian minister. Mr. Ekong was not sent to any denominational institution in particular, but Divine Providence so led him that, after he had attended other schools, he found his way to Immanuel Lutheran College at Greensboro. Through him his people established contact with the Synodical Conference.

The Synodical Conference at its convention in 1930 ordered the Missionary Board to elect a committee to do the preliminary work necessary for exploring the possibilities in Nigeria. This committee gave attention to the appeals which were coming from the Ibesikpo United Church, Uyo District, Nigeria. In 1934 the Synodical Conference resolved to send a committee of three to investigate the claims of the native Nigerian Christians.

H. Nau

The committee, Dr. H. Nau and Pastors I. Albrecht and O. C. A. Boecler, traveled to Africa early in 1935, returning in time to submit their report to the Delegate Convention of the Missouri Synod at Cleveland, 1935. Synod resolved: "that on account of the urgency of the call to this work as many of the constituent synods of the Synodical Conference as shall express themselves in favor of undertaking the work take steps as soon as possible to begin and carry on the work under the direction of the Missionary Board of the Synodical Conference until the next meeting of the Synodical Conference in 1936." The other synods concurred, and Dr. and Mrs. Nau were sent to Africa as the first missionaries, sailing on March 4, 1936.

The task was not an easy one, but God granted consecration and wisdom and blessed the efforts of Missionary Nau abundantly. While Dr. Nau busied himself especially with the indoctrination of the natives by preaching and by instructing and guiding the teachers of the various schools, Mrs. Nau directed her attention, as time permitted, to the native women, teaching them in religion and instructing them in domestic duties.

Dr. Nau served 32 preaching stations and during the eighteen months of his stay in Africa was privileged to baptize more than 400 persons. Demands for the missionary's

Missionaries and Native Teachers in Nigeria, Africa
Dr. Nau, center; Rev. Wm. H. Schweppe, right;
Rev. V. Koeper, left

services increased so rapidly that the Missionary Board was compelled to provide assistance. Early in 1937 Wm. H. Schweppe and Vernon Koeper with their wives and a deaconess, Miss Helen Kluck, R. N., sailed from New York, arriving in Africa in April, 1937. In June, 1939, Candidate and Mrs. J. P. Kretzmann and Miss Christine Rapier, teacher, landed in Africa. Missionary Schweppe returned for his second term in Africa in May, 1944. In June, 1944, Mis-

Congregation in Afaha, Nigeria, Africa

Nung Udoe Dispensary, Nigeria, Africa

sionary Carl Rusch and wife, and since June, 1945, Missionary Louis Konz and wife began working in Nigeria. In 1946 the following missionaries were added to the staff: Rev. and Mrs. Norbert Reim; Rev: and Mrs. Robert Stade; Mr. and Mrs. Walter F. Stahlke (principal of high school); Rev. and Mrs. Willard Baringer.

The Lutheran Church in Nigeria has grown to 59 stations with a total of 10,011 baptized members and 3,569 communicant members. There are 59 churches and 57 schools in the ten fields operated by the Synodical Conference. Native pastors are J. U. Ekong and D. U. Ekong.

Two deaths, in particular, filled the hearts of the members of Synod with grief, that of Dr. Pieper and that of Dr. Pfotenhauer. Francis August Otto Pieper was born June 27, 1852, at Carwitz, Pomerania. Coming as a young man to America, he entered Northwestern College at Watertown, Wisconsin, from which he was graduated in 1872. He completed his theological studies at Concordia Seminary, St. Louis, in 1875. A member of the Wisconsin Synod, he served two congregations of that body, Centerville, Wisconsin, 1875—1876, and Manitowoc, Wisconsin, 1876—1878. At the convention of the Missouri Synod in 1878 he was elected to a professorship at the St. Louis seminary. Upon the death of Dr. Walther in 1887 he was elected president of the institution, an office which he held until the day of his death. He was President of the Missouri Synod for four terms, from 1899 to 1911. He received the title of Doctor of Divinity from Northwestern College, Watertown, Wisconsin, and from Luther College, Decorah, Iowa. After a lingering illness he departed this life June 3, 1931, in St. Louis.

After a brief service in the home the remains were transferred to Holy Cross Church on June 6. At the funeral service Dr. F. Pfotenhauer spoke on John 17:14. Dr. L. Fuerbringer represented the faculty of Concordia Seminary and the educational institutions of Synod. Dr. R. Kretzschmar addressed the mourners in the name of the Seminary Board, and Pastor J. Oppliger as pastor of the sainted Doctor. Burial was in Immanuel Cemetery, St. Louis.

In addition to the work which Dr. Pieper performed as teacher at the seminary for 53 years, as member of many boards and committees, as President of Synod, he was active in a literary way through the publication of countless articles and editorials and essays dealing with Christian doctrine. His lifework was the *Christliche Dogmatik,* a monumental work in three volumes. "In the clarity of his style and cogency of his argumentation there has not been the equal of Dr. Pieper in the American Lutheran Church. His literary ability, his eloquence, his deep personal piety combined to make him a character rare in the history of the Church which has produced so many noble characters." [14]

At the convention of the Western District, June 15—19, 1931, the delegates assembled resolved "that the memory of our sainted teacher be honored and confession be made of the faith of true Lutheranism by sending a copy of the Brief Statement of the Missouri Synod to every Protestant pastor in the United States or to as many as funds will permit."

The Honorary President of the Missouri Synod, Dr. F. Pfotenhauer, was translated into the eternal rest of the children of God in 1938. Frederick Pfotenhauer was born at Altencelle, Hanover, Germany, April 22, 1859. His father, Pastor Hermann Pfotenhauer, who represented the seventh successive generation of Lutheran ministers, died when Frederick was 15 years old. Soon after, Frederick Pfotenhauer entered the *Progymnasium* conducted by Pastor Fr. Brunn at Steeden, Germany. He emigrated to the United States in 1875, completed his studies at Fort Wayne in 1877, and was graduated from the seminary at St. Louis in 1880.

From 1880 to 1887 he was a traveling missionary in the Northwest, making his headquarters at Odessa, Minnesota. After serving the congregation at Lewiston, Minnesota, 1887 to 1894, he was called as pastor of the congregation at Hamburg, Minnesota, to which he ministered until 1911. In 1891 he was elected president of the Minnesota and Dakota District, which at that time embraced the States of Minnesota, North and South Dakota, Montana, and all of Canada west of Fort William, Ontario. 1908—1911 he served Synod as its First Vice-President. He was President of the Missouri Synod from 1911 to 1935, making his home in Chicago, where he died October 9, 1938.

Funeral services for Dr. Pfotenhauer were conducted in Holy Cross Church. Pastor A. Both spoke to the children of the congregation on October 11, and Pastor E. G. Nachtsheim had devotions for the family on the morning of October 12. In the public service Dr. J. W. Behnken preached in English on 2 Tim. 4:7-8, and Dr. L. Fuerbringer in German on Ps. 84:6-8. Eleven representatives of Synod's boards, seminaries, and colleges gave brief addresses. Interment was in Bethania Cemetery, Chicago.

Dr. Pfotenhauer was "a leader among leaders. He towered above others. He recognized his responsibilities and was aware of his limitations. He took an uncompromising stand on the Bible in all matters of doctrine and life. He was not an opportunist, not a church politician, easily swayed by temporary advantages, but a man of principle. The welfare of our Synod and the Lutheran Church at large was close to his heart. He was a wise general, well informed on all matters pertaining to his great office. He did not parade his leadership, he placed confidence in his assistants, in the various committees and boards of Synod. He was fearless and firm, yet humble. He was a Christian gentleman, a true Israelite, in whom there was no guile." [15]

This brief history has dealt with the work and activities conducted by the Missouri Synod as a body. For the sake of completeness a number of projects sponsored by congregations or by other groups within the Missouri Synod are added.

A. EDUCATIONAL

A Lutheran high school was opened in St. Louis in 1867 under the auspices of the local congregations. It was divided into a *Hoehere Buergerschule* and a *Hoehere Toechterschule*. The school was called Concordia Academy in 1880 and the Lutheran High School in 1881. After 1887 it was known as Walther College. It was discontinued in 1917.

Pastor A. F. Hoppe opened a school in New Orleans in 1881 to prepare boys for Fort Wayne or Springfield. The academy, supported by the Southern District, was closed in 1887, after Professor Hoppe had gone to St. Louis in 1886 to edit Luther's works. In 1904 the Southern District opened Concordia College, a four-year academy, in New Orleans. The institution was discontinued in 1918 because of lack of students.

The Cleveland *Progymnasium* (Grades IX and X) was operated 1890—1892 by Pastor O. Kolbe. It was a private institution, supported by the Cleveland congregations, and served as a feeder chiefly for Fort Wayne.

High schools maintained by associations of congregations or by individual congregations are Lutheran High School, Milwaukee, Wisconsin; Luther Institute, Chicago, Illinois; Lutheran High School, Detroit, Michigan; Concordia Lutheran High School, Fort Wayne, Indiana; Lutheran High School, Racine, Wisconsin; Trinity Lutheran High School, Fort Lauderdale, Florida; Trinity Lutheran High School, Oregon City, Oregon; Lutheran High School, St. Louis, Missouri.

Early in 1925 the Lutheran University Association purchased Valparaiso University, Valparaiso, Indiana, and set itself to the task of developing the institution into a Lutheran university. Dr. W. H. T. Dau of Concordia Seminary, St. Louis, served as the first president. At his inauguration in the auditorium of the university, Dr. Pieper of St. Louis delivered a Latin address and the Bach Chorus of Chicago provided suitable music. Special trains had to be chartered, and the attendance reached 5,000. Dr. Dau was succeeded by Pastor O. C. Kreinheder (1930), who filled the office of president until 1939, when failing health compelled him to resign. Since 1940 Prof. O. P. Kretzmann is at the head of Valparaiso University.

B. PUBLICATIONS

Practically every District of Synod publishes a District paper. At the present time 25 Districts are using District Supplements in the *Lutheran Witness* and *Der Lutheraner* for this purpose.

From 1857 to 1858 Pastor Fr. Lochner of Milwaukee issued the *Notwehr-Blatt* to combat hierarchical tendencies within the Lutheran Church of America. Prof. F. A. Schmidt of Decorah, Iowa, edited *The Lutheran Watchman,* 1866 to 1867, to supply members of the Missouri Synod who found difficulty in reading German with wholesome reading matter.

The American Lutheran Publicity Bureau, organized in 1914, has for its objective "to make known the teaching, principles, practice, and history of the Lutheran Church by lecture courses, through the public press, and by other publicity methods." The Bureau maintains a Free Tract Fund and a Free Bible Fund. Since 1917 it publishes *The American Lutheran.*

The Confessional Lutheran Publicity Bureau, established in 1940, issues tracts and other literature "in the interest of ecumenical Lutheranism." Its monthly periodical, *The Confessional Lutheran,* is edited by Pastor Paul H. Burgdorf.

C. WELFARE WORK

The first hospital opened by a Missouri Lutheran is the Lutheran Hospital at St. Louis. It was founded by Pastor J. F. Buenger on December 1, 1858. A training school for nurses was organized at this hospital in 1898. Encouraged by the success of the St. Louis hospital, other Lutheran centers erected similar institutions. Hospitals controlled by members of Synod and of the Synodical Conference are established at Alamosa, Colo., Beaver Dam, Wis., Brooklyn, N. Y., Chicago, Ill., Cleveland, Ohio, Fort Wayne, Ind., Hampton, Iowa, La Crosse, Wis., Mankato, Minn., Norfolk, Nebr., Omaha, Nebr., Red Wing, Minn., St. Louis Convalescent Home, St. Louis, Mo., St. Paul, Minn., Sheboygan, Wis., Sioux City, Iowa, Wheat Ridge, Colo., York, Nebr. The total bed capacity of these hospitals is 1,930. The value of the property is estimated at $5,610,420.

Homes for the Aged are maintained at Arlington Heights, Ill., Baltimore, Md., Brooklyn, N. Y., Buffalo, N. Y., Cleveland, Ohio, Kendallville, Ind., Cabot, Pa., Monroe, Mich., Omaha, Nebr., St. Louis, Mo. (2), Wauwatosa, Wis. The capacity of these homes is 784. Property value: $1,100,600.

Child Welfare is carried on in institutions at Addison, Ill., Baltimore, Md., Bay City, Mich., Buffalo, N. Y., Cabot, Pa., Cleveland, Ohio, Fort Wadsworth, N. Y., Fremont, Nebr., Indianapolis, Ind., Fort Wayne, Ind., Des Peres, Mo., Minneapolis, Minn., New Orleans, La., San Francisco, Calif., St. Louis, Mo., Wauwatosa, Wis., Winfield, Kans. The property value is estimated at $1,508,610.

Institutional missions are conducted in 38 cities by 49 full-time and 66 part-time workers. 621 institutions were served, and 310,077 calls were made during 1944. The property value amounts to $236,794.

At the Associated Lutheran Charities Convention of 1911 the question of training deaconesses was discussed, and eventually, in 1919, the Lutheran Deaconess Association of the Evangelical Lutheran Synodical Conference of North America was organized. A Deaconess Home to train deaconesses was opened in Fort Wayne (1921) in connection with the Lutheran Hospital. Similar institutions were established at Beaver Dam, Wisconsin (1922), Wauwatosa, Wisconsin (1925), Hot Springs, South Dakota (1927). The four schools were consolidated in the Central Training School for Deaconesses at Fort Wayne in 1935. Since 1943 the facilities of Valparaiso University are used for the training of deaconesses. 136 deaconesses have been graduated by the Association since 1922. The Deaconess Conference meets annually. The publication of the association is *The Lutheran Deaconess*.

The Evangelical Lutheran Institute for the Deaf was established in 1874 and is under the auspices of an association of Lutheran congregations of Greater Detroit. The school consists of a nursery, kindergarten, primary, intermediate, and grammar grades, thus offering an eight-grade course of study. The children are taught to speak and to read lips. The Gloria Dei Clara Elizabeth Knudsen Chapel is the gift of General Wm. Knudsen.

14

THE CENTENNIAL OF 1947

More than 100 years have passed since the fathers and founders of the Missouri Synod came to America, and soon the centennial of the organization of this body will be at hand. Acting under resolutions of the convention of 1941, President Behnken appointed Drs. Theo. Hoyer, L. Fuerbringer, H. B. Hemmeter, Pastor E. T. Lams, Prof. F. H. Schmidt (replaced by Mr. A. H. Kramer), Pastor H. W. Romoser, and Mr. G. A. Fleischer members of the Centennial Committee, which is concerning itself chiefly with "the spiritual objectives of the anniversary celebration — thus to stimulate the proper spiritual approach of gratitude and thanksgiving to the Centennial." The centennial will be observed by Synod, God willing, at its convention in 1947 in Chicago.

A review of the history of the Missouri Synod reveals the manifold blessings it has received from the Lord. From an insignificant group it has grown to a body of more than 1,500,000 members. It is working either alone or in affiliation with fellow Lutherans on every continent of the earth. It has four theological seminaries, four normal schools, and twelve colleges in North and South America besides institutions in India and in China for the training of workers in the Church. 1,093 Christian day schools taught by 2,342 men and women are maintained by its congregations. In Concordia Publishing House it possesses the largest strictly denominational publishing concern in the world. Through Radio Station KFUO and by means of the Lutheran Hour Missouri is privileged to bring the Gospel to millions. The value of the congregational and synodical property is estimated at $107,230,471. But the most brilliant gem in its radiant diadem of blessings is the pure and unadulterated Word of God which it has been privileged to preach, teach, and confess for nearly 100 years and which, by the grace of God, it has been able to apply in its work.

God forbid that Missouri glory in these blessings as though they had been merited by its own efforts and consecration or achieved through its own ingenuity and labor. The history of the Missouri Synod has also its dark sides. There have been neglected opportunities, slothfulness in doing the Lord's work, lack of initiative, indifference to God's Word, and base ingratitude. On the day of the centennial the members of Synod will approach the throne of grace in deepest humility and say with the Psalmist:

> Not unto us, O Lord, not unto us,
> But unto Thy name give glory
> For Thy mercy and for Thy truth's sake.

The centennial of Synod calls upon its members to examine their attitude toward faithful adherence to the Word of God and to the Confessions of the Lutheran Church. It was Luther who said that Church history teaches that the Gospel seldom remained pure and unadulterated in one place for more than one or two generations. The Missouri Synod is now entering upon the fourth generation. May its members heed the Word of the Lord as spoken by the Prophet Jeremiah (15:19-21): "Therefore thus saith the Lord, If thou return, then will I bring thee again, and thou shalt stand before Me; and if thou take forth the precious from the vile, thou shalt be as My mouth. Let them return unto thee, but return not thou unto them. And I will make thee unto this people a fenced brazen wall; and they shall fight against thee, but they shall not prevail against thee, for I am with thee to save thee and to deliver thee, saith the Lord. And I will deliver thee out of the hand of the wicked, and I will redeem thee out of the hand of the terrible." If the history of Synod teaches anything, it is the truth of Isaiah's words, chapter 66:2: "But to this man will I look, even to him that is poor and of a contrite spirit, and trembleth at My Word."

Finally, the centennial of Synod must stimulate its members to reconsecrate themselves to the work of the Lord. By the grace of God the Missouri Synod has the message of justification by faith in Jesus, the message of salvation solely in the blood of the crucified Savior. The Lord, who has preserved unto this body the purity of the teachings of His Word, certainly has done this for a specific purpose, namely, that it preach this Gospel in its truth and purity to a sin-stricken world. The first fifty years of Synod's existence was a period of ingathering and indoctrination. The work was done almost exclusively in the German language. World War I served to tear down the walls of language with which many of the congregations had surrounded themselves and stimulated them to reach out to the unchurched Americans in the language of our country. Since 1918 the pastors of the Missouri Synod have confirmed 189,945 adults. World War II has been called the Global War. May one not draw the inference of global missions? "Unto whomsoever much is given, of him shall much be required," Luke 12:48. If the Missouri Synod, bountifully equipped with spiritual and material resources, refuses to discharge its obligations as a missionary agency, the Lord can and will call forth a Church to do His bidding, for "this Gospel of the Kingdom shall be preached in all the world for a witness unto all nations; and then shall the end come," Matt. 24:14.

The prayer of Missouri on the day of its centennial is:

"The Lord our God be with us as He was with our fathers. Let Him not leave us nor forsake us, that He may incline our hearts unto Him to walk in all His ways and to keep His commandments and His statutes and His judgments which He commanded our fathers" (1 Kings 8:57-58). "Let Thy work appear unto Thy servants and Thy glory unto their children. And let the beauty of the Lord our God be upon us; and establish Thou the work of our hands upon us, yea the work of our hands, establish Thou it" (Ps. 90:16-17).

NOTES

Chapter 1
1. W. G. Polack, *Fathers and Founders.* St. Louis. 1938. P. 47.
2. D. H. Steffens, *Doctor Carl Ferdinand Wilhelm Walther.* Philadelphia. 1917. P. 78 ff.

Chapter 2
1. Ludwig Fischer, *Das falsche Maertyrertum oder die Wahrheit in der Sache der Stephanianer.* Leipzig. 1839. P. 7 ff.
2. *Concordia Historical Institute Quarterly.* St. Louis. 1939. P. 24.
3. Translation by Prof. G. Eifrig in *Lutheran Witness,* LVII, 189.
4. *Lutheran Witness,* LVII, 140.
5. Ludwig Fischer, *op. cit.* P. 210.
6. For additional information on the attitude of the German newspapers of St. Louis see Carl E. Schneider, *The German Church on the American Frontier.* St. Louis. 1939. Pp. 30, 33 ff.
7. *Mitteilungen des Vereins fuer Geschichts- und Altertumskunde zu Kahla und Roda.* Kahla. 1912. VII, 158 ff.
8. G. A. Schieferdecker, *Geschichte der ersten deutschen lutherischen Ansiedlung in Altenburg, Perry County, Mo.* Wartburg. 1865. P. 15.
9. J. F. Koestering, *Auswanderung der saechsichen Lutheraner im Jahre 1838.* St. Louis. P. 32.
10. D. H. Steffens, *op. cit.* P. 145.

Chapter 3
1. Martin Guenther, *Dr. C. F. W. Walther.* St. Louis. 1890. P. 5.
2. C. F. W. Walther, *Kurzer Lebenslauf des weiland ehrwuerdigen Pastor Joh. Friedr. Buenger.* St. Louis. 1882. P. 17 ff.
3. Martin Guenther, *op. cit.* P. 10.
4. C. F. W. Walther, *op. cit.* P. 32.
5. J. F. Koestering, *op. cit.* P. 38.
6. Martin Guenther, *op. cit.* P. 36. Translated by Dr. P. E. Kretzmann in *Concordia Theological Monthly.* St. Louis. XII, 166 ff.
7. J. F. Koestering, *op. cit.* Pp. 43—45. Translated by Dr. P. E. Kretzmann. *Concordia Theological Monthly.* St. Louis. XI, 169 ff.
8. J. F. Winter, *Ein Brief aus dem Jahre 1839* (?). Winter-Mennicke. 1925. P. 9.
9. D. H. Steffens, *op. cit.* P. 234.

Chapter 4

1. H. C. Wyneken, *Lebenslauf von Adolf Fr. Th. Biewend.* St. Louis. 1896. P. 28.
2. W. G. Polack, *op. cit.* P. 56.
3. Geo. J. Fritschel, *Quellen und Dokumente zur Geschichte und Lehrstellung der ev.-luth. Synode von Iowa u. a. Staaten.* Chicago. P. 44.
4. *Ibid.* P. 45.

Chapter 5

1. Geo. J. Fritschel, op. cit. Pp. 5 ff.
2. *Zum 50jaehrigen Jubilaeum des praktischen evang.-lutherischen Concordia-Seminars zu Springfield, Ill.* St. Louis. 1896. P. 21.
3. *Ebenezer.* St. Louis. 1922. P. 82.

Chapter 6

1. W. Sihler, *Lebenslauf.* St. Louis. 1879. Vol. I. P. 84.
2. *Ibid.* P. 142.
3. C. Spielmann, *Abriss der Geschichte der ev.-luth. Synode v. Ohio u. a. Staaten.* Columbus. 1880. P. 124.
4. *Ibid.* P. 114.

Chapter 7

1. *Briefe von C. F. W. Walther.* St. Louis. 1915. Vol. I, p.11.
2. *Ibid.* P. 15.
3. *Kirchliche Mitteilungen aus und ueber Nord-Amerika.* 1845. P. 12.
4. *Concordia Historical Institute Quarterly.* St. Louis. VII, 77 ff.
5. Martin Guenther, *op. cit.* P. 70.
6. *Ibid.* Pp. 71 ff.
7. W. Sihler, *Lebenslauf.* New York. 1880. Vol. II, 72.
8. *Concordia Historical Institute Quarterly.* St. Louis. IX, 17.

Chapter 9

1. *Allgemeine Synodalberichte.* St. Louis. P. 99.
2. *Ibid.* P. 242.
3. *Ibid.* P. 46.
4. *Ibid.* P. 128.
5. *Concordia Historical Institute Quarterly.* XV, 67.
6. *Zum 50jaehrigen Jubilaeum des praktischen evang.-lutherischen Concordia-Seminars zu Springfield, Ill.* St. Louis. 1896. P. 88.
7. *Allgemeine Synodalberichte.* P. 175.
8. *Zehnter Synodalbericht der Allgemeinen Synode v. Missouri, Ohio u. anderen Staaten.* St. Louis. 1860. P. 65.
9. Johannes Deindoerfer, *Geschichte der Ev.-Luth. Synode v. Iowa u. anderen Staaten.* Chicago. 1897. P. 17.
10. *Ebenezer.* St. Louis. 1922. P. 165.
11. *Ibid.* P. 169.
12. *Allgemeine Synodalberichte.* St. Louis. 1876. P. 271.
13. *Ebenezer.* St. Louis. 1922. P. 16.

NOTES

Chapter 10
1. *Lehre und Wehre.* St. Louis. 1856. P. 186.

Chapter 11
1. *Proceedings of the Twenty-Second Regular Convention.* 1893. P. 83.
2. *Proceedings of a Free English Lutheran Conference.* Columbus. 1873. P. 1.
3. *Ibid.* P. 2.
4. *Proceedings of the Eighth Annual Convention of the Evang. Luth. English Conference of Missouri.* St. Louis. 1880. P. 20.
5. *American Lutheran Almanac and Year Book.* 1899. Pittsburgh. P. 19.
6. Chr. Hochstetter. *Die Geschichte der Evangelisch-lutherischen Missouri-Synode in Nord-Amerika.* Dresden. 1885. P. 354.
7. *Ebenezer.* St. Louis. 1922. P. 408.
8. Chr. Hochstetter, *op. cit.* P. 355.
9. *Lutherske Vidnesbyrd.* 1882. P. 60.
10. *Grace for Grace.* Mankato, Minn. 1934. P. 172.
11. *Proceedings of the Twenty-First Regular Convention.* 1890. P. 85 ff.
12. *Der Lutheraner.* XXXII. P. 10.
13. *The Concordia Cyclopedia.* St. Louis. 1927. P. 704.

Chapter 12
1. Translated by Dr. Theo. Graebner in *Concordia Seminary, Its History, Architecture, and Symbolism.* St. Louis. 1926. P. 22.
2. *Der Lutheraner.* LXXIII. P. 292.
3. *Proceedings of the Thirty-First Regular Convention.* 1920. P. 237.
4. *Proceedings of the Twenty-Eighth Regular Convention.* 1911. P. 31.
5. *Ibid.* P. 33.
6. *Ibid.* P. 35 ff.
7. *Proceedings of the Thirty-First Regular Convention.* 1920. P. 104.
8. *Proceedings of the Twenty-Eighth Regular Convention.* 1911. P. 205.

Chapter 13
1. *Lutheran Witness,* LIV, 236.
2. *Proceedings of the Thirty-Second Regular Convention.* 1933. P. 51 ff.
3. *Proceedings of the Thirty-Sixth Regular Convention.* 1935. P. 221.
4. *Proceedings of the Thirty-Seventh Regular Convention.* 1938. P. 38.
5. *Proceedings of the Thirty-Eighth Regular Convention.* 1941. P. 279.
6. *Ibid.* P. 301.
7. *Proceedings of the Thirty-Ninth Regular Convention.* 1944. P. 248 ff.
8. *Proceedings of the Thirty-Third Regular Convention.* 1926. P. 236.
9. *Proceedings of the Thirty-Fourth Regular Convention.* 1929. P. 118.
10. *Proceedings of the Thirty-Seventh Regular Convention.* 1938. P. 161.
11. *Proceedings of the Thirty-Eighth Regular Convention.* 1941. P. 212.
12. *Proceedings of the Thirty-Fourth Regular Convention.* 1929. P. 5 f.
13. *Proceedings of the Thirty-Seventh Regular Convention.* 1923. P. 84.
14. *Lutheran Witness,* L, 198.
15. *Lutheran Witness,* LVIII, 443.

A CENTURY OF GRACE

OFFICERS, BOARDS, AND COMMITTEES OF THE MISSOURI SYNOD

A. GENERAL OFFICERS

President: The Rev. J. W. Behnken, D. D.
First Vice-President: The Rev. H. Harms.
Second Vice-President: The Rev. A. Brunn, D. D.
Third Vice-President: The Rev. H. A. Grueber, D. D.
Fourth Vice-President: The Rev. F. A. Hertwig.
Secretary: The Rev. M. F. Kretzmann, D. D.
Treasurer: Mr. W. A. Schlueter.
Corresponding Secretary for Foreign Relations:
    Prof. L. Fuerbringer, D. D.
Statistician and Chronologist: The Rev. Armin Schroeder.
Transportation Secretary: The Rev. Martin Piehler.
    Board of Directors: The President, the Secretary, and the Treasurer, *ex officio;* Revs. Paul Schulz, D. D., and Paul Koenig; Messrs. E. J. Gallmeyer, J. W. Boehne, Jr., Martin A. Salvner, Theo. Schlake.

B. MISSION BOARDS

Home Missions in North America: Revs. Harry E. Olsen, E. T. Bernthal, E. H. Buchheimer, Walter H. Storm; Messrs. E. W. Engel, Geo. A. Grits, Ferd. Korneffel. — Rev. F. C. Streufert, D. D., Executive Secretary.
Missions for South America: Revs. Hy. Blanke, C. F. Lehenbauer, P. Harre, W. Roth; Messrs. E. W. Schumm, E. Tatge, Hy. Gieseke. — Rev. F. C. Streufert, D. D., Executive Secretary.
Home Missions in Europe: Revs. A. F. Bobzin, L. T. Buchheimer, A. G. Dick, P. G. Sander; Messrs. F. Schurmann, H. Thien.
Foreign Missions: Revs. A. M. Kuehnert, C. Peters, K. Kurth, R. G. Lange, R. J. Torgler; Prof. W. Arndt, D. D.; Teacher Th. Struckmeyer; Messrs. H. F. Voertman, Theo. Hanser, Louis Prange, Alvin A. Welp. — Rev. Frederick Brand, D. D., Director and General Secretary; Rev. O. H. Schmidt, Executive Secretary.
Board of Missions to the Deaf and Blind: Revs. H. A. Gamber, E. H. Bertram, C. J. Hoffmann, J. Schumacher; Messrs. G. F. Kruse, J. P. Miller.

C. VARIOUS BOARDS

Board for Parish Education: Prof. P. Bretscher, Ph. D.; Revs. P. Juergensen, C. T. Spitz; Teachers L. J. Dierker, H. F. C. Roehl, W. Schroeter; Messrs. V. Eggerding, J. Goodbrake, R. Steinmeyer. — Arthur A. Miller, Executive Secretary; A. C. Stellhorn, Secretary of Schools; Wm. A. Kramer, Assistant; Rev. A. C. Mueller, Editor, Sunday School Literature; Dr. J. Weidenschilling and Arthur W. Gross, Assistants; Rev. Oscar E. Feucht, Secretary of Adult Education.
Board for Higher Education: Dr. H. A. Grueber, Dr. O. P. Kretzmann; Rev. M. Walker; Superintendent S. J. Roth; Prof. W. Gast; Messrs. E. Wengert, E. Buenger. — Prof. M. J. Neeb, Executive Secretary.
Board of Appeals: Prof. P. Koehneke; Revs. W. C. Wangerin, M. Mayer, F. L. Oberschulte; Messrs. E. C. Jacobs, C. Thrun, T. Markworth.

Board of Support and Pensions: Revs. O. Fedder, B. W. Janssen, G. W. Lobeck; Teachers A. W. Obermann, E. A. Groth; Messrs. S. Machina, C. H. Dehning, Theo. Doering, A. C. Sommer. — Rev. F. G. Kuehnert, Executive Secretary.

General Relief Board: Revs. W. Klausing, F. Wambsganss; Mr. P. E. Wolf, Jr.

Board for Young People's Work: Rev. Clarence Peters, Prof. R. Jesse; Teachers Th. Hillmann, H. C. Gruber; Mr. M. J. Roschke.

Student Service Commission: Rev. W. C. Birkner; Prof. E. M. Plass; Mr. H. J. Meier. — Rev. R. W. Hahn, Executive Secretary.

Church Extension Board: Revs. F. Niedner, Theo. H. Roschke; Teachers W. Brauer, Geo. C. Stohlmann; Messrs. C. Burde, W. Kroehnke.

Committee on Constitutional Matters: Drs. L. Fuerbringer, J. H. C. Fritz; Mr. O. Rentner.

Bureau of Information on Secret Orders: Dr. Theo. Graebner, Rev. O. F. Engelbrecht, Dr. P. Bretscher.

Army and Navy Commission: Dr. P. L. Dannenfeldt, Revs. O. A. Sauer, F. C. Proehl, K. Schleede, O. E. Sohn; Messrs. Th. Schlake, O. C. Rentner. — Rev. P. Mehl, Executive Secretary.

Board of Directors of Concordia Publishing House: Rev. R. H. C. Meyer; Messrs. R. C. Obermann, O. P. Brauer, Harry J. W. Niehaus, A. Leimbach, A. J. Meyer, J. Grundmann.

Synodical Press Committee: Revs. A. F. Meyer, Wm. F. Bruening; Mr. J. F. E. Nickelsburg.

General Literature Board: Revs. A. Doerffler, W. H. Eifert, W. E. Hohenstein, O. Nieting; Wm. A. Kramer; Dr. E. Seuel, O. A. Dorn, advisory members.

Young People's Literature Board: Dr. J. T. Mueller; Revs. R. C. Delventhal, A. Herpolsheimer; Teachers C. Tucker, A. H. Stellhorn.

Committee on Church Architecture: Revs. F. R. Webber, A. J. Stiemke; Messrs. F. Wegner, J. A. Richter, H. Bernhard, Theo. Steinmeyer, J. J. Zink.

Committee on Hymnology and Liturgics: Dr. W. G. Polack; Prof. L. Blankenbuehler; Revs. O. Kaiser, O. H. Schmidt; Superintendent B. Schumacher.

Catechism Committee: Rev. E. Kurth; Prof. O. C. Rupprecht; Teacher J. M. Runge.

Committee on Finnish Relations: Dr. Paul Schulz; Revs. E. C. Wegehaupt, R. Herrmann.

Synodical Radio Committee: Drs. J. H. C. Fritz, G. V. Schick; Rev. J. Oppliger; Messrs. Theo. Heinicke, Geo. Stohlmann, Wm. Drees, Wm. Pfaff, P. Weeke, O. Selle, R. Niedner; Dean R. A. Jesse (*ex officio*); Rev. A. Doerffler (*ex officio*); Director H. H. Hohenstein (*ex officio*).

Synodical Centennial Committee: Dr. Theo. Hoyer; Rev. H. W. Romoser; Drs. L. Fuerbringer, H. B. Hemmeter, E. T. Lams; Teacher A. H. Kramer; Mr. G. A. Fleischer.

Committee on Doctrinal Unity: Drs. Wm. Arndt, J. H. C. Fritz; Prof. W. A. Baepler; Revs. F. H. Brunn, W. H. Jurgens, G. J. Meyer; Messrs. J. C. Wegner, H. W. Knopp.

SYNODICAL OFFICERS, DISTRICTS, AND DISTRICT PRESIDENTS
1847–1947

A. OFFICERS OF THE GENERAL BODY

PRESIDENTS

C. F. W. Walther	1847–1850	H. C. Schwan	1878–1899
F. C. D. Wyneken	1850–1864	F. Pieper	1899–1911
C. F. W. Walther	1864–1878	F. Pfotenhauer	1911–1935
		J. W. Behnken	1935–

VICE-PRESIDENTS

(Note: 1847–1851 Synod had one Vice-President; 1851–1854, two Vice-Presidents; 1854–1874, one Vice-President; 1874–1905, two Vice-Presidents; 1905–1908, three Vice-Presidents; since 1908 four Vice-Presidents.)

Wm. Sihler	1847–1854	F. Pfotenhauer	1908–1911
Theo. J. Brohm	1851–1857	J. W. Miller	1908–1929
H. C. Schwan	1857–1860	J. Strasen	1908–1914
Theo. J. Brohm	1860–1864	J. Hilgendorf	1911–1920
Wm. Sihler	1864–1869	H. Speckhard	1914–1917
Theo. J. Brohm	1869–1874	F. Brand	1917–1929
Wm. Sihler	1874–1878	H. P. Eckhardt	1917–1926
C. J. H. Fick	1874–1878	G. A. Bernthal	1920–1926
R. Lange	1878–1881	Wm. Dallmann	1926–1932
C. Gross	1878–1899	F. J. Lankenau	1926–1939
O. Hanser	1881–1884	J. W. Behnken	1929–1935
Chr. H. Loeber	1884–1887	Fr. Randt	1929–1937
H. Succop	1887–1890	H. A. Grueber	1932–
H. Sauer	1890–1893	K. Kretzschmar	1935–1938
J. P. Beyer	1893–1899	H. Harms	1938–
C. C. Schmidt	1899–1908	A. Brunn	1941–
P. Brand	1899–1917	G. Chr. Barth	1941–1945
H. Succop	1905–1908	F. A. Hertwig	1946–

SYNODICAL OFFICERS

SECRETARIES

F. W. Husmann	1847–1850	G. Kuechle	1866–1874
L. W. Habel	1850–1854	A. Rohrlack	1874–1905
F. W. Husmann	1854–1860	R. D. Biedermann	1905–1920
J. A. F. W. Mueller	1860–1866	M. F. Kretzmann	1920–

TREASURERS

F. W. Barthel	1847–1857	J. F. Schuricht, Jr.	1902–1914
F. Boehlau	1857–1863	E. Seuel	1914–1942
J. F. Schuricht, Sr.	1863–1881	W. H. Schlueter	1942–
C. F. W. Meier	1881–1902		

B. DISTRICTS AND DISTRICT PRESIDENTS

(Note: Names of Districts in brackets have been changed during the course of years.)

Alberta and British Columbia, 1921, branched off from the Minnesota District.

Aug. J. Mueller	1921–1930	W. C. Eifert	1930–

Argentine District, 1927, branched off from Brazil District.

A. T. Kramer	1927–1928	A. C. Kroeger	1941–1942
G. Huebner	1928–1941	S. Beckmann	1942–

Atlantic District, 1906, branched off from Eastern District.

E. C. L. Schulze	1906–1918	Geo. Koenig	1941–1942
H. Birkner	1918–1930	H. J. Rippe	1942–
Arthur Brunn	1930–1941		

Brazil District, 1904.

Wm. Mahler	1904–1910	J. Kunstmann	1921–1922
Ad. Vogel	1910–1913	J. Busch	1922–1924
Aug. Heine	1913–1916	Con. F. Lehenbauer	1924–1930
E. Mueller	1916–1921	A. Heine	1930–1942
		R. Hasse	1942–

California and Nevada District, 1899, branched off from Western District in 1887, called California and Oregon District until 1899, when Oregon and Washington organized a new District.

J. M. Buehler	1899–1903	J. W. Theiss	1920–1924
G. Runkel	1903–1906	Arthur Brohm	1924–1945
G. A. Bernthal	1906–1920	C. Fickenscher	1945–

A CENTURY OF GRACE

[*California and Oregon District*, 1887], branched off from Western District.

J. M. Buehler 1887–1899

[*Canada District*, 1879], branched off from Northern District, name changed to Ontario District in 1923.

A. Ernst	1879–1882	G. Eifrig	1906–1909
Chr. Hochstetter	1882–1883	W. C. Boese	1909–1918
F. Dubpernell	1883–1888	P. Graupner	1918–1921
F. Bente	1888–1893	F. Malinsky	1921–1923
J. W. Weinbach	1893–1906		

Central District, 1854.

Dr. Wm. Sihler	1854–1860	Wm. Moll	1915–1919
H. C. Schwan	1860–1878	J. A. Schmidt	1919–1920
W. S. Stubnatzi	1878–1880	J. D. Matthius	1920–1927
J. H. Niemann	1880–1909	W. F. Lichtsinn	1927–
J. H. Wefel	1909–1915		

Central Illinois District, 1907, part of Illinois District, which branched off from the Western District in 1875.

F. Brand	1907–1917	Ph. Wilhelm	1932–1933
F. W. Brockmann	1917–1918	W. E. Hohenstein	1933–1935
W. Heyne	1918–1928	J. C. Schuelke	1935–1942
Paul Schulz	1928–1932	Alb. C. Bernthal	1942–

Colorado District, 1921, branched off from the Kansas District.

O. Luessenhop	1921–1930	F. W. Obermeier	1932–1942
O. K. Hensel	1930–1934	E. J. Friedrich	1942–

Eastern District, 1854.

E. G. W. Keyl	1854–1870	W. Broecker	1921–1928
C. Gross	1870–1875	J. K. E. Horst	1928–1931
J. P. Beyer	1875–1888	F. C. Verwiebe	1931–1938
P. Brand	1888–1899	O. A. Sauer	1938–1939
H. H. Walker	1899–1915	P. Fretthold	1939–1945
F. C. Verwiebe	1915–1921	C. A. Behnke	1945–

English District, 1911.

H. P. Eckhardt	1911–1912	G. Schuessler	1927–1936
M. S. Sommer	1912–1915	P. Lindemann	1936–1938
J. A. Detzer	1915–1918	Martin Walker	1938–1945
O. C. Kreinheder	1918–1927	H. Bartels	1945–

[*Illinois District*, 1879], branched off from Western District.

H. Wunder	1875–1891	H. Engelbrecht	1903–1907
H. H. Succop	1891–1903		

SYNODICAL OFFICERS

[*Iowa District,* 1879], branched off from the Western District.

J. Lorenz Craemer	1879–1888	E. Zuerrer	1906–1909
Ph. Studt	1888–1891	A. D. Greif	1909–1914
Fr. Brust	1891–1894	Theo. Wolfram	1914–1927
E. Zuerrer	1894–1900	H. Harms	1927–1936
O. Cloeter	1900–1906		

Iowa District East, 1936, half of the Iowa District.

H. Harms	1936–1938	C. Hesse	1938–

Iowa District West, 1936, half of the Iowa District.

Ad. Schwidder	1936–1945	H. Berner	1945–

Kansas District, 1888, branched off from Western District.

F. Pennekamp	1888–1894	Chas. F. Lehenbauer	1919–1932
C. Hafner	1894–1906	W. Mahler	1932–1939
F. Droegemueller	1906–1912	W. H. Meyer	1939–
Theo. H. Juengel	1912–1919		

Manitoba and Saskatchewan District, 1922, branched off from Minnesota District.

Paul Wiegner	1922–1924	J. Lucht	1930–
C. T. Wetzstein	1924–1930		

Michigan District, 1882, formerly the Northern District.

Jos. Schmidt	1882–1891	E. A. Mayer	1914–1924
G. Spiegel	1891–1912	John Schinnerer	1924–1942
Theo. Engelder	1912–1914	A. Zeile	1942–

[*Minnesota and Dakota District,* 1882], branched off from the Northwestern District.

O. Cloeter, Sr.	1882–1885	F. Pfotenhauer	1891–1908
Fr. Sievers	1885–1891	H. Schulz	1908–1910

Minnesota District, 1910.

H. Schulz	1910–1912	H. J. Bouman	1930–1933
R. Koehler	1912–1918	J. C. Meyer	1933–1942
H. Meyer	1918–1930	R. G. Heyne	1942–

[*Nebraska District,* 1882], branched off from Western District.

J. Hilgendorf	1882–1900	C. F. Brommer	1915–1922
C. H. Becker	1900–1915		

North Dakota and Montana District, 1910, branched off from the Minnesota and Dakota District.

T. Hinck	1910–1924	A. Jordan	1941–1942
J. P. Klausler	1924–1941	A. H. Grumm	1942–

North Dakota District, 1945.

A. H. Grumm   1945–

Montana District, 1945, branched off from North Dakota District.

P. Freiburger 1945–

[*Northern District,* 1854], Canada District branched off in 1879; name changed to Michigan District in 1882.

O. Fuerbringer	1854–1873	O. Fuerbringer	1875–1882
J. A. Huegli	1873–1875		

Northern Illinois District, 1907, part of former Illinois District.

H. Engelbrecht	1907–1909	Alex Ullrich	1927–1936
W. C. Kohn	1909–1913	E. T. Lams	1936–1945
Fr. Brunn	1913–1927	A. H. Werfelmann	1945–

Northern Nebraska District, 1922, part of former Nebraska District.

W. Harms	1922–1923	W. E. Homann	1939–
M. E. Mayer	1923–1939		

[*Northwestern District,* 1875], branched off from the Northern District; reorganized in 1882 as Minnesota and Dakota District and Wisconsin District.

K. J. A. Strasen 1875–1882

North Wisconsin District, 1916, part of former Wisconsin District.

J. G. Schliepsiek	1916–1918	W. L. Kohn	1936–
H. Daib	1918–1936		

Oklahoma District, 1924, branched off from Kansas District.

Hy. Mueller	1924–1939	P. Hartenberger	1942–1943
C. Matthies	1939–1940	O. Hoyer	1943–
E. Hauer	1940–1942		

Ontario District, called Canada District until 1923.

F. Malinsky 1923–

Oregon and Washington District, 1899, branched off from California and Oregon District.

H. A. C. Paul	1899–1903	J. A. Rimbach	1918–1921
W. Luessenhop	1903–1906	W. Janssen	1921–1936
W. H. Behrens	1906–1909	F. M. L. Nitz	1936–
L. Stuebe	1909–1918		

Southeastern District, 1939, formed of parts of the Eastern and the English Districts.

George J. Spilman	1939–1945	O. A. Sauer	1945–

South Dakota District, 1906, branched off from Minnesota and Dakota District.

A. F. Breihan	1906–1912	F. W. Leyhe	1921–1936
J. D. Ehlen	1912–1919	Walter Nitschke	1936–
E. G. Jehn	1919–1921		

SYNODICAL OFFICERS

Southern District, 1882, branched off from Western District.

Tim. Stiemke	1882–1889	G. J. Wegener	1891–1927
G. Birkmann	1889–1891	M. W. H. Holls	1927–

Southern California District, 1930, branched off from California and Nevada District.

G. H. Smukal	1930–1942	W. F. Troeger	1942–

Southern Illinois District, 1907, part of former Illinois District.

F. W. Brockmann	1907–1909	C. Thos. Spitz	1934–1945
U. Iben	1909–1912	E. H. Bohrer	1945–1946
J. G. F. Kleinhans	1912–1934	P. Juergensen	1946–

Southern Nebraska District, 1922, part of former Nebraska District.

C. F. Brommer	1922–1924	A. J. C. Moeller	1936–1938
W. Cholcher	1924–1930	I. C. Heinicke	1938–
H. E. Meyer	1930–1936		

South Wisconsin District, 1916, part of former Wisconsin District.

Ed. Albrecht	1916–1921	J. F. Boerger	1932–1936
H. Grueber	1921–1932	F. A. Schwertfeger	1936–

Texas District, 1906, branched off from Southern District.

A. W. Kramer	1906–1909	J. W. Behnken	1926–1929
C. A. Waech	1909–1912	C. M. Beyer	1929–1942
G. Birkmann	1912–1920	E. A. Heckmann	1942–
H. Studtmann	1920–1926		

Western District, 1854.

G. A. Schieferdecker	1854–1858	J. J. Bernthal	1901–1919
G. Schaller	1858–1863	J. H. C. Fritz	1919–1920
J. F. Buenger	1863–1875	Fr. Brust	1920–1921
J. F. Biltz	1875–1891	R. Kretzschmar	1921–1939
C. C. Schmidt	1891–1898	P. Koenig	1939–1945
P. Roesener	1898–1901	E. L. Roschke	1945–

[*Wisconsin District*, 1882], branched off from the Northwestern District.

K. J. A. Strasen	1882–1885	J. Strasen	1894–1900
H. F. Sprengeler	1885–1891	Cl. Seuel	1900–1906
J. Herzer	1891–1892	H. Daib	1906–1916
B. Sievers	1892–1894		

Synod of Missouri and Other States, organized 1888, until 1891 called the General English Evangelical Lutheran Conference of Missouri and Other States. Joined Missouri Synod as the *English District* in 1911.

F. Kuegele	1888–1897	A. W. Meyer	1901–1905
Wm. Dallmann	1897–1901	H. P. Eckhardt	1905–1911

PRESIDENTS OF THE EVANGELICAL LUTHERAN SYNODICAL CONFERENCE OF NORTH AMERICA

C. F. W. Walther	1872–1873	(Missouri Synod)
W. F. Lehmann	1873–1876	(Ohio Synod)
H. A. Preuss	1876–1877	(Norwegian Synod)
W. F. Lehmann	1877–1880	(Ohio Synod)
P. L. Larsen	1880–1882	(Norwegian Synod)
J. Bading	1882–1912	(Wisconsin Synod)
C. Gausewitz	1912–1927	(Wisconsin Synod)
L. Fuerbringer	1927–1944	(Missouri Synod)
E. Benj. Schlueter	1944–	(Wisconsin Synod)

A BRIEF STATEMENT OF THE DOCTRINAL POSITION OF THE EVANGELICAL LUTHERAN SYNOD OF MISSOURI, OHIO, AND OTHER STATES

OF THE HOLY SCRIPTURES

1. We teach that the Holy Scriptures differ from all other books in the world in that they are the Word of God. They are the Word of God because the holy men of God who wrote the Scriptures wrote only that which the Holy Ghost communicated to them by inspiration, 2 Tim. 3:16; 2 Pet. 1:21. We teach also that the verbal inspiration of the Scriptures is not a so-called "theological deduction," but that it is taught by direct statements of the Scriptures, 2 Tim. 3:16; John 10:35; Rom. 3:2; 1 Cor. 2:13. Since the Holy Scriptures are the Word of God, it goes without saying that they contain no errors or contradictions, but that they are in all their parts and words the infallible truth, also in those parts which treat of historical, geographical, and other secular matters, John 10:35.

2. We furthermore teach regarding the Holy Scriptures that they are given by God to the Christian Church for the foundation of faith, Eph. 2:20. Hence the Holy Scriptures are the sole source from which all doctrines proclaimed in the Christian Church must be taken and therefore, too, the sole rule and norm by which all teachers and doctrines must be examined and judged. — With the Confessions of our Church we teach also that the "rule of faith" (*analogia fidei*) according to which the Holy Scriptures are to be understood are the clear passages of *the Scriptures themselves* which set forth the individual doctrines. (Apology. *Triglotta*, p. 441, § 60; Mueller, p. 284.) The rule of faith is not the man-made so-called "totality of Scripture" (*"Ganzes der Schrift"*).

3. We reject the doctrine which under the name of science has gained wide popularity in the Church of our day that Holy Scripture is not in all its parts the Word of God, but in part the Word of God and in part the word of man and hence does, or at least might, contain error. We reject this erroneous doctrine as horrible and blasphemous, since it flatly contradicts Christ and His holy apostles, sets up men as judges over the Word of God, and thus overthrows the foundation of the Christian Church and its faith.

OF GOD

4. On the basis of the Holy Scriptures we teach the sublime article of the Holy Trinity; that is, we teach that the one true God, Deut. 6:4; 1 Cor. 8:4, is the Father and the Son and the Holy Ghost, three distinct *persons,* but of one and the same divine *essence,* equal in power, equal in eternity, equal in majesty, because each person possesses the one divine essence *entire,* Col. 2:9; Matt. 28:19. We hold that all teachers and communions that deny the doctrine of the Holy Trinity are outside the pale of the Christian Church. The Triune God is the God who is *gracious* to man, John 3:16-18; 1 Cor. 12:3. Since the Fall no man can believe in the "fatherhood" of God except he believe in the eternal Son of God, who became man and reconciled us to God by His vicarious satisfaction, 1 John 2:23; John 14:6. Hence we warn against Unitarianism, which in our country has to a great extent impenetrated the sects and is being spread particularly also through the influence of the lodges.

OF CREATION

5. We teach that God has created heaven and earth, and that in the manner and in the space of time recorded in the Holy Scriptures, especially Gen. 1 and 2, namely, by His almighty creative word, and in six days. We reject every doctrine which denies or limits the work of creation as taught in Scripture. In our days it is denied or limited by those who assert, ostensibly in deference to science, that the world came into existence through a process of evolution; that is, that it has, in immense periods of time, developed more or less out of itself. Since no man was present when it pleased God to create the world, we must look for a reliable account of creation to God's own record, found in God's own book, the Bible. We accept God's own record with full confidence and confess with Luther's Catechism: "I believe that God has made me and all creatures."

OF MAN AND SIN

6. We teach that the first man was not brutelike nor merely capable of intellectual development, but that God created man *in His own image,* Gen. 1:26, 27; Eph. 4:24; Col. 3:10, that is, in true knowledge of God and in true righteousness and holiness and endowed with a truly scientific knowledge of nature, Gen. 2:19-23.

7. We furthermore teach that sin came into the world by the fall of the first man, as described Gen. 3. By this Fall not only he himself, but also his natural offspring have lost the original knowledge, righteousness, and holiness, and thus all men are sinners already by birth, dead in sins, inclined to all evil, and subject to the wrath of God, Rom. 5:12, 18; Eph. 2:1-3. We teach also that men are unable, through any efforts of their own or by the aid of "culture and science," to reconcile themselves to God and thus to conquer death and damnation.

OF REDEMPTION

8. We teach that in the fullness of time the eternal Son of God *was made man* by assuming, from the Virgin Mary through the operation of the Holy Ghost, a human nature like unto ours, yet without sin, and receiving it into His divine person. Jesus Christ is therefore "true God, begotten of the Father from eternity, and also true man, born of the Virgin Mary," true God and true man in *one* undivided and indivisible person. The purpose of this miraculous incarnation of the Son of God was that He might become the *Mediator* between God and men, both fulfilling the divine Law and suffering and dying in the place of mankind. In this manner God has reconciled the whole sinful world unto Himself, Gal. 4:4, 5; 3:13; 2 Cor. 5:18, 19.

OF FAITH IN CHRIST

9. Since God has reconciled the whole world unto Himself through the vicarious life and death of His Son and has commanded that the reconciliation effected by Christ be proclaimed to men in the Gospel, to the end that they may *believe* it, 2 Cor. 5:18, 19; Rom. 1:5, therefore faith in Christ is the only way for men to obtain personal reconciliation with God, that is, forgiveness of sins, as both the Old and the New Testament Scriptures testify, Acts 10:43; John 3:16-18, 36. By this faith in Christ, through which men obtain the forgiveness of sins, is not meant any human effort to fulfill the Law of God after the example of Christ, but faith in the Gospel, that is, in the forgiveness of sins, or justification, which was fully earned for us by Christ and is offered in the Gospel. This faith justifies, not inasmuch as it is a work of man, but inasmuch as it lays hold of the grace offered, the forgiveness of sins, Rom. 4:16.

OF CONVERSION

10. We teach that conversion consists in this, that a man, having learned from the Law of God that he is a lost and condemned sinner, *is brought to faith in the Gospel*, which offers him forgiveness of sins and eternal salvation for the sake of Christ's vicarious satisfaction, Acts 11:21; Luke 24:46, 47; Acts 26:18.

11. All men, since the Fall, are dead in sins, Eph. 2:1-3, and inclined only to evil, Gen. 6:5; 8:21; Rom. 8:7. For this reason, and particularly because men regard the Gospel of Christ, crucified for the sins of the world, as foolishness, 1 Cor. 2:14, faith in the Gospel, or conversion to God, is neither wholly nor in the least part the work of man, but the work of God's grace and almighty power alone, Phil. 1:29; Eph. 2:8; 1:19; Jer. 31:18. Hence Scripture calls the faith of man, or his conversion, a raising from the dead, Eph. 1:20; Col. 2:12, a being born of God, John 1:12, 13, a new birth by the Gospel, 1 Pet. 1:23-25, a work of God like the creation of light at the creation of the world, 2 Cor. 4:6.

12. On the basis of these clear statements of the Holy Scriptures we reject every kind of *synergism*, that is, the doctrine that conversion is wrought not

by the grace and power of God alone, but in part also by the co-operation of man himself, by man's right conduct, his right attitude, his right self-determination, his lesser guilt or less evil conduct as compared with others, his refraining from willful resistance, or anything else whereby man's conversion and salvation is taken out of the gracious hands of God and made to depend on what man does or leaves undone. For this refraining from willful resistance or from any kind of resistance is also solely a work of grace, which "changes unwilling into willing men," Ezek. 36:26; Phil. 2:13. We reject also the doctrine that man is able to decide for conversion through "powers imparted by grace," since this doctrine presupposes that *before* conversion man still possesses spiritual powers by which he can make the right use of such "powers imparted by grace."

13. On the other hand, we reject also the *Calvinistic* perversion of the doctrine of conversion, that is, the doctrine that God does not desire to convert and save all hearers of the Word, but only a portion of them. Many hearers of the Word indeed remain unconverted and are not saved, not because God does not earnestly desire their conversion and salvation, but solely because they stubbornly resist the gracious operation of the Holy Ghost, as Scriptures teach, Acts 7:51; Matt. 23:37; Acts 13:46.

14. As to the question why not all men are converted and saved, seeing that God's grace is universal and all men are equally and utterly corrupt, we confess that we cannot answer it. From Scripture we know only this: A man owes his conversion and salvation, not to any lesser guilt or better conduct on his part, but solely to the grace of God. But any man's non-conversion is due to himself alone: it is the result of his obstinate resistance against the converting operation of the Holy Ghost, Hos. 13:9.

15. Our refusal to go beyond what is revealed in these two Scriptural truths is not "masked Calvinism" ("Crypto-calvinism"), but *precisely* the Scriptural teaching of the Lutheran Church as it is presented in detail in the Formula of Concord (*Triglot,* p. 1081, §§ 57-59, 60 b, 62, 63; M., p. 716 f.): "That one is hardened, blinded, given over to a reprobate mind, while another, who is indeed in the same guilt, is converted again, etc., — in these and similar questions Paul fixes a certain limit to us how far we should go, namely, that in the one part we should recognize God's *judgment.* For they are well-deserved penalties of sins when God so punished a land or nation for despising His Word that the punishment extends also to their posterity, as is to be seen in the Jews. And thereby God in some lands and persons exhibits His severity to those that are His in order to indicate what we all would have well deserved and would be worthy and worth, since we act wickedly in opposition to God's Word and often grieve the Holy Ghost sorely; in order that we may live in the fear of God and acknowledge and praise God's *goodness,* to the exclusion of, and contrary to, our merit in and with *us,* to whom He gives His Word and with whom He leaves it and whom He does not harden and reject. . . . And this His righteous, well-deserved judgment He displays in some countries, nations, and persons in order that, when we are placed alongside of them and com-

pared with them (*quam simillimi illis deprehensi, i. e.*, and found to be most similar to them), we may learn the more diligently to recognize and praise God's pure, unmerited grace in the vessels of mercy. . . . When we proceed thus far in this article, we remain on the right way, as it is written, Hos. 13:9: 'O Israel, thou hast destroyed thyself; but in Me is thy help.' However, as regards these things in this disputation which would soar too high and beyond these limits, we should with Paul place the finger upon our lips and remember and say, Rom. 9:20: 'O man, who art thou that repliest against God?'" The Formula of Concord describes the mystery which confronts us here not as a mystery in man's heart (a "psychological" mystery), but teaches that, when we try to understand why "one is hardened, blinded, given over to a reprobate mind, while another, who is indeed in the same guilt, is converted again," we enter the domain of the unsearchable judgments of God and ways past finding out, which are not revealed to us in His Word, but which we shall know in eternal life, 1 Cor. 13:12.

16. Calvinists solve this mystery, which God has not revealed in His Word, by denying the *universality* of grace; synergists, by denying that salvation is by grace *alone*. Both solutions are utterly vicious, since they contradict Scripture and since every poor sinner stands in need of, and must cling to, both the unrestricted *universal grace* and the unrestricted "by grace *alone*," lest he despair and perish.

OF JUSTIFICATION

17. Holy Scripture sums up all its teachings regarding the love of God to the world of sinners, regarding the salvation wrought by Christ, and regarding faith in Christ as the only way to obtain salvation, in the article of *justification*. Scripture teaches that God has already declared the whole world to be righteous in Christ, Rom. 7:19; 2 Cor: 5:18-21; Rom. 4:25; that therefore not for the sake of their good works, but without the works of the Law, by grace, for Christ's sake, He *justifies*, that is, *accounts* as righteous, all those who believe in Christ, that is, believe, accept, and rely on, the fact that for Christ's sake their sins are forgiven. Thus the Holy Ghost testifies through St. Paul: "There is no difference; for all have sinned and come short of the glory of God, being justified freely by His grace, through the redemption that is in Christ Jesus," Rom. 3:23, 24. And again: "Therefore we conclude that a man is justified by faith, without the deeds of the Law," Rom. 3:28.

18. Through this doctrine alone Christ is given the *honor* due Him, namely, that through His holy life and innocent suffering and death He is our Savior. And through this doctrine alone can poor sinners have the abiding *comfort* that God is assuredly gracious to them. We reject *as apostasy from the Christian religion* all doctrines whereby man's own works and merit are mingled into the article of justification before God. For the Christian religion is the faith that we have forgiveness of sins and salvation through faith in Christ Jesus, Acts 10:43.

19. We reject as apostasy from the Christian religion not only the doctrine of the *Unitarians*, who promise the grace of God to men on the basis of their moral efforts; not only the gross work doctrine of the papists, who expressly teach that good works are necessary to obtain justification; but also the doctrine of the *synergists*, who indeed use the terminology of the Christian Church and say that man is justified "by faith," "by faith alone," but again mix human works into the article of justification by ascribing to man a co-operation with God in the kindling of faith and thus stray into papistic territory.

OF GOOD WORKS

20. Before God only those works are good which are done for the glory of God and the good of man, according to the rule of the divine Law. Such works, however, no man performs unless he first believes that God has forgiven him his sins and has given him eternal life by grace, for Christ's sake, without any works of his own, John 15:4, 5. We reject as a great folly the assertion, frequently made in our day, that works must be placed in the fore, and "faith in dogmas" — meaning the Gospel of Christ Crucified for the sins of the world — must be relegated to the rear. Since good works never precede faith, but are always and in every instance the *result* of faith in the Gospel, it is evident that the only means by which we Christians can become rich in good works (and God would have us to be rich in good works, Titus 2:14) is unceasingly to remember the grace of God which we have received in Christ, Rom. 12:1; 2 Cor. 8:9. Hence we reject as unchristian and foolish any attempt to produce good works by the compulsion of the Law or through carnal motives.

OF THE MEANS OF GRACE

21. Although God is present and operates everywhere throughout all creation and the whole earth is therefore full of the *temporal* bounties and blessings of God, Col. 1:17; Acts 17:28; 14:17, still we hold with Scripture that God offers and communicates to men the *spiritual* blessings purchased by Christ, namely, the forgiveness of sins and the treasures and gifts connected therewith, only through the external means of grace ordained by Him. These means of grace are the Word of the Gospel, in every form in which it is brought to man, and the Sacraments of Holy Baptism and of the Lord's Supper. The Word of the Gospel promises and applies the grace of God, works faith and thus regenerates man, and gives the Holy Ghost, Acts 20:24; Rom. 10:17; 1 Pet. 1:23; Gal. 3:2. Baptism, too, is applied for the remission of sins and is therefore a washing of regeneration and renewing of the Holy Ghost, Acts 2:38; 22:16; Titus 3:5. Likewise the object of the Lord's Supper, that is, of the ministration of the body and blood of Christ, is none other than the communication and sealing of the forgiveness of sins, as the words declare: "Given for you," and: "Shed for you for the remission of sins," Luke 22:19, 20; Matt. 26:28, and "This cup is the New Testament in My blood," 1 Cor. 11:23; Jer. 31:31-34 ("New Covenant").

22. Since it is only through the external means ordained by Him that God has promised to communicate the grace and salvation purchased by Christ, the Christian Church must not remain at home with the means of grace entrusted to it, but go into the whole world with the preaching of the Gospel and the administration of the Sacraments, Matt. 28:19, 20; Mark 16:15, 16. For the same reason also the churches at home should never forget that there is no other way of winning souls for the Church and keeping them with it than the faithful and diligent use of the divinely ordained means of grace. Whatever activities do not either directly apply the Word of God or subserve such application we condemn as "new methods," unchurchly activities, which do not build, but harm, the Church.

23. We reject as a dangerous error the doctrine, which disrupted the Church of the Reformation, that the grace and the Spirit of God are communicated not through the external means ordained by Him, but by an *immediate* operation of grace. This erroneous doctrine bases the forgiveness of sins, or justification, upon a fictitious "infused grace," that is, upon a quality of man, and thus again establishes the work doctrine of the papists.

OF THE CHURCH

24. We believe that there is *one* holy Christian Church on earth, the Head of which is Christ and which is gathered, preserved, and governed by Christ through the Gospel.

The members of the Christian Church are the *Christians*, that is, all those who have despaired of their own righteousness before God and believe that God forgives their sins for Christ's sake. The Christian Church, in the proper sense of the term, is composed of believers only, Acts 5:14; 26:18; which means that no person in whom the Holy Ghost has wrought faith in the Gospel, or — which is the same thing — in the doctrine of justification, can be divested of his membership in the Christian Church; and, on the other hand, that no person in whose heart this faith does not dwell can be invested with such membership. All unbelievers, though they be in external communion with the Church and even hold the office of teacher or any other office in the Church, are not members of the Church, but, on the contrary, dwelling-places and instruments of Satan, Eph. 2:2. This is also the teaching of our Lutheran Confessions: "It is certain, however, that the wicked are in the power of the devil and members of the kingdom of the devil, as Paul teaches, Eph. 2:2, when he says that 'the devil now worketh in the children of disobedience,'" etc. (Apology. *Triglot*, p, 231, § 16; M., p. 154.)

25. Since it is by faith in the Gospel alone that men become members of the Christian Church, and since this faith cannot be seen by men, but is known to God alone, 1 Kings 8:39; Acts 1:24; 2 Tim. 2:19, therefore the Christian Church on earth is *invisible*, Luke 17:20, and will remain invisible till Judgment Day, Col. 3:3, 4. In our day some Lutherans speak of two sides of the Church, taking the means of grace to be its "visible side." It is true, the means of grace are necessarily related to the Church, seeing

that the Church is created and preserved through them. But the means of grace are not for that reason a part of the Church; for the Church in the proper sense of the word consists only of *believers*, Eph. 2:19, 20; Acts 5:14. Lest we abet the notion that the Christian Church in the proper sense of the term is an external institution, we shall continue to call the means of grace the "marks" of the Church. Just as wheat is to be found only where it has been sown, so the Church can be found only where the Word of God is in use.

26. We teach that this Church, which is the invisible communion of all believers, is to be found not only in those external church communions which teach the Word of God purely in every part, but also where, along with error, so much of the Word of God still remains that men may be brought to the knowledge of their sins and to faith in the forgiveness of sins, which Christ has gained for all men, Mark 16:16; Samaritans: Luke 17:16; John 4:25.

27. *Local Churches or Local Congregations.* — Holy Scripture, however, does not speak merely of the *one Church*, which embraces the believers of all places, as in Matt. 16:18; John 10:16, but also of churches in the *plural*, that is, of *local churches*, as in 1 Cor. 16:19; 1:2; Acts 8:1: the churches of Asia, the church of God in Corinth, the church in Jerusalem. But this does not mean that there are *two kinds* of churches, for the local churches also, in as far as they are churches, consist solely of believers, as we see clearly from the addresses of the epistles to local churches; for example, "Unto the church which is at Corinth, to *them that are sanctified* in Christ Jesus, called to be *saints*," 1 Cor. 1:2; Rom. 1:7, etc. The visible society, containing hypocrites as well as believers, is called a church only in an improper sense, Matt. 13:47-50, 24-30, 38-43.

28. *On Church Fellowship.* — Since God ordained that His Word *only*, without the admixture of human doctrine, be taught and believed in the Christian Church, 1 Pet. 4:11; John 8:31, 32; 1 Tim. 6:3, 4, all Christians are required by God to discriminate between orthodox and heterodox church bodies, Matt. 7:15, to have church fellowship only with orthodox church bodies, and, in case they have strayed into heterodox church bodies, to leave them, Rom. 16:17. We repudiate *unionism*, that is, church fellowship with the adherents of false doctrine, as disobedience to God's command, as causing divisions in the Church, Rom. 16:17; 2 John 9:10, and as involving the constant danger of losing the Word of God entirely, 2 Tim. 2:17-21.

29. The orthodox character of a church is established not by its mere name nor by its outward acceptance of, and subscription to, an orthodox creed, but by the doctrine which is *actually* taught in its pulpits, in its theological seminaries, and in its publications. On the other hand, a church does not forfeit its orthodox character through the casual intrusion of errors, provided these are combated and eventually removed by means of doctrinal discipline, Acts 20:30; 1 Tim. 1:3.

30. *The Original and True Possessors of All Christian Rights and Privileges.* — Since the Christians are the Church, it is self-evident that they alone *originally* possess the spiritual gifts and rights which Christ has

gained for, and given to, His Church. Thus St. Paul reminds all believers: "All things are yours," 1 Cor. 3:21, 22, and Christ Himself commits to all believers the keys of the kingdom of heaven, Matt. 16:13-19; 18:17-20; John 20:22, 23, and commissions all believers to preach the Gospel and to administer the Sacraments, Matt. 28:19, 20; 1 Cor. 11:23-25. Accordingly, we reject all doctrines by which this spiritual power or any part thereof is adjudged as *originally* vested in certain individuals or bodies, such as the Pope, or the bishops, or the order of the ministry, or the secular lords, or councils, or synods, etc. The officers of the Church publicly administer their offices only by virtue of delegated powers, conferred on them by the original possessors of such powers, and such administration remains under the supervision of the latter, Col. 4:17. Naturally all Christians have also the right and the duty to judge and decide matters of doctrine, not according to their own notions, of course, but according to the Word of God, 1 John 4:1; 1 Pet. 4:11.

OF THE PUBLIC MINISTRY

31. By the public ministry we mean the office by which the Word of God is preached and the Sacraments are administered *by order and in the name* of a Christian congregation. Concerning this office we teach that it is a *divine ordinance;* that is, the Christians of a certain locality must apply the means of grace not only privately and within the circle of their families nor merely in their common intercourse with fellow Christians, John 5:39; Eph. 6:4; Col. 3:16, but they are also required, by the divine order, to make provision that the Word of God be publicly preached in their midst, and the Sacraments administered according to the institution of Christ, by persons qualified for such work, whose qualifications and official functions are exactly defined in Scripture, Titus 1:5; Acts 14:23; 20:28; 2 Tim. 2:2.

32. Although the office of the ministry is a divine ordinance, it possesses no other power than the power of the Word of God, 1 Pet. 4:11; that is to say, it is the duty of Christians to yield unconditional obedience to the office of the ministry whenever, and as long as, the minister proclaims to them the Word of God, Heb. 13:17; Luke 10:16. If, however, the minister, in his teachings and injunctions, were to go beyond the Word of God, it would be the duty of Christians not to obey him, but to disobey him, so as to remain faithful to Christ, Matt. 23:8. Accordingly, we reject the false doctrine ascribing to the office of the ministry the right to demand obedience and submission in matters which Christ has not commanded.

33. Regarding *ordination* we teach that it is not a divine, but a commendable ecclesiastical ordinance. (Smalcald Articles. *Triglot,* p. 525, § 70; M., p. 342.)

OF CHURCH AND STATE

34. Although both Church and State are ordinances of God, yet they must not be commingled. Church and State have entirely different aims. By the Church, God would save men, for which reason the Church is called the "mother" of believers, Gal. 4:26. By the State, God would

maintain external order among men, "that we may lead a quiet and peaceable life in all godliness and honesty," 1 Tim. 2:2. It follows that the means which Church and State employ to gain their ends are entirely different. The Church may not employ any other means than the preaching of the Word of God, John 18:11, 36; 2 Cor. 10:4. The State, on the other hand, makes laws bearing on civil matters and is empowered to employ for their execution also the sword and other corporal punishments, Rom. 13:4.

Accordingly we condemn the policy of those who would have the power of the State employed "in the interest of the Church" and who thus turn the Church into a secular dominion; as also of those who, aiming to govern the State by the Word of God, seek to turn the State into a Church.

OF THE ELECTION OF GRACE

35. By election of grace we mean this truth, that all those who by the grace of God alone, for Christ's sake, through the means of grace, are brought to faith, are justified, sanctified, and preserved in faith *here in time,* that all these have already from eternity been endowed by God with faith, justification, sanctification, and preservation in faith, and this *for the same reason, namely,* by grace alone, for Christ's sake, and by way of the means of grace. That this is the doctrine of Holy Scripture is evident from Eph. 1:3-7; 2 Thess. 2:13, 14; Acts 13:48; Rom. 8:28-30; 2 Tim. 1:9; Matt. 24: 22-24 (cp. Form. of Conc. *Triglot,* p. 1065, §§ 5, 8, 23; M., p. 705).

36. Accordingly we reject as an anti-Scriptural error the doctrine that not alone the grace of God and the merit of Christ are the cause of the election of grace, but that God has, in addition, found or regarded something good *in us* which prompted or caused Him to elect us, this being variously designated as "good works," "right conduct," "proper self-determination," "refraining from willful resistance," etc. Nor does Holy Scripture know of an election "by foreseen faith," "in view of faith," as though the faith of the elect were to be placed before their election; but according to Scripture the faith which the elect have in time belongs to the spiritual blessings with which God has endowed them by His eternal election. For Scripture teaches, Acts 13:48: "And as many as were ordained unto eternal life believed." Our Lutheran Confession also testifies (*Triglot,* p. 1065, § 8; M., p. 705): "The eternal election of God, however, not only foresees and foreknows the salvation of the elect, but is also, from the gracious will and pleasure of God in Christ Jesus, a cause which procures, works, helps, and promotes our salvation and what pertains thereto; and upon this our salvation is so founded that the gates of hell cannot prevail against it, Matt. 16:18, as is written John 10:28: 'Neither shall any man pluck My sheep out of My hand'; and again, Acts 13:48: 'And as many as were ordained to eternal life believed.'"

37. But as earnestly as we maintain that there is an election of *grace,* or a predestination to salvation, so decidedly do we teach, on the other hand, that there is no election of wrath, or predestination to *damnation.*

Scripture plainly reveals the truth that the love of God for the world of lost sinners is universal, that is, that it embraces all men without exception, that Christ has fully reconciled all men unto God, and that God earnestly desires to bring all men to faith, to preserve them therein, and thus to save them, as Scripture testifies, 1 Tim. 2:4: "God will have all men to be saved and to come to the knowledge of the truth." No man is lost because God has predestinated him to eternal damnation. — Eternal election is a cause why the elect are brought to faith in time, Acts 13:48; but election is *not* a cause why men remain unbelievers when they hear the Word of God. The reason assigned by Scripture for this sad fact is that these men judge *themselves* unworthy of everlasting life, putting the Word of God from them and obstinately resisting the Holy Ghost, whose earnest will it is to bring also them to repentance and faith by means of the Word, Acts 13:46; 7:51; Matt. 23:37.

38. To be sure, it is necessary to observe the Scriptural distinction between the election of grace and the universal will of grace. This universal gracious will of God embraces all men; the election of grace, however, does not embrace all, but only a definite number, whom "God hath from the beginning chosen to salvation," 2 Thess. 2:13, the "remnant," the "seed" which "the Lord left," Rom. 9:27-29, the "election," Rom. 11:7; and while the universal will of grace is frustrated in the case of most men, Matt. 22:14; Luke 7:30, the election of grace attains its end with all whom it embraces, Rom. 8:28-30. Scripture, however, while distinguishing between the universal will of grace and the election of grace, does not place the two in opposition to each other. On the contrary, it teaches that the grace dealing with those who are lost is altogether earnest and fully efficacious for conversion. Blind reason indeed declares these two truths to be contradictory; but we impose silence on our reason. The seeming disharmony will disappear in the light of heaven, 1 Cor. 13:12.

39. Furthermore, by election of grace, Scripture does not mean that *one* part of God's counsel of salvation according to which He will receive into heaven those who persevere in faith unto the end, but, on the contrary, Scripture means this, that God, before the foundation of the world, from pure grace, because of the redemption of Christ, has chosen for His own a definite number of persons out of the corrupt mass and has determined to bring them, through Word and Sacrament, to faith and salvation.

40. Christians can and should be assured of their eternal election. This is evident from the fact that Scripture addresses them as the chosen ones and comforts them with their election, Eph. 1:4; 2 Thess. 2:13. This assurance of one's personal election, however, springs only from faith in the Gospel, from the assurance that God so loved the world that He gave His only-begotten Son, that whosoever believeth in Him should not perish, but have everlasting life. For God sent not His Son into the world to *condemn* the world; on the contrary, through the life, suffering, and death of His Son He fully *reconciled* the whole world of sinners unto Himself. Faith in this truth leaves no room for the fear that God might still harbor thoughts of wrath and damnation concerning us. Scripture inculcates that in Rom.

8:32, 33: "He that spared not His own Son, but delievered Him up for us all, how shall He not with Him also freely give us all things? Who shall lay anything to the charge of God's elect? It is God that justifieth." Luther's pastoral advice is therefore in accord with Scripture: "Gaze upon the wounds of Christ and the blood shed for you; there predestination will shine forth." (St. Louis Ed., II, 181; on Gen. 26:9.) That the Christian obtains the personal assurance of his eternal election in this way is taught also by our Lutheran Confessions (Formula of Concord. *Triglot*, p. 1071, § 26; M., p. 709): "Of this we should not judge according to our reason nor according to the Law or from any external appearance. Neither should we attempt to investigate the secret, concealed abyss of divine predestination, but should give heed to the revealed will of God. For He has made known unto us the mystery of His will and made it manifest through *Christ* that it might be preached, Eph. 1:9 ff.; 2 Tim. 1:9 f." — In order to insure the proper method of viewing eternal election and the Christian's assurance of it, the Lutheran Confessions set forth at length the principle that election is not to be considered "in a bare manner (*nude*), as though God only held a muster, thus: 'This one shall be saved, that one shall be damned'" (Formula of Concord. *Triglot*, p. 1065, § 9; M., p. 706); but "the Scriptures teach this doctrine in no other way than to direct us thereby to the *Word*, Eph. 1:13; 1 Cor. 1:7; exhort to repentance, 2 Tim. 3:16; urge to godliness, Eph. 1:14; John 15:3; strengthen faith and assure us of our salvation, Eph. 1:13; John 10:27 f.; 2 Thess. 2:13 f." (Formula of Concord. *Triglot*, p. 1067, § 12; M., p. 707). — To sum up, just as God in time draws the Christians unto Himself through the Gospel, so He has already in His eternal election endowed them with "sanctification of the Spirit and belief of the truth," 2 Thess. 2:13. Therefore: If, by the grace of God, you believe in the Gospel of the forgiveness of your sins for Christ's sake, you are to be certain that you also belong to the number of God's elect, even as Scripture, 2 Thess. 2:13, addresses the believing Thessalonians as the chosen of God and gives thanks to God for their election.

OF SUNDAY

41. We teach that in the New Testament God has abrogated the Sabbath and all the holy days prescribed for the Church of the Old Covenant, so that neither "the keeping of the Sabbath nor of any other day" nor the observance of at least one specific day of the seven days of the week is ordained or commanded by God, Col. 2:16; Rom. 14:5 (Augsburg Confession. *Triglot*, p. 91, §§ 51—60; M., p. 66).

The observance of Sunday and other church festivals is an ordinance of the Church, made by virtue of Christian liberty. (Augsburg Confession; *Triglot*, p. 91, §§ 51—53, 60; M., p. 66. Large Catechism; *Triglot*, p. 603, §§ 83, 85, 89; M., p. 401.) Hence Christians should not regard such ordinances as ordained by God and binding upon the conscience, Col. 2:16; Gal. 4:10. However, for the sake of Christian love and peace they should willingly observe them, Rom. 14:13; 1 Cor. 14:40. (Augsburg Confession, *Triglot*, p. 91, §§ 53—56; M., p. 67.)

OF THE MILLENNIUM

42. With the Augsburg Confession (Art. XVII) we reject every type of Millennialism, or Chiliasm, the opinions that Christ will return visibly to this earth a thousand years before the end of the world and establish a dominion of the Church over the world; or that before the end of the world the Church is to enjoy a season of special prosperity; or that before the general resurrection on Judgment Day a number of departed Christians or martyrs are to be raised again to reign in glory in this world; or that before the end of the world a universal conversion of the Jewish nation (of Israel according to the flesh) will take place.

Over against this, Scripture clearly teaches, and we teach accordingly, that the kingdom of Christ on earth will remain under the cross until the end of the world, Acts 14:22; John 16:33; 18:36; Luke 9:23; 14:27; 17: 20-37; 2 Tim. 4:18; Heb. 12:28; Luke 18:8; that the second visible coming of the Lord will be His final advent, His coming to judge the quick and the dead, Matt. 24:29, 30; 25:31; 2 Tim. 4:1; 2 Thess. 2:8; Heb. 9:26-28; that there will be but one resurrection of the dead, John 5:28; 6:39, 40; that the time of the Last Day is, and will remain, unknown, Matt. 24:42; 25:13; Mark 13:32, 37; Acts 1:7, which would not be the case if the Last Day were to come a thousand years after the beginning of a millennium; and that there will be no general conversion, a conversion *en masse*, of the Jewish nation, Rom. 11:7; 2 Cor. 3:14; Rom. 11:25; 1 Thess. 2:16.

According to these clear passages of Scripture we reject the whole of Millennialism, since it not only contradicts Scripture, but also engenders a false conception of the kingdom of Christ, turns the hope of Christians upon earthly goals, 1 Cor. 15:19; Col. 3:2, and leads them to look upon the Bible as an obscure book.

OF THE ANTICHRIST

43. As to the Antichrist we teach that the prophecies of the Holy Scriptures concerning the Antichrist, 2 Thess. 2:3-12; 1 John 2:18, have been fulfilled in the Pope of Rome and his dominion. All the features of the Antichrist as drawn in these prophecies, including the most abominable and horrible ones, for example, that the Antichrist "as God sitteth in the temple of God," 2 Thess. 2:4; that he anathematizes the very heart of the Gospel of Christ, that is, the doctrine of the forgiveness of sins by grace alone, for Christ's sake alone, through faith alone, without any merit or worthiness in man (Rom. 3:20-28; Gal. 2:16); that he recognizes only those as members of the Christian Church who bow to his authority; and that, like a deluge, he had inundated the whole Church with his antichristian doctrines till God revealed him through the Reformation, — these very features are the outstanding characteristics of the Papacy. (Cf. Smalcald Articles, *Triglot*, p. 515, §§ 39—41; p. 401, § 45; M., pp. 336, 258.) Hence we subscribe to the statement of our Confessions that the Pope is "the very Antichrist." (Smalcald Articles. *Triglot*, p. 475, § 10; M., p. 308.)

OF OPEN QUESTIONS

44. Those questions in the domain of Christian doctrine may be termed open questions which Scripture answers either not at all or not clearly. Since neither an individual nor the Church as a whole is permitted to develop or augment the Christian doctrine, but are rather ordered and commanded by God to continue in the doctrine of the apostles, 2 Thess. 2:15; Acts 2:42, open questions must remain open questions. — Not to be included in the number of open questions are the following: the doctrine of the Church and the Ministry, of Sunday, of Chiliasm, and of Antichrist, these doctrines being clearly defined in Scripture.

OF THE SYMBOLS OF THE LUTHERAN CHURCH

45. We accept as our confessions all the symbols contained in the Book of Concord of the year 1580. — The symbols of the Lutheran Church are not a rule of faith beyond, and supplementary to, Scripture, but a confession of the doctrines of Scripture over against those who deny these doctrines.

46. Since the Christian Church cannot make doctrines, but can and should simply profess the doctrine revealed in Holy Scripture, the doctrinal decisions of the symbols are binding upon the conscience not because our Church has made them nor because they are the outcome of doctrinal controversies, but only because they are the doctrinal decisions of Holy Scripture itself.

47. Those desiring to be admitted into the public ministry of the Lutheran Church pledge themselves to teach according to the symbols not "in so far as," but "because," the symbols agree with Scripture. He who is unable to accept as Scriptural the doctrine set forth in the Lutheran symbols and their rejection of the corresponding errors must not be admitted into the ministry of the Lutheran Church.

48. The confessional obligation covers all doctrines, not only those that are treated *ex professo*, but also those that are merely introduced in support of other doctrines.

The obligation does not extend to historical statements, "purely exegetical questions," and other matters not belonging to the doctrinal content of the symbols. All *doctrines* of the Symbols are based on clear statements of Scripture.

TOPICAL INDEX

Abbetmeyer, Dr. C., St. Paul, 225.
Abendschule 151.
Achenbach, Pastor W., succeeds C. S. Kleppisch in Fort Wayne, 125.
Adams County, Ind., 104, 105.
Addison, Ill., Teachers' Seminary 126, 177; additions to faculty (1905—1922) 222 f.
Africa 275.
Aged, Homes for the, 352.
Ahlbrand, A. H., 251, 280.
Alaska 300 f.
Albrecht, I., 344.
Albrecht, Max, 176, 224, 225.
Albrecht, W., 285.
Alexandria, Va., 112.
Allwardt 200, 203.
Alpha Synod 164.
Alsace 302.
Altar fellowship 157, 322, 329.
Altenburg, debate, 47 f., 89, 138; institution, appeal for financial aid, 102, 105, 106, 116; institution transferred to St. L. 118; institution passed under control of Synod 1850, 118; Altenburg faculty 118.
Altenburger Bibelwerk 121
Altes und Neues, F. A. Schmidt's periodical, 201.
American Lutheran 351.
American Lutheran Church 320 to 327, 329 f, 332.
American Lutheran Conference 324, 325, 326.
American Publicity Bureau 351
Ann Arbor, Mich., 72, 91.
Anniversaries 339 f.
Antichrist 147, 322, 328.
Anzeiger des Westens 30 f., 33, 36.
Appelt, T. C., 286.
Arcadia, Mich., 317.
Argentina (District 1927) 243, 246, 275, 305 f.
Army and Navy Board 264 f.
Army and Navy Commission 334 ff.

Arndt, E. L., Prof. 178; China 233; seminary 234; death 294, 295.
Arndt, Walter (China) 234.
Arndt, Wm., 220, 226, 321.
Assignment of calls 277.
Athanasian Confession 332.
Atlanta, Ga., congregation organized, 275.
Auch, J., 72 f., 91, 128 ff.
Augsburg Confession 58.
Austin (Texas) College 281, 283, 288.
Australia 188 f., 241 f., 304.

Bachmann, Paul (India), 233.
Backhaus, Prof. J. L., 175.
Bading, J., 160, president of Syn. Conf. 163.
Baepler, A., called by Western District as English missionary 193; opens St. Paul's College at Concordia, Mo., 176; head of Fort Wayne College 175; Prof. at Concordia, Mo., 226.
Baepler, W. A., 229, 285, 288.
Baierlein, E., 73, 128 ff.; recalled by Leipzig Mission Society 131.
Bakke, N. J., 164, 165.
Baltimore 55, 62, 79, 84; English church established 190; English mission started (1887) 195; F. A. Schmidt 199.
Baringer, Willard (Africa), 347.
Bartels, G., 58, 83.
Barth, G. Chr., succeeds Max Albrecht at Milwaukee 225; assumes presidency at Springfield 285, 308.
Barthel, F. W., 39, 43, 47, 91, 103, 106, 127.
Barthel, M. C., 209.
Bartling, V., 286.
Bartling, W., 160.
Battenberg, Oscar H., 243.
Baumgart 83, 87.
Baumstark, H., called to pro-seminary, becomes Catholic, 125.

Baur, J. C., 281.
Beck, W. H., 286.
Becker, L. H., 262.
Behnken, Dr. J. W., elected to succeed Dr. F. Pfotenhauer as President of Synod 278 f., 283, 338, 339, 349, 355.
Behrens, W. H., 262, 285.
Bente, Prof. F., 175, 224, *Triglotta* 262, 269.
Bente, Paul F., Prof., Fort Wayne, 225.
Benton County, Mo., 83.
Bentrup, H. (China), 234.
Bentrup, H. A., mission among deaf 185.
Berg, F., Doescher's successor, St. Paul's Colored Luth. Ch., Little Rock, 164.
Berger, J., 287.
Bergheim, India, 232 f.
Bergmann, A. E., Prof., Milw., 225.
Berlin, 25, 58, 75, 303.
"Berliner" 32, 34.
Bertram, M. H., Prof., Fort Wayne, 225.
Bethany, most promising station of Indian Mission, 130 f.
Bethesda Hospital, Ambur. See "India".
Beto, G. F., 288.
Beyer, J. P., 160; first secretary of Syn. Conf. 161.
Bible women 289 f.
Bickel, L. G., 286.
Biewend, A. F. Th., Wyneken's letter to 54; accompanies Wyneken on the latter's return to America 61; Washington, D. C., 112; added to St. L. faculty 121; dies 121, 123.
Biedermann, R., 222.
Biegener, E. (Stockbridge Indians), 240.
Biltz, F. J., 37, 106, 160.
Birkner, H., 213.

Bischoff, R. A., 112; to Fort Wayne College, 126, 175; the *Lutheran Pioneer* 165.
Bischoff, W. O. (Conover), 226.
Blaess, G., to New Zealand, 179.
Blankenbuehler, Prof. L., St. Paul, 225; Portland 228; C. P. H. 317, 319.
Board for Foreign Missions 235.
Board for Higher Education 284.
Board for Home Missions 168 f. 277.
Board for Parish Education 313.
Board for Young People's Work 315.
Board of Appeals (1941) 279.
Board of Assignment of Calls 277.
Board of Control, General 230.
Board of Directors, the first, 219; 280.
Board of Missions to Deaf and Blind 297 f.
Board of Support and Pensions 252 f., 312.
Boards, various 362 f.
Boecler, O. C. A., to Springfield 222; to St. L. 285, 344.
Boehne, J. W., 251.
Bohm, Edmund, first president, N. Y. *Progymnasium* 176 f.
Bongarzone, Andrea, mission among the Italians in West Hoboken, N. J., 238.
Book of Concord 77, 81, 103, 294, 340.
Boriack, L., (India) 232.
Bosse, Benjamin, 219, 230, 251.
Boston, Mass., 112.
Both, A., 349.
Braille 297.
Braeunsdorf, Saxony, 25.
Brand, F., mission director 235; visits India 290; China 294.
Brand, P., 112.
Brandhorst, C. T., 286.
Brandt, E. H., (Portland) 229.
Brauer, Mr. A. G., 221, 251.
Brauer, E. A., professor, St. L., 125, 209.

Brauer, K., teacher, becomes professor at Addison, 126.
Brazil 243—248, seminary 247 f., 304 f.
Bredemeyer, H. G., 286.
Bremen 25, 26, 32, 58.
Bremer Zeitung 26.
Bremerhaven 28.
Bremervoerde 54.
Brenner, J., 264.
Breslau 75.
Bretscher, P., 285.
Bretschneider, K. G., general superintendent at Gotha, 22.
Brief Statement 320, 321, 322, 323, 324, 328, 329, 371—384.
Broders, J. C., 245.
Brohm, Theo. J., 25, 30, 37, 42, 43, 47, pastor in New York City, entertains Craemer and his emigrants 72; 83, 87, 91, 95, 103, 112, 118, 138; Publishing House 149, 152; first in Synod to preach an English sermon 190; stressed importance of using English language 191; death 211, 253.
Brohm, Theo., (Addison) 224.
Brohm, Theo., (Oakland) 229.
Brommer, C. F., 230, 286, 321.
Bronxville, N. Y., 227, 230, 287.
Brunn, Arthur, 264.
Brunn,, Friedrich, Steeden, Nassau, his great work sending students 126, 151; Saxon Free Church 186, 187.
Brunn, F. H., 321.
Brux, A. A., 290.
Buchheimer, L., joins Conover faculty 197.
Buchheimer, L. T., (New York) 339.
Buchroth, C. F., (Letts and Estonians) 236.
Budget for 1946, 309.
Buehler, J. M., 110.
Buehler, W. R., colored mission at Meherrin, Va., 164.

Buenger, H., 37.
Buenger, J. F., his biography by Walther 9, 25; arrives in Perry Co. from N. Y. with 95 "Berliner" 32, 37, 42, 43, 49, 83, 89, 95, 103, 107, 110, 118, 119; colored mission 163; Young Men's Society 209; death 212, 253, 352.
Buenger, Theo., first president of Concordia College, St. Paul, Minn., 178.
Buenos Aires, Concordia Seminary 306.
Buerger, E. M., obtains a pastoral charge through his patron, Count von Schoenberg 8; 20, 25, 28, 30 34, 39, 47, 83, 138.
Buffalo, N. Y., 83, 105.
Buffalo Synod 5; controversy with 137—142; Missouri's lengthy negotiations with 155.
Burgdorf, Aug., Bethlehem congregation, colored, New Orleans 164.
Burgdorf, Paul H., 351.
Burger, Geo., 4, 67, 68, 82, 83, 87, 88, 95; his widow 253.
Burhop, W. C., Prof., Fort Wayne, 225; returns to ministry (1937) 286.
Buszin, W. E. 286.
Buuck, L. A., 293, 296.

Caemmerer, R., 285.
Call-of-the-Cross movement 308.
Camp meeting, as Wyneken described it, 60.
Canada 167.
Candidates of theology, emigrants, 25.
Carino, Alvaro, 302.
Carondelet 125, 151.
Catechism, the new, 319; anniversary (1929) 339.
Centennial of 1947, 355—358.
Ceremonies, uniformity of, 101.
Ceylon 292.

TOPICAL INDEX

Chaplaincies in the Army and Navy 334 ff.
Chemnitz 41.
Chicago, size of city (1847) 97; congregation, host of Synod 97, 105.
Child Welfare 352.
China Mission 233 ff.
Christ Church Cathedral, emigrants worship in basement 29.
Christian Day School 207 ff.
Christian liberty 77, 101, 139.
Church and Ministry (Doctrine) 89, 138, 144; Cloeter 145, 158.
Church and State, separation of 208.
Church discipline, unable to function under State rule 8, 10.
Church Extension Board 248.
Clergy vestments, etc., bought for emigration 22.
Cincinnati, O., 91, 107.
Civil War 122, 124, 136, 157.
Cleveland, Ohio, 85, 93; Cleveland *Progymnasium* 350.
Cloeter, Ottomar, Indian mission in Minnesota 134 ff., 145.
Coates, Thomas, 288.
College in Perry Co., announcement in *Anzeiger des Westens* 37.
Colporteurs 108.
Columbus, Ohio, 70, 78, 79; seminary 81, 85; conference at 157; Colloquy 158.
Columbus Theological Magazine 202.
Committee of Thirteen 283 f.
Committee on Higher Education 284.
Committee on Curriculum 284.
Committee on Hymnology and Liturgics 319.
Committee on Lutheran Church Union 321, 325; "Committee on Doctrinal Unity in the Lutheran Church of America" 327, 329, 332.
"Committee 16" 321, 323.

Communal form of living 33.
Concordia Academy 350.
Concordia Cyclopedia 317.
Concordia Magazine 209.
Concordia, Mo., college 176, 226, 284.
Concordia Publishing House 209 f., 261—263, 356.
Concordia Synod of Pennsylvania and Other States 162; (C. A. Frank) 202.
Concordia Theological Monthly 317.
Concordia Theological Seminary at Hankow 294.
Concordia Theological Seminary, St. Louis. (See also "Missouri Synod"). Number of students graduated by 1872 127, 282 f., 285.
Concordia Theological Seminary, Springfield, Ill., begun by Sihler and Roebbelen 70; number of students graduated by 1872, 127; 171 f., 284 f.; enrollment limit raised 285. (See also "St. Louis", "Fort Wayne", "Missouri Synod").
Confessional Lutheran, The, 351 f.
Confessional Lutheran Publicity Bureau 351.
Conover, N. C., college 197, 226, 284.
Contact key pastors 338.
Continuance of negotiations 326 f., 328, 329.
Conversion, Doctrine of 206, 251, 319, 321.
Correspondence Course at St. Louis Seminary 339.
Coyner, M. H., Professor, Conover, 226, 285.
Coyner's Congregation in Augusta, Co., Va., 194, 195.
Craemer, August F., 69, 70, 71 ff.; offers his services to Loehe, becomes pastor of small mission congregation organized at Neuendettelsau 72; marriage 72; at

TOPICAL INDEX 389

Frankenmuth 84, 87; Michigan Synod 90 f.; report on third preliminary meeting 92 f., 95, 102, 103, 104, 114; professor 123, 125; correspondence with Brunn 126; Indian mission 127 ff., 141, 142; represents Synod 155, 172, 173, 213; death 214.
Craemer, Henry, 128, 132, 133, 135.
Crespo 305.
Cresset 317.
Crull, A., 160, 174; Fort Wayne 175; English Lutheran Hymnal 191, 196.

Dallmann, Wm. called to Webster Co., Mo., 194; Baltimore 195 ff.; editor of *Lutheran Witness* 198; *Sunday School Hymnal* and Church hymnbook 198, 230.
Daniel, Andrew, 238.
Dannenfeldt, P. L., 336.
Dau, W. H. T., president Conover College 197; A. L. Graebner's successor 220; *Triglotta* 262; months overseas 241; first president of Valparaiso U. 251, 269.
Day and Klauder, architects 281.
Deaconesses 289, 353.
Deaf Mission 184 ff.; *Deaf Lutheran* 298.
"Declaration" (A. L. C.) 321, 322, 323, 325.
Decentralization, Process of, Perry Co., 33.
Dede, A., 287.
Deffner, E. H., 286.
"Definite Platform" of General Synod leaders 156.
Deindoerfer, "History of the Iowa Synod" 143, 144, 145, 146.
Delitzsch, Franz, 102.
Demme, Pastor in Philadelphia, secretary of Pennsylvania Ministeriam 59, 79.
Democratic form of government 94.

Detroit, Mich., 73; convention (A. L. C., 1940) 325.
Detzer, Adam, 72; missionary at large, headquarters Fort Wayne 84, 87, 95.
Dick, A. G., 335.
Diederich, H. W., Prof., Fort Wayne 126.
Dierks, H., missionary at Maxwelltown, New Zealand, among Maoris 179.
Dietz, teacher Normal School, Milwaukee, 123.
Diesing, A. E., 286.
Director of Publicity 277.
Districts and their presidents 1899 to 1922, 217 f., 364 ff.
Dobberfuhl, W. A., 287.
Doctors of medicine emigrating 25.
Doctrinal Affirmation 326, 327, 332.
Doederlein, Dr. Theo., 233, 289.
Doege, A., 287.
Doescher, J. F., 110; first man called by Missionary Board for work among the Negroes 163 f.
Dorn, L., Prof., Fort Wayne, 225.
Dorn, O. A., 317.
Dorsch, Caspar, St. L. graduate called to Adelaide 189.
Dresden (Saxony). Dresden Committee 22, 24, 34, 38; emigrants leave D. 26; Wyneken's visit 60, 66; Sihler 76; Dresden Mission Society 77; 78; H. Ruhland, pastor in 187, 303.
Dresden (Perry Co.) 34.
Drewes, C. F., 268.
Drignat, Peter, (Lithuanian mission) 236.
Duden, Dr. Gottfried, his book directed attention to the State of Missouri 23.
Duemling, Dr. H., joins teaching staff at Addison, Ill., 126; Fort Wayne 175.
Dulitz, Pastor, normal school opened in Milwaukee 123.

TOPICAL INDEX

Eckhardt, H. P., 257.
Eckhart, Theo. W., 265, 281, 307.
Edmonton, Alberta, college 229, 281, 283, 288.
Educational institutions 116–127, 170–179, 220–230, 281–288, 350 f.
Educational standards, raising of 283.
Edwards Law (against private elementary schools) 207.
Efik 343.
Ehlers, A., (India) 231.
Eichenberg, Saxony, 24.
Eifert, R., (Oakland) 229.
Efrig, G., Addison Teachers College 224.
Einsiedel, Count Carl von, employs Craemer as tutor 71.
Einsiedel, Count Detlev von, 8, 20, 45; Sihler 77.
Eirich, Pastor, (Predestinarian Controversy) 203.
Eissfeldt, C., 263.
Eissfeldt, Theo., working with Missionary Baierlein 131.
Ekong, D. U., 347.
Ekong, Jonathan Udo, 343, 347.
Election (See also Predestinarian Controversy") 319; "in view of faith" 206 f.
Elementary Education 249.
Ellermann, Miss L., (India) 232.
Ellwanger, Pastor W. H., 343.
Emergency men 68 ff., 74.
Emergency Planning Council 338 f.
Engel, R., joins faculty, Fort Wayne 125.
Engelbrecht, E. H. (Addison), 224, 261, 316.
Engelbrecht, H. C., (Bronxville) 227.
Engelbrecht, O. F., 334.
Engelder, Th., Springfield 222; St. L. 285, 319, 321.
English Academy 123, 124.
English language, in parish schools 153; spread periodicals, books, etc. among English population 161; exclusive use of German in conventions 189; first E. sermon preached 190; an E. confirmation 190; *Lutheraner* (1855) urges younger generation to become familiar with E. language 190. (See also Language Question.)
English Lutheran Conference of Missouri 191 ff., 196.
English Synod of Missouri, Ohio and Other States 162; organization 195 ff.; union with the German Mission Synod 253–261.
Enshih 294.
Erdman, F., 160.
Erlangen, Wyneken visiting 60; Craemer's university 71.
Ernst, Pastor, Predestinarian Controversy 203.
Ernst, Prof. A. E. (Wisconsin Synod), 160.
Ernst, J. A., Loehe's first missioner, 4, 67, 68, 82, 83, 84, 87, 88, 89, 90, 91, 95, 104, 107, 215.
Esthonians 235.
"Evangelical Lutheran Mission for China" 233.
Evangelists 108, 289.
Eversmann, Louis, 23.

Faculties 116–127, 170–179, 220–230, 281–288.
Federal Communications Commission 310.
Fehner, Prof. H. B., Seward, 226.
Female College and Normal School Association 171.
Feth, Henry, Director Edmund Bohm's successor, Hawthorne College, 177; succeeded by G. A. Romoser 227.
Feucht, Oscar, 314.
Fick, C. J. H., 103, 105, 127.
Field work, obligatory for all St. L. students 285.
Finances of Synod 307–309.

TOPICAL INDEX 391

Finland 303.
Finnish Ev. Luth. National Church in America 340.
Finns, work among the, 237.
Fiscal Conference 307, 309.
Fischer, Henry, 33, 39, 47.
Five Million Dollar Peace Thankoffering 309.
Fleischer, Mr. G. A., 355.
Fleischmann, Pastor, opening of Normal School, Milwaukee 123; returns to the ministry 126.
Foehlinger, F. W., 112; care for immigrants 136.
Foelber, E. E., 286.
Foreign-Tongue Missions 237.
Forster, F., (India) 231.
Fort Wayne, Ind., Wyneken 55 f., 56, 58, 61, 83, 84; preliminary meeting 90, 91 ff., 104, 105, 106; institution opened 1846 116; document of transfer 117; instructors 123; pro-seminary 123; English Academy 123; Normal School of Milwaukee transferred to Fort W. 123 f.; Indian mission property transferred to Concordia College 133; military training 225.
Four Hundred Years, Centennial book, 1917, 271.
Francke, A. G. G., president of Addison Teachers' Seminary 126.
Franconian Centennial 340.
Frank, C. A., *Lutheran Witness,* 196, 202.
Frankenhilf 73, 147.
Frankenlust 73, 109, 147.
Frankenmuth 73, 84, 104, 106, 147.
Frankentrost 73, 147.
Frankfurt, Revolution 1833, Craemer involved 71.
Franzmann, M. H., 285.
Freche, Missionary, 230.
Frederick William III, king of Prussia, 11.
Free Church of Denmark 241.
Free Church of Hermannsburg 188.

Freiburger, P., 276.
French Ev. Luth. Congregation on Saminaque, Ill., 104.
Frey, A. E., 180.
Friedmann, Nathaniel, missionary among the Jews 183, 239; Catechism into Yiddish 240.
Friedrich, E. J., 285.
Friedrich, J. A., 235.
Frieling, R. M., Alaska, 300 f.
Frincke (Fricke), C., "Visitor", 62, 87, 102, 103, 106; accepts call to an established parish 107.
Fritsche, G. D., 189.
Fritschel, G., 199.
Fritschel, S., 146.
Fritz, J. H. C., 220, 281, 304, 310.
Fritze, A. (India), 232.
Fritze, J. A., 110.
Froehlich, E. F. A., 25, 83.
Frohna, Saxony, 25, 38.
Frohna, Mo., 101, 193.
Fuerbringer, A. O., 286.
Fuerbringer, L., 175, 188, 221, 243, 285, 319; president of Syn. Conf. 341, 348, 349, 355.
Fuerbringer, O., 25, 34, 37, 49, 83, 89, 90, 91, 95, 97, 103, 105, 116, 118; at meeting of Indianapolis Synod 155, 200; death 215.
Fuerth, near Nuernberg, 59.

Gaenssle, Prof. C., Milw., 225.
Gaertner, Prof. H. C., 224.
Gausewitz, Pastor C., 341, 342.
Gebhardt, A. H. (China), 234.
General confession and absolution 101.
General Council (1867) 157.
General Officers 362.
General Synod 5, 57, 59, 61, 62, 63.
Georgi, Miss A. (India), 232.
Gerding, H., 177.
"German" dropped from Synod's name 219.
German prisoners of war 338 f.
German university **training 89.**

TOPICAL INDEX

Germantown, Ohio, 80.
Germany 1846—1871, political aspect, 7; Church controlled by State, 7 f.
Geyer, C. L., 25, 34, 49, 83, 101, 106.
Gienapp, J. H., 287.
Gienapp, N., 287.
Gieseler, C. A., 287.
Gihring, H. (China), 234.
Gehrke, Wm. H., 343.
Glock, H., 288.
Goenner, J., 25, 83, 118; from Altenburg to St. Louis 119; leave of absence, to edit *Altenburger Bibelwerk,* 121; returns 122.
Goerss, R. W. (India), 231.
"Gospel Voice" 311.
Gossner, Pastor in Berlin, 58.
Gotsch, G. M., 111.
Grabau, J. A. A., emigrates with 1,000 Lutherans to America 12; controversy with 137—142.
Graebner, A. L., 174, 175, 180, 210, 214, 220; to Australia 241; death 272.
Graebner, C. F. (Australia), 241.
Graebner, J. Ph., 73, 108.
Graebner, Prof. M., Milw. 225, 226; (St. Paul) 287.
Graebner, Th., 220; *Luth. Witness* 260; first Juvenile Lit. Board 261, 262; Young People's work 314; Lodge information 334.
Graetzel, Pastor H., first president of Synod in Iowa 110.
Gravelton, Mo., 191.
Greensboro, N. C., 270, 344.
Gross, A. W., 314.
Gross, C., 160, 174.
Gross, H. H., 286.
Grossmann, A. A., 261, 263.
Grossmann, G. M., 145.
Gross-Oesingen 303.
Gruen, Miss Olive (China), 234.
Gruett, Jim, interpreter for missionaries among Indians 127 ff.

Grunnet, N. P., Copenhagen 241.
Guebert, A., 288.
Guebert, A. W. C., 285.
Guenther, Prof. M., 175, 209.
Guericke, H. E. F., 12, 24.
Grunau, H., 287.

Haase, Prof. Karl, Seward, 226.
Hackstedde, F. W., 178.
Haentzschel, Prof. Ad., Concordia, Mo., 226; Valparaiso 350.
Haentzschel, C. E., 175.
Haesbaert, J., 55, 56; resigns charge in Baltimore 62.
Hagedorn, O., 264.
Hagen, W., 219, 241.
Halle 24, 34.
Hamann, E., 176.
Hamann, H., 231.
Hankow 234, 294, 296.
Hannover 34, 59, 68.
Hansen, Aug., 301.
Hansen, Prof. W. A., Fort Wayne 225.
Hanser, C. J. Otto, Boston, 112; Fort Wayne 126, 175, 180, 213.
Hardt, C. A., 287.
Hardt, Prof. H. L., Seward, 226.
Harless, G. C. A. von, 12, 57, 63, 102.
Harms, Claus, leader of Confessional Lutheran School, 12.
Harms, H., 275.
Harms, J. (India), 231.
Harms, Pastor Theodore, 151.
Hartmeister, J. (Brazil), 247.
Hassler Settlement, Ill., 104.
Hassold, E. C. (Bronxville), 227.
Hattstaedt, E., 287.
Hattstaedt, Otto, 174, 176.
Hattstaedt, W. G. C., 70, 71, 73, 83, 84, 87, 88, 90 f.; report on third preliminary meeting 94, 95.
Hausmann, Theo. W. (Bronxville), 227; survey director 284.
Hawaiian Islands 301 f.
Hawthorne, N. Y., College, 177, 227.

TOPICAL INDEX 393

Heckel, P. (India), 232.
Hein, B., missionary among Poles, 237.
Hein, J., free Church at Wiesbaden, 187.
Heinrichsmeyer, L., 227.
Heintze, R. W., 177, 285.
Hellwege, W., 286.
Hemmeter, H. B., Conover, 226, 256. 288; Springfield 285, 355.
Hengstenberg, E. W., 12.
Henkel, Andrew, Pastor and Freemason, 81.
Henkel, P. C., attends Gravelton, Mo., meeting 191; founder of Conover College, 197.
Henrichs, K. H., 286.
Heresy 85.
Hermannsburg Free Church joins the Saxon brethren 188.
Herreilers, J. H., 288.
Herold, Miss E. (India), 233.
Herrling, W. G., 286.
Herzer, Prof. J., 160, 173, 222.
Heuer, C. J., Prof., St. Paul, 225.
High Schools 350.
Hildner, V., 286.
Hinz, H. A., 294, 296.
Hirtenbrief, by Grabau, 138.
Hochstetter, Chr., 44.
Hoehere Buergerschule and *Hoehere Toechterschule* 350.
Hoelter, L., 230.
Hoenecke, A., 160.
Hoffmann, C. J., 222.
Hoffmann, F. A. ("Hans Buschbauer"), 106.
Hoffmann, O., 287.
Hohenstein, H. H., 311.
Holls, W. M. H. (London), 242 f.
Holston Synod 191.
Homaun, Prof. E., (Addison), 175.
Homann, E., of Australia, 189.
Homiletisches Magazin 209
Hommel, Friedrich, 69.
Honolulu 275, 301, 302.
Hoover, Jesse, 55 f.
Hope, R., 287.

Hoppe, Prof. A. F., 350.
Horse Prairie, Ill., 83.
Horst, Henry W., 219, 251, 280.
Hospitals 352.
Hoyer, A., 112.
Hoyer, Th., 285, 287, 355.
Huchthausen, P., 286, 288.
Huebener, A. (India), 231.
Huebener, G. (India), 231.
Huebschmann, E., 288.
Huegli, A. G., 286.
Huge, A. W., auditor, 307.
Husmann, F. W., 58, 61, 87, 95; secretary of Synod 99, 103, 104.
Huth, Prof. C., first instructor at Milwaukee Concordia College 176.

Ibibios 343.
Ichang, China, 234.
Illinois Synod 159.
Immanuel Lutheran College, Greensboro, N. C., 270, 342.
Immigrant Mission 136 f.; Loehe's plan of an immigrant hostel 145; S. Keyl and Restin 238; A. H. Winter, Philadelphia, 239.
Immigration, surge of, 2; why Lutheran Church (U. S.), in 1846, was unable to meet the challenge of Lutheran immigration 4; during 19th century millions of German emigrants arrived at American ports 7, 107; Synod followed imm. step by step 152.
"In the light of" 323, 329.
India, Naether and Mohn, 180 ff., 230—233; forces in India, 1922—1945.
Indianapolis, Ind., 91; Indianapolis Synod 155.
Indians (Chippewas) in Michigan, mission work among 71, 73 ff., 91, 102, 127—136; Stockbridge Indians 240.
Indifferentism, in General Synod 61; in Walther's age and ours 270 f.
Inspiration, Doctrine of, 231, 324.

Institute for the Deaf 353.
Institutional Missions 352.
Intersynodical conference at St. Paul 251.
Iowa District East; Iowa District West (1936) 275.
Iowa Synod organized 146; "Open questions" 147 f.; colloquy with Missouri 148.
Irmo, S. Carolina, congregation organized 1932, 275.
Itinerant missionaries 108 f, 168 f.

Jaebker, J. H., 62, 95, 105.
Jaeckel, Gustav, 33, 39, 47.
Jahn, Dr. J. N. H. (Bronxville), 227.
Jank, R., 232.
Janzow, C. L., .installs A. Baepler at Frohna 193, 194; chairman of Board of English Missions 195.
Japan, Synod resolves to open a mission 179 f.; change from Japan to India 180.
Jena, University of, 76.
Jenne, E. A., 287.
Jensen, G., 58, 61.
Jesse, F. C. W., succeeds President Weller 226, 249; re-enters ministry 286.
Jesse, R. A. (Dean, 1940), 262, 285.
Jesudason, G. (India), 231, 232.
Jews, mission among 182 f., 239 f.; general conversion of 322, 328.
Johannes, Pastor, 107.
Jones, Lawrence C., 342.
Jubilee 1872, 151–153.
Jurksaitis, G., translated Catechism into Lithuanian 236.
Juvenile Liberature Board 262.

Kaeppel, A., 175.
Kaeppel, J. H. C:, 176; death 287.
Kahmeyer, F. W., 109.
Kaiser, O., 319.
Kalbfleisch, H., 150.
Kalender 150.
Kauffeld, P. (India), 232

Kauffung, F., delegate from Freystadt, Wis., 103, 106.
Kavel, A. L. C., left Prussia for Australia 12, 188.
Keinath, H. O. A., 286, 319.
Kellerbauer, O. (India), 181 f., 231.
KFUO 283, 309, 356.
Kemper, Jackson, bishop, reads notice to his congregation permitting Saxons to worship in Christ Church 29.
Keyl, E. G. W., appointed pastor at Niederfrohna by Count Einsiedel 8, 20, 25, 28; appointed by Stephan to officiate as pastor at Christ Church Cathedral 30; leaves for Perry Co., 30, 34, 45, 76, 77, 83, 88, 89, 91, 95, 109, 116, 118; Publishing House 149, 211.
Keyl, Stephanus, 136 f., 182.
Kilian, Joh., 111.
Kinder-und Jugendblatt 209.
Kindermann, G. A., 137.
Kirchenlamitz 65.
Kirchliche Mitteilungen aus und ueber Nord-Amerika 64, 144.
Kitzerow, W. G., 286.
Klein, H., missionary in China 296.
Klein, H. A., called to Springfield presidency 222; fatally injured 285.
Klemmer, C., Esthonian 237 f.
Kleppisch, C. S., college assistant 125, 192.
Kliefoth, Dr. T. F. D., ordains Craemer 72.
Klinck, A., president of Teachers College, River Forest, 286.
Kloster, I. J. (Winfield), 228.
Kluck, Miss Helen (Africa), 345.
Kluegel, G., Candidate, 23, 25, 39, 46, 47, 83.
Klotz, J. W., 286.
Knabenschuh, H. S., 164.
Knape, A. F., missionary 58, 59, 95.

Knippenberg, K. (London), 242.
Koch, G. (Australia), 241.
Koch, Dr. H., 287.
Kodaikanal 231.
Koehler, Ed., Addison Teachers College 224, 319.
Koehneke, P. F., 286.
Koenig, F., 175.
Koenig, H. A., 286.
Koenig, P., 313.
Koepchen, Wm. 224.
Koeper, Vernon (Africa), 345.
Koestering, J. F., 36, 45 f., 47.
Kohn, W. C., to Addison 224; 249, 263.
Kolarik, Jos., first Slovak missionary 238.
Kolbe, Pastor O., Cleveland *Progymnasium* 350.
Konz, Louis (Africa), 347.
Koren, U. V., 160.
Kories, E., Lithuanian 236.
Kornbausch, teacher, Loehe man 83, 87.
Kosciusko County, Ind., 105.
Kraeft, W. O., 286.
Kramer, A. T., 275.
Kramer, G. M. (colored mission), 343.
Kramer, Wm. A., 314.
Krause, L. F. E., 103, 109, 137 ff.
Krauss, E. A. W., 175, 220, 224.
Kraussold, Konsistorialrat 59.
Kreinheder, O. C., Valparaiso, 351.
Kreinheder, O. W., Conover, 227.
Kreiss, F. C. (Paris), 303.
Kretzmann, J. P. (Africa), 345.
Kretzmann, K., 321.
Kretzmann, O. P., 285, 316; Valparaiso (1940) 351.
Kretzmann, P. E., Prof., St. Paul, 225; St. Louis 285, 313, 339.
Kretzmann, R. (Stockbridge Indians), 240.
Kretzschmar, R., 235, 348.
Kroening, Prof. G., Springfield, 171, 173; Milwaukee, 176.

Krishnagiri 292.
Krueger, Prof. Ottomar, Concordia, Mo., 226; president 287; Fort Wayne 286.
Kruger, Obert, 287.
Kruse, W. F., 286.
Kruse, Prof. W. H., Fort Wayne, 225.
Kuechle, Geo. (India), 231.
Kuegele, F. (English Missouri Synod), 194 f., 259.
Kuegelgen, Frau von, 76.
Kuehn, Candidate, 42.
Kuehn, Pastor H. (Frankenhilf), 73.
Kuehn, Professor H. (Bronxville), 227.
Kuehnert, Theo., 286, 313.
Kuerbel, Louise, 76.
Kuhlmann, G. A., 287.
Kuling, China, 235, 294.
Kunstmann, J., St. Louis graduate, Prof. at Murtoa Seminary, Australia, 189; Brazil, S. America, 248.
Kunstmann, Prof. J. G., Fort Wayne, 225.
Kuntz, A. H., 297.
Kunzmann, A. E. (Winfield), 228.
Kuring, H., first resident Missouri pastor in Alaska 300.
Kurth, Pastor K., Executive Secretary of the Missionary Board 343.
Kurth, W., 301.
Kurtz, Dr. B., of Baltimore, 21, 63, 79.
Kurtz, Daniel, installs Wyneken in Baltimore 62.
Kweifu 294.

Laetsch, Th., 285.
Lamprecht, Theo. H., 251, 256.
Lams, E. T., 265, 355.
Lancaster, Ohio, 79, 85, 105.
Landeck, Prof. C. A., 178.
Landeck, H. F., 261.
Landsmann, Daniel, mission among the Jews 182 f.

TOPICAL INDEX

Lang, Otis (Stockbridge Indians), 240.
Lange, B., 288.
Lange, F., colporteur 108; publishing house 150.
Lange, F. W., first missionary in Kansas 110.
Lange, Louis, 150, 151, 180.
Lange, R. A., 286.
Lange, Rudolph, called as professor 122, 125.
Langenchursdorf, Saxony, 25, 41.
Language question (See also "English language") 81 f., 82, 153; transition from German to English practically completed 276; World War I 357.
Lankenau, F. C., 269, 287.
Larsen, D. (Stockbridge Indians), 240.
Larsen, Lauritz, joins St. Louis faculty as the Norwegian professor 122; president of Syn. Conf. 163, 201, 213.
Lash, W. H., 269.
Last Things, Doctrine of the, 321.
Lehenbauer, A., Buenos Aires 306.
Lehmann, A., 95, 201.
Lehmann, W. F. (Ohio Synod), 160; vice-president of Syn. Conf. 161, 163, 201.
Lehre und Wehre 149, 155; invitation for general conference of all Lutherans who accept the Augsburg Confession as a true presentation of the doctrines of the divine Word 156 f.; Australian brethren find Missouri Synod through *L. U. W* 189; Predestinarian Controversy 199 ff.
Leipzig 25.
Lenk, E., 187.
Lenski, R. C. H., on "the spirit of Missouri." 13.
Leonhardt, Pastor E., 101.
Leonhardt, E. W., 150.
Leonhardt, Mr. R., 180.

Leschen, J. A. (L. L. L.), 251.
Letts, mission, 235.
Levihn, H. (India), 232.
Lewerenz, E. C., 286.
Liebe, Frederick, first missionary at large 108.
Lillegard, Geo. (China), 234.
Lindemann, Prof. F., 175.
Lindemann, J. C., ·175.
Lindemann, Paul, 264.
Lindemeyer, O. W. H., 288.
Link, G., 169, 214.
Link, Prof. J. T., Seward, 226.
Lithuanian mission 236.
Lobeck, H., Prof., Concordia, Mo., 226.
Lochner, F., report of Wyneken's visit to Germany 59; Mecklenburgers provide transportation to America 69, 70; en route to Michigan 72; stationed at Toledo, Ohio, 84, 87, 88; marriage 90; Michigan Synod 90 f., 95, 109; opens normal school in Milwaukee 123; Syn. Conf. 160; *Missionstaube* 165, 272.
Lochner, Louis, 244.
Lochner, M., Addison Teachers College 224.
Loeber, Chr. H., 37, 169, 175.
Loeber, G. H., becomes pastor at Eichenberg through his brother, G. F. Loeber, a "Patron," 8, 20, 24; Stephan's vicar in St. Louis 30, 33, 34, 36, 39, 76, 83, 88, 91; reports on third preliminary meeting 92, 93, 95, 98, 103, 105, 118, 138 f.; characterized by Vehse 153; his death 119, 153.
Loeber, Martha, 37.
Loehe, W., 4; with K. v. Raumer publishes Wyneken's *Aufruf* 60; Wyneken's visit with 61; Wyneken's letters 63 f., 65–74; instructs Emergency men 67, 69; *Kirchliche Mittheilungen* 68; surveys Luth. Ch. in America 70;

TOPICAL INDEX

Springfield Concordia 70; Indian mission in Michigan 71; Franconian colonies 73; work this man did for the Missouri Synod within the space of a decade (summarizing paragraph) 73 f.; Sihler's visit 78, 84; his "instructions" 89; Indian missions 91, 93, 128 ff.; Hattstaedt to Loehe, democratic form of synodical government 94; Synod requests L. to relinquish rights to Fort Wayne institution 102, 104, 116, 117; his high opinion of Craemer 123; break with Craemer 126, 143 ff.; Walther and Wyneken visit L. 144; Grabau and Rohr call on L. 144; his official farewell to pastors and congregations of Saginaw Valley 146; church fellowship 145.

Loehe men (See also "Nothelfer," "Sendlinge") 15, 52, 82; where at work in 1845, 83, 84; resolve to leave Ohio Synod 85; meet in Cleveland 87; Fort Wayne 91; travel to Chicago 98, 137.

Loesel, Lorenz, 71.
Loesel, W. G., 286.
Log-cabin college 37.
London, England, Missouri Synod comes to 188; Pastors who served there, Teacher Vornsand, 242 f.
Lord's Supper, unionistic formula 81, 82.
Lorenz, K., 288.
Loy Matthias, 5, 160; declines chair of English theology, St. L., 198, 203.
Loyalty 336.
Ludwig, Eric (India), 231.
Ludwig, H., Publisher, 103.
Luecke, E. W., 287.
Luecke, Geo., joins Conover faculty 197.
Luecke, M., 224; president Fort Wayne College 225.
Luecke, W. H., 287.

Luedtke, H. A., 251.
Lueker, E. L., 287.
Luke, Wm. H., editor of Sunday school literature 313.
Lussky, Prof. E., St. Paul 225.
Luther, the works of, 89; Small Catechism 103; his Works in the German language, the most ambitious project of Concordia Publishing House 262, 356.
Luther College, New Orleans, 342; Selma, Ala., 342.
Lutheran Annual 262.
Lutheran Chaplain, The, 336.
Lutheran Church in America hundred years ago 4; lack of confessional Lutheranism 8.
Lutheran Education Week 314.
Lutheran Guide 262.
Lutheran High School (1881) (See also "High Schools") 356.
Lutheran Hour 311 f.
Lutheran Hymnal 317, 319.
Lutheran Laymen's League 251 f; Lutheran Hour 311; "continue negotiations" 326.
Lutheran Pioneer, The, 165.
Lutheran Union movement 250 f; 319—332.
Lutheran Watchman 351.
Lutheran Witness 193, 195; its first editor, Pastor C. A. Frank, presents it to English L. Synod of Missouri 196, 255, 260, 262, 351.
Lutheran Women's Missionary League; organization; first regular convention 280.
Lutheraner, first number 51; a "frank and honest name" 52; Wyneken receives copy of 52, 62; interested Loehe men 84, 93; Fort Wayne draft 95; announcement of first session at Chicago 97; offered to Synod 102 f.; congregation in London 188; jubilee issue 213; Supplements 351.
Lutherans from Berlin 25.

Lutherische Hochschule, St. L., 272.
Lutherische Kirchenzcitung 55, 57. Sihler's "Letters to the German Lutherans in America" 80.
Lutz, A. J. (India), 231.

Mahler, Wm. (Brazil), 246.
Maier, F., 91; Indian mission 128, 129.
Maier, W. A. (Lutheran Hour), 220, 261, 312, 316.
Mailender, E., 164.
Maltzan, Karl von, Councilor, zealous co-worker of Loehe 68.
Manitoba 167.
Manning, E. (Bronxville), 287.
Marbach, Dr. F. A., 20, 21, 23, 25, 30, 39, 46, 48.
Marcis, J., Slovak, 238.
Martens, P. R., 294, 296.
Martyrs, Physical resurrection of 322, 328.
Matuschka, P., 265.
Matzat, Geo., Lithuanian, 236.
Maurer, A. V., 286.
Mayer, F. E., 285.
Mayer, Pastor Herman (Bay City), 339.
Means of Grace, the public administration of the 321.
Mecklenburg 68.
Meherrin, Va., colored mission 164.
Meier, E. F. W., 150.
Membership of Synod by 1872 according to States 113.
Memorials, convention of 1941, 326, 327; convention 1944, 330.
Mendota convention (1942), 329.
Mensing, H. D., 286, 335, 336.
Merz, A. G., 262.
Methodists 55, 59, 60, 61, 79; missionary Auch harassed by 129, 132.
Mexico Mission, German and Spanish, 299 f.
Meyer, A., 287.
Meyer, Adolph R., 302.

Meyer, A. W., 174, 184, 194, 195; to presidency of Winfield College 198, 256; retired 287.
Meyer, E. L., 286.
Meyer, H., 286.
Meyer, Lawrence (China), 233, 234; appointed Director of Publicity 277; to Europe 339.
Mezger, Geo., 175; to Germany 302.
Michael, J. M., Hamburg and Denmark 241.
Michigan, Craemer's group en route to 72.
Michigan City, Mich. (Wyneken), 56.
Michigan Synod 5; Craemer, Hattstaedt, Lochner, joined Mich. S., 70; leave this synod 90; Mich. Syn. becomes member of Syn. Conf. 163; District Synod of Michigan 163.
Miessler, E. G. H., missionary to Indians 130 ff.; leaves the mission field 133.
Mikulski, C., mission among Poles 237.
Military training, Fort Wayne, 225.
Millennium 147, 157, 322, 328.
Miller, Prof. Alb., 224.
Miller, Dr. E., Baltimore, Md., 198.
Miller, Mr. Fred., Baltimore, Md., 198.
Milwaukee, Wis., 59; Concordia College 175 f., 225.
Ministerium of Pennsylvania 6.
Minneapolis 109; Minneapolis Meeting (A. L. Conference 1940) 325; Theses 323.
Minnesota, 109; Minnesota Synod 159.
Miracles 54.
Mishawaka, Ind., 105.
Mission Boards 168 f.; mission activities (1869 ff.) 179—186.
Mission department at St. L. Seminary 285.

Mission work among Indians in Mich. 71.
Missionaries at large 108.
Missionaries in all States of the Union 275.
Missions, among Indians 127–136, 240; Immigrants 136, 182, 238; Japan 179; India 180–182, 230, 288–293; Jews 183, 239 f.; Deaf 184–186; China 233–235; Letts 235; Esthonians 236; Lithuanians 236; Poles 237; Persians 237; Finns 237 f.; Italians 238.
Missionstaube, Die, 165.
Missouri Synod, organization 2; original territory 2; secret of its growth and achievements 13; charter members 15; most of Loehe's "Sendlinge" join the M. S. 69; preliminary meetings leading to organization 83–95; organization 97–106; constitution 99 f; merely an advisory body 99; six conference circuits 103; roster of first Synod 104–106; expansion: Wisconsin 109; to Minnesota 109; Iowa 109 f.; Kansas 110; Nebraska 110; California 110; Louisiana, Texas, Arkansas, Tennessee, Alabama, 111; Maryland, Massachusetts, Pennsylvania, Virginia, Washington, D. C., Connecticut, Rhode Island, 112; New Jersey, Canada, 113; Division of Synod into Districts 113; Membership by 1872, 113; 1854 last annual convention of General Body 115; Delegate Convention 115; Districts in 1854, 115; educational institutions 116–127; how institutions were located in 1860, 124; reasons for combining the two seminaries under one faculty 124; college section moved to Fort Wayne, practical seminary to St. L. 125; "Missourians," term coined by Grabau 139; Colloquy with Iowa 148; jubilee, 25 years, 152; founders not Separatists 155; free conferences 156; conferences at Columbus, Ohio, Pittsburgh, Cleveland, Fort Wayne 157; W. 1860; colloquy at Columbus (1868) 158; organization and first convention of Synodical Conference 159; growth up to 1872, 167 f.; changes of Districts 167 f.; a President of Synod no more to be a full-time pastor of a congregation 169 f; practical seminary removed to Springfield 170–173; dedication of building on Jefferson Ave., St. L. (1883), 173; Statistics (1897) 217 f.; first Board of Directors 219; the word "German" dropped from Synod's name 219; "Budget System" 220; financial secretary (Theo. W. Eckhart) 220; new seminary buildings needed 221 f.; Springfield seminary 222; statistics (1922) 275; new Districts 275; educational institutions 220–230; new Seminary, De-Mun Ave., 281.

Missouri Synod conventions and the Luth. union movement (1923) 319; (1929) 319; (1932) 319; (1935) 320; (1938) 321 ff., 332; (1941) 325 ff.; (1944) 329 ff.

Modernism, makes reason the arbiter of religious truth, is rationalism 9.

Moeller, A. J. C., president of St. Paul's College, Concordia, Mo., 287.

Moenkemoeller, Prof. Wm., St. Paul, 225.

Mohn, F. J. (India), 180 ff., 231.

Moll, W. E., 249.

Moll, Prof. W. L., Fort Wayne, 225.

Monroe, Mich., 71, 73, 83, 105.

Montana District (1945) 276.

Moon type 297.

Morris, J. G., Baltimore, 79.

Moser, Jonathan R., 191.
Muehlhaeuser, John, 28.
Mueller, A. C., 313, 314.
Mueller, Prof. G. W. (Milw.), 176.
Mueller, Hy., 275.
Mueller, J. A. F. W., 37.
Mueller, J. T., 220, 363.
Mundinger, C., president of St. John's College, 287.

Nachtsheim, E. C., 349.
Naether, Theo. (India), 180 ff., 231.
Nagercoil, theological seminary, 231, 289.
Nau, Dr. H. (India), 231; (Africa), 344 f.
Naumann, Geo., 231.
Neeb, M. J., 284, 288.
Negroes, mission work among, 163, 268 f., 342.
Neitzel, R. C., 222, 319.
Neuendettelsau, near Nuernberg, 65, 72, 78.
Neuendettelsau, Ohio, 83, 104.
Neumelle, Mo., 105, 133.
New Orleans 108, 111, 164; English preaching 195, 350.
New York City 32, 34, 61, 72, 78, 91, 105.
New York Pastoral Conference, Immigrant Mission 136; *Progymnasium*, St. Matthew's Church, 176; Daniel Landsmann 182.
New Zealand 179, 242.
Nickel, Th., preaches and teaches among Stockbridge Indians 240.
Nigeria 344—347.
Nitschke, C. J. O., 25, 119.
Noerdlingen 66, 67.
Noffke, E. A. (India), 232.
Nollau, L., 28.
Nonfundamental doctrines 323, 324, 328, 330.
Normal school opened in Milwaukee 123.
Northern District, divided, 167 f.
Norwegian Synod 158, 162, 325, 330.

Norwegians, agreement with Synod reached 1857 with reference to a Norwegian professorship at St. Louis 122; Missouri delegates to conventions of N. Synod 155.
Nothelfer (emergency men) 67.
Noticiero Luterano 300.
Nuelsen, J. J., 57.
Nuernberg 59, 65, 71; Central Mission Society, 102.

Oakland, Calif., college 229, under control of Synod 287.
Obermeyer, C. F., 230.
Oertel, Maximilian, 28, 32; leaves Perry Co. for New York, there turns Catholic, 34.
Oberheu, G., 232.
Oesel (Island) 78, 303.
Office of the Keys 140, 141.
Officers, Boards, Committees 362.
Ohio Synod 4, 5; found orthodox by Loehe 70; Sihler joins 80; convention 1845, 82.
Oklahoma District (1924) 275.
"Old Lutherans" 12.
Ontario District 276.
Open Bible Thankoffering 308.
Oppliger, J., 348.
Ordination, Sihler's, 80 f.; *Hirtenbrief* 138; answer to *Hirtenbrief* 139; Loehe 144.
Otterbeinians 55.
Otto, E. J., 287.
Otto, L. C., 287.
Overn, O. B., Prof., St. Paul, 225.
Oxford University 71.

Pahl, Ed. J., letter to A. Reinke 184.
Paitzdorf, Perry Co., 38.
Paitzdorf, Saxony, 25, 37.
Pankow, E. A., 176.
Paraguay 243, 306.
Pardieck, E., 220, 226.
Parish schools (See also "Christian Day School") 249 f.
Pascha, J., missionary among the Persians, 237.

TOPICAL INDEX

Pascha, Philip, missionary among Persians, 237.
"Patronatssystem" 8.
Peace Thankoffering 309.
Pearl Harbor 327.
Pennsylvania Ministerium 55, 59.
Persians, Mission among, 237.
Peters, J. W., to New Zealand, 179.
Petri, Dr. L. A., pastor of city church, Hannover, 68, 102.
Pfau, Gustav, colporteur, 108.
Pfotenhauer, F., President of Synod 219, 249; succeeded by Dr. J. W. Behnken 278—283, 339, 341; death 347 f.
Philadelphia, Pa., 59, 79, 112.
Philippi, F. A., Sihler's colleague in Blochmann's Institute, 76.
Philippine Islands 302.
Pieper, Franz, 174, 175, 178, 180; Predestinarian Controversy 203; President of Synod 218 f., 224, 228; for South America Lutherans 243 f.; *Christliche Dogmatik* translated into Chinese 294 (See also "Concordia Publishing House"); 347—348; death 284, 347 f.; 351.
Pieper, R., 173, 214, 222.
Pietism 8 f., 20.
"Pilgerhaus," Lutherisches, 137; no longer serving its purpose, is sold 339.
Piney Woods Country Life School 342.
Pinkert, Max, Seamen's Mission, 239.
Pittsburgh 55, 61.
Pittsburgh Agreement 324, 329.
Planena 24, 34.
Plass, E. M., 287.
Poch, Bruno (London), 242.
Poehler, W. A., 287.
Poeschel, candidate, wrote pamphlet defending Stephen, 21.
Poeschke, F. W., 103, 104.
Polack, W. G., 263, 285, 319.

Polish Lutherans, mission among, 236 f.
Pomeroy, Ohio, 52, 79, 83.
Popular Commentary (P. E. Kretzmann) 262.
Population during century 1.
Portland, Oregon, college, 228, 284; taken over by Synod 288.
Practice, Christian, agreement in, 325, 327.
Prayer fellowship 324, 329.
Precht, F. L., 285.
Predestinarian Controversy 162, 198—207; doctrine of predestination 321.
Preliminary meetings, Cleveland, 85—87; St. Louis, 88—90; Fort Wayne, 91—95; list of signers 95.
Press Committee (1926) 276.
Preuss, E., succeeds Baumstark 125; editor of *Kalender* 151; oration, dedication of Synodaldruckerei 151.
Preuss, H. A. (Norw.), 160.
Price, Columbus, log-cabin college student 37.
Priesthood, Spiritual, of the believers, 139, 141.
Pritzlaff, Fred. C., 219, 251.
Proehl, F. C., 335, 336.
Proehl, H. E., 287.
Prokopy, O., 227.
Prokopy, P. G., 316.
Prussian State Church 243.
Prussian Church Union 11, 12, 91.
Pulpit fellowship 322, 329.
Punga, a Maori, missionary 242.

Quadricentennial of the Reformation (1917) 271.

Rader, Rev. Andrew, 191.
Radio station 309 ff.
Rapier, Miss Christine (Africa), 345.
Rationalism 4; in State-controlled Church 9; havoc caused by it 9 ff.; in General Synod 61.

Raumer, Karl v., 60.
Razokas, J. J. D., Lithuanian mission, 236.
Rebane, H., 235.
Rechlin, Prof. F., 175.
Reese, A. W., 286, 287, 300.
Reformed Church (Wyneken), 58; (Sihler) 78, 79.
Rehfeldt, Prof. L. C. (Porto Alegre), 246.
Rehwaldt, A. C., 286.
Rehwinkel, Miss A. (India), 233.
Rehwinkel, A. M., 229, 285, 287.
Reifschneider, G. H., 286.
Reim, Norbert (Africa), 347.
Reinke, Aug., 184.
Rentner, Mr. O. C., 336.
Repp, A. C., Executive Secretary of Board for Parish Education 313, St. L. faculty member 285.
Restin, O. H., Immigrant Mission 238 f., 264.
Reuter, Prof. P., Seward, 226.
Revivalism 61, 79.
Richmann, Wm., 82.
Richmond, Va., 112.
Riedel, Erhard (China), 234.
Riedel, M. W., 288.
Riep, A. R., 288.
Riga 78.
Rincker, L. C., president of Milwaukee College 286.
Rippe H. J. (Bronxville), 227.
Ritzmann, Prof. G., Seward, 226.
River Forest Seminary 224.
Roebbelen, K., 70, 122 f.
Roeder, candidate, sent to help Missionary Auch 128; comes to Bethany 132.
Roehrs, W. R., 285, 287.
Roemer, C., member of Trinity, St. Louis, houses students 120, 150.
Roesener, P., 230.
Rohlfing, R. T., 286.
Rohr, H. v., 137, 142; with Grabau calls on Loehe 144.
Rolf, E., of St. Paul, conducts first German Lutheran service in Western Canada 167.
Roman Catholic Church 78, 80.
Romanowski, Eduard, 72, 83, 87, 88.
Romoser, Prof. Geo. A., Conover, 197; Bronxville 227; dies 287, 334.
Romoser, Pastor H. W., 355.
Rosel, P., 286.
Ross, Prof. C., 176.
Rudelbach, A. G., 12, 25, 44, 63, 77, 78, 80.
Rudisill, Henry, 56, 61, 62.
Ruhland, H., Pastor at Pleasant Ridge, Ill., called to Dresden, Germany, 187; Planitz 187.
Ruperti, Justus, pastor of St. Matthew's, N. Y., 53.
Rupprecht, Dr. F., C. P. H. editor 317.
Rupprecht, O. E., 287.
Rusch, Carl (Africa), 347.
Rusch, O. F., Addison Teachers College, 224.
Rusch, W. H., 286.

Sachsen-Altenburg, good effect of emigration on, 27.
Saginaw, Mich., 72, 73; churches beautify cemetery of former Indian mission 133 f.
St. John's College, Winfield, 197, 227.
St. Joseph, Mich., Wyneken 56.
St. Louis, center of industrial life in West, 3; Saxons' Church in 30, 33, 34; becomes center of Lutheran orthodoxy 50; Trinity Church, constitution and name 50; Loehe men meet with St. L. congregation 90, 104; St. L. Pastoral Conference 115; cornerstone, new seminary (1849), 119; dedication (June 11, 1850) 120 (see also "Concordia Theological Seminary, St. L.").

TOPICAL INDEX

St. Paul, Minn., 109; Concordia College 177 f.
St. Paul's College, Concordia, Mo., 176.
Salonen, Pastor K. E., 340 f.
Salvner, J. L., 298.
Sandusky Resolutions 323, 325.
Sandy Creek, Mich., 83.
Sapper, C. F. W., 163, 180.
Sattelmeier, F., mission among Polish Lutherans 237.
Sauer, G. H., first Missouri Synod pastor at Mobile, Ala., 112.
Sauer, O. A., 336.
Saupert, A., 82, 84, 87.
Saxer, Mr. A., joins St. L. faculty 121; director 122, 125; resigns at Fort Wayne 125.
Saxon Free Church 187 ff., 241, 302.
Saxons, 700 leave for America 12; wholesome effect on many who remained in Germany 12; the S. and the Loehe men 15; resolution to emigrate 22; meetings of Stephan's followers anent emigration 23; Paragraph Two in emigration regulations: cause, end, and aim, 24; Stephan sends word: "The hour has struck," 24; excitement of preparation 24 f.; number of souls participating 25; candidates of theology 25; schoolteachers, doctors of medicine, lawyers, farmers, artisans, craftsmen emigrating 25; list of candidates 25; embarkation; names of ships and their pastors 28; arrival in St. Louis 29; land bought in Perry Co. 29; church services until Dec. 4, 1842, in St. L. 29; severe blow 32; bewilderment 33; depleted treasury 33; decentralization; five congregations 33; distressing times 36; confusion 39; pastors and teachers —where working in 1845, 83; stand aloof from all synodical groups 84; aversion to synodical organization waning 86, 137, 139; Centennial 340.
Saxony, confessional Lutheran laymen in spiritual distress 10; church Union never became effective in 12.
Scaer, Prof. Chas., 198.
Scaer, C. S., 286.
Scaer, E., 288.
Scandinavian immigrants 107.
Schaller, Gottlieb, 112, 116, 145, 174, 190, 272.
Schaller, J., 269.
Schaller, W., Prof., Concordia, Mo., 226.
Schelp, Paul, Porto Alegro, 248.
Scheuermann, E. A. (teacher), 82.
Schick, G., of Chicago, joins faculty, St. L., 121, 125.
Schick, Geo. V., Prof., Fort Wayne, 225; St. L., 285.
Schieferdecker, G. A., 25, 29, 34, 36, 48, 49, 83, 89, 91, 95, 115, 120.
Schlake, Theo., 336.
Schlake, Mr. W., 241.
Schleede, K. W. F., 336.
Schlerf, K. G., 265.
Schleiermacher, F., his church services attended by Sihler 76.
Schlichten, A. v., ministered to Persians 237.
Schlueter, A., Prof., St. Paul, 225.
Schlueter, E. Benj., president of Syn. Conference 341.
Schlueter, Pastor Th., J. S. Simon's successor 222.
Schlueter, W. H., treasurer of Synod 280.
Schmieding, Prof. A., 224.
Schmidt, A., 87, 88, 95.
Schmidt, F., 55, 57, 58, 72, 73, 90 f.
Schmidt, F. A., 159, 160, 172, 174; attends Gravelton meeting 191 f., 203; *The Lutheran Watchman* 351.
Schmidt, Pastor G. A. (Piney Woods), 343.

Schmidt, Geo. F., 265.
Schmidt, Geo. P., Prof., Fort Wayne, 225.
Schmidt, J., 180; relinquishes presidency, Fort Wayne, 224.
Schmidt, J. E. R., Professor, Milwaukee, 287.
Schmidt, Karl, 244.
Schmidt, O. H., visits India 290; Executive Secretary 297, 302, 319.
Schmidtke, L., 227.
Schmitt, F. H., Addison Teachers College 224.
Schnedler, Prof. E., Fort Wayne, 225.
Schneider, J. E., signs Fort Wayne report 95.
Schoede, A. H., 176.
Schoenfeld, Wm., 264.
Scholz, C. F. W., 95.
Schoof, D. H., pastor of Meherrin, Va., colored flock 164.
Schoolteachers emigrating 25.
Schroeder, E. T., 287.
Schroeder, Geo. (India), 232.
Schroedel, Geo. C., 287.
Schubert, Theo., 37.
Schuelke, Prof. Aug., Seward, 226.
Schulblatt 150 f.
Schulz, P., 319, 336.
Schulze, F. W., called to London 188, 242.
Schumacher, B., 319.
Schuricht, J. F., Treasurer, 253.
Schuster, G. K., Loehe emissary, pastor 83, 87, 95, 105.
Schwan, H. C., 53, 160, 165; President of Synod: biographical notes 169, 180, 200, 213, 218; his death 272; Catechism 319.
Schwartzkopf, L. (China), 234.
Schwermann, A. M., president, Edmonton, 229 f.
Schweppe, Wm. H. (Africa), 345.
Schwidder, Ad., 275.
Schwoy, Prof. J., 227.
Seamen's mission 239.

Secret Societies 148 f., 157, 333 f.
Secretary of Missions 278.
Seelitz (Perry Co.) 34, 39.
Selle, C. Aug., 82, 87, 95, 97, 98, 108, 110, 149.
Seminario Concordia at Porto Alegre 248.
Sendlinge, Loehe's 68 f.
Separation of Church and State 335.
Service centers 337.
Seuel, E., 251, 262, 280, 317.
Seward Teachers College 177, 225 f., 286.
Seyffarth, Dr. G., gives his services to St. L. College without compensation 121; resigns 122.
Shawano, Wis., Stockbridge Indians 240.
Shinanfu 234; Shinan 294.
Sibiwaing, Mich., 91, 129.
Siebert, E. G. R., 287.
Sieck, Dr. L. J., follows Dr. Fuerbringer as president of St. L. Seminary 285.
Sieker, L. H., president Minnesota Synod 159 f.
Siemon, O., 175.
Sievers, Ferdinand, 73, 108, 109; serves Indian station of Bethany 131; opening of mission among Indians in Minnesota 134 f.; foreign missions 179, 180.
Sievers, F. jun., 180.
Sihler, Dr. E. G., 176.
Sihler, W., 52; breaks with Ohio Synod 70, 75—82; early life 75 ff.; Ph. D. 76; tutor, Institute of Dr. Blochmann, Dresden, sudden conversion 76; Wyneken's "Appeal," Sihler comes to America, 78; Pastor at Pomeroy, Ohio, 79; his "Letters to the German Lutherans in America" and "A Dialog of Two Lutherans on Methodism" 80; joins Ohio Synod 80; ordained 81; receives his first copy of *Der Lutheraner* 82; be-

TOPICAL INDEX 405

comes Wyneken's successor at St. Paul's in Fort Wayne 82; severs connection with Ohio Synod 82, 83, 84, 87, 88, 89, 90, 91; on third preliminary meeting 93 f., 95; first Treasurer of Synod 99, 103, 104, 108, 115, 122, 124, 125; convention of Tennessee Synod 155; Syn. Conference organized 160; custodian of treasury to provide for needs of itinerant missionaries 168; death 212.

Sillak, J., missionary among Letts and Esthonians 236, 238.

Slovak Ev. Luth. Church 238, 329.

Smith, C. O., Conover, 226. 238, 329.

Smukal, G. H., 275.

Sohn, Prof. J. G., Fort Wayne, 225.

Sohn, O., 336.

Sommer, M. S., 220, 290.

Sonntagsblatt (Wucherer) 66.

South America, 243—248; visitors 304.

South Bend, Ind. (Wyneken), 56.

Southeastern District (1939) 276.

Southern California District (1930) 275.

Speckhard, G., 183 f.

Spiegel, C. W., 285.

Spilman, Geo., 264, 276.

Spitz, Lewis W., 285, 287.

Springfield, Ill., 59; seminary 170 f. (See also "Concordia Theological Seminary, Springfield.").

Stade Mission Society 58; Biewend 61, 65.

Stade, Robert (Africa), 347.

Stahlke, Walter F., principal of high school, Africa, 347.

Stallman, H. (India), 231.

Statistical Yearbook 167.

Steeden Academy 126.

Steege, M. J., 285.

Steffens, D. H., 263, 265.

Stein, Prof. Henry E. A., 177.

Steiner, L., 198.

Steinmeyer, H., 150.

Stellhorn, A. C., 250, 314, 319.

Stellhorn, F. W., 175, 202; Predestinarian Controversy 203.

Stelzer, Theo., 286.

Stephan, M., 12; his education 15—33; his farewell to Germany 27; persuades fellow passengers to elect him bishop 28; unworthy 32; false teaching 38 f., 39, 44, 45, 76, 77, 83, 153; death 33.

Stockbridge Indians 240.

Stoeckhardt, Dr. G., 174; comes to Holy Cross Church 189; Predestinarian Controversary 203, 220, 273; sermons translated into Chinese 295; death 273.

Stoeppelwerth, J. H., 198.

Stoeppelwerth, Prof. M., Fort Wayne, 225.

Stohlmann, Dr., 72, 79.

Strasen, B. (India), 232.

Strasen, C. A., 160.

Streckfuss, F., 173.

Streckfuss, G., 103, 105.

Streufert, A. C., 287.

Streufert, F. C., Secretary of Missions, 263, 278, 301, 304.

Strieter, Prof. F., Seward, 226.

Stub, H. G., 269.

Student Welfare Committee 276.

Subcommittees of Missouri Synod and A. L. C. 330, 332.

Sullivan, J., 287.

Sunday (doctrine) 147 f. 321.

Sunday schools 313 f.; S. S. Board 313.

Supplements to *Lutheran Witness* 318.

Survey Committee 230.

Sutermeister, Mr. A., headed English academy 124.

Sylwester, F. W. J. (Portland), 228.

Synod of Missouri, Ohio, and Other States, see Missouri Synod.

Synod of West 5; Wyneken 61, 62.

Synodical allegiance 331.

Synodical Conference 155—165; organized 159 f., 266, 323—327, 329, 340—347.

Teacher-catechists 289.
Tennesee Synod 6, 155, 191, 197.
Theiss, H. W. (China), 234.
Theiss, O. H., 288, 316.
Theological Monthly 207, 262.
Theological Quarterly 209, 262.
Thiemeyer, Mr. H., 256.
Thode, E. H., 293, 296.
Tirmenstein, Martin, 209.
Tjernagel, H. M., serves Stockbridge Indians 240.
Toledo, Ohio, 84, 91, 92.
Tractarian Movement 71.
Trailer missions 338.
Transoceanic Relations 186—189, 241 ff.
Trautmann, Ph. Jak., Loehe "Sendling," 70, 77; Danbury, Ohio, 84; 90 f., 95.
Travancore 292.
Tresselt, F., 230.
Triglotta 262.
Trinity Church, "Old Trinity," constitution and name, 50.
Trivandrum 292.

Umbach, E., 316.
Umbach, J., colporteur, 108; Board for work among the Negroes 163.
Union of the English and the German Missouri Synods 253 ff.
Unionism 5; in State-controlled Church 9, 11, 22; Wyneken at first not yet a firm stand against 58; but does so strongly after his visit to Germany 61; Baltimore church 62; Sihler's abhorrence for 78, 79, 81, 82, 85.
United Lutheran Church 324, 325.
Unity of the Spirit 114 f.
Unser Erbteil, 400th anniversary of the Reformation, 271.
Uruguay 306.

Valparaiso University 350 f.
Van Wert Co., Ohio, 83, 105.
Vaniyambadi 291 f.
Vehse, Dr. C. E., 20, 25, 33, 39, 47, 153.
Venedy, Ill., 83.
Verein zur Kirchl. Unterstuetzung der Deutschen in Amerika 60.
Viehweg, G., 288.
Visible and Invisible Church 140, 144; "visible side of the Church" 321, 322.
Volck, George, 111.
Volkening, L., 180.
Vornsand, J., Teacher, London, 247.
Voss, K. E., 294, 296.

Wabash Canal 93.
Wagemann, Dr., 177.
Wagner, A., 160, 169.
Wahlers, Prof. F., St. Paul, 225.
Wahlers, L. F., 287.
Walker, M., Professor, Hawthorne, 227.
Walker, Mr. F. C., 230.
Wall, G., Evangelical pastor, 49.
Walle, O. T., 287.
Walther, C. F. W., appointed pastor at Braeunsdorf by Count Einsiedel 8; his detailed account of the destruction rationalism worked in Saxony 9, 16, 20, 24, 25; why he did not board the *Amalia* 28; remains in St. L. with Buerger and Loeber 30; sent by St. L. clergy to Perry Co. to confront Stephan 32; serves congregation at Dresden and the "Berliner" group 34; college announcement 37; the instrument in God's hand to dispel doubts 40; birth, education 41 ff.; ill health, interruption of studies 45; recuperating at home, studied Luther's work 45; continued at university 45; private tutor 45; at Dresden and Johannisburg (Perry Co.) 46;

TOPICAL INDEX

affliction after Stephan's removal 46; illness, confined to house of Keyl, studied Luther 47; Altenburg debate 47 f.; called to St. L., his health restored 49, 62, 83, 84; letter to Loehe men 85 ff., 89, 90, 91, 92, 93, 94, 95, 97; first President 99; editor of *Der Lutheraner* 102, 103, 104, 111, 112, 116, 118, 119, 120, 121, 125; visits Brunn 126; *Hirtenbrief* 139, 143; journey to Europe 144; jubilee sermon 152; has hope for a united Luth. Ch. 156; greater part of 1860 in Germany to regain health 157; organization of Synodical Conference 160, first president 161; relieved of his duties as President 169; Gospel sermons 188; eager to promote English work 190, 191; Ohio Synod confers upon W. the title of Doctor of Divinity 198; Predestinarian Controversy 199 ff.; death 212 f.; Walther Centennial 269 ff.

Walther, C. F. W., his Gospel sermons translated into Chinese 295.

Walther College 272, 350.

Walther League 210, 261, 263; builds residences at Kuling, China, 294; 310.

Walther League Messenger, The, 261.

Walther, O. H., 20, 25, 27, 28; leaves St. L. for Perry Co. 30; serves congregation in St. L. 33, 37, 39, 46; called as minister by emigrants remaining in St. Louis 49; died (age 31) 49, 83, 252.

Waltke, Louis H., 308.

Wangerin, Tr. missionary among the Deaf 185.

Wanhsien 294.

Washington, D. C., Biewend, 61, 167.

Watertown, Wis., 106.

Wedig, Pastor Wm., 343.

Wefel, J., returns call as Director of Missions 180.

Wege, E. J. M., 25, 83.

Wegehaupt, E. C. (Brazil), 247.

Weidenschilling, Dr. J., 314.

Weiherman, W. F., 317.

Weis, E. C., 287.

Weiss, C. A., joins Conover faculty 197.

Welfare work 352 f.

Weller, G., first professor, Seward, 178, 249.

Wenchel, J. F., 263, 265, 335.

Wenger, F., 285.

Wenger, G. K., 293.

Wente, W. H. (Winfield), 228.

Werling, H. F., 286.

Werling, J. W. (Winfield), 228.

Wermelskirch, Pastor, 77.

Wernle 87.

Wessel, L., 173.

Wessling, A., 288.

Westcott, Pastor E. A., 343.

Western District, divided and redivided, 167 f.

Wheat Ridge, Colo., 352.

Wibracht, E. J., 286.

Williems, J. (India), 231.

Winfield, Kans., J. P. Baden, St. John's College, 197.

Winkler, Fr., severs connection with Ohio Synod 82, 87.

Winkler, M. (Australia), 241.

Winter, A. H., Immigrant mission, Philadelphia, Pa., 239.

Winter, J. F. F., 24, 25.

Wisconsin Synod 159; unites with Minnesota and Michigan Synods 163, 325, 330.

Wisler, Pastor L. A., 343.

Wismar, Prof. O. W., Concordia, Mo., 226.

Witte, H. G., 288.

Wittenberg on Mississippi 34, 88.

Wolbrecht, W. F., 286.

TOPICAL INDEX

Wolf, C. W., went with Wyneken to America 55, 95.
Wolfram, E. A., 287.
Wollaeger, H. W. F., Prof, St. Paul, 225.
Wolter, C. L. A., 70, 103, 105, 123.
Woman suffrage 341.
World War I 263–266, 357; World War II 303, 334–339, 357.
Woy, P., 287.
Wucherer, J. F., editor of *Sonntagsblatt*, 66 f.
Wuerffel, L. C., 286.
Wunder, H., 175.
Wunderlich, L. C., 287.
Wurmb, Marie von, 37.
Wurm, Sarah von, 37.
Wurmb, Theobald von, 37.
Wyneken, F. C. D., describes physical hardships of pioneers 3, 5; leaves General Synod 6; "Thank God, there are still Lutherans in America" 52, 53–64; private tutor 53; resolves to go to America 54; Haesbaert 55; Pennsylvania Ministerium 55; "Father" Buuck 55; Fort Wayne 55; St. Joseph, Mich., Michigan City, Mich., Mottville, Niles, Crawfordsville, Ind., 56; his correspondence 57; personal visit to Germany 58 f., 68; marriage 59; his vivid descriptions, lecturing in Germany, 59; describes a camp meeting 60; visiting Erlangen, Dresden, Leipzig, 60; contact with confessional leaders in Germany strengthened his confessional position 61; returns to Fort Wayne 61; emphasizes difference between the Lutheran and the Reformed Confessions 61; called as Haesbaert's successor 62; his appeal: *Distress of the German Lutherans in N. America* 60, 63, 72, 78; severs connection with General Synod 63; standing alone 64, 82; his reports stir Loehe; Stade Mission Society 65; at Baltimore 84, 87, 88, 110, 115; called to Trinity, St. Louis, 116; President of Synod 116; health failing, call to Cleveland, 116, 120; ordains and installs Miessler as missionary to Indians 131; visits Loehe with Walther 144, 155, 160; dies 211; Wyneken Centennial 340.
Wyneken, H., begins work among the colored people at Springfield, Ill., 164; joins Springfield faculty 173.
Wyneken, M., 111.

Ylvisaker, Prof. S. C., St. Paul, 225.
Young Lutheran's Magazine 209.
Young People's Work 314–317.
Young, Rosa, 268.
Youth Building, Chicago, 317.
Yuma, Arizona, congregation organized (1939) 275.
Yurawitz, E. (Letts and Esthonians), 236; (Indians in Minnesota) 240.

Zanesville, Ohio, 79, 81, 83; C. A. Frank, 196.
Zanow, P., 286.
Zehlendorf, theological institution. 241, 302.
Zeitblaetter (Ohio Synod organ) 206.
Zeitschrift fuer Protestantismus u. Kirche 57, 62.
Zetzer, Alb., 236.
Ziegler, A. H., 293, 296, 297.
Zimmermann, E. C., 293, 296.
Zschiegner, Max (China), 234, 294, 295.
Zschoche, M., 301.
Zorn, C. M., 180.
Zorn, H. M., visits India, 290.
Zschech, E. Wm. (Australia), 241.
Zucker, Prof. F., 175, 180; 231 (India; mission director 235.
Zwerner, Loehe man, colporteur, 83.

www.ingramcontent.com/pod-product-compliance
Lightning Source LLC
Chambersburg PA
CBHW031249230426
43670CB00005B/95